WITHDRAWN

THE FOREST AND THE FIELD
Changing theatre in a changing world

THE FOREST AND THE FIELD
Changing theatre in a changing world

CHRIS GOODE

OBERON BOOKS
LONDON

WWW.OBERONBOOKS.COM

First published in 2015 by Oberon Books Ltd
521 Caledonian Road, London N7 9RH
Tel: +44 (0) 20 7607 3637 / Fax: +44 (0) 20 7607 3629
e-mail: info@oberonbooks.com
www.oberonbooks.com

A catalogue record for this book is available from the British Library.

PB ISBN: 9781849434751
E ISBN: 9781849438605

Cover design and text layout by Konstantinos Vasdekis

Printed, bound and converted
by CPI Group (UK) Ltd, Croydon, CR0 4YY.

Visit www.oberonbooks.com to read more about all our books and to buy them. You will also find features, author interviews and news of any author events, and you can sign up for e-newsletters so that you're always first to hear about our new releases.

Contents

Within the theatre, find its outside.[1]

— Augusto Corrieri

Acknowledgements

This book has its origins in a paper setting out some early thoughts on the topic of 'incorporative dissidence', on which I expand in chapter 4 here. For the invitation, back in March 2007, to deliver that paper to a Graduate Seminar at the Central School of Speech and Drama, my thanks to Andy Lavender and Simon Shepherd.

I susbsequently developed those ideas into a paper called 'The Forest and the Field', which was delivered at the Miscellaneous Theatre Festival at the University of Cambridge Faculty of English; my thanks to Jeremy Hardingham for that invitation.

That paper then became a performance lecture, with the same title, which was first presented at Camden People's Theatre, London, in 2009, as part of the *Lean Upstream* festival of my work. Thank you to Matt Ball, who was then the director of CPT; and to Sébastien Lawson, who performed so beautifully in the piece, and David Palmer, for lighting and technical management. The piece was revisited and substantially redeveloped in 2013 for Chris Goode & Company; I am particularly grateful to the Touchstone Trust, and especially Paul Hains, for their extraordinarily generous support of that show. My thanks also to the creative team for the tour: designer Naomi Dawson, lighting designer Kristina Hjelm, stage manager James Lewis, and all the guest cats, especially Antonio. And thank you above all to my talented and intrepid co-performer Tom Ross-Williams; and everyone at Ovalhouse.

Chapters 3 and 4 develop ideas that I first explored in a 2004 essay: '"These facts are variously modified": American writers in an information economy', written for *Edinburgh Review* at the invitation of Sam Ladkin and Robin Purves. My thanks to both of them, and to Sam for the great generosity of his continuing support, not least inside the rehearsal room, where he is always an exceptionally stimulating guest whenever schedules permit his attendance.

In respect of this present publication I'm profoundly grateful to everyone at Oberon, and especially my editor Andrew Walby, whose consistent support, integrity, and apparent serenity have been frankly superhuman.

More than any other, one figure looms particularly large in this book, and not only in those passages where I refer to him by name: that is Keston Sutherland, currently Professor of Poetics at the University of Sussex. I can hardly begin to express adequate gratitude for his agitating and comradely friendship over many years, and for his extraordinary example as poet, scholar, correspondent, provocateur and fellow-traveller.

I want to record my thanks to the two collaborators who have most frequently directed me in my own performance work, and contributed to so many other productive processes and conversations: namely, Wendy Hubbard and Jamie Wood. They have enlarged my thinking and challenged my complacencies with a perfectly balanced combination of rigour and cheerful good humour, and I have learned more from them than I could ever begin to recount, let alone repay.

Not much that I do would be imaginable, let alone practically possible, without the support and the joyous companionship of my colleagues in Chris Goode & Company: my amazing producer, Ric Watts, and our (licensed) resident critic, Maddy Costa. They teach me new and surprising things every day, whether I want it or not. Fondest thanks are due also to Giles Smart and Andy Gout at United Agents for their invaluable part in keeping the show on the road.

I was extremely fortunate to be encouraged and formed by a number of brilliant teachers and mentors early on, and I constantly find myself tracing lines of thought in this book back to their origins in mind-expanding encounters with Gillian Beer, Anne Bowler, Roland Clare, the late Mike Drew, Peter Holland, John Lennard, the late Derek Lucas, Mick Mangan, Rod Mengham, J.H. Prynne, the late David Selwyn, and Ceri Sherlock.

A comprehensive list of all those friends and colleagues who have influenced my thinking and enhanced and enlivened my work would need its own separate volume. Without their various modes and threads of collaboration, this book would be a good deal thinner in every way, and I am greatly indebted to them for the pleasures of their company. I cannot feasibly name them all, so I do what I can: thank them all, and name a few (in addition to those acknowledged in the paragraphs above and below): Rebecca Atkinson-Lord, Julia Lee Barclay-Morton, Nigel Barrett, Michael Basinski, Gerard Bell, Caroline Bergvall, Iain Bloomfield, Andrea Brady, Rachel Briscoe, Gemma Brockis, Akeim

Buck, Jeff B. Cain, Chris Campbell, the late Ken Campbell, Joel Chalfen, David F. Chapman, cris cheek, Karen Christopher, Linda Clare, Angela Clerkin, Jo Clifford, Ed Collier, Nic Conibere, Dennis Cooper, Alison Croggon, Tim Crouch, Matt Davis, Naomi Dawson, Jeni Draper, Clare Duffy, Lucy Ellinson, Andy Field, Harold Finley, Emma Frankland, Harry Gilonis, Rupert Goold, John Hall, the late Rod Hall, Jeremy Hardingham, Andrew Haydon, the late Corrin Helliwell, Maggie Henderson, Katja Hilevaara, Kristina Hjelm, Kirsty Housley, Tom Hughes, George Hunka, Kieran Hurley, George Irving, Elizabeth James, Karl James, Tim Jeeves, Gareth Kieran Jones, David Jubb, Simon Kane, Alex Kelly, Lynne Kendrick, Judith Knight, Alan Lane, Peter Larkin, Richard Lee, Amy Letman, James Lewis, Joe Luna, Tom Lyall, Phelim McDermott, Greg McLaren, Peter Manson, Pauline Mayers, Clive Mendus, Mervyn Millar, Tim Miller, C.J. Mitchell, Hannah Nicklin, Cis O'Boyle, Robin Oakley, Anthony Paraskeva, Malcolm Phillips, Ben Power, David Prescott, Dan Rebellato, Philip Ridley, Finlay Robertson, Christian Roe, Tom Ross-Williams, Scottee, Rajni Shah, Ian Shuttleworth, Hannah Silva, Lee Simpson, Andy Smith, Simon Stephens, Tassos Stevens, Simon Stokes, Toke Broni Strandby, Lou Sumray, Martin Sutherland, Alex Swift, Jennifer Tang, Chris Thorpe, Catherine Tilley, Nikki Tomlinson, Matt Trueman, Mischa Twitchin, Heather Uprichard, Lawrence Upton, Michelle Walker, Rick Warden, Paul Warwick, Anna Watson, Katharine Williams and Melanie Wilson.

My dear friend and housemate Susanna Ferrar has done far more than anyone knows (including her) to make my life feel remotely possible; she has consistently inspired and humbled me with her kindness, her patience, her vigilance and – not least – her musicianship. And I am deeply and abidingly grateful to my parents for their unwavering support and their wholehearted encouragement all the way along. Not once did they suggest I might be happier with a proper job: they must have known as well as I did that I wouldn't be.

Finally, I want to acknowledge, thank and celebrate above all the two people who, during the period when the ideas in this book were forming, were, consecutively, my closest collaborators: Theron Schmidt and Jonny Liron. Words could never contain my admiration for their talents and my gratitude for their generosity in sharing them with me so thoughtfully, intimately and courageously; I am sorry we couldn't go on – and yet, somehow, we do.

Introduction

This is a story about us.

About you and me; and about how – and where – we might think about who we are to each other.

About a bigger 'us', and how and where we meet.

About the big us; and about the little us, the two of us specifically, and what we might want.

I wonder where you are. I wonder how you're doing. I wonder what it's like being you.

Let's see how this story starts. Who are we going to be to each other, now?

———

This book about theatre begins with another book about theatre.

Not long ago, a brilliant director, Katie Mitchell, wrote a book called *The Director's Craft*,[1] and another brilliant director, Nicholas Hytner – the then artistic director of the National Theatre – wrote the foreword.

By the time I picked up *The Director's Craft* I'd already been a director (and a maker of theatre in other ways, other roles, as a writer, a performer, a composer and sound designer sometimes, a sort-of-but-not-quite choreographer, a sort-of-but-not-quite lots of things) for well over a decade. But, never having trained as a director and never having assisted more experienced directors (which is how many directors really learn their trade), I still secretly felt there were huge gaps in my knowledge. There was this constant anxiety, that I was going to embarrass myself, any minute now, by yet again mixing up downstage and upstage, or by not knowing the proper name for a doodah.

So I bought this book by Katie Mitchell – a director I have sometimes loved and always revered – in the hope that it would plug those gaps. And to some extent it has, though I still feel the anxiety of not being quite 'proper'. (I suspect a lot of directors, and in fact a lot of theatre workers of all stripes, secretly feel similar doubts.)

But I nearly didn't get as far as the main body of Mitchell's text. I almost got snagged on Nicholas Hytner's foreword. Hytner introduces the book by noting how Mitchell "rigorously insists on the practical necessities"[2] (which is exactly what I wanted her to do). In making this point, Hytner contrasts his description with some of the other kinds of books that *The Director's Craft* might have been, but isn't. In particular, he says, "There are…many inspirational books about the purpose of theatre."[3] I can't think of all that many, actually, but that wasn't what bothered me about the distinction that Hytner seems to be wanting to make.

This is not, he seems to be saying, a manifesto. Don't go in there expecting a call-to-arms, don't hope for intense and passionate rhetorical flights. On the contrary, here only – thank goodness – is what is "rigorous" and "practical".

Reading Mitchell's nuts-and-bolts book, it's obvious what Hytner means, but his account is nonetheless misleading. Every handbook, every user's manual, especially on a subject like theatre where so much is subjective and intangible, is also – implicitly, perhaps, but incontrovertibly – a manifesto. Every proposed model of how things ought to be done is loaded with information about "the purpose of theatre": but the information is rendered invisibly, between the lines, like adware downloading silently behind a dodgy computer application. Every methodological tenet has its ideological payload, not merely unacknowledged but actively disclaimed.

Whatever else you may find going on in this book, I hope it is pretty honest about what it's up to. *The Forest and the Field* is certainly a kind of manifesto, and it is certainly a book about "the purpose of theatre". (Whether or not it is inspirational is for you to decide.) It may also be of some use to the practitioner, not as a handbook exactly – though many of its proposals can easily be translated into ideas for practical work – but more as a series of jumping-off points for any number of explorations in thought and practice. Only its procedural quality, which I describe below, may be vulnerable to a charge of disingenuousness; I hope not. My intentions in this regard are, at least, virtuous. What I hope to describe is a structure that can be put to thoughtful use. An important element in that structure is an alertness around the ways in which images, especially those constructed in language, can encode ideological positions without their users necessarily being aware that they are doing so. Images which contrast the central and the marginal, for example, are prevalent in our everyday discussion both around theatre and around society – both have 'fringes', for a start; likewise, the normative is set against the extreme case, in ways that necessarily assume too much about where we start from, and who 'we' are in the first place; perhaps most perniciously of all, the establishment of some positions can often involve a claim to neutrality (as Hytner more or less does for Mitchell). I'm sure many readers will notice me falling in to exactly these traps from time to time: we can all take better care.

The case of Hytner seeking to present Mitchell as somehow transcending ideology – or (even more questionably) avoiding it *through the application of rigour* – recalls in some ways a longstanding controversy arising from the difficulty of mapping the world onto a two-dimensional plane. We are so accustomed to imagining the world 'looking like' the familiar Mercator projection that it is very hard to comprehend the degree of distortion that Mercator installs at the core of our cultural perceptions.

In a brilliant sequence[4] in my favourite TV drama show of recent years, *The West Wing*, White House Press Secretary C.J. Cregg is visited by the (fictional) 'Organization of Cartographers for Social Equality', who demonstrate how Mercator's Eurocentric bias, which also favours North America, makes that projection a woefully unreliable guide to the actual proportional relationships of land areas. What's more, they suggest, the bias is compounded by placing the northern hemisphere at the top of the map and the southern at the bottom, with all the associations of power and prestige that 'top' and 'bottom' connote.

"But wait," C.J. objects. "Where else could you put the northern hemisphere but on the top?"

The socially-concerned cartographer clicks his remote for the next slide, and there on the screen is C.J.'s answer.

The world turned upside-down.

<hr />

We come in peace, they said, to dig and sow
We come to work the lands in common
and to make the waste ground grow
This earth divided we will make whole
So it will be a common treasury for all

— Leon Rosselson, from 'The World Turned Upside Down'

The question towards which this book makes its way is the one that lies in wait for any theatre maker who dares to profess some concerted political ends for their practice: a question asked frequently by sceptics, seldom by those who hear within it a promise rather than an accusation: namely, "Can theatre change the world?" It appears usually to be a trap. The idea such a claim might be made on behalf of theatre is assumed to be ridiculous, and consequently anyone making it is easily taken to be ridiculous too; yet if theatre *cannot* seriously hope to change the world, it quickly comes to be seen as ridiculous itself, an act whose pretensions to significance, should it dare to essay them, are everywhere and always overwhelmed by futility.

One not wholly evasive response that I and others will sometimes make to this terrible question – sometimes as a route in to a more developed answer, which (or a template of which) is what I hope this book may offer – is one based in personal testimony. Theatre, we say, has certainly changed *us*. We can muster some anecdotal evidence to support this assertion, and it at least holds the question ajar for a while: because if we can be changed by theatre, maybe anyone (and everyone) can.

With this in mind, I want to mention four crucial moments in my own relationship with theatre. (The first chapter begins by describing a fifth, and there are certainly others I might have liked to discuss.) This is done in the interests of disclosure, rather than any hope to persuade the reader of anything at this stage. You should know something about where I'm coming from.

I was, and am, an only child, who from very early on lived out daily the mortifying cliché of being torn between, on the one hand, a shyness and physical timidity that kept me from football and tree-climbing, and on the other, a compulsion to impress, to be at the centre of (particularly adult) attention, especially on stage. I was an infant Prince Charming and First Wise Man, a revoltingly precocious budding impressionist and showman who would, at the drop of the flimsiest hat, teach other children to tap-dance (a discipline in which I had no skills or training whatsoever, but an almost psychotic amount of *chutzpah*), or gamely dress up in a frock and pearls for a school assembly. At home, I bullied my friends into concert parties and cast them without their consent in my ersatz gang shows. I was never a stage school moppet, and I loathed the bogus practised smiles of the television kids who were; I was much more the class clown and clever-dick who created for himself a safer and more habitable existence than the rough and chaotic world of other children at play.

This sense of feeling at home as a star turn (or as totally invisible, but nothing in-between) continued well into my teens, and it's concisely indicative that when I turned up to audition for the school play that was being mounted in the autumn term following my fifteenth birthday, the director's response – not unreasonably – was to check: "You do know it's not a comedy, don't you Chris?" The play in question, called *The Earth Divided* (the title borrowed from Leon Rosselson's great song 'The World Turned Upside Down'), was an example of what would now be called 'new writing': a robustly anarcho-socialist historical drama by Mick Mangan, which had had one professional production three years earlier at the Riverside Studios in London under the direction of a young Stephen Daldry; as such, it was by any standards a bold and unexpected choice as a main stage production at a relatively conservative independent school in a posh part of Bristol. Despite his initial misgivings, the director, English teacher Roland Clare, managed to locate in me during the audition some obscure capacity for seriousness and subtlety, and I was cast – not, in fact, wholly against type – as a repressed and disdainful Puritan hellfire preacher.

CG, centre, as disdainful Puritan, with Cathie Ackroyd and Daniel Pearce, in Mick Mangan's *The Earth Divided*. Bristol Grammar School, 1988
© South West Picture Archive.

The experience of working on *The Earth Divided* turned out to be something of a political awakening: not, or not principally, because of the play's cheerfully radical content, but more because working on it required me to orient myself within a zone of collective responsibility the like of which I'd never encountered. In preparation for the practical tasks of staging this play, a spirit of collaborative endeavour was fostered in us. Apart from anything else, it was a grown-up experience: as the youngest in the cast, I was suddenly spending much of my time with sixth-form students of unimaginable coolness, and talking with Roland and the other adults around the production as if we were proceeding on an equal footing. Suddenly, the hierarchies I had learned to shape to my individual advantage were softening of their own accord, and my habitual strategies for impressing the grown-ups were worthless. There was nothing to which I could apply my competitiveness. What was valued here instead was thoughtfulness, kindness, openness. Co-operation. A gentle candour. A willingness to share. We were working together to make something, and part of what we were making was our togetherness. It was an incredibly romantic atmosphere, and sure enough I fell unspeakably in love – with one of the older boys, yes, very quietly, but also with the sense of the collective: the sense not least that the revolutionary instincts of Mick's play were somehow being expressed through the tender rule-breaking and border-crossing of our friendships and our conversations, the unaggressively radical cell we seemed to be forming at the heart of an establishment institution whose mores, I was now realising for the first time, were not necessarily my own. And in that light, also for the first time, I saw how theatre was larger than the stage on which my focus had always been trained: it was also a kind of way of being in the world – an activity without walls, a space that could be lived in.

The second of the formative events I want to describe chimes with the first. Four years later, part way through my first term at university, a friend and I took the train down to London to see Théâtre de Complicité's *The Street of Crocodiles* at the Cottesloe. I can't now think what had alerted us to it, or why it was this rather than any other production that drew us to London; I've no idea what expectations I might have had about what we were going to see. But almost before I'd got comfortable in my seat, I was captivated by the stage world; within four or five minutes of the show starting, I was ready to give up fighting back tears. For the remainder of the duration of the show I was so totally engrossed, so deeply involved, that re-entering the world afterwards felt ugly and crass:

my friend and I travelled back to Cambridge in silence, and went our separate ways – for my part, back to my college room, where I stayed up until daybreak, scrawling an outburst of questions, observations, objections even, with which I ended up covering the walls. How had they done it? How had *The Street of Crocodiles* done what it did to me?

Théâtre de Complicité, *The Street of Crocodiles* © Joan Marcus.

This experience was – and remains – important to me for three reasons. One: it was the first time I ever saw professional theatre and was genuinely moved by it: not making an effort to engage because I thought I should, but because I had no choice other than to yield to its extraordinary power and lyricism. (I don't suppose I've felt that more than a dozen times since: but maybe that's more than enough.) Two: it inculcated in me a reflex that has served me well: to want to take apart what I don't understand: to analyse it with all the tools at my disposal, at least attempting to apply some kind of careful or rigorous thought to what may initially appear to resist analysis altogether. By dissecting *The Street of Crocodiles* in that geeky way, overnight I learned things about theatre that still matter to me today, and which will show up later in this book. Three: it encouraged in me, as someone who saw himself (and still does) as a writer and an artist who works dedicatedly with words, a fascination in what lies beyond words, and before them, and behind them. In how *The Street of Crocodiles*, which has a perfectly fine authored text (you can buy a copy of the script, after all), did so much of its most emotionally enthralling work in a space where language is too crude or overbearing a technology to do justice to the fluid complexity of human experience. How, in fact, it is quite often the failure of words in the face of our lived (and imagined) experience that creates the physical rush of intensity, the bodily sensation of our profoundest longing and most potent desires. And how it was partly through the evident but inexpressible *complicité* – exactly – of that ensemble, the shared rhythms and the sub- (or pre-)linguistic quasi-telepathic simpatico of that company at that time, that I came to some early understanding of how the sustained and concentrated fellowship that I had felt in the process of making *The Earth Divided* could show up excitingly, tantalisingly, on stage for an audience who had no knowledge of how that sense of togetherness could possibly have been achieved.

Back at university, I continued to write plays, as I had done right from the start (hiding in my room throughout Freshers' Week, too shy to venture out, knocking up a one-act play as a pretext for meeting some like-minded students). But play-writing was an activity that was already becoming strange to me. I was trying to come to terms with the influence not only of *The Street of Crocodiles* but also of the dance-theatre works I was coming to admire, the chronically underrated Yolande Snaith above all; the contemporary visual art, especially the installation work, I had started to enjoy seeing at the Arnolfini in Bristol, or at Kettle's Yard in Cambridge, or at the (then) Museum of Modern Art in Oxford; leftfield films like David Byrne's *True Stories* or Gus van Sant's *My Own Private Idaho* (both of which remain key reference points for me); and live art by the likes of Station House Opera and the Damned Lovely. Increasingly, inspired by these artists and dozens more, I was thinking in images, I was dreaming movement; I was becoming more immediately interested in how people looked and what they were doing than in the words they might be saying to each other. By the time I came to write what became my first professionally produced full-length stage play, *Kissing Bingo*, it was clear that a tension was growing between what I wanted to see on stage and how effective a medium the play-script could be for capturing those ideas. To put it simply, my stage directions were getting longer and longer. Three scenes of *Kissing Bingo* had no dialogue at all, just written choreographies. The language that came most readily to me was one that had more in common with eighties art-pop videos, or Charles Atlas and Michael Clark's thrillingly edgy dance films for late-night Channel 4, or fashion shoots in style magazines, or Derek Jarman's Super-8 movies, or Bob Cobbing's ecstatically smudgy visual poetry, than with tight little English plays in which people talked to each other in neat rows of small words.

One response to this state of affairs – and one that seemed expedient rather than at all visionary or ideological – was for me to start directing my own work. Helen Raynor made a very nice job of *Kissing Bingo* at the Finborough in 1996, but by that time I had pretty decisively moved into a practice where writing was just one of a number of elements that were created, as far as possible, in the rehearsal room; in trying things out with actors and harnessing their own inventiveness and their willingness to play; in relating visual ideas and movement ideas and sound ideas without having to capture these, let alone pre-empt their discovery, in plain text on the page. In other words, I started devising without quite knowing what I was up to; it didn't occur to me that anyone else made work like this, but neither did I suppose that I was doing anything unusual. At that time it was simply about getting the work made, in as rich and honest and enjoyable a way as I could imagine, both for myself and for the actors I worked with. There didn't seem to be a choice that needed to be made, a privileging of one approach over another. In 1995, while still a student, I made for the first time a full-length piece (called *River Phoenix on the Sidewalk*) that had no script at all, except for eight one-sheet monologues. But on the other hand, by this time I also had a literary agent, and my next production was a scripted play called *Weepie* – which had in it, along with a lot of words of various lengths, three scenes without dialogue again. At least now I didn't have to write absurdly detailed stage directions: those scenes would be devised with the actors, in the room, in response to a particular performance venue and context.

My work continued to occupy (quite comfortably, as far as I was concerned) this middle-ground for the next little while, through the setting up of my first company, Signal to Noise, and the beginnings of my association with the Leeds-based company Unlimited Theatre, who were interested in exploring a similar vein of writing-centred ensemble devising, and with whom I went on to make a piece called *Neutrino* which in some respects exemplified that approach. The next move I was to make, however, critically reframed some of the artistic questions that I was working with at the time.

In November 2001, I was appointed to run Camden People's Theatre, a pioneering – and, needless to say, perpetually struggling – fringe venue in central London. CPT had been founded in 1994 by a group of practitioners whose common ground was a commitment to collaborative making practices and to a theatrical aesthetic and language that privileged physical and visual elements over verbal ones. In both these respects, the originators of CPT had ideological reasons for their programme: they were seeking to make work in ways that felt consistent with their political beliefs; perhaps less obviously, their attachment to movement, gesture and image-driven work was rooted in an impulse to make their theatre as open as possible to the broadest, most diverse audience, with a particular eye on the local community, which had large immigrant and transient populations with whom the company sought to engage. If those potential audiences didn't speak English at home, why should they be expected to do so when they went out for an evening's entertainment?

In fact, as subsequent research seemed to indicate, what those audiences really wanted was not culturally non-specific, non-text-based clown/mime shows, but text-based narrative drama with dialogue in their own first language, exploring issues that were relevant to their daily lives. In other words, CPT couldn't even lead that particular horse to water, and as such, it tended (in those days at least) to be seen more as an eccentric player on the fringe circuit, offering niche fare to a specialist audience that was often, frankly, vanishingly small. Nonetheless, becoming the venue's custodian for three years compelled me for once to come down on one side of the argument around text-driven theatre and, by uncomfortable extension, against the other side.

From the distance of just a decade it is difficult to remember how different the ecology of London theatre (and to some extent British theatre in general) felt at that time. Although the centrality of 'new writing' in the culture was to some extent being challenged in the early/mid 2000s by emerging companies such as Shunt, Filter and Gecko, as well as more established outfits such as Complicite, Improbable, Kneehigh and Frantic Assembly – and of course the likes of Forced Entertainment and Stan's Cafe just a few inches to their left; and notwithstanding that all these companies' work was frequently distinguished by superb writing that paradoxically failed to register on most critics' and opponents' perceptual apparatus precisely because, unlike a lot of mainstream play-writing at the time, it was so smartly and imaginatively tailored to theatrical, rather than literary, modes of production and inscription: nonetheless, it still felt at that time compulsory, and bracingly assertive, to taxonomise this non-standard work as 'physical theatre', 'devised theatre', 'visual theatre' and so on. (These now outmoded terms still seem to have a surprisingly extended half-life in the discourse of various institutions: it's a good way of monitoring their basic conservatism.) So, for example, Unlimited and I took our first collaborative venture to BAC's 'Festival of Visual Theatre' in 2000, while CPT's annual Sprint Festival had been straplining its dedication to 'physical, visual and unusual theatre' since 1997. (I swiftly and silently dropped the 'unusual' when I took over: it seemed to me a pretty meagre way of distinguishing what the venue sought to do.) These appellations represented a decent stab at managing expectations, but they inevitably led to a sense of quarantine around the work they were intended to describe and make more available, and the embedding in the culture of a demonstrably inaccurate and weirdly obdurate 'two tribes' mentality. When in 2001 BAC rebranded its festival as Octoberfest, the move seemed both admirably pragmatic and tinged with defeatism: how could a coherent promotional narrative be spun around work whose only common factors were an unwillingness to be hidebound by dominant models, and being existent in the month of October?

At any rate, CPT's programming policy was clear. We were emphatically not a 'new writing' venue. (This didn't stop us receiving several unsolicited scripts every week, many of which were so irredeemably bizarre that I often had to talk myself sternly out of wanting to put them on.) There were enough – more than enough – new writing venues at every level of the industry. We wanted to be a haven for something different. Looking back, I'm as glad now as I was then to be fighting this particular corner, albeit from the unhappy starting-point of saying what we didn't do rather than what we did: but out of that commitment two awkward problems gradually emerged. Firstly, it reasserted and entrenched a binary which has always been specious, when we could have been questioning the premise of the division; nowadays, more mainstream figures are trying to testify to the phoneyness of the war, which certainly mirrors the reality that many if not most makers currently experience, but doesn't seem to alter – in fact possibly intensifies – some influential playwrights' determined insistence that they are intrinsically entitled to their centrality and the prestige that manifestly goes with it. Secondly, more personally, it placed me in an acutely conflicted relationship with my own work. Every one of the shows I created at CPT involved writers (including

myself) – in fact, *Past the Line, Between the Land* in 2003 included specially
solicited texts by several writers, ranging from Forced Entertainment's
Tim Etchells to poet Allen Fisher to the Japanese cyberpunk author
Kenji Siratori. The clear implication was not that devised or experimental
theatre had no time for writing, but that, more disquietingly, soi-disant
'new writing' had no time for *this* writing.

Certainly, my very happy spell at CPT finally reinforced my sense that
I couldn't get on with much 'new writing', not because I had little use for
writing but, on the contrary, because I wanted writing to work so much
harder. I was, at this time, deeply involved in London's experimental
poetry scene – indeed I invited the long-running Sub Voicive reading
series and the even longer-running Writers Forum Workshops (which
had been started by Bob Cobbing in the 1950s) in to the theatre, and
curated myself two festivals under the name Total Writing London, with
a view to programming interesting poets alongside live art which engaged
closely with exploratory language practices, as well as leftfield music,
and especially free improvisation, with which experimental poetry has
had a fascinatingly entangled history. Inspired perhaps above all by J.H.
Prynne's devastating short essay 'A Quick Riposte to Handke's Dictum
about War and Language',[5] I increasingly distrusted the use to which
many playwrights seemed pleased to put their words, as a supposedly
stable and transparent carrier of narrative and fictive information, often
with an intermittent strenuous lyrical uplift that spoke directly to the
vacuously reverberant epiphanic gruel which then (as now) characterised
much 'official' British poetry. I was becoming much more interested – as
I think I had been to some extent for a long while – in text as texture and
as tone generator, in modernist and materialist perspectives on language
as a much more complex producer of meaning and identification.

This appointment, then, was the third in this series of (what were for
me) significant movements in my understanding of what theatre might
be. But its consequences are, in a way, hard to track. My tenure at CPT
ended with a production called *Escapology*[6] which had a lot of fun with
the slipperiness and absurdity of language, not least by requiring its six
intrepid actors to improvise much of the script afresh each night; the
unreliability of language structures in that piece, and the pressures that
were built up in this way, certainly led directly to a two-hander, *Longwave*,
for Tom Lyall and Jamie Wood, the actors who had so gorgeously played
the squabbling Montgolfier Brothers in *Escapology*. *Longwave* was, in
fulfilment perhaps of a trajectory that I couldn't see so clearly at the

time, a play without words; or, at least, it was billed as such, because neither of the characters ever spoke. In fact, *Longwave* was full of words, which spilled out of the play's antagonist, a malign radio. (No, really.) Not only did it not matter that much of what that radio 'said' was in Finnish or Italian: it was vitally necessary that audiences were invited from the very beginning to listen to its speeches for tone, for colour, for rhythm, rather than for narrative data.

Perhaps, somehow, *Longwave* cleared the decks for me. Certainly, when, not long after, I was approached by the Theatre Royal in Plymouth, with a view to my making something for their Drum space, the idea that most excited me was the challenge of writing a 'proper' play. In fact I have now written three plays to commission for the Drum – *Speed Death of the Radiant Child*, *King Pelican*, and *MAD MAN* (after Gogol) – and while none could reasonably be called conventional textbook plays, all of them behaved in many ways like pieces of 'new writing' probably should. There have been other plays too, but I admit I can never quite bring myself to write a play that doesn't, somehow, eat itself or harm itself; the structure is always purposely undermined, the scripted world suffused with a sense of constraint and paranoia, the weight of artifice constantly threatening (and usually ultimately managing) to collapse the whole construction.

These written plays are, in a sense, simply a flipside of the pieces I make at the other end of the (still disputed) axis, in which I am able to feel more relaxed, and allow more of an openness: an acknowledgement of togetherness, and a glad dependence on the networks of feeling that a sense of that togetherness can so often release in an audience: in other words, the theatrical situation is acknowledged from within the operations of the work, rather than suppressed or suspended as it generally has to be, although unsustainably and ultimately self-destructively, in the scripted plays.

One particular thread of this 'other' work originated, by my reckoning, in 2003, while I was still at CPT. I had wanted to direct a production of *Macbeth*, to make retroactively a Shakespeare trilogy with my previous stagings of *The Tempest*, which I made with a cast of six for performance in audiences' own homes, a project that began as a sort of undergraduate prank in 1994 and gradually became a serious and fundamental part of my artistic offering over several years, as well as being the project that first won me the critical attention of the national press; and *Twelfth Night*, which I had very happily directed at CPT the summer before I took over as artistic director (the day-to-day reality being, of course, that, whatever its programming policies might be, CPT often had to take whatever work could pay the rent.)

Macbeth, however, was turned down for Arts Council funding, which made it impossible to produce. My reaction to this disappointing news was to want to make something much smaller by way of a ritual, almost, in memory of this lost project. Reconfiguring my overview of *Macbeth* to focus, or fixate even, on the minor character of Fleance, Banquo's young son who has to flee for his life, I worked with the performer Theron Schmidt, who was at that time a frequent collaborator, to develop a solo for him to perform, which we came to call *his horses*. This was a piece which sought to create a certain tone, and a kind of spaciousness or reflectiveness, with Theron at its centre (or sometimes on its periphery, even, despite his being the sole performer) occupying a softly ambiguous role, for the most part working through a series of apparently simple tasks and self-(re)stagings. We arrived at a rule for text: anything that would have been spoken the same way in every performance would be pre-recorded; whatever was spoken live would be improvised. There was dance-like material, including a sequence reflecting Theron's interest at that time in Butoh; and there was talking; but mostly there were small, unshowy – though pictorial – events: dressing and undressing; combing hair; burning a leaf; putting on make-up; painting a wall; drawing diagrams and writing out equations on the floor; eating an apple; finally, going to sleep – in which mode Theron ended the performance, with audiences leaving only when they were ready to do so. The aim was to create a feeling

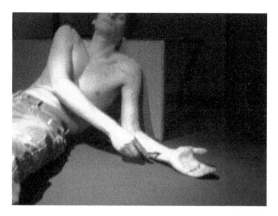

Theron Schmidt in *his horses*. Camden People's Theatre, 2003 © Rajni Shah.

of gentle intimacy through which it might be possible to tune in to a sense of loss, an awareness of time, perhaps a summoning of ghosts; this was enough. My work to this point had always been notoriously packed, even overloaded: yet in this case it was clear that less could also be more.

Theron and I showed *his horses* at CPT again the following year, in a version billed as a 'remix' of the original piece; and when I left the venue at the end of 2004 I wanted to pick up with Theron where we'd left off. For the next three years, on and off, we continued to work together, not (at least initially) with a particular production in mind, but simply wanting to continue what felt like a valuable collaborative dialogue. Mostly we worked either in a spare room in the house I shared, or in Theron's flat: small, squeezed domestic environments which afforded all of the intimacies of my home performances but also all of their constraints. It was hard to keep up the momentum, especially without scheduled targets – public performances, sharings, whatever – to which I was reluctant to commit while it felt like we were still so much in transit and the work we were doing was so fragile. Eventually, in 2008, as the vectors of our respective interests started to diverge and the difficulty of the work we were doing began to feel intractable, we reluctantly called it quits.

At the time, the breach seemed terminal, and personally as well as professionally painful, and I was ruefully certain that the line of thought that I was pursuing and which had become matchlessly important in my sense of my own praxis would have to end abruptly in that moment; I have always felt that my 'body' of work is necessarily, but perilously, dependent upon its 'embodiment' by particular collaborators with whom I hope to work over long periods, accruing certain idiosyncratic kinds of expertise. I had by this time developed a sense of the material that I wanted the next piece in this vein to draw on: the life and work of the American anarchist philosopher and sociologist Paul Goodman, and in particular the way in which his erotic attachment to young men was evidently grievously injured and disarrayed when his son, Mathew Ready Goodman, was killed in a climbing accident in 1967 at the age of just twenty-one.

For a while I feared that, with Theron having withdrawn, that piece was now unmakeable. But I happened to remember seeing on the Edinburgh Fringe the previous summer an actor called Jonny Liron, who had been performing in *Apollo/Dionysus*, a curious but in many ways remarkable play written and directed by Daniel Austin. Jonny was evidently an actor capable of performing with incredible insouciance and an enviable pleasure in his own physical confidence and charisma.

I managed to track him down, and we started a conversation; four months later, he was in London, and we were embarking on the (Arts Council funded) process of making together my Goodman piece, now called *Hey Mathew*.

Nothing in my body of work is as hard to assess as *Hey Mathew*, even now that more than six years have passed since we showed it. It was a piece, and a process, in which the normal boundaries that are supposed to keep makers and audience alike in a place of safety simply – or not at all simply – broke down: not least because Jonny and I, in the heady thrill of meeting each other and revelling in the excitement of a new working relationship that seemed able to be uncommonly intrepid, chose to ignore, or perhaps to leap over, those boundaries. In doing so, it is certainly possible that we took too little care of our other collaborators, and of our audiences, and perhaps of ourselves; at the same time, in creating that piece Jonny and I thought and spoke about little other than wanting to take the best possible care of our audiences and our co-workers precisely by crafting a space which we hoped would be warmed and illuminated by an exceptional degree of openness and candour.

For some, there's no doubt that the intense intimacies of *Hey Mathew* were too much: what we were doing seemed to them alarming and consequently aggressive. For others, a willingness to be seduced in the November evening performances by the gentleness of tone with which we hoped to alleviate the challenging nature of some of the content was superseded, in the cold light of the following day, by confusion and concern: a sharp experience of the morning after the night before. For others still, I think it's fair to suggest that the work was, and remains, an example of brave and generous (and perhaps upsetting) theatre-making. I certainly remember the presence of all of these types of audience member, and feel especially fondly about all those who found themselves somewhere in-between, embracing each other in the foyer afterwards, as if to say (or actually saying): "Are you OK?"

It is certainly true that I am in some ways more proud of *Hey Mathew* than of anything else I've made, though almost everything I've done before or since has been more unequivocally liked by more people. It is also true that the process was to some extent injurious. I'm never sure whether perhaps it had to be; it was, as all creative processes are (and as all worthwhile theatrical productions are, for good or ill), a record of who we were when we were making it, and of what we did in the conviction that, whatever it was, we were doing it for the best. If nothing else, it was the start of a creative and personal relationship that radically shaped and underwrote everything I did for the next five years, a relationship in which the distinction between 'doing some work' and 'just hanging out' was seldom clear: in which ambiguity rests much that I think is productive, as this book will hope to suggest.

If the making of *Hey Mathew*, for all of its turbulences, is the fourth and last of the formative passages that I intend to recall here, it's because, way more than any other project I've ever initiated, it bore out the hunch I've had ever since *The Earth Divided*: that, at its best, you can live inside theatre, in the way that you might feel that you live inside a set of political or religious commitments: the feeling that you don't contain such commitments – they contain you. Thus theatre becomes a way of looking at the world, a way of forming and deepening relationships, a way of connecting the intellectual and the romantic, the political and the sexual, the individual and the collective, the civic and the visionary, the present and the future. To borrow what the poet Roy Fisher said (of Birmingham)[7]: theatre's what I think with. Seen always as a hybrid art and a social practice, theatre will expand to accommodate whatever you bring to it; everything can be taken to the work, nothing is necessarily excluded. This gives it a reach and a valency that can be daunting, the power not only to enlighten but to consume.

Jonny Liron in *Hey Mathew*.
Theatre in the Mill, 2008
© Simon Warner.

In a way, the worst thing that happened in the making of *Hey Mathew* was that I forgot my dad's birthday. For the first time in my life, and by miles, by days and days, because I was so immersed in the work, I forgot his birthday. I still feel bad about that.

––––––––

The great and fondly-missed theatrical troublemaker and mind-expander Ken Campbell, with whom I was fortunate to spend some time in the late 1990s, used to say that he didn't believe in believing things, but that he was prepared to *suppose everything.*[8]

Beneath its many scenic turns, this book proceeds as methodically as any book on theatre could be expected to, through a series of single steps which I describe below. But it hardly needs saying that, right from the point of embarkation, our task is problematic in the first place because we lack any kind of common ground from which to make our departure. Even my closest colleagues would take issue with some of the assumptions that I don't even know I've already made, but which will tacitly inform the journey ahead.

For that reason, I want to do what I can to describe the three basic suppositions that I'd invite you to set out with. No reader need fully believe even these first principles, but so as to not waste your time altogether I would encourage you to entertain the possibility that one might suppose them, for the time being, and proceed from there.

The first is this: that theatre is worth taking seriously, and that one way of taking it seriously is to think about it.

I imagine that for most readers who have already got this far with my introductory remarks, or even who have picked this book up in a shop or library and are flipping through it to see what it's made of, this first point is a truism that hardly needs stating. But it is perhaps worth reminding ourselves that we are not representative of the whole population of theatre makers in Britain, let alone beyond. There remain, in both amateur and professional sectors, plenty of busy and successful artists and creatives, and large audiences too, for whom the idea of theatre as an intellectual pursuit is abhorrent and infuriating. They have a cheerfully pragmatic approach to the business of staging and watching plays, the shorthand of which is familiar to all: learn your lines and don't bump into the furniture; give 'em the old razzle-dazzle; bums on seats and pass the Maltesers, it's only a bit of fun. I don't actually find this attitude at all despicable – it has a great deal more to recommend it than some of the smug and joyless approaches that pass unexamined from generation to generation in many of our drama schools and major institutions, passing for a mainstream orthodoxy. It is an attitude with its sights trained on entertainment: which is among the highest aspirations with which theatre can be made.

We might also recognize that lighter shades of the same dispositions persist in far more (supposedly) elevated situations. I've been told many times by theatre people of some standing that I'm 'overthinking' a question of staging or approach; and I've heard more than once that my writing on theatre is 'pretentious' in its intellectual exertions. And of course I know what they mean and recognize some of their fears. To think *at the expense of* movement, to worry away at some nicety such that instinct is suffocated and intuition is crowded out, to wander through abstraction into a kind of deep-space remoteness, is all too easy: and when I say above that theatre is what I think with, part of what I'm getting at is that I like the very various kinds of thinking that a fully theatrical process will foster: thinking with and through the body, thinking on your feet in the room with others in conversation and play, thinking with a beating heart and a reckless romantic attachment to one's co-workers. The reason I like exploring philosophical ideas in my work is that I suspect the answers that emerge through thinking within theatre are often more human – richer and more dimensionalized – than those which are squeezed out in solitary and sedentary pondering. I enjoyed a recent remark[9] by the poet Ian McMillan that he found it helpful to read difficult poetry in a swivel chair: the movement helped him to process what he was reading. Likewise it often seems to me that really good theatre, like great dance, achieves its brilliance by having the right balance of craft, confidence and spontaneity to be able to move at the same speed as the thought within it: much as Ian Patterson writes of J.H. Prynne's poetry "catching the instant on the wing and flying with it."[10]

But the movement that matters most (to me) is not this "flying" in itself, but the motion between the mode of spontaneous discovery and the application of a careful and rigorous attention to a process of reflection on that discovery. In this reflective state I am trying to listen, in an almost devotional way, to what theatre is telling me about itself. If it is true (and I certainly think it is) that making theatre, like all creative acts, is first and foremost an art of wanting – of wanting something to exist, or to take its place in the world, that is not yet there, or is not yet seen to be there – then part of my wanting is the desire to understand what *theatre* wants. If this sounds mystical, its truth is almost comically quotidian: in the making process – the process of travelling from what we think we want to make, to watching in the end what it is that we've made – many things inevitably change: and in those shifts are countless clues as to what kinds of wants theatre can accommodate and be hospitable to, and what desires conversely are extraneous and interferent, and have to do with us rather than it. Most makers will recognize the truth of this, but often we are too quick to shrug and blame circumstances, or to concede the notion that as creative artists we are simply throwing a bunch of ideas at a wall and seeing what sticks. My approach has always been more methodical, more forensic; more curious, ultimately. The rubbish left behind at the end of a project which has partly worked and partly not contains within it the possible beginnings of a dozen more projects. There is at the base of my contention that part even of the most wilful manifesto for theatre must be a concern with what theatre wants to tell us about itself a very simple and unglamorous resourcefulness, a measure of expediency.

For these reasons, I like to think as deeply and carefully as I can about theatre: I think it makes me make better theatre, for all that the questions that come to the surface, and those that lurk naggingly and inarticulably just beneath, can sometimes feel overwhelming. I might, however, associate with this first principle a disclaimer. I am not by any means a theatre academic. I appreciate scholarship and I think I apply to my work in theatre certain critical skills that I learned from my undergraduate degree in English and my musical studies. But I cannot claim a command of, or indeed an especially close interest in, the academic territories of theatre and performance. In fact I am frequently puzzled by academic books and essays on theatre – most of which focus on a small coterie of international practitioners who have a particular currency in the academy, and are written by people who seem to have very different relationships with the whole idea of theatre than my own, let alone those of casual theatre-goers. To those who can make use of such discourses, I've no doubt they are enriching rather than obfuscating; and certainly there are academic theatre writers whom I find immensely lively and stimulating, though even they are seldom of much use in the moments where theatre actually happens.

So to my earlier warning about my not having trained as a director or learned by assisting, I must add this further disclaimer that I am not a trained thinker-about-theatre either. I do read a lot of books by other directors and makers, and my experience over the years has been that of (presumably) many autodidact practitioners: the insight that arrives suddenly and with the force of a wholly original discovery in rehearsal on a Wednesday afternoon will turn up, apparently quite coincidentally, much more concisely and cogently expressed, five days later in the book you've been reading between tube stops for the past month. My own book, then, is sure to do the same for some readers, though as its author I can see only the awful flipside: everything I say in these pages will surely already have been proposed in some other book I haven't read yet, and comprehensively disputed in another. Well, for the sake of being able to write anything at all, so it goes. Often at the beginning of a devising process these days I'll find myself in a room with a group of collaborators some of whom are vastly more experienced in the industry than others, and some of whom furthermore may be much more experienced than me; sometimes it's good to remind everyone on the first day that nobody present, including myself, is any more experienced than anyone else in the process of making *this* show, because we haven't started making it yet. If that observation can be stretched across to excuse the lacunae in this book – which will appear different to every reader, of course – then that's a great help: and on that basis, I cordially invite you to enjoy those passages that follow wherein it's quite evident that you know more about the topic at hand than I do.

If with my first assumption – 'thinking about theatre is a good thing' – I am preaching to the choir, my second may require more of a leap of faith. An otherwise unspoken principle which underscores the argument of this book is that theatre should be *as much like itself as possible*.

I think I can only explain what I mean by recourse once again to personal experience. At about the time that I was starting out professionally, in the mid 1990s, theatre was being pronounced dead or dying, as it almost always is or has been from some quarter. Normally the moribundity is evidenced through a more-or-less specious connection being drawn between dwindling audience numbers, or the underrepresentation of certain demographics in the composition of audiences, and a concomitant increase in the popularity of some other cultural pastime or lifestyle choice; and the inference is drawn that, in order to survive, theatre must make itself over so as to more closely resemble whatever the popular thing is at that moment. So, for example, at the point that I was beginning to think seriously about theatre, there was from some quarters an urging that, in order to secure its continued relevance, theatre should be more like club culture, because clubs were full of young people spending money, and theatres were not.

My instinctive resistance to this line of thought – theatre should be more like clubbing, or television, or the internet, in order to appeal to a wider constituency – expresses itself in an obvious and clearcut rejoinder: in order to maximize its appeal, theatre should actually be *less* like other cultural forms, and *more like itself*. The problem that this position acknowledges is, in part, that theatre can only ever be a bit like those other things. Theatre is already too much like television, for example, but also not enough: it concentrates on modes of linear storytelling and varieties of psychological realism that TV does brilliantly; partly TV does those things because it also has a syntax of framing and cutting and mobility, of different kinds of camera movement that allow the viewer's attention to be very specifically directed, of shots that can instantly create intimacies and disconnects at once more subtle and more assertive than anything that can be achieved on stage, even when theatre consciously mimics that grammar and maybe even incorporates screens and live video feeds into its presentational apparatus.

The difficulty with identifying what it is that distinguishes theatre *as opposed to* any other format or platform is that, if any particular quality does, then it's surely its hybridity. Asking theatre to be 'more like itself' brings to mind Caroline Bergvall's brilliant poem/text 'More Pets', which starts by setting out a speculative yearning for:

> a more — cat
> a more — dog dog
> a more — horse
> a more — rat
> a more — canary
> a more — snake[11]

and so on, but quickly moves into more complex chimerical specifications:

> a more — turtle cat
> a more — turtle — more — cat dog
> a more — dog — more — cat horse
> a more — dog — less —horse — less — cat rat

and finally:

> a lessplus — notrat — monlapin — dogless — horsecheval not
> a plusnot — notnot — notrat — goldfish — cancan canary

– *et cetera*. This tendency towards multiplicity of language, polyphony of voice, and polymorphism of image and relation seems, paradoxically, distinctively theatrical in its insistence on the complexity of meaning-generation and the fluency of play. A 'more — theatre', to borrow Bergvall's formulation, is surely more compendious, more expansive, more connective. (We can, however, recognize that this may be so, but equally be aware that a commodious theatre is not always a successful theatre, and that a rather celibate theatre, which does one small thing perfectly, can seem to be using the medium with great refinement and understanding.)

Furthermore, the problematic nature of this proposition is compounded by the third assumption I want to bring in to play: that another part of theatre's distinctiveness (it cannot be the whole of it because it's a quality that obtains in other forms too) is its liveness, its happening only and entirely in the moment of its enaction. As Andrew Upton, the artistic director of Sydney Theatre Company, says:

> Theatre is now. It is of now and therefore, inevitably about now.
> That is the most abiding characteristic of the form for me.
> 'Now' is its it-ness. It happens now, in front of you and is gone forever. Forms of recording drama have evolved mighty quickly into other forms in their own right.
> Theatre remains. Now only.[12]

To the extent that this is true – and I wholly share Upton's belief in the vital importance of this characteristic quality of theatre – it follows that theatre cannot always be the same; that it changes not, or not solely, through the efforts of innovating artists or in response to the pressure of audiences' shifting tastes and the currents of fashion, but in response (and by contradistinction) to its social, cultural and political environment. What it means now to 'put a play on', to stage an event, to make a piece of theatre, is not what it might have meant five, let alone fifty, years previously. (It is partly for this reason that I am unconvinced by arguments for the cultural centrality of writing-centred theatre that appeal to custom or heritage. What it meant for Christopher Marlowe to be a playwright is not what it means now for, say, Inua Ellams to write for theatre; what it meant for someone like Howard Brenton to work as a playwright in the 1970s is vastly different to what it means now, for reasons that extend far beyond whatever may have changed in his personal and professional circumstances, and the relationship that he has with theatre both as an industry and as an artistic practice is greatly altered.)

I have now been at work long enough to be able to plot some changes in my own sense of what I'm doing. A very clear example leaps out when I look back at the manifesto I wrote in 1999 when we launched Signal to Noise. The programme for our debut production that year carried a text which made much of the (as I then thought) crucial importance of sincerity, as a quality which, at that time, seemed to me to be not only largely missing in the work of the experimental theatre sector in Britain, but the object of contempt and disdain. For my part, as a young maker with a much more lyrical view of what theatre could do, the prevailing thrall to irony had become just another marker of that culture's political nullity and risk-aversion – what artist and critic Andrew Gellatly had brilliantly described earlier that year as "hip fatigue – the ironist's love of his cage."[13] What was required, I wanted to affirm, was the (implicitly moral, as well as artistic) courage to make work in a mode of sincerity.

Just four years later, the illegal and profoundly immoral US/British assault on Afghanistan and invasion of Iraq were being justified by their proponents in part by the 'sincerity' of George W. Bush and Tony Blair's conviction that their criminal actions were merited and proportionate. Disagreement could be tolerated, it was said, but that 'sincerity' was not to be impugned. And so, with the building of a whole rhetorical edifice of neocon righteousness on the foundations of that word, what it meant to be 'sincere' (as opposed to 'ironic', in my somewhat faulty construction) entirely shifted, and though what I wanted artistically had not much changed, how those ideas could be positioned in the wider culture would need radical rethinking. (In fact this process of rethinking, considered particularly in the long aftermath of 9/11, was essentially the starting point for much of what follows in these pages, especially in chapter 4.)

Looking back over the past twenty years of my work in theatre, it's easier to see the constant alterations, the responses, the kinks in the trajectory: and the process of writing this book has allowed me for the first time to try and form those movements retrospectively into something approaching a single argument or narrative. But I offer this train of thought only as a model, nothing more. To write a book about theatre is by extension to write about current affairs; in fact the 'now'-ness of theatre to which Andrew Upton points can only undermine and constrain the effectiveness of any attempt to set down on paper a consideration of the nature of theatre: the only part that will remain true is the bit about change, which is the bit a paper publication can least successfully reflect. That being so, this book has in one sense an expiry date perhaps not more than a few months after the moment of its initial publication; but I hope the questions it poses will remain pertinent even when the answers I offer have ceased to present any vital signs.

Aside from and lurking beneath these three operating principles – which we might combine into a single statement of intent: something like: 'it is worth thinking carefully about what theatre distinctively is, right now' – there is a final set of assumptions we should name before we embark on our journey together. We quickly run into feedback problems in trying to say what theatre is, at a point in time when the range of practices and approaches that might be considered 'theatre' is broader and more diverse than ever before: a situation that is variously seen, from different perspectives, as the happy pluralism of a 'broad church', or as a battleground on which certain values are to be defended and promoted in competition for a finite pool of producing resources and media coverage, or as a variegated territory in which only one or two small sectors might properly be considered to qualify for the appellation 'theatre'.

It is probably true that the default liberal position is the wish to be as inclusive as possible: whoever says they are making theatre is making theatre, whether or not their work sits comfortably with our own priorities. But I dare say many makers will recognize the feelings of panic and dismay that at some point may have seized them when they know that they are discussing their work with someone who is orienting themselves in the conversation by means of reference points that are painfully out of sync: whether it's the family member at a Christmas get-together who has only ever seen *Starlight Express* and *Mamma Mia*, or who happens to know Felicity Kendal's dentist, and whose expectations (and in particular their assessment of what it might mean to be successful in one's work) are impossibly remote from one's own; or the blood-letting performance artist whose immediate response to the very idea of theatre is an open disdain coloured by frustratingly outmoded (though, admittedly, not wholly unfounded) visions of decrepit velvet curtains being laboriously hoisted over a proscenium arch stage and posh people talking inconsequentially about their tedious heterosexual entanglements behind a pristine invisible wall.

It can be similarly painful, perhaps even more so, when visual artists working with performance, such as Marina Abramović or Tino Sehgal, express their contempt for and revulsion at the very idea of 'theatre'. Here's Abramović in an online interview with Robert Ayers in 2010:

> This is what I think: to be a performance artist, you have to hate theatre. Theatre is fake: there is a black box, you pay for a ticket, and you sit in the dark and see somebody playing somebody else's life. The knife is not real, the blood is not real, and the emotions are not real. Performance is just the opposite: the knife is real, the blood is real, and the emotions are real. It's a very different concept. It's about true reality.[14]

I find this hard to take for all sorts of reasons. Firstly, the binary 'performance' vs 'theatre' is surely untenable, as is 'real' vs 'fake': both the theatre maker and the performance artist are concerned with staging constructed events, in which there is (if they are not to be completely inert) some degree of tension between the ways in which that event is 'real' and the ways in which it is, if not fake exactly, then fictive, or speculatively manufactured. Secondly, the version of theatre she describes is partial at best, and in so far as it describes something that actually occurs, I probably dislike that kind of theatre as much as she does. Thirdly, however I might on any given day choose to define or describe 'theatre', I think I would always want it to be able to include works such as Abramović's 'The Artist is Present' (which I discuss more fully in chapter 3), or Sehgal's remarkable 'These Associations', his piece for the Unilever series of commissions for Tate Modern's Turbine Hall. "[Theatre] is for me a problematic format," Sehgal told the *Guardian*'s Charlotte Higgins: "because it belongs to another time, a more collective time. For me, politically, to sit people down, shut them up and ask them to look in one direction, somehow doesn't belong to our times."[15] To which, many theatre makers, including myself to some extent, would say only: Amen. Certainly, 'These Associations' is, to my mind, one of the best pieces of theatre I've ever seen. If Sehgal says so emphatically that it's not, my only argument is that when he and I talk about theatre, we must be talking about two different things; and yet when he describes theatre in that dismissive thumbnail sketch, I can only recognize that, sure enough, he is talking about theatre: and so theatre is both the thing that he says it is, and also something profoundly different. The key, perhaps, is his opening assertion that theatre "belongs to another time": it could be argued that the theatre he describes really does belong to another time, really is outmoded (which is not the same thing as it not being around any more), and that when I think about theatre, I'm thinking about theatre *now*: a theatre that I think might be more palatable to him because it is already showing, in some regions, the influence of relational artists such as him – and, for that matter, of new-school European dance companies such as Les Ballets C de la B, with whom Sehgal started his career in the late 90s.

A problem arises, though, when we try to define theatre in this almost gerrymandering way, constantly redrawing the boundaries so that everything we like and approve of falls within them, and everything we dislike or are embarrassed by is neatly excluded. A problem arises; but also, perhaps, a space opens up, a more generous and curious and intelligent space, a possibility of enlargement and inquiry.

In 2007 I set out on a project (which will at long last be realised in 2015) to create a theatre 'adaptation' of the blog maintained by the American novelist, poet and theatre writer Dennis Cooper. Cooper's blog[16] is fascinating for many reasons: he generally posts there every day except Sundays, and the great majority of posts, rather than being directly 'about' Cooper himself or his reflections on work and current events, present material relating to a topic in which he has – or is prepared to suppose – an interest: perhaps an overlooked author, or a survey of bands relating to a particular scene, or rollercoasters, say, or crazy golf courses, or (regularly every month) an assortment of online personal ads placed by young men working as escorts. Due in part to Cooper's smart and intensely loyal fanbase, and in part to his willingness to interact attentively with readers in a daily postscript to the main post, an ad hoc community of significant size gathers at the blog every day to discuss, in the blog's comments field, the day's post, and also their own work and thoughts and (in some cases) the minutiae of their daily lives. It is a community characterised by flux and, especially in its earlier years, a good deal of 'performance', but some commenters have been around the blog for a long time and have become friends and colleagues offline as well as on. (When we made *Hey Mathew* in 2008, the contributors included Cooper himself as well as the novelist and poet Thomas Moore and the visual artist Kier Cooke Sandvik, both of whom I had met through Dennis's blog.)

Members of this blog community frequently submit guest 'days' where they will take over the curation of a particular post: and when I wanted to introduce to the readers the idea I'd had to create a theatre adaptation of the blog – and, somehow, of the community structure that had arisen organically and anarchically around Dennis's posts – I chose to do so through a guest day which, with tongue not far from cheek (but not firmly pressed into it), I entitled "The young anarchosyndicalist's guide to theatre space"[17]. Picking up on the multimedia bricolage approach that Dennis has used so effectively on the blog, I presented (without commentary, except for an introduction to the project which I relegated to the end of the post) a range of items that I felt would sit interestingly in relation to the day's stated theme. There were prose extracts from Blaise Cendrars and Italo Calvino; images by Jean-Michel Basquiat and Jannis Kounellis; an excerpt from Berio's *Sinfonia* and a song by Scott Walker; a little snatch from an episode of Derren Brown's TV show *Trick of the Mind*, and an old commercial for Ariston kitchen appliances; YouTube clips of skateboarding and parkour; a visual poem by Maggie O'Sullivan, a scene from Derek Jarman's *Jubilee*, and Philippe Découflé's video for New Order's 'True Faith'; a bit of Shakespeare next to the Flash game 'Grow Island'; a few minutes of a video in which a young male model participates in an erotic photoshoot; and so on. Only one of the two-dozen items I presented actually showed what might objectively be thought of as theatre: an extract from Sidi Larbi Cherkaoui's dance piece *Foi* (for Les Ballets C de la B).

To present these collaged materials as if they all self-evidently had some claim to be, or to show, 'theatre space', was of course deliberately provocative (though in practice perhaps less provoking to that blog community than it would have been in front of an audience of theatre specialists). Clearly there was some ambiguity in the set-up: what exactly was I proposing about the idea of theatre space, with this selection box of paintings, pop songs, poetry and porn – and only a little scrap of 'theatre' (and that, at any rate, a dance piece)?

The truth is, I didn't really know. I had a stab at a gloss in my commentary note at the foot of the post, noting of these various 'spaces' that: "…all of them suggest to me something of how meaning (and usable sensation) is created within the acts and instances of theatre at its fullest."[18] There followed a list of the "characteristics and values" I saw in these different shreds and patches – which I won't quote here, for fear of pre-empting some of what lies ahead; but it would be fair to say that it was also, pretty much, a list of the things I like art to do, or to show. In a way, then, this is an entirely circular and self-supporting position: theatre is valuable because it is characterised by these excellent virtues; wherever I see these virtues enacted, I read an instance of theatre. This is to turn the blindest of eyes to that great majority of theatre that's being presented at any one time, that exhibits none of those qualities.

Nonetheless, there is a kind of information that is often induced out of this sort of category play. If theatre-making is a variety of wanting, then it is not *only* fanciful or erroneous to want theatre to be more like, say, Calvino's novel *Invisible Cities*, or a painting by Jean-Michel Basquiat, or an erotic photoshoot; it may be interesting and productive to intuit that something which is not in fact theatre as such may nonetheless be saying more about theatre than something that, merely by dint of some uninvigilated industrial-aesthetic consensus, is theatre.

This is not, perhaps, helping us towards a clear understanding of what I might mean, and not mean, by 'theatre': but what does come through is the degree of elasticity that now obtains in the word. 'Theatre' as an idea is now not only so capacious as to cover every denomination to be found within our present 'broad church' (including many who wouldn't be seen dead in its grounds), but also so contested that it could conceivably be applied to practices that have literally nothing in common. This being so, how can 'theatre' as a notion be sufficiently robust and distinct that we can put it to any use?

I can only answer this question by examining the uses to which I put the word – not least in this book – and by trying to describe the conditions which underwrite that usage. In passing and by way of an entry route I should mention a couple of other words whose meaning may also be contested or ambiguous. Obviously I cannot speak to the preferences of other users, including you.

Generally I use the words 'actor' and 'performer' interchangeably, though they do not have quite the same redolences. I want to say that an actor is simply someone who acts, who undertakes actions, who enacts a text or proposition, who interacts with others. I don't see that a 'performer' who has been asked simply to walk from one side of the room to the other is not (or not also) an actor undertaking an action. So, I mean when I say 'actor' to imply no *a priori* assessment of the degree to which we should or should not read her action as 'real' – or, contrarily, as 'fictive'.[19]

It is sometimes useful to think of non-human elements in a constructed event as actors, too. This is an expansion I have borrowed from the

Serbian film director Dušan Makavejev, whose intensely interesting tussles with the actor Simon Callow (on the set of Makavejev's film *Manifesto*) regarding the nature of film acting are recorded with nail-biting candour in Callow's book *Shooting the Actor*. At one point Makavejev asserts:

> In the theatre the actor is always on *stage* and *in the foreground.*
> In film, as soon as the camera moves closer than medium shot,
> the actor becomes the *stage*. When a *tear* rolls down the actor's
> face, the tear is the actor and his *facial skin* is the stage, while
> his face is the *background*. Anything in the film can *act*, the tree,
> the boiling milk, the fly on somebody's nose.[20] [emphases in
> original]

Broomer the rabbit, Gemma Brockis and Melanie Wilson
in ...*SISTERS*. Gate Theatre, 2008 © Simon Kane.

For my part, though I understand it and the thinking behind it, I don't accept Makavejev's distinction between theatre and film here. Of course he is talking about a film syntax to which theatre does not ordinarily have access (unless it imports film technologies so as to open up this sort of mobility); but this is a question of scale, not of register. On the whole I tend to think that anything capable of compelling an audience's attention can be an actor. Certainly the two rabbits which lolloped about the stage in the final scene of my version of *Three Sisters* were actors every bit as much as the six human performers; but so too, I'd argue, were the spinning bottle at the beginning of the third act, and the amber light that came up at the back of the stage at the end of that act. The radio in *Longwave* was an actor, and the photocopier in *Speed Death of the Radiant Child*, and the ceiling fan in my production of Pinter's *Landscape*. (A real diva, that fan, but capable of brilliance.) The moving lights for whom a whole routine was beautifully choreographed in Tim Crouch's *The Author* were some of the best actors I've ever worked with.

The idea of the 'performer' and the 'performance' are less appealing to me than the action of an actor. The principal connotation of 'performance' for me is that of the task. Behind every performance is some kind of template or target, and the task of the performer is to work through whatever instruction or invitation has been issued to them, as best they can. Etymologically, 'performance' is about completing something, carrying it out and seeing it through; and certainly, when we evaluate performance, we tend to check first for adequacy, and then, depending on the context, we may look for expertise (*vide* 'performance-related pay'). But neither adequacy nor, in fact, expertise may produce interesting effects for an audience. As I suggest more expansively in chapter 3, excess and shortfall – two different kinds of failure in performance – can often make for exciting theatre; a bad actor may be extremely interesting, but a bad performer is just bad.

Theatre, then, crucially, to begin with, is not at all congruent with performance. Performance may be one (or many) of the things that take place within an instance of theatre. Theatre is a complex system whose many elements establish – and are (ideally) continually re-establishing – relations with each other. These elements are present both substantially, say as bodies or objects or sounds, and intangibly, as expectations or memories or contextual information or legal structures.

We might imagine this complex as a network of crosshatching lines which are able somehow to connect material realities with emotional and psychological states, cultural values and social customs, entire histories and geographies of interdependence. And if we are able to imagine this, albeit in the vaguest and most generalised of ways, then we have described some kind of place, or rather a diagram of a place – even if we take that diagram to be a most unreliable and distorting map-projection.

It feels both obvious and peculiar to describe theatre as a place. Peculiar because, particularly as a young upstart maker, I was keen to impress on anyone who'd listen that theatre was not – or was not just, or not principally – a place. As *Guardian* critic Lyn Gardner wrote of Signal to Noise's home performances on the Edinburgh Fringe in 2000: "This production of *The Tempest* is a sharp reminder of something we so often forget: theatre is an experience that you have, not a place that you go."[21] What we meant, of course, was to free ourselves from the tyranny of the theatre seen first and foremost as a building of that name. My friend and sometime collaborator Jeremy Hardingham described his 1997 show *Incarnate* as "theatre rushing out of its own emergency exit",[22] which perfectly encapsulates the impulse. (There is a fire exit from the auditorium at Camden People's Theatre which opens directly onto a busy street; it represents a challenge, and a nagging invitation, that many makers over the years – myself included – have been unable to resist, and numerous shows consequently have burst out of their allotted space into the world beyond, for better or worse.)

Street theatre, guerrilla performance, site-specific work: none of these are new, and the excitement they can generate in audiences – quite often, audiences who would not otherwise identify as theatre-goers – has increasingly been noted by large organizations that might be expected to be heavily invested in building-based models: a tendency that in this generation has reached an apogee with the proud self-advertisement of the National Theatre of Scotland as a "theatre without walls", resistant to what it calls "bricks-and-mortar institutionalism".[23]

And this energetic propulsion away from the idea of the building may indeed help us to perceive more accurately what exactly constitutes an act of theatre, and how intangible some of those constitutents may be. If theatre and performance are not congruent, then, in a sense, theatre might be said to be everything that's left over if the performance were somehow to be lifted out. The incomplete, and the overspill; everything that drew your attention away from the efficient, the competent, the fulfilling; those extraneous elements that the event seemed somehow to bring in or to reach towards, and which perhaps you reproached yourself for noticing or caring about; everything that made the performance more complicated than the text or contract that originated it, and everything that made it personal to you; everything that made that single performance unrepeatable and unrecoverable. These scattered and residual traces can feel so partial, so contingent, that it's sometimes hard to track them at all, let alone read them topographically: they seem more constitutive of a non-place than of a viable 'somewhere'.

Yet it is with reference to this idea of place – however speculative or provisional, however little like a building – that I customarily use the word 'theatre', and in (shifting) relation to which this book is conceived. At base, again, is the etymology: at its ancient Greek roots, 'theatre' (θέατρον) is a 'beholding-place': a place you go to in order to see what is shown. My proposal, as explored in the following chapters, is precisely not that this definition has become superseded by contemporary changes in how theatre may be sited and where 'shows' meet their audiences (or, one might rather say, spectators, given that, strictly speaking, 'audiences' hear and 'spectators' see); instead, I want to suggest that acts of theatre, by necessity, create their own species of place: that, literally, these are events which 'take place': and that what we imagine theatre to be able to do, what we think its social and cultural and political meanings and aspirations might be, depends critically on how we imagine the place(s) that theatre takes.

Essentially, then, my project here is to wonder about the nature of the place of theatre. In order not to overwhelm – and thereby short-circuit – this inquiry with my own needs and desires, my aim is to try to come to an understanding of the logic of theatre: what *it* needs and desires, in order to be most fully itself; and my approach to that question is as methodical as I can make it.

So, inspired in a way by a variation on one of the basic philosophical questions: 'Why is there something rather than nothing?', we start with as close to nothing as we can imagine: that is, in inherited theatrical terms, the idea of the 'empty space'. Examining this problematic notion and its relation with 'place', we then, in chapter 2, introduce an actor into this space, so that it more unambiguously begins to be activated as a theatrical site. In chapter 3, we go further still, by inviting in a whole audience (or group of spectators), to see how these additional presences change the nature of the encounter. At this point we have something very like a conventional theatre situation: a bunch of people watching a show. Chapter 4 then opens wider the scope of our investigation, to consider the possible relationships between that theatre situation and the 'real' world that surrounds it on all sides: and positing along the way three kinds of place – the forest, the field and the archipelago – that may consciously inform and give shape to our conception of theatre's relationship with its social and cultural environments. Finally, I arrive again at the question of theatre's political utility, and its capacity for creating (or holding open a space for) meaningful change.

———

Some readers will have noticed a particular reference – I intend it almost like a musical sample – in the opening lines of this introduction. I invite you to start thinking with me about the kind of place where "we might think about who we are to each other". To those who know it, this is clearly an echo of the mission statement of that venerable American anti-institution, the Living Theatre, which begins:

> Our mission
>
> To call into question
> who we are to each other in the social environment
> of the theater...[24]

I have found this provocation a constant source of inspiration since I first came across it: an inspiration that is in no way compromised or debilitated by the ambiguity I detect within it. It is not quite clear to me from these words whether we are to question who we are to each other *while we are within* the social environment of the theatre (that we might not be when we are *not* in that environment); or whether the social environment of the theatre permits us to question who we are to each other in all times and places. Knowing the work of the Living Theatre, their long and valorous commitment to being the very model of a 'theatre without walls', intervening in the midst of many other kinds of social environment, I suspect it is the latter. But the ambiguity is productive: indeed, it contains much of the tension by which this book is animated. If theatre is a special category of place, one in which a certain license pertains that can throw into question the normative construction and condition of our social relations, how then can what is discovered within the bounds of that license be exported into our everyday lives? How can it change us for good, when the very factors that open up that possibility of change belong to the distinctive speciality of theatre's own operating terms?

Coming to this writing, from the start I have been more than a little haunted by the figure of Paul Goodman, the writer and thinker whose biography and body of work gave rise to the piece *Hey Mathew* I described earlier. Goodman was an early associate of the Living Theatre: he was friendly with that company's founders, Julian Beck and Judith Malina, and a prominent figure in its milieu more generally in the 1950s; and the Living Theatre staged some of Goodman's plays, including, in 1955, *The Young Disciple*, which is probably the most interesting of them and certainly the least bad. (At least, as far as one can tell without actually staging it, as I have long hoped to do at some point.)

When Random House published a collection of three of his plays[25] in 1965, Goodman prefaced it with a short essay written the previous year called 'Art of the Theatre', which is instructive in two ways: it is, at once, the most brilliantly lucid, radical, sensible few pages of writing about theatre that I know; and, at the same time, a typically painfully candid, passive-aggressive report of Goodman's failure – as he (probably correctly) perceived it – to be acknowledged as the serious theatre maker he wished to be:

> To me, writing for the theatre is the only kind of writing that is not lonely, and if I had my choice I would write mainly for the theatre. But I have not had the choice because the theatre has not been willing to have me.
>
> To write for the theatre means to belong to a company for whose known actors I make appropriate speeches that ring beforehand in my ears; at whose rehearsals I swiftly tailor a scene so that they may all shine at their best. I do not have such a company. And the company does not have me.[26]

Poignantly, Goodman goes on to say, mostly to himself perhaps as some kind of consolation, that: "After a while – after I am good and dead – I stoically count on being a statue in the park."[27] Well, who knows: this may yet come to pass: after many years of being overlooked, all but forgotten, Goodman, who died in 1972, has recently been more visible again, and his writing and thought – which contain much that would be of use to us now in our present predicaments – properly if quietly celebrated. But even in this resurgence of interest, Goodman's work in theatre remains pretty much invisible. In so far as his plays survive at all, they have dated badly – I suspect because they speak too directly and too particularly to the moment and the milieu in which he wrote them. He is hoist by the petard of his own now-ness.

I am a good deal luckier than Goodman ever was. I have a company, and I am able to make a fair proportion of the work that I want to make, and I have hardly ever had to make work that I didn't want to make. It has often felt that the theatre establishment has not been 'willing to have me', but, to be fair, I have often not been willing to have it, either, or I have wanted it to be different and to do better; either way, I am aware that, for every theatre maker or afficionado who has kept an eye on my work in recent years, there are very many more who will not know me or my work, and who perhaps will wonder at my presumptuousness in writing a book like this.

Paul Goodman © Getty Images.

If Goodman is both admonitory spectre and mascot of this writing project, I cherish his example (whilst admittedly fearing his fate) because of his outsider status, which he certainly relished, at least sometimes, as much as he was dismayed by it. It seems to me that he knew, not only in his plays but across the extraordinary span of his life's work, the vital importance of going outside and doing your best to stay there.

Likewise, at a time in which British theatre is delighting in its own plurality, its supposed willingness to accommodate whatever it thinks is the acceptable face of pretty much anything, it may seem particularly perverse to be pursuing the question of what theatre *ought* now to be doing – especially if its conclusions seem to offer a narrower vision, paradoxically in the name of enlargement.

But pluralism can use its magnanimous hospitality, its genial character, as a weapon, crowding out and stifling more stubborn lines of dissent. What shows up in the marketplace as a pneumatically exuberant freedom may appear on other maps as a bullying hegemony that constrains and disempowers. It is true, all the while, that if I am discontent with our present theatre culture, I have also been the frequent beneficiary of its privileges, not only in making my own work but as a keen member of hundreds of audiences, in most of which I am glad to have taken my place. But I cannot wholeheartedly join with my friends and colleagues who celebrate from within that culture its apparent diversity and polyphony, as if these were enough. To them, and to you, I offer this book as the beginning of another kind of conversation, along different lines.

1. Space and place

"I can take any empty space and call it a bare stage. A man walks across this empty space whilst someone else is watching him, and this is all that is needed for an act of theatre to be engaged."[1]

— Peter Brook

"There is no such thing as an empty space or an empty time."[2]

— John Cage

One reason to be optimistic about theatre – and about life, I suppose, if you like that sort of thing – is that sometimes the smallest and most apparently insignificant moments can turn out to be life-changing.

In the spring of 2001 I ran a series of workshops at Chisenhale Dance Space in east London, the focus of which was cross-form improvisation. I was becoming interested in how artists from different disciplines – actors, dancers, performance artists; but also musicians, visual artists, poets – might be able to improvise together, across the imaginary boundaries that make their artistic practices distinct. I wondered whether there was a shareable language, or a set of common perceptions and impulses, that would allow such a diverse range of practitioners to meet each other and to work spontaneously together in a coherent field of interaction. Each week, six or eight people would gather at Chisenhale – in the studio, thrillingly, which had passed for my hero Michael Clark's apartment in Charles Atlas's film *Hail the New Puritan* some years earlier – and we would try to explore these ideas collaboratively, necessarily taking the rough of frustration and misunderstanding with the smooth of excited recognition and inspiration.

Perhaps halfway through the workshop series, the group one week included the brilliant young poet and academic Keston Sutherland.

Keston's adventurous and ecumenical attitude, coupled with his highly acute political sensibility, which was (and remains) far more intricately and robustly developed than my own, made him a particularly attractive invitee for the workshop series, though I think neither of us knew when he arrived for the day's session what he'd make of it.

Often, due more to a kind of nervous reticence than anything else, the workshops began in discussion, where we tried to establish some parameters and jumping-off points for whatever we wanted to explore in our time together. The nature and temperature of these conversations varied considerably from week to week, and on this occasion it was clear from the start that we were going to struggle to find enough of a *lingua franca* to enable our first steps together. In particular, I was aware, as we discussed some of the practical exercises we might want to undertake in the course of the session, that Keston, sitting in the periphery of my vision, was becoming increasingly agitated. We had only been talking about what we actually wanted to do in the space; it wasn't clear to me what was discomfiting him. And so, in the end, I asked him what was wrong. His answer – objecting to my use of that phrase, 'in the space' – was as concisely and cogently expressed as you could possibly want any life-changing utterance to be.

"People don't live in spaces," said Keston. "They live in places."

At the time, I can't say I registered at all what I now take him to have been saying. In the midst of this difficult conversation, I thought he was merely articulating one among many possible examples of the linguistic glitches that make collaboration across disciplines so ticklish, the terminological obstacles on which it's easy to trip and stumble. As a poet, I thought, he obviously wouldn't know that theatre people talk about 'spaces' all the time: that this rehearsal room is a sympathetic 'space', that that performance venue is a difficult 'space' to play, that the actor's task in any particular moment may be about how she inhabits the available 'space'. This usage seemed to be so universally accepted that no one, as far as I knew, ever questioned it. Certainly we didn't question it at that moment, despite Keston's implicit suggestion that we should.

For some reason, though, the moment stuck in my mind – perhaps because I know better than to dismiss out-of-hand any objection that Keston might have to the unthinking deployment of some piece of conceptual apparatus. As the days and months and years went by, his observation underscored much of the thinking I did about what theatre is and about what we're making when we make it. And before

I'd even made much of a start on unpacking this complex and crucial proposition and its theoretical premises, I was instinctively reaching towards a commitment. If it is true that 'space' and 'place' are not, after all, casually synonymous, then I wanted to dedicate my own practice to making work that happened in places rather than spaces. I wanted, in conceiving and constructing the environments in which my work would unfold – not just the physical environments, but the psychological situations and perceptual fields that at once gave rise to and arose out of the work – to create places, *as opposed to* spaces; to make work that people could really live inside: not visit, in a state of holiday, or peer into from the temporary exile of some theoretical 'beyond'-space, but inhabit fully and creatively. Mindful straight away that the 'people' I was thinking about were actors and other makers, as well as audiences and other participants, it was clear that the differences between those roles were circumstantial rather than fundamental, and that all were included in my basic aspiration for the theatre I made: I wanted to create places fit for living in.

Michael Clark in *Hail the New Puritan,* showing Chisenhale
Dance Space main studio © Electronic Arts Intermix.

What this might actually mean, in practice – in the conception of projects, in the creation of working 'space', in the building and sharing of theatrical events – continues to move in and out of focus. The presence of the question is, as so often, more valuable than the achievement of a stable answer. But at the times that the provocation itself feels especially present, it can be put to good work.

Only a few months after that Chisenhale workshop, I was appointed artistic director – and in a more general and perhaps more weighty sense, I became day-to-day custodian – of Camden People's Theatre. It was both a thrilling and an onerous position. Onerous not simply because, as the sole paid member of staff, my duties included a fair bit of toilet-unblocking, flood-repelling and ladder-scaling (not my strong point) to change bulbs in the houselights, but because I had inherited an existing organization, which, like most organizations, wanted change and welcomed it in theory but resisted and resented it in practice; in particular, there was at that time not only an artistic policy for which I was not a perfect match but also a resident company of actors and makers who could not have been more hospitable – or more daunting, in so far as they embodied an unmanageably huge range of (mostly unspoken) hopes and expectations.

The first few days in the post were almost overwhelming – absurdly so, perhaps, given that I'd taken charge of a cheerfully scrappy fifty-seater fringe venue, not the Royal Shakespeare Company – and I vividly remember the Friday at the end of my first week. Left alone for the first time, I went and sat in the empty theatre, with my head in my hands, and tried to tune into this particular space. I'd made one show in this room – though it had only run for a week, and we'd made it offsite, rehearsing in an actor's dad's friend's deserted office or *ad hoc* in car parks and on fire escapes around the South Bank – and seen a couple more. What did this room want from me? And to what extent were those wants aligned with the needs of the resident company? And of the audiences who already knew about CPT, and those whom we needed to start drawing in? And, anyway, what did *I* want?

I wanted, in that moment, in the 'empty space', to really look, and to really listen – for clues, for information. The most obvious indication was that, in those days, the theatre itself was painted dark blue, rather than the black of a typical 'black box' fringe space. What did that mean? The fact that it was contrary to expectation at all suggested a degree of the unorthodox, an attitude of wanting to create something different from the norm. To most users, a (literally) black box-shaped theatre is likely to seem 'neutral', the blackness of an unspoilt blackboard, blank and limitlessly receptive, ready effectively to disappear behind any kind

of action or event; but CPT's deep blue immediately made that black
seem far from neutral, but rather earnest, even severely abstinent in its
refusal to be colourful in itself – and, of course, a bit pretentious (a
vastly overused adjective and one that should generally raise suspicion,
but justified here in that the signalling of neutrality is always a pretence at
some level). The distinctive blue of CPT – at one time, the organization
even considered renaming itself 'The Blue Box' – was, by comparison,
warm, pleasing, and above all present. It said: people made this choice;
it said: this is a place where people live.

And as I got up from my seat and walked around, looking carefully
at the walls and the floor, and up at the lighting grid, there were traces
everywhere, signs of life: scars and scabs and scratches, obscure fixtures,
inadvertent impasto, long meandering cracks and inexplicable orifices,
the temporary patches of bodged repair that in time became permanent:
all the marks of human habitation that come to form a relief map of
an engaged life in a room just as on a body. And though there were
many evenings of repainting and many more bodged repairs over the
three years of my tenure, most of those inherited marks remained in
some form, and some of them are still there now, as intimately and
expressively familiar as the tender blemishes on the skin of a longtime
companion.

As the custodian of such a space, there is always a tension between
wanting to make good these imperfections, so as to offer to a visiting
company or an artist on a one-night stand a performance area that's
smart and pristine, and wanting those same imperfections to speak
welcomingly to the visitor. It's hard to say which is the more hospitable
approach, perhaps – just as you either tidy your house impeccably when
friends come to stay, or you figure that it's warmer, kinder somehow, to
ask them to take you as they find you.

As well as looking carefully, almost forensically, around on that first
afternoon alone in the theatre, I wanted to listen. The impulse itself was
nearly fanciful, a vague sense of wanting somehow to commune with
the ghosts of previous occupants. (I was deeply in thrall at that time to
Gavin Bryars's *The Sinking of the Titanic*, a piece of music partly inspired
by the telegraphic pioneer Marconi's belief, near the end of his life, that no
sound ever faded completely to nothing, but that extremely faint signals
continued to permeate the atmosphere, such that, given the appropriate
equipment to isolate and amplify its trace, it would still be possible, for
example, to listen to Christ delivering the Sermon on the Mount.[3])

If, however, any such echoes or whispers from the past did come through, they would certainly have been drowned out by the ambient sound from outside the venue. Camden People's Theatre sits on the junction of two busy roads, and two of the sides of the blue 'box' are exterior walls, so a background (at least) of traffic noise, sporadically adorned with pedestrian conversations, will often be present to performers and audience alike; when an emergency vehicle tears down Hampstead Road, or a car held at the traffic lights is pumping out bass-heavy music, or a drunk guy on a Saturday night shouts obscenities at the frail moon over London, the show inside can be all but obliterated.

Quickly, the 'problem' of extraneous noise became a useful litmus test for me in understanding the needs and attitudes of visiting companies presenting their work. There were those for whom it was, without question, a black mark against the venue, a failure to show proper respect for their work by protecting and insulating it from the crude and inevitable (but unpredictable) intrusions of the urban environment around us; and there were those who accepted it with patience and equanimity and perhaps a little curiosity as to what would be visited on them in the next performance and how, if at all, they would respond. For myself, I did, I think, the best thing I could have done: for my first show as artistic director, *Napoleon in Exile* in the spring of 2002, I rigged a couple of microphones outside the theatre, which picked up the street noise and relayed it back to our sound desk, where I filtered it softly through a harmonizer and played it at low level into the auditorium, layering it under the elaborate sound score for the show itself. Later I discovered a sort of precedent in John Cage, who liked to say that he had started including radios as a sound source in his compositions because he had moved to an apartment in a noisy area where the residents customarily put their transistor radios in their windows and played loud music: which Cage initially found annoyed him; but how could he be disturbed if his neighbours were, in effect, playing his own compositions? This sense of 'making friends' with the intrusive and the unsought, by inviting it in to the room and enlarging the language of one's practice so as to accept and absorb what would otherwise tend to despoil, is a key element in the management of relationships that make a 'place' liveable.

Cage's refusal of the 'empty space', so much at odds with Peter Brook's dependence on exactly that notion as a *sine qua non* of his praxis, is resolutely expressed in his 1957 talk 'Experimental Music', where it functions as a quasi-axiomatic introduction to the following anecdote regarding a formative research experience:

> For certain engineering purposes, it is desirable to have as silent a situation as possible. Such a room is called an an-echoic chamber, its six walls made of special material, a room without echoes. I entered one at Harvard University several years ago and heard two sounds, one high and one low. When I described them to the engineer in charge, he informed me that the high one was my nervous system in operation, the low one my blood in circulation. Until I die there will be sounds.[4]

Here, Cage posits an attentive reality against a theoretical or fictive construct: exactly as he had already done in 1952 with his celebrated composition *4'33"*. This piece (in three movements) famously requires of its performers that they do not play, within the time parameters specified by Cage; it is, as such, a 'silent' piece. But the experience of hearing, or of performing, *4'33"* is never an experience of silence: it is, just as Cage intended, a way of inviting in and befriending the sounds we customarily depreciate and ignore. No two performances of any other single composition have probably been less alike. (It is, for example, instructive to listen to the two contrasting renditions of *4'33"* on the album *Non Stop Flight* by the Deep Listening Band; or even simply to consider the existence of the compilation album *45'18"*, which collates nine performances of *4'33"* by various artists such as Thurston Moore and Keith Rowe.)

If we come to Peter Brook's conception of 'empty space' via Cage, it becomes possible to see the wilfulness, the violence even, of its premises. Brook's intent – if we take it at face value – is anything but; he seeks simply to create a means of communication between people who may have little or nothing in common culturally. The 'empty space' is marked perhaps by a rolled-out carpet: nothing more, none of the trappings and conventions of the traditional proscenium-arch stage which still dominated the theatre in which Brook took his first professional steps in the 1940s, and which – as we too easily forget – still dominate, or at least shape and inflect, the power structures of much theatre today (and not only the mainstream). Brook's vision of the 'empty space' makes room for what he describes, in the closing chapter of *The Empty Space*, as 'The

Immediate Theatre', and it is in pursuit of this vision that he established the International Centre for Theatre Research in 1970. This model, in the name of a truly egalitarian and intellectually cogent accessibility and of communication and collaboration across cultural and linguistic borders, presents itself as, exactly, enlightened: unencumbered (to much general relief) by the heavy baggage of nationally, historically and politically determined identities. It is a perfect picture of liberal downsizing, in which the accumulated clutter of interferent realities can be jettisoned in favour of a quieter life, a life shorn above all, as Brook himself says, of context:

> The reason we started the [International] Centre was to start working outside of contexts. My own work and the work I've been in contact with has always been within a context. The context is either geographical, cultural or linguistic, so that we work within a system. The theatre that works within a system communicates within a system of reference. We set out to explore what the conditions were through which the theatre could speak directly.[5]

The position Brook espouses is reminiscent of some strains of practical criticism, which promote a close readerly attention to the operations of the text without admitting any consideration of the historical or cultural conditions surrounding its production. In an encounter with a text there can be benefits to such an approach: but it is clear, always, that by insisting that so much evidence is inadmissible right from the start, the reader creates and imposes an unreal picture.

Likewise, Brook's work since the 1970s has been profoundly controversial in many quarters precisely because it advances its apparently frictionless multiculturalism through the suppression of context: that is to say, through a willed or performed erasure of the specific histories and political circumstances in which particular cultures are formed and confront other cultures. To work, as Brook often has, from texts and forms originating in cultures other than his own, and with actors and collaborators from a diversity of backgrounds, is one thing; to imagine that he can will into being a space in which the context of those differences coming into relation with each other can be silenced so that "theatre [can] speak directly" is for many observers an extremely disquieting act which simply replays and extends much of the colonial and imperialist history that Brook wishes to evade.

Ultimately, the question that arrests us is this: if the theatre really could "speak directly", unburdened by any system of reference or cultural position, what on earth would it say? How could it have a thought in its empty head? In whose voice would it speak? And who would I be, as a spectator watching it, with my own ineluctable social background, my class and my race, my gender and my sexual orientation, having paid however-much for a ticket to (say) the Barbican in London, which is so-much less than the people in the best seats or so-much more than those with a restricted view? How can the theatre "speak directly" to me if I've just paid four fifty for a sandwich?

Having seen only a couple of Brook's productions in this mode, I can attest to there being much that is blandly attractive about his work; he likes handsome actors, and a measured pace that can become seductive in its rhythms, and there is the kind of modest wit and quietly fluent movement that flatters an audience into thinking it is obviously as sophisticated and refined as the show it is bearing with. But there is something terrible going on: because nobody lives there. The work does not create a place, it stakes out a space. It proceeds from a simulation of emptiness, which presumes to delete in an arrogant slow-motion panic all the turbulent data contained in the life-system that Brook wishes to transcend. In his empty space, he wants no context; the crucial problem is not that the world outside the theatre is teeming with context, but that theatre itself *is* context. Theatre is only and entirely context: and without context, theatre is nothing.

Brook's fantasy of the empty space is, perhaps, forgiveable: maybe we all make the theatre we'd like to live in, and who doesn't sometimes quietly yearn for a space where our uncomfortable histories and our present unwarranted privilege and our complicity with systemic injustice can all be suspended and we can enjoy the sexy easygoing pleasure of each other's company without our difference and our misunderstanding getting in the way. But in the absence of the long, slow, painstaking, sometimes gruelling work of dialogue and reparation, that space is no more viable and no more life-supporting than John Cage's early pursuit of absolute silence.

Eventually, as we have seen, Cage concluded that the empty space (or time) was impossible, and that what we might, in the terms of our present inquiry, consider a place fit for living in could be created only "if, at the parting of the ways, where it is realized that sounds occur whether intended or not, one turns in the direction of those he does not intend."

For all that Peter Brook's staking out of an empty space may be deeply
problematic, it's nonetheless true that the *idea* of the blank slate, the
tabula rasa, is not only seductive but may be, with regard to theatre
at least, profoundly necessary. For example, I am fond of quoting,
particularly to students (who can be surprisingly conservative in their
outlook), biographer Leroy Leatherman's observation of the pioneering
American choreographer Martha Graham that she "took over the stage
as if nothing had ever happened on it before".[6] It is exciting to read
this not as a description of one individual and idiosyncratic genius,
but rather as exemplary, an imperative for all theatre and performance
makers to take to heart.

What makes all the difference, of course, is the nature and context
of that "as if". For Brook – a white middle-class man using the idea of
the 'empty space' as a passport to what some critics see as a systematic
project of transcultural appropriation – the "as if" is carefully obscured,
in the effort to evade or transcend the specifics of geography, language,
politics and so on: an effort which of course initially anticipated,
and now flows easily downstream alongside, the liquid movements of
neoliberal globalized capitalism. For a figure like Graham, the stimulating
permissiveness of "as if nothing" is not traded off against context. The
blank page on which she makes her mark is the stage, and nothing in the
impulse towards 'starting over' requires an emptying-out of the specifics
of the place in which her work is enacted: whereas for Brook, the emptying
of the stage-space is utterly dependent on the erasure of any detailed
apprehension of what he calls the "system" that surrounds the stage.

Having made this distinction we can begin to see how the idea of
'space' is not *in itself* deleterious to the making of theatre, but that the
conceptual technology connoted by that vital pivot "as if" can create
or imply a register of theatrical site that, accurately perceived, may be a
viable temporary working environment.

One text I have returned to often since coming across it early in
my career is a 1996 pamphlet by the wonderful poet and visual artist
Thomas A. Clark, called 'Some alternatives to the white cube'. Across
the four pages of a single folded sheet of card, Clark places two dozen
thumbnail descriptions of different imaginary 'spaces' that, according
to the proposition of the title, might initiate the conceiving of other
kinds of gallery space than the 'white cube' – which is, of course, art's

equivalent to the black box of the standard-issue fringe theatre. So, the
text begins:

> a space flooded with natural light

> a space where many acts of attention
> have contributed to the stillness

> a space where things come and go
> where people come and go
> a space of change

> a space which has been ordered
> and re-ordered many times but where
> no order is thought to be absolute[7]

– and so it goes on.

A number of things strike me about Clark's intensely beautiful text.
Although he is describing 'spaces', I am in many cases able to picture a *place*
that seems to fulfil the micro-brief: sometimes these are imagined places,
such as the room I visualise in response to the opening proposition, "a
space flooded with natural light" (which seems pretty much designed
to elicit a visually imaginative response even though it could hardly be
less specifically detailed); sometimes these pictures are recollections, or
slight adaptations, of real galleries or theatre 'spaces' I know: Kettle's
Yard in Cambridge, Inverleith House in Edinburgh, rehearsal room
Studio 5 at the Jerwood Space in Southwark, York Hall in Bethnal Green
where Improbable host their annual Devoted & Disgruntled events, and
so on; in a few cases, somewhere (apparently) completely different comes
to mind: a dental hospital I went to a couple of times, an impossibly big
department store I dreamed about as a child, a particular region of Changi
Airport in Singapore, an architectural model of an urban square: and these
real and semi-real places are thrown up as pictures in my imagination in
response to maybe a single word or tiny fragmentary phrase: "come and
go", "practical", "a clearing"[8]. Perhaps, if you retrace your steps, you
will notice that even the first four of the spaces in the extract above are
similarly projecting different places in your mind, vividly or fuzzily, arising
out of your own experiences and imaginative resources.

I notice that some of the spaces I imagine in reading Clark's text are populated and some are not; and that the longer I think about any one of these spaces (and it seems to be a text that asks to be read quite slowly, though not necessarily in a linear or methodical way), the more likely it is for there to be people in the picture, either still or, more often, moving: blurrily perhaps, and certainly not distinctly enough for individuals to be discerned (though your experience may well differ), but creating a sense of presence, of habitation. If it is true, *pace* Keston, that "people don't live in spaces", then it seems not to follow that every space is devoid of people, or of an impression of, or simulation of the presence of, people. What they are doing is not exactly 'living' because they are not exactly there; but they can follow the shapes of living, they can indicate and in a way help to preserve the sense of what might happen if such a space were somehow made real.

Thirdly, and perhaps most interestingly for our present inquiry, I start to wonder how many spaces *in total* Clark is describing. Were we to obscure the title of the poem for a moment, we could imagine reading this as a set of twenty-four descriptions of a single space; certainly, even holding ourselves to the promise of "[s]ome alternatives", we needn't see these as twenty-four separate proposals. And this, then, gives rise to a number of questions about contradiction, about competing claims, and therefore, finally, about preference, about the ideas that seem to chime most resonantly with our own desires. So, for example, Clark later invokes "a space flowing out into other spaces", but also "a space within parenthesis / sheltered from the world". Do these spaces contradict each other, tend away from each other? Or could this be a single space described two ways? Could the two apparently opposed concepts be realized in one site to which different users responded in different ways, or at different times of day, or depending on their route through it? Do we not, in fact, expect most buildings to be both of these spaces, simply by dint of their having both walls and roofs to shelter us, and doors and windows which open out into the beyond?

These sorts of questions, it will already be clear, register politically, even though we are locating our considerations in imaginary space. Even before (and after) Clark describes, among his twenty-four variations, "a space having specific dimensions, / a history, a politics, a poetics" – a space vitally unlike Brook's conception – a political context and narrative are already forming around relation and priority, and therefore around power. In Clark's matrix of possible spaces, class is already present, and desire is already present; what we see in our mind's eye on the basis of a word or two, what comes most readily to our imagination, has to do with what we want: with what we habitually want, and perhaps with what we secretly or inarticulably or even unconsciously want. On its surface, Clark's text presents us with a matrix of equal choices, as if it were serenely and equitably unconcerned with our navigation of the constructed freedom of movement and opportunity that the larger space of the entire text inscribes. But as soon as we engage with it as readers – that is, as operators of our own conceptual spaces – we are quickly confronted with the exigencies of wanting as they ramify in our lives at their realest.

In a sense – a sense, I want to suggest, that is particularly activated by the premises of theatre-making – wanting is the common term through which the imagined or conceptualised space and its real-world place (or placeholder) become meaningfully contiguous. As theatre makers we involve ourselves in the imagining of places that do not yet exist, or at any rate are not here-and-now with us; what we want of those places is what is not found in that immediate, local world which, it follows, we 'find wanting'. And the act by which we effect some contingent transition between the imaginative space of our wanting and the real – that is, not least, the contextually inflected – place in which our wanting takes shape (finds its form, is given voice) is the beginning of an act of theatre.

For some theorists of space, the denomination of place *as distinct from* space, which Keston Sutherland asserted (topically and, it must be said, in relatively casual conversation) in my improvisation workshop using the idea of inhabitation ("liv[ing] in") – not, I think, entirely metaphorically – as the contrasting factor, is reflected, broadly if not exactly, in the contraposition of two different categories of space. For instance, in O.F. Bollnow's classic *Human Space* – at least in Christine Shuttleworth's translation – 'experienced space' is distinguished from 'mathematical space'[9]; like Sutherland, Bollnow expresses a preference for the phrase 'lived space' rather than 'experienced space', but is thwarted by the constraints of conventional usage: "'living' is an intransitive verb … one cannot say that man lives *something*, such as space or time…"[10]. For Henri Lefebvre, writing a little later, this contrast is most powerfully expressed in terms of the "*mental* space"[11] produced by a "theoretical practice"[12] which, for those theorists, operates outside ideology (as Brook's 'empty space' does, or professes to) and at a remove from what Lefebvre calls "social practice"[13], in an interesting chime with a term now commonly used in proximity to ideas such as 'relational art' and 'participatory art'.

So, common to all these different descriptions and perspectives is the aim of distinguishing between the kind of space that has no one in it (other than, perhaps, in some sense, the imagining agent), and the kind of space (or place) that does, that is "lived" or "experienced" or has a "social" life. We might, however, pursue this just one step further by returning to that snapshot where I'm sitting in the otherwise 'empty' theatre auditorium at Camden People's Theatre, gradually tuning in to the traces and residues and echoes of previous – and, without exception, transient – 'inhabitants' of that space. The filmmaker Peter Greenaway opens an essay on the idea of place with a distinction that might appear to contradict our present identification of place with habitation but that quickly and productively resolves that tension:

> Place in preference to people. I know my enthusiasms to be stronger for a sense of place than for a sense of people. Yet I like crowds. Perhaps that is not so contradictory. Sufficient numbers of people on a flat and empty plane make a place, a *genius loci* with its own shape. And smell. And temperature. And when the crowd disperses, you are left with a pregnant void that's tangible enough.[14]

It would be true to say that CPT, at least during my time there, was not often obliged to accommodate "crowds", exactly. But what the theatre is hospitable to – exceptionally so, in fact – is the crowd *across time*. The marks left behind on the walls and floor of the performing space (to say nothing of the dressing rooms) – notwithstanding frequent attempts at repair and redecoration – are a record of several years of shows and rehearsals and get-ins and -outs and after-show parties and arguments and burglaries and vandalism and outbursts of spontaneous dancing: groups perhaps of half a dozen people here, two dozen there, this or that individual, constituting a crowd only when considered across a span of many months. Yet this is not, or not only, a fanciful construction. Notice how Greenaway's "flat and empty plane", resembling the flat carpet of Brook's "empty space", becomes a "place … with its own shape" only with the weight of "[s]ufficient numbers of people": a crowd which, in theatre, gathers across time and only through a feat – specifically a social feat – of memory, establishing in that space a sense of history, of time passing and time past as well as present; fostering acts not only of witnessing, in the here and now, but of remembrance and commemoration, and of a kind of (re-)collective storytelling.

Almost an inverse of the array or litany of imagined but realizable spaces in Thomas A. Clark's 'Some alternatives to the white cube', *The Dust Archive* by Alexander Kelly and Annie Lloyd is, as its subtitle says, 'A History of Leeds Met Studio Theatre'[15]: but it is a history of a theatre that is rendered in a form that itself feels exceedingly suffused with the properties of theatre-as-place. This publication, produced in 2008 to mark the closure of Leeds Met Studio, a significant smallscale theatre venue for many years, is a beautiful book, square and spiral bound, the main body of which is a sequence of sixty-three translucent pages on each of which is drawn a floorplan of the theatre, and, in the appropriate place on each of these plans, a hand-lettered description of a moment from one of the shows that had been presented there since 1990. Most of the descriptions are layered over the stage space, but not all: some describe audience responses; some are descriptions of acts performed outside the space, outside the building even. So, a handful of captions taken more or less at random:

> As the audience come in, a silver remote-control airship is navigating slowly around the theatre.[16]

> A suitcase, open, full of turf. Jon and David stand on the turf, in the suitcase, for the whole show.[17]

> Feathers. Tomatoes. Mole in a bear suit.[18]

> Anthony as a vampire hanging in chains on the 9th floor pretending to be Johnny Rotten.[19]

> A girl in the audience crying silently.[20]

> Jamie leaves through the Fire Exit with a walkie-talkie, reporting back live as he circumnavigates the building. / He comes back in through this door.[21]

As with Clark's text, these brief (and some not-so-brief) descriptions may fire the visual imagination, though these encapsulations are on the whole far more specific, which may mean that they throw up images more readily or considerably less so. An additional complication for some readers will be knowing either the Leeds Met Studio venue, or having seen some of the referenced shows, either in that theatre or elsewhere. In most cases, though, and regardless of these variables, these captions are remarkably reverberant: even if they don't produce specific images for the reader (or elicit particular memories), they very effectively create or release certain tonal qualities – perhaps closer to Greenaway's invocation of smell, and of temperature. And in the case of *The Dust Archive* this effect is amplified in two ways. Firstly it happens through the decisions made by Kelly and Lloyd about format and aesthetic: the use of tracing paper, allowing several layers of memories to overlap or merge or echo much as they might have done for frequent visitors to the venue; the minute variations in each hand-drawn iteration of the floorplan, capturing something of the humanity and fallibility of the building as used socially rather than as theorised; the deferral of attribution to an index at the back of the book so that no companies or authors are identified on the page itself, unless the reader happens to know the reference for themselves; above all, the fragmented, elliptical descriptions themselves, which seem to signify both loss and incompletion, and the use throughout of the present tense, as if to suggest that all these performances, if they survive in the memory at all, continue to do so on the basis of theatrical (rather than archival) premises: that is, they occupy a perpetual 'now' rather than a past rendered remote and stable by the technologies of closure. Secondly, that resonance is supported – even guaranteed – by the circumstances of the production of the book and the sad decommissioning of the venue itself, which layers over the whole object an additional poignancy, a filter of evacuation or redundancy, that would not have arisen from the book in quite the same way had it been published, for example, to celebrate a milestone anniversary in the venue's continuing operation.

There is, though, a third factor here which merits consideration: that is, how performance works – some, indubitably, more than others – achieve the kind of theatricality that we are connecting here with the 'lived' or 'experienced' space. In other words, in terms of *The Dust Archive*, one of the things that makes Alex and Annie's fragmentary recollections of nearly two decades of performances in the Studio so 'reverberant' (to continue to use that slightly imprecise word) is that in staging those moments, their makers were able somehow to anticipate their appeal to reverberation. No matter how powerful or mundane, aggressive or docile, surprising or inevitable, these moments of action somehow contain within themselves something that fixes them both in that moment and in the memory of a spectator, such that they work thereafter on parallel tracks, being immediately lost to the present (except in narrative reconstruction after the fact) and at the same time available to recollection. This is work that depends in part on its own transience to enable its persistence, albeit in a radically decentred and unstable form.

One way of describing this interdependence of the specifics of presence in place and time, and the way that that interdependence ramifies both for individual spectators and for participants in what the Living Theatre call "the social environment of theatre"[22], is 'liveness'. It is a quality that is frequently invoked in relation to theatre, and particularly to theatre as a 'special' case, distinct from other forms of artistic and cultural production; on the whole it is described forensically but badly and inertly by performance theorists, and often horribly vaguely and superstitiously but sometimes nonetheless accurately (or at least recognizably) by theatre makers and audiences. It is a 'liveness' that seems in general to be different from the liveness of, say, live television, or a constantly updated online news feed, though it is arguably present in live music, or in sport, or in stand-up. It also, presumably, must have something in common with the 'liveness' of life as it is lived by the

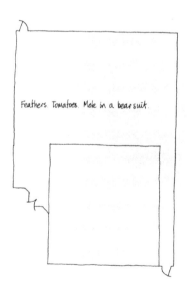

A page from *The Dust Archive* © Alexander Kelly and Annie Lloyd.

living. Perhaps, then, in order to draw closer to an understanding of theatre as place, or as inhabited space, we need to consider how the 'live' of theatrical 'liveness' interacts productively (and definitively) with the 'live' of "People … live in places."

———————

One of the most exciting openings to any theatre work I know (though I've never seen it performed live) is the beginning of Judith Weir's chamber opera *The Consolations of Scholarship*. This opera is something of a mini-epic, whose limited resources – a nine-piece instrumental ensemble and a single mezzo-soprano, performing a work of not much more than twenty minutes' duration – belie the widescreen ambition of its narrative and imaginative scope. The soloist alternates between singing and speaking the libretto, and in fact the very first lines are spoken, with the ensemble accompaniment exactly matching the rhythms of the mezzo's speaking, so that the effect is rather like that of, say, Laurie Anderson speaking through a harmonizer in some of the tracks on *Big Science*. With no musical introduction, we are immediately drawn into the heart of the matter.

"Look!", she says. "There in the distance…"[23]

And we're off. The appeal to the audience is direct and – if it's possible to say so without pejorative overtones – remarkably efficient.

It begins with a clear invitation, delivered with some of the force of a bald imperative but actually feeling in practice more like the friendly ushering-in of a storyteller, like a peculiarly compact version of "Once upon a time…". "Look!" she says, and our likely (unspoken) reflex response is, firstly, "Yes! OK," and secondly, "Look where?"

"There," she says. And in this single gesture, the premise of our relationship is established. If "Look!" tells us that she will be our guide, our navigator, then the qualification "There" indicates something about the kind of guide she will be: we will be relating to her as narrator, not (or not principally) protagonist. This is not the "Look at me!" of first-person performance, but the "Look at this!" of third-person storytelling, in which the speaker's job is to direct attention away from herself and towards something else that we and she will observe together, with her guidance helping to stimulate and shape our perceptions. This sense is already subtly reinforced by the fact that our gaze is directed "there" rather than 'here': away towards an elsewhere that is, in this moment, no more hers than ours: so that we, as an audience, are already sharing the space of "here" with the speaker – we are not separate from her, but together.

But what, or who, is "there"? The word helps us orient ourselves in relation to the speaker but it only *signals* specificity. Even if, in a staged production of the opera, the soloist is, say, pointing in a particular direction as she says "Look! There…" (which anyway sounds like pretty crummy direction), at this point we can only understand it as not-here; we still do not have quite enough data to understand what she means by "there" and what it is that she wants us to look *at* when we look there.

But this last piece of information falls quickly into place, as "there" is immediately qualified: "[t]here in the distance". *That* "there". And this, now, requires some fast and radical adjustment. Both the direct appeal of "Look!" and the aligning gesture of "there" have helped to create a strong sense of here-and-now; but by invoking "the distance" the speaker has at a stroke not only enlarged the field in which our attentions are being marshalled, but propelled us into a zone we can attend to only imaginatively, in the space of fiction: because we know as well as we are "here" that, even on the main stages of the world's largest opera houses – where *The Consolations of Scholarship* is unlikely to be heard – it would be stretching a point to suggest that anywhere within the concrete space of the auditorium could be thought of as being "in the distance". "[T]he distance" has to be supplied by us, collaborating now in the storytelling act by lending to it our capacity to extend a real space so that it can contain and refer to imaginary space without contradiction.

What Weir does here is, essentially, to foreground the construction of the spatial apparatus on which any fully theatrical act depends. It might be imagined as a three-dimensional 'mathematical' space, with the x-axis being the line-of-sight implied by the invitation "Look!", the y-axis being the separation out of 'here' and 'elsewhere' that permits the location of a "there" (which is, at least potentially, where 'we' are not), and the z-axis which opens up into the third dimension being the gesture towards a distance that can only be imagined, and which necessarily entails the positive of a fictive space in relation to the space we have thus far been able to equate with our moment-to-moment experience. In other words, Weir starts with a point (albeit one containing multitudes), which is the place where 'we' are, where 'we' originate; that point is extruded into a line, then into a plane, and finally into a three-dimensional space, like a room. (It is important to be clear that the third dimension opens up with 'distance' not because it requires an act of enlargement beyond the real space of here-and-there, but because it necessitates recourse to a register of the imaginary.) In less than five seconds, Weir takes us methodically through the elements of theatrical spatiality: and this matters not because we end up somewhere new, but because we seldom show our workings as to how we got there. The theatrical space that Weir takes pains to elucidate is very often taken as read, and for granted, through the transmission of various orthodoxies that it is all too easy never to re-examine once they are learned.

It seems to me that this capacity for explication is a particular (if not quite unique) function of direct address: in fact it might be argued that the space implied in the rapid motion of Weir's arresting opening line is also one way of mapping the logic of direct address as a technology. When an actor on-stage (and an actor is always on-stage, even if they happen, for example, to be sitting amid the audience, as the actors in Tim Crouch's *The Author* do; the stage need not be one continuous generalised container for all the action of a play, it can be localized and multiple) speaks directly to an audience whose presence she necessarily acknowledges, the following indications are being offered: that she, the actor, and we, the audience, are all inhabitants of a single lived space (notwithstanding our experience of it as however-many individuals will be abundantly various); that that space is a 'here' and that, it follows, other spaces are 'not-here', are specifically 'there' or generally 'elsewhere'; that 'here' in this moment of performance is also a 'now'; and that if other spaces are 'not-here' then there are also species of 'not-now' – different kinds of past and future that may be posited: but that it can also be 'now' 'elsewhere': which is not a kind of space we can experience directly, because we are here-and-now, but we are instinctively aware that we can imagine those spaces. In other words, every instance of direct address contains subtextually the idea: "Look! There in the distance…".

Looking over my resumé – which at the time of writing I am a bit startled to find lists about seventy different productions (not all of full-length works) that I've been involved in making over the past two decades – just half a dozen do not include some form or measure of direct address: and of those six exceptions, three or four refuse it as a deliberate strategy to help something else happen. But on the whole, direct address is the closest thing I can find to a common factor across all my work; on reflection I see that I think of it principally as a basic courtesy: which is to say that it has a political or ethical component as well as an aesthetic and formal significance. We begin with some acknowledgement of the space we share, because in doing so – in saying "Look!" and "[T]here" and "in the distance", in redescribing the three dimensions of our meeting-place – we re-state the fundamental importance of liveness as a premise of our gathering: the liveness of being specifically here, and precisely now, and actually together, and of being able to extend our here-and-now into imaginative space (but also to reconcile, or to want to reconcile, our imaginings with the material facts and contexts of our here-and-now).

Most often these days, particularly if I'm performing in a show, it starts with a kind of direct address which marries extreme simplicity with a seed of ambiguity out of which something complex and challenging can grow. It starts with me saying "Hello." (Often the pattern is something like: "Hello. Thank you for being here. My name's Chris. This is a show called [title].") What I find interesting and quietly provocative about starting with this kind of 'hello' is not just that it can be disarmingly low-key relative to an audience's expectations, but that it creates a degree of disorientation. Is this part of the performance, or a preamble to it? The answer to both questions seems, self-evidently, to be 'yes'. But how can this be both the thing and at the same time not-yet the thing? How do you tell the difference, how do you draw the line, between what is 'in' the performance and what is extraneous to it? What is authorially constructed and what falls out just as it is?

Having been interested in this question of saying 'hello' for some years, I was delighted to be introduced to Julian Beck's extraordinary book *The Life of the Theatre*, in which he writes:

> I do not like the Broadway theatre because it does not know how to say hello. The tone of voice is false, the manner-isms are false, the sex is false, ideal, the Hollywood world of perfection, the clean image, the well pressed clothes, the well scrubbed anus, odorless, inhuman, of the Hollywood actor, the Broadway star. And the terrible false dirt of Broadway, the lower depths in which the dirt is imitated, inaccurate.[24]

For Beck, then, saying 'hello' is akin to a shibboleth, an act through which we might guarantee the access of theatre to what is 'true' or 'real' or whatever we think might be the antithesis of "false, imitated", inaccurate". This language of authenticity and its opposites is never less than ticklish in the context of performed action and constructed space, but there is at least some overlap here with the idea of "lived space" or "experienced space", the kind of place that supports habitation in all its complexity. For me, "hello" is simply how we begin a conversation on the 'outside', and to use it as a marker for starting (or, some might think, for being about to start) is partly a sign of wanting to show how the social patterns of our everyday interactions need not be suspended within the 'special' domain of theatre. 'Why should they be?', we might ask, as if it is odd that anyone would suppose otherwise; and yet the conventions of theatre work against us, whether we ourselves choose to work with or against them (or, as so often, a bit of both). It is still quite normal for audiences to be asked – compelled, even – to sit silently, and still, in the dark, while others speak, and move, and are lit; and while this massive imbalance of power, or at least of license, may have its uses – "It's a play when some do and others watch,"[25] writes Paul Goodman, and this seems a reliable starting-point, for all its incompleteness – it is a space that seems designed in every one of its facets and qualities to prohibit exactly the conversation that saying "hello" is presumably intended to initiate.

Nonetheless, experience shows that the action of saying "hello" can be sufficient to overwrite all those contrary signs, because more often than not, at least some of the audience will say "hello" back. I'm always pleased by this, but it's not necessary. The point has been made from the stage: an explicit acknowledgement of the presence of the audience, and hence the liveness of the event, is enough to indicate that that presence is in some way consequential. It matters that some are here to "watch" what others "do"; it matters – and an audience may perhaps understand this at some level, but it is vital that actors and makers apprehend it too – that watching is itself a kind of doing: that an engaged mode of watching is actually not, as it is so often characterised now, a passive state: and moreover that, as actors, we also "watch" to see what the audience will "do", as an intrinsic element of the liveness we depend upon. Everyone is watching, everyone is doing, and the state of togetherness this creates – no matter how variant or atomised that togetherness may be or seem – is part of the complex of liveness, and the collaboration it represents is part of the livedness, the liveability, of the place that theatre takes.

One example that comes to mind is that of a production I directed, at the Ustinov Studio in Bath at the beginning of 2011, of Harold Pinter's

Landscape. Here, the idea of direct address and the idea of the lived space
came together (to my mind) very satisfactorily and very truly.

Landscape, a lesser-known but crucial one-act play written by Pinter
during 1967, and performed first on BBC radio in 1968 before receiving
its theatrical premiere in 1969, is a poetic drama for two voices, in which
for the first time perhaps in Pinter's work the poetry takes a certain
precedence over the drama: which is to say that, although it has narrative
threads in it that are not wholly ambiguous or irrecuperably unreliable,
Pinter's main interest in the play is in the liquidity of memory and in what
can be done with tone and with the reverberation of the incomplete and
the fragmentary. There are two characters: "DUFF: a man in his early
fifties. BETH: a woman in her late forties."[26] They speak in intercutting
monologues, and though Duff appears to be recalling and describing
aspects of his relationship with Beth, it is not quite clear whether Beth,
in the story she tells, is talking about Duff or about another man. The
ambiguity in the staged situation is encapsulated in Pinter's directorial
note:

> DUFF refers normally to BETH, but does not appear to hear
> her voice.
>
> BETH never looks at DUFF, and does not appear to hear his
> voice.
>
> Both characters are relaxed, in no sense rigid.[27]

In staging the piece, we came quickly to an arrangement where Duff
sat at the head of a long table, looking at Beth, while Beth, perching lightly
on the edge of the table, looked out in the direction of the audience.
Both, then, were – inevitably, it seemed – separated from 'us' by the
familiar fourth wall that seems to be present in all Pinter's plays (albeit
it will sometimes flicker or feel fragile). If anything, Beth was doubly
insulated, not just by that conventional barrier but also by a bubble of
nostalgic introversion and withdrawal – a sense that was strong in my
mind particularly, perhaps, because I knew the play through recordings
of three different radio productions, but had never seen it staged; on
radio, Pinter's specifications regarding the visual relationship between
the characters can only be implied, and Beth's disattachment from Duff
could take a number of forms: for example, within the grammar of
radio, it cannot absolutely be established that we are not hearing two
interior monologues – indeed, this is one of the most obviously faithful

ways of 'staging' Pinter's directions, which place the two characters together but apparently unable to hear each other (or choosing not to). The actor's experience, however, is always instructive – and often decisive. Maggie Henderson, the wonderful actor playing Beth, found the situation I was asking her to play, of facing the audience but not 'seeing' them, so strenuously difficult as to be practically unviable. The effort of imposing not just the standard-issue fourth wall but the kind of wilful blindness that would enable her to achieve the necessary combination of absolute interiority and recollective projection left her exhausted, faint, dizzy sometimes. I can't now remember the route by which we got there but I will always remember the terrible nervous excitement of the afternoon when I started to wonder if it might be possible to follow an instinct that seemed to have more to do with me than with Pinter: to allow Maggie to *see* the audience, to address her cut-up monologue directly to them, to be telling them the story rather than retracing it in her own mind. Something would obviously be lost – the poignancy of that very palpable 'bubble' around Beth – but something even more interesting replaced it: the idea that, as a result of making this shift, our staging of *Landscape* would present two separate theatrical situations, one superimposed on the other: Duff, trapped (perhaps comfortably) behind a fourth wall that Beth had somehow penetrated. Was the audience then in Beth's mind? (When a stage event is ineluctably fictive, it can sometimes help hugely to 'fictionalise' the audience too, so that the possibility of everyone being together in the same space is not lost.) Were two different worlds being overlaid, and in what ways might that ramify for an audience?[28]

Probably, not many audience members even consciously read this (to us) radical, potentially jarring reimagining of the theatrical space of *Landscape*. Certainly, no critic picked up on it. Maybe it mattered only to us. The fact that it made Maggie's nightly task bearable, if still far from easy, was important: a play has to work for the context and conditions of its staging, not the other way around, because the priority has to be what is made here-and-now: and when that alignment is finally achieved, it can often illuminate something unexpected in the play, a facet which would not have been lit under other circumstances.

For me, what happened with this staging of *Landscape* – one which, essentially, and perhaps unprecedentedly, was able to say 'hello' to its audience – was a clarifying of something that had previously been only the vaguest hunch about Pinter's use of silence. That Pinter uses stage directions indicating "Pause" and "Silence" (including at one point near the end of *Landscape*, "Long silence") is one of the better known features of his stage writing ("Even those who rarely set foot inside a theatre have heard of the Pinter pause," avers Michael Billington): it shows up particularly in parodies and shorthand jokes – the particular focus of which is often a perceived pretentiousness in his differentiation between the 'pause' and the 'silence'; in fact a 'silence' is often considered to be not much more than a long pause, long enough perhaps to allow for some sense of transition.

In a theatrical situation where the stage space is continuous with the audience space, however – where the fourth wall is not, or not consistently, present – another consideration is possible. A 'pause', it strikes me, may be something enacted by an actor; a 'silence', however, is not an action, but a quality or state in the space as a whole. One person alone can, with the most basic consent of an attentive audience, produce a pause; one person alone cannot produce a silence. A silence – or, to be more accurate, a feeling of silence – is produced communally, and created through a process of instinctual agreement.

This, then, is what I asked the actors in *Landscape*. That their pauses were their own business, and had to do with rhythms they could themselves control and behavioural patterns they might wish to consider; but that they would have to seek out their silences. That silence was to be listened for, patiently and honestly – that is, for as long as it might take. That something about their internal selves had to come in to alignment with the life of the space around them, the space that we had invited an audience into, so that only when a silence in themselves matched, or found itself reflected by, a silence in the room, would I want them to continue.

This was not an easy task, and it was one that took some getting used to; in notes after each performance, I remember, I would talk about the silences I had found I agreed with and those I had not, and the degree of subjectivity in the recognition of silence felt unmanageable sometimes. But it was at least active, which is what most actors mostly like – a call to activity, even when that means active listening, active stillness, active waiting – and when it was truthfully pursued, the silence in that room could be extraordinarily deep, unforgettably so. We remember, of course, from Cage, that there is no such thing as silence, just as there is no such thing as empty space (or time); but it was quite something to feel those actors almost physically leaning in to the room, waiting to hear not the cold conceptual silence of empty space but the lived silence of a place inhabited by a group of people engaged in an active, searching collaboration: a real place, not just lived-in but fully and abundantly alive with the high buzz of nervous systems and the low hum of circulating blood.

———————

> Derek [Jarman] could really throw a party. Since his death he is remembered for his films, his painting, his writing, his set designs and, sometimes, even his gay rights political actions. No one ever mentions his great parties. The ones I went to were at his loft studio in Butler's Wharf overlooking Tower Bridge. There was never anyone on the door, in fact the door was usually wide open. *If you knew about the party you got in.*[29]
>
> — Simon Barker, 'A Jarman Party' in *Punk's Dead* [my emphasis]

To those makers who recognize the significance of liveness in the construction of liveable theatre places, who wish to hold up the theatrical here-and-now to scrutiny and admiration, the category of the 'site-specific' has a particular and understandable appeal.

In practice, and notwithstanding the eagerness of marketing departments and the authors of media coverage to use the term, genuinely site-specific work – as opposed to that which is merely presented in sites not normally used as locations for performance – is pretty rare. A more useful term may be 'site-responsive', but the two are not synonymous; nor, however, have rigid definitions yet emerged, so it is perhaps useful to say a little about what I think I mean when I use these words, by reference to a particular project.

In 2005 I was invited to create a new show for performance in domestic venues – a niche in which my then company Signal to Noise had developed a modest reputation. The project had two phases: the piece devised by the company would be seen first at the Harley Gallery in Welbeck, where a temporary exhibition of contemporary craft and design for the home[30] was being displayed in something like a stage set: visitors moved through spaces which suggested different rooms – kitchen, dining room, living room, bedroom – but retained also a greater sense of artifice, of openness and provisionality, than would be found in most domestic interiors. The piece would then tour a number of real homes in Nottinghamshire (and in fact it went on to other regions).

To some considerable extent, it seems to me, the Harley Gallery 'version' of the piece can fairly be said to be site-specific, in that the show was created with that particular location in mind, and the exhibition on which the performance was overlaid dictated much about the form and shape of the piece. So, for example, the narrative of the show took the audience on a journey, starting in the kitchen and ending in the bedroom, which mirrored the natural flow of visitors through the defined spaces of the exhibition: in other words, the layout of the site was projected decisively onto the structure of the story we would tell. More fundamentally, the show – which we called *Homemade*, and in which, just under the surface of an uncomplicated story about love and bereavement, we explored some ideas about how the spaces in which we live influence our behaviours and our aspirations – would never have been made without the existence of that site and the questions which arose from it.

Once *Homemade* went on tour, the nature of its engagement with its performance situation changed somewhat. In common with the company's previous home-based work, we would arrive at our host's house or apartment just a few moments before the designated start-time. While the last of our host's guests arrived – we would normally play to an audience of ten or twelve, usually the host's family and friends – and often had wine and nibbles and mingled (more or less apprehensively), the company would quickly set up the bagful of props and items of technical apparatus that we had brought with us, and make a few on-the-hoof decisions about how and where certain scenes and moments would be played. The aim was that within no more than ten minutes, I'd be able (in my role as company manager) to announce to the chattering audience in the living room that the show had already begun: which it had, with the image of actor Lucy Ellinson sitting in the dark kitchen staring mournfully into – and lit only by – a refrigerator with its door ajar. They'd then follow the action through the same four rooms as the exhibition had used, in the same order, until, in common with all our home pieces, at the end the whole company disappeared into the night, leaving behind us as unobtrusively as possible a few bits and pieces – the odd photograph or postcard or memento – which would linger in the house long after the show was over.

This touring version of *Homemade* was – necessarily, and, to my mind, excitingly – acutely 'site-responsive'. Though the narrative of the show never really changed, the dialogue was improvised more or less from scratch every night, around a skeleton of plot points, an intermittent sequence of four monologues, and a few fleeting moments that it was possible to craft with great precision. So there was an uncommon degree of latitude, which permitted (and indeed required) the performers to tell stories about, or simply make passing references to, details of that particular home and its contents, only a very few of which had been introduced into the site by the company; but there was also a level of intricacy that allowed these moments – which the watching audience knew must be being improvised right before their eyes – to intertwine with very carefully prefabricated events that did not advertise themselves as such. The effect was the creation – when it worked (which it certainly didn't always) – of a kind of magical serendipity, of very specific things happening that seemed ineffable, even impossible, to the audience. (This was enhanced by their gradual realisation that, of the three characters in the story, only one could apparently 'see' them and address them, while the other two inhabited a theatrical layer in which the audience was not present to them; while those two appeared to 'live in' the house where the performance was taking place in front of its actual residents, the third character, who spoke to the audience, turned out to be, in the world of the story, a dead man. As with the later, very similar layering of spaces I describe above in my production of *Landscape*, there is something uncanny about the simultaneity, which is at once jarring and yet strange in its refusal to signal itself as a 'problem' needing to be resolved.)

The 'site-responsiveness' of the touring version of *Homemade* is clearly very keen, albeit at one level rather superficial, incorporating unforeseen variables into its storytelling structures, in the manner of improvisational comedy for example. Nonetheless, these simple techniques, cleverly and softly deployed, can become quite load-bearing in their impact on an audience.

If the two phases of the *Homemade* project make for a serviceable example of one possible way to distinguish 'site-specific' from 'site-responsive' work, they also point towards a more broadly applicable and important observation. On tour, that piece is infinitely adaptable from site to site, and as such the specific details of each site are both profoundly significant, in the moment of performance, and of no lasting significance at all. In Thursday night's performance, five minutes of brilliant material might be generated from the presence of, say, a nude portrait of a young woman above the fireplace in the living room; on Friday night's performance, not only is there no painting, there's no fireplace: but perhaps instead there's a kitsch figurine of a flamenco dancer on the sideboard, and that will be the source of the equivalent story that night, which may or may not go as well as the night before. The experience of an audience may have much to do with the idea of a particular 'place', especially one they know (or thought they knew) well, such as their own home – with which, of course, they may actually be so familiar in so quotidian a way that they have ceased to consciously experience it as a place at all; but in the resilience and the sustained affordance of the show itself, the 'space' of the piece as an effectively adaptable format counts for much more than any single instance of its temporary layering over a particular place.

'Site-specific' theatre and performance often benefits from the inflationary hypervigilance of promoters and media commentators who are desperate for any 'angle' that speaks to a constant market-driven need for novelty (often dressed-up, justifiably or otherwise, as 'innovation'). A disused toothpaste factory may look wonderful in pictures; the meagre redolences of an evacuated pantry in a disrepaired stately home can always be spun into euphoric brochure copy. But 'site' is, in syntactical if not in logistical terms, a cinch. The crucial, radical challenge that site-specificity poses to theatre makers and thinkers is really in the idea of the 'specific'.

The appeal to specificity is one that theatre should take in its stride. After all, 'specificity' is cognate with the 'spectator': the 'specific' (related of course to 'species') presents its specialness as something to be beheld, discriminatingly; to be accurately seen for just what it is. And yet, the ways in which theatre is customarily conceived, made, presented, re-presented, and documented, all tend towards a minimizing of the work's capacity for specificity – that is, the precision and sensitivity of its active consequential liveness.

The most glaringly obvious way in which theatre makers reject specificity is in the standard division of the process into a preparatory phase ('rehearsal') and a delivery phase ('performance'). This immediately establishes a situation in which almost all the pertinent decisions are made *in anticipation of* an event that has not yet happened, namely the exposure of a prepared production to an audience. This advance work has therefore to be undertaken in front of an *imaginary* audience – often one that 'includes' critics – in an atmosphere of fraught second-guessing and mild-to-moderate dread, which arises, as fear so often does, out of a state of not-knowing. The process, even in the most apparently carefree devising, often requires that a script or text or score is settled early on; most likely by that time, the set design has been agreed too, and marketing copy for the show may have been determined weeks or even months before that. It is seldom now the case that directors arrive at the beginning of the rehearsal period with a whole show pre-blocked, as they might well have fifty or seventy years ago; but a settled methodology of read-through, discussion, analysis, 'actioning' maybe, and so on (or an equivalently orthodox prescription for how devised work is made), takes its place: against the unknowability of the moment of live performance are shored up these reliable certitudes. By the time the work meets its first audience, decisions have been taken about every aspect of its presentation, and it falls more or less entirely to the actors – whose presence on-stage is about the only element that has about it even a modicum of liveness (responsiveness, fluidity, non-fixedness): and it may be a pretty scant modicum at that – to mediate between the prepared work, which has of apparent necessity concerned itself with the generic and the anticipated, and the here-and-now of a particular audience.

That audience, meanwhile, feels compelled to subdue its experience of its own specificity, in order to enter in to that negotiation. Individuals arriving at a theatre space (whether or not that space is usually agreed to be a theatre) tend to be very aware at some level of their own individuality. They have taken a particular journey in order to be present; commingled with whatever sense of anticipation of this event they are carrying with them, are dozens of private narratives: the car park, the babysitter, the price of a gin and tonic at the bar; the stressful situation at work, that elderly relative that no one knows what to do with; the sexual confusion, the class anxiety, the fear of dying. All of this has to be quietened down, because none of these things are what this event is 'about': and so they will create unwelcome interference with the experience that has been promised by the marketing copy that was written six months ago about what would happen tonight. The upshot is that makers and audience alike are trying to bring their respective nonspecificalities into a kind of sad pragmatic alliance – notwithstanding that both parties might well, if you asked them, attest to the importance of liveness as a particularly special and delightful element in the experience of theatre.

One way the seemingly impossible challenge of specificity shows up in current theatre discourse, especially among sleepless artistic directors and agitated literary agents, is in its coarse allotrope, 'relevance'. It's not hard to see why: it would hardly ever occur to most people, especially young people and working-class people, to go to the theatre, except maybe to the odd musical or panto. Programmers recognize that a big part of the alienation that keeps these potential audiences away is exactly that sense that our putative audience member in the paragraph above is taking in to the auditorium with them: the sense, as telegraphed by so many elements in the mix, that this work is *not about you*. But the attempt to use 'relevance' (which is almost invariably taken to be a question of content, not of form) as a weapon with which to bludgeon theatre into a pose of specific care is doomed to an extraordinarily uninteresting kind of failure. What is relevant to the moment of a theatrical encounter is the set of conditions in which artists and audience conspire together in an act of collective making; everything else – including, for example, any narrative content, or the physical design of the show – has to do with the ways in which those conditions appeal (or don't) to the attention of the conspirators.

Site-specificity, then, can be seen as part of an ironic system, in that it (or its designated driver) is set to work in order to capture the imaginations of an audience who are feeling rejected or alienated by more obviously 'conventional' theatre; yet the quality of specificity that's missing in their experience of standard theatre may well be equally missing in their experience of a novelty site. And it's worth stating the flipside of this observation, too: staged work that is able to apply itself to the specific conditions of the encounter it initiates will cause its audience to feel that that work is, for once, *about them*. It will have something to say about their lives, even if, for example, it's a story about people with whom they might think they have nothing apparently in common.

Etymologically, 'relevance' is closely linked to 'relief': both have to do with the idea of lightness and of uplift. Perhaps, then, we might better comprehend the relevance we seek – the sense that theatre is not remote from us, but involves us and depends (somehow *specifically* in the here-and-now) upon our reciprocal involvement with it – if we think about that relevance as having to do not with what we bring to the experience, but with what we leave out of it; how, even in the midst of wanting to think about what might seem 'heavy' questions, we can create a sense of lightness that allows for a fully developed engagement to take place, a sense of ourselves inhabiting this temporary place that isn't immediately weighed down, squashed by the burdensome density of prefabricated art.

Shomit Mitter writes interestingly about the place in the work of Peter Brook, and of Brook's forebear Jerzy Grotowski, of the idea of 'wholeness'. Mitter portrays both figures as seekers after wholeness, an aspiration which serves to confirm (and perhaps to advertise) the special conditions under which the theatrical encounter is lived out. For Grotowski, "the actor ... transcends the phase of incompleteness, to which we are condemned in everyday life"[31], while Brook's pursuit of wholeness tends finally towards the proposition of "an alternative system of ethics in which 'good' and 'bad' are replaced by 'whole' and 'incomplete'."[32] Mitter tracks this movement through both directors' attempts to enact or inspire reconciliation within each of a series of posited binaries: in the first place, 'mind' / 'body' (which also shows up as 'intelligence' / 'feeling', or 'consciousness' / 'flesh'), but also 'soul' / 'body' (or 'inner' / 'outer' or 'internal' / 'external'), and 'appearance' / 'substance'. These pairings ideally having been smoothed into balanced productive unities, the "integrated"[33] self then meets its 'other': which might take place in contact with another actor, or in an encounter between the actors and the 'other' of their audience; or there is some more numinous, spiritually configured 'otherness' to be confronted. For Brook, building on Grotowski's impulse towards wholeness, these apparently exhaustive efforts at extension and rehabilitation nonetheless fall short, at least in practice, because they create an aesthetic programme that appears characteristically pious or "esoteric" and into which, Brook avers, the introduction of rougher, dirtier, more 'popular' notes is necessary, for any claim to 'wholeness' to be valid.

It is straight away obvious, without any further analysis, that these projects, in their apparent advance towards a horizon of wholeness that is, as it were, *terminally* whole, or somehow *absolutely* complete, are heavily loaded with ideological freight, expressed most distinctly perhaps in Grotowski's point of departure: the idea that 'incompleteness' is a state to which, in our daily lives, human beings are 'condemned'. It need not be disputed that that 'incompleteness' is a fact, and any individual or group of individuals may find that predicament more or less congenial, more or less like an experience of having been condemned: but the idea that 'incompleteness' is a problem to be solved is a comment on sociality and interdependence whose political index is clear – and to wish to take that problem into the realm of theatre (of all places) to be worked on and finally "transcended" is at best perverse.

This is not to suggest that the experience – especially the communal experience – of incompleteness is not problematic; in the next chapter, we'll think a bit about Bataille and the category of the erotic, which is definitively tied to the problem of incompleteness in a way that (I would argue) is very potently theatrical. But to *feel* the problem of incompleteness is not to wish to *solve* it – or to "transcend" it. And in its way, Grotowski's – and by extension, Brook's – will to transcend the material complexities of social incompleteness and the forces that create and sustain that incompleteness is no different than Brook's violent refusal of context: at its heart is a quintessentially colonial attitude, where what cannot be controlled must be risen above. To attain wholeness, in this construction, is to absorb difference and neutralize its power to disturb; it is an acquisitive fantasy, feeding off imperialist narratives and a valorization of 'peace' in a political vacuum, attained at the expense of 'others' the details of whose lives we transcend at too high an altitude to be able to make out.

To say all this more positively: wholeness is not a theatrical value (let alone a virtue), because the relationality at the core of theatre and theatrical structures depends on the consequential presence of an 'other' that is always partly unknown or unpredicted: whether that otherness is embodied in the unsettled presence of another actor whose own life experience ramifies variously in the work she does (rather than being 'checked' at the door of the rehearsal room or minimized in the service of the 'vision' of an absent writer, say), or in the always partly incomprehensible presence of a heterogeneous and variegated audience; or whether its effects enter simply through the multiple contingencies and serendipities of a fully live event, wherein, it might be argued, that sense of 'liveness' is both a metaphor for and a generator of the signs of difference and otherness by which any social constellation might be discriminated. Perhaps, to some viewers, the admission and promotion of such variability into the theatrical event may be seen as the last (or merely a next) step in the journey towards a fully conclusive 'wholeness'; others, including myself, will see this as an icky self-harming paradox, and prefer to seek a theatre that, in its hospitality to a difference which is not ours to 'know' or to subsume within the expanses of our authority and privilege, guards vigilantly against any suggestion of wholeness or completion, for the sake of its viable life.

It is perhaps instructive, and certainly illustrative, that all the acts of harmony and inclusiveness proposed by Grotowski and Brook in their pursuit of wholeness concern themselves with the activity of adult humans. It is as if they mean tacitly to endorse the adage usually credited to the comedian W. C. Fields: "Never work with children or animals": a truism to whose apparent common sense we might readily accede. But what this famous injunction speaks to, plainly, is our desire (as makers) to control – or at least to be able to control – what happens 'on stage', not only in the moment of its happening but also in our anticipation of it, and our wish to depend on the accuracy of that anticipating rendition: in other words, our liking to diminish the specific and contingent quality of any single event or set of events, and to prefer the predictable, the generic and the intentional. Audiences, of course, don't necessarily agree: they love signs of liveness: whether these are manifested in functional errors in prestige dramas – the door-handle that comes off in John Gabriel Borkman's hand one Thursday matinee; or carnivalesque treats on a panto stage – the wisecracking snot-nosed moppety kid brought up from the audience, the defecating Shetland pony in the background. The particular anxiety, for the maker and especially for the actor, has to do with being 'upstaged', or (almost as bad) the seriousness of their endeavour being undermined, their dignity as an actor – a special case of the pristine completeness that Grotowski fancies – being collapsed by circumstances beyond their control.

What underscores these positions is a template of what we might call the 'fully achieved', in which a distinctly singular vision is faithfully translated with maximum efficiency and minimal variance into an enaction that appears at some level to be 'lived' (or 'lived-in', genuinely inhabited, as places often are), that still hopes to signal 'liveness' through means of simulation or decoration. Yet audiences are often extraordinarily sensitive to the differences between the actually live and the merely imitative, and to them, on these terms, the signs of liveness that they love will almost always show up in moments of (what is taken to be) failure or unforeseen excess.

The persistence of this inadequate template certainly reflects the extent to which authority is normally construed in theatre as both identical with and, therefore, inevitably, always falling (perhaps painfully) somewhat short of a literary model of authorship, in which what is made is 'set down': as if a playwright – or, for that matter, a director, probably of the variety known disparagingly in English-speaking cultures as an *auteur* – could write as directly onto the stage, or into the theatre, as she might onto the page, or into the space of the text. Although many writers and directors – and, for that matter, actors – for the stage would quickly recognize (and insist) that most making processes are a good deal more collaborative than this suggests, it's also true that those collaborations are commonly organized in service and protection of exactly that authorial model. The choices available are plainly seen to be stark: either one exerts control through the exercise of authority, or one abdicates that authority, control is lost, and, in the words of one iconic performing animal – the wounded fox in Lars von Trier's film *Antichrist* – "chaos reigns".[34]

But in fact, where the will to control is relaxed, authority is not weakened but extended, in a way that resonates with a half-hidden root meaning of 'authority', the idea of the making of *increase* (as in the cognate 'augmentation'). In this picture, authority becomes inclusive: what is authored is not the event, but the space in which the event takes place – in other words, authoring here is an act in which the 'space' of the event as conceived undergoes its transition into a 'place' which, ideally, teems with life, not all of the carriers of which can consciously 'serve' to realize the makers' imaginative anticipation of the event, but all of which can assist in and enrich the process of transition. In this model, the craft of the making and contributing artists is neither to assert control nor to abandon control, but to accept – preferably, to welcome, and ideally, to be able to harness – the co-authoring role played by chance and by contingency. This does not amount to a dilution or a dissipation of the will of the author, but an enlargement of it.

Some years ago, in a discussion of the problem of specificity in the construction of the 'site-specific' performance, I proposed what has come to be known as 'the cat test':

> Let loose a cat in the performance space: if the piece can ac-commodate and include and refer to the cat, in all its feline unpredictability and unwillingness to comply with the struc-tures of performance, then you've got a specific piece.[35]

In this thought-experiment (though, as I am about to explain, it is not *only* an experiment to be conducted in thought), the cat embodies all that we cannot control: a dog in the performance space would signal entirely differently, in that dogs are frequently engaged in certain kinds of performance, if only in our day-to-day interactions with them as 'owners', in which role we may hope to commission their obedience, or at least their acknowledgement: whereas cats are notoriously difficult to train or even to coerce into behaviours that are convenient to us. So in any theatrical system that depends on control structures and predictable response patterns, a cat is a problem, a challenge: not least because it is not in any meaningful sense *rebelling* against those structures – if it were, some shared premise might permit negotiation; as it is, the cat is sublimely oblivious to the syntax surrounding it. As Nicholas Ridout puts it in his intensely useful (if sometimes dispiriting) *Stage Fright, Animals, and Other Theatrical Problems*:

> The theatre…is all about humans coming face to face
> with other humans and either liking it or not liking it.
> The animal clearly has no place in such a communication…
> [I]t shouldn't be there because it doesn't know what to do
> there, is not capable of performing theatrically by engaging a
> human audience in experimental thinking about the condi-
> tions of their own humanity… The impropriety of the animal
> on the theatre stage is experienced very precisely as a sense of
> the animal being in the wrong place.[36]

What's vital, though, is the careful retention of a distinction between hospitality and absorption – in other words, between multiplicity and wholeness – in the actions through which we might "accommodate and include…the cat". Imagine, for example, a cat wandering onto the stage while a stand-up comedian is performing. To a certain sort of comic, this is not a breach to be deplored, a 'failure' to be brushed aside, but rather it's a veritable gift. He can get ten minutes of material out of the cat: he can talk to it, he can tell us what it's thinking, he can imitate it, anthropomorphize it, turn its presence to his advantage. His improvisational élan will amuse and delight; the whole episode will end up on YouTube and everyone will admire the comedian's virtuosity. This is exactly the kind of co-option that I tend to disdain, at least for theatre, because it seeks (and in this instance succeeds) to *solve* the problem that the cat represents. The cat is 'won over' by the comedian, in the same way that his job is to 'win over' his audience.

In my theatre piece *The Forest and the Field*, out of which this book grew, I wanted first and perhaps foremost to create a physical environment in which audiences could experience very directly some of the ideas around space and place that I have found suggestive in my work. With this in mind, clearly the opportunity was there to bring the 'cat test' out of its conceptual hiding-place and into the system of an actual show. Audiences entering the theatre found an environment organized in the round, with chairs, cushions and platforms for seating at different levels, surrounding on all sides a space for 'acting', which, initially at any rate, contained only an island-like patch of earth and a large branch we'd found; there were domestic lamps and pot-plants, but also fluorescent tubes, stage lights, a microphone. (Our reference points had mostly been Arte Povera artists such as Mario Merz, Jannis Kounellis and Giuseppe Penone.) The two human performers, the actor Tom Ross-Williams and myself, and the technical operator James Lewis, sat amid the audience, at least initially, hoping neither to draw nor to deflect attention, but merely to be present alongside all the other elements of the performance. And somewhere in the room was a cat, whom I would introduce, along with the rest of the team, at the beginning of each show.

The piece toured to four UK venues, in London, Bristol, Plymouth and Ipswich, which necessitated finding a different participant cat in each city; the owners with whom we were put in touch all asked (often slightly baffled) versions of the same question: "What would you want my cat to do?" To which the only response we could give, not entirely satisfactorily perhaps, was: "Just be a cat." This answer was both complete in itself and seriously deficient in practice: cats don't know what you might mean by "be a cat". With our first guest star, Antonio, we were spoiled: as a dweller in a warehouse community occupied by artists and party animals (mostly, but not exclusively, human animals), he was utterly unfazed by the whole apparatus and rigmarole of theatre, including the presence of the audience. During rehearsals and on the first night, he would walk into scenes, watch them *in media res*, play happily with Tom, climb ladders, and even position himself centre-stage and, with enviable unselfconsciousness, thoroughly and explicitly clean himself. Probably in traditional terms Tom and I were repeatedly 'upstaged': if so, we were delighted.

By the night of the second performance, however, Antonio's insouciance had shaded into apparent boredom, and he spent most of the evening asleep on a ledge. The audience knew he was there, and reported afterwards that their knowledge of his presence had still informed their viewing of the piece: but there was no doubt that we felt a little disappointed, a bit robbed. This, though, was the pattern for the whole tour: we were always glad of the presence of our four feline collaborators (I use that word not entirely facetiously), and audiences were too, but Antonio's note-perfect first-night demonstration of the affordances of an onstage cat would never quite be matched, and as time went by, I began to be guiltily aware that "Just be a cat" was a wholly disingenuous stage direction. I might have meant "Be an exemplary cat": except that that was, of course, what each cat did. The cat in Bristol who appeared, brilliantly, exactly as I spoke her name, and then clambered out of sight and never showed her face again; the cat in Plymouth who sat all night by the exit patiently waiting to be let out, and who on another occasion mewed in apparent distress from an invisible position beneath a seating bank, sounding like a forlorn ghost, though her owner assured us afterwards that she was absolutely fine; the cat in Ipswich who was considerably more nervous than any of the others, and ended up sitting on her owner's lap, out of sight of the audience, throughout: all of these were being exemplary cats, just as much as was the coolly extrovert Antonio.

"Be careful what you wish for," then, is perhaps the moral of this story: or, as one frequent collaborator is kind enough to remind me when rehearsals go through a sticky patch: "Well, you invited it all in."[37] But I'm very glad we enacted the cat test for real, and I'd certainly be keen to work with a cat in the room again. While my assumptions, my unexamined imaginative projections, around the scripted task of "being a cat" may have been shown up for their reductiveness and casual speciesism, the impulse behind 'inviting in' those radically uncontrollable presences feels right. Essentially, our interest had been – and remains – in

Tom Ross-Williams and Antonio the cat in *The Forest and the Field*. Ovalhouse, 2013
© Richard Davenport.

setting against itself Nick Ridout's perception of "a sense of the animal being in the wrong place". If a cat on stage is in the wrong place, but also a cat embodies and enacts so much that theatre needs in order to be fully live and actually specific in space and time, then it would seem that the responsible course of action is not to guard against working with cats (or with children and animals more generally), but to observe that theatre itself, when it takes place, most often takes "the wrong place": that either the primary conceptualisation of theatre space is awry, or that the process of moving those spatial concepts into placed and inhabited realities is too often an inaccurate or unfaithful translation.

We might pause to notice that even the act of 'inviting in', with its connotations of openness and inclusivity, depends upon a position of cultural privilege: 'we' are already here, and it is our choice to 'invite' people or animals or elements or chance occurrences into the room, or not. (We may not be able to keep some of those visitors out – especially chance, which, as I've already indicated, will make its presence felt whether we want it or not, which is why it makes sense to at least try to want it.) Quite often in theatre, especially in designated theatre buildings, we start from a 'place' of privacy, of private ownership, even though as artists we may be motivated by or compelled towards acts of public speech, and wish to participate in the sharing of public space. Privacy is one of capitalism's bluntest instruments, and again, it behoves theatre artists to consider their own dependence on it as an element in the apparatus of control. To make theatre is very often to seek a legitimate public life for acts commissioned and created in private, but the two states are inevitably wretchedly mixed up in each other's operations.

I have been fortunate to see in a few different versions a performance lecture by the brilliant academic and artist Theron Schmidt, called (after a line of Susan Sontag) *Some people will do anything to keep themselves from being moved.* About two thirds of the way through the piece, Theron props open the doors to the room in which his performance is taking place, and they stay open for the rest of the duration, admitting – inviting in – sounds (and potentially other elements: smells, say, or air currents) from outside, whether that exterior is 'the outside world', as it was when I saw his performance at Siobhan Davies Studios in London, or simply the foyer to the auditorium, as at The Bike Shed Theatre in Exeter. Shortly afterwards, he explains that this action refers back to the same action in another show: Karen Christopher and Gerard Bell's piece *So Below*, which Theron and I both saw at the Chelsea Theatre. As he explains:

> You could say that the performance itself has an everyday quality
> – there's a gentleness and an absence of pretence to Karen and
> Gerard's actions, their fragments of speech, their small acts of
> kindness – and so there's a pleasing harmony with the sounds of
> the everyday that seep in from outside… But watching them, I
> felt there was something more than just reality seeping in, lend-
> ing its unpredictability to the events in the room. For theirs was
> a performance made out of careful attention… And so with the
> doors open, I felt not only the outside everyday seep in, but this
> careful attention work its way out.[38]

There is an appealing porosity to the situation Theron describes, and
I absolutely recognize the sense of flow he identifies; it's not far from
being an economic relationship, in which hospitality, invitation – the
outside world, "reality seeping in" – has its recompense in the export
of an unusual quality of attentiveness. This is, of course, a subjective
perceptual construct: or at any rate it is hard to know whether, and how,
someone outside the room would detect the emanation from it of "this
careful attention". But one can easily understand – indeed, I would
happily vouch for – the spectator's sense of their own attentiveness
extending into the zone beyond the performance space, meeting and
perhaps somehow irradiating the aural information that is for its part
streaming towards us and into our territory. That the doors are open is
not, by any means, an empty or shallow gesture: it signifies abundantly
and with some precision.

All the same, however, we might notice how the sense of *freedom* in
this exchange – the sense that information is free to enter the space we
occupy and, at least on an imaginative or speculative level, can freely leave
it – is secured by a concentric set of perimeters that hold that exchange
within the protective seclusion of essentially private activity. Sound,
for example, or ambience more generally, may come and go; but the
movement of people, certainly, is exactingly constrained: a ticket must be
bought from a box office in another part of the building; front of house
staff will later check this ticket. The movement of some animals would be
even more tightly controlled, where possible: a fly might make it in to the
auditorium; a guide dog might be welcome, a stray dog almost certainly
not. But this is only the most palpably transactional guarantee of a safe
context in which to leave the doors open. Imagine if a random number
generator produced a series of global coordinates that would determine

where on earth the next twelve performances of *So Below*, or of Theron's piece, would take place. At a guess it seems unlikely that more than one or two of those tour dates would provide the kind of environment that would allow for the porousness that artists and audiences alike find so pleasant. Even confining the same exercise to within the boundaries of London might not produce a higher proportion of viable sites. These artists depend, as do I, for the free flowing movements to which we're so attracted, on many different sets of closed doors through which only certain people may pass. Notice, for example, how some of the characteristics Theron identifies in the performed actions of *So Below* – "gentleness", "kindness" – are described first as "everyday" qualities. Hadn't we better pause for a moment to wonder whether gentleness and

Some People Will Do Anything... © Theron Schmidt.

kindness are part of the lived experience of 'every day' for everybody? In fact, the structure of the piece as Theron sets it out would seem to ask the same question: if gentle and kind acts promote an unusual level of attentiveness, and this quality of attentiveness is so unusual as to be a notable production arising from the work, this would seem to imply that the space in which the work happens is somehow discontinuous with the everyday, but rather is a site operating under special conditions, or within which it is possible to work in ways that are not quotidian: and is, in fact, in that sense, a space of privilege, in which the door can safely be left open, in tacit confidence that guards both nameless and dismally familiar patrol the borders of these grounds.

At base, these observations have to do with access, and as such are hardly revelations. Economic and class obstacles, both real and perceived, and the self-harming participation of theatre – one might nearly say *even* theatre – in a culture defined substantially by the conditions of commodity and exchange value, taken together make for an intractable edifice of barriers to entry, which is further complicated by the ways in which, for example, 'plays' or 'drama' might be taught in schools, or 'actors' portrayed in the broadcast media, or 'theatricality' reduced in common currency to an egregious concoction of ludicrous shabby glitz and nauseating self-indulgence. Even its most ardent supporters do not necessarily see, or understand, or feel able to articulate (without embarrassment, at least) the ways in which theatre is distinct in its affordances: meaning that it merely takes its place among an array of leisure options, and promises so little and at such an unacceptable level of risk versus outlay as to be, in most cases, a terrible prospect. These problems in turn may be compounded by other related issues – despite the efforts of many worthwhile organizations, rural and non-metropolitan audiences are often ill-served, as are potential users with special access needs.

Any account, then, of what theatre 'invites in' as it takes its place, must not – even if it theoretically could – seek to separate out the systematic openness of its aesthetic and formal imperatives from its responsibility to engage with the question of how it can be actively open to all who want or need it. Only in a theatre that radically responds to the entanglement of these propositions will it be possible for an actor meaningfully to say 'Hello' to an audience, and for an audience genuinely to say 'Hello' back.

In the spring of 2011, Chris Goode & Company developed a piece called *Open House*, in response to an invitation from West Yorkshire Playhouse [WYP] to participate in their inaugural 'Transform' season, part of an Arts Council-funded initiative to find new models for developing relationships between makers and audiences. As with many complex and unpredictable offerings, the basic substance of *Open House* can be simply described, in two sentences. One: the company – as represented by a small ensemble of performing makers, writers, designers and technicians – arrives in a rehearsal room early on Monday morning, and will spend the rest of the week devising from scratch an entirely new show, the 'finished' version of which will be performed on the Friday evening. Two: anybody who wants to can come into the rehearsal room and engage with that process in whatever way they wish – from a five-minute drop-in on a lunchbreak, to an afternoon spent chatting informally with the team and other visitors, to a deep involvement in the making of the show, which might even include performing in it alongside the company. (In this first *Open House* week, the 'professional' ensemble that arrived on Monday morning numbered five; the combined cast of Friday's final show, sixteen.) The situation thus created is one in which any dependable separation between 'makers' (or 'artists') and 'audience' is quickly and irrecuperably destabilized, but in which distinct roles can still be assumed, sometimes in flux, sometimes in dazzling clarity: host, witness, actor, companion, ringleader, 'outside eye', interlocutor, partner, caregiver, archivist, anarchist, trickster, dancer, enthusiast, model, clown; and so on. The need for any of these roles to be occupied in any moment seems to be read – by company artist and visitor alike – from the place of the event, its social life, rather than from the structure of the process (which visitors will not necessarily comprehend): but it is the authored permissiveness of the space, and the emergent sense that all present are custodians of that permission, that fosters the interactions through which the work is collectively made.

Chris Goode & Company, *Open House*. West Yorkshire Playhouse, 2011
© CG&Co Archive.

It would be wrong to overstate the resilience of *Open House* as a portable format: a second week, with a different company, for Mayfest in Bristol, was in many ways less successful, though still worthwhile; the difference had much to do with material factors such as the shape and ambience of the work room, and the location of the piece within the festival context and particularly within the city. Though there may be further week-long experiments with *Open House* as a standalone piece, the applications we are now most interested in have to do with longer creative projects and rehearsal processes: so, a production of an existing text, or the devising of a wholly original piece, might include a few days, perhaps, or a week, 'in Open House' – in other words, harnessing the fecundity of the porous and sometimes heavily (perhaps even chaotically) populated environment that will tend to arise from those particular conditions of engagement and permission.

Another extension of the ideas behind *Open House* could be seen in *9*, Chris Goode & Company's follow-up project for Transform 2012 at WYP. For *9* we put out an open call across West Yorkshire, inviting anyone – but especially those with no prior experience of performing – to contact us and tell us about themselves; of those who got in touch, we invited about fifty to come and meet us over the course of a weekend, and then selected nine with each of whom we worked one-on-one, pairing them with one of three directors from the company (Kirsty Housley, Jamie Wood and myself), to develop an eight-minute solo performance for them to present as part of an anthology show at WYP's beautiful but formidable 350-seat Courtyard Theatre. Over the course of several weeks, we worked with our nine guests on pieces that reflected their own personalities, interests, cultures and life-stories, aiming at all times (on the whole successfully, I think) to treat them as serious artists and collaborators. This was emphatically not an 'outreach' project or a 'community theatre' project – at least, it had none of the sense of quarantine that those phrases often connote. The production values were high, the quality of attention and engagement that was both given to our collaborating subjects and required of them was profound, and we tried to shape for them an adventure that I described to WYP during our initial pitch meeting as a "golden ticket"[39] experience, in which they would be consistently supported and rewarded for their courage in stepping up and asking to be involved.

9 was conceived partly out of the sole frustration that arose from the previous year's *Open House*: in such a teemingly busy and unstable creative environment, it was all but impossible to refine the work that emerged, and consequently the culminating performance was as rough and underachieved as it was energetic and good-natured. For all that the idea of craft in theatre-making may have been recentred around the holding open of certain kinds of space and hospitality, as opposed to assertive expressions of authorship, nonetheless, certain compositional gestures and editorial interventions remain crucially important in the apparatus of relationality, and when these are missing or obscured, the work that emerges can feel too provisional, too constrained by its internal operations to communicate productively with its audience. In *9*, then, we had recourse to a more apparently orthodox methodology in the collaborative partnerships we sought, in order to preserve and enjoy the possibilities in craft and refinement, while other elements in the system continued to feed in signals of openness and contingency: above all, the presence throughout the project of a visual artist, Lou Sumray, who was generally with us in rehearsal, drawing, sketching: both documenting the processes of creating the performances, and feeding back into those processes images of movement, glimpses, fleetingness, the perpetual disappearance of our moment-to-moment negotiations and improvisations.

The company of Chris Goode's *9*. West Yorkshire Playhouse, 2012
© Richard Davenport.

The aim in both *Open House* and *9* is not to eliminate any distinction between audience and participants, though with the former especially the border can be erased or suspended in an instant: rather, it's to make that distinction somehow radiant and tantalising. The audience saw the cast of *9* as belonging to *them*, rather than to the 'us' of the established theatre; but that belonging also brought messages *from* the theatre, about care taken, support given, different kinds of beauty given room. And beneath those messages, an implied provocation – which also belonged much more actively, naggingly even, to the rehearsal room of *Open House*, and indeed to the various spaces in which most of our work now happens: this all has to do with what you want.

At the beginning of this section, the photographer Simon Barker describes a party – a typical, rather than a particular, party – thrown by the late artist and filmmaker Derek Jarman during the late 1970s in London. "[T]he door was usually wide open," he says: no guest-list, no gatekeepers. Similarly, it was often said of Jarman when he was making a film – especially one of his more improvisatory works such as *The Last of England* or *The Garden* – that anyone who wanted to be in the movie would simply have to show up at the start of the day's shooting, and some use would be made of them. But this 'open door' policy – like our *Open House* policy – is only open up to a point. "If you knew about the party, you got in," says Barker; likewise, you're welcome to attend *Open House*, on terms that are shaped as much by you as by us, but you have to know it's there and be willing to make the journey. More testingly, the invitation that's open to everyone (except professional theatre makers) in *9* is an invitation to ask for admission to quite a privileged zone of access: working directly and intimately on a genuinely collaborative basis with experienced makers; getting to see what happens backstage at a major regional theatre; having some time in the spotlight in front of a large and enthusiastic audience. Aside from its capping at nine participants, that admission is essentially selective on one criterion only: how much you want it, how ready you are. It is true that your capacity to articulate your readiness and your desire to participate, and your confidence in understanding that the invitation might apply to you in the first place, are determined by many of the factors that shape the contours of (what we perceive as) social inclusion and exclusion; at the same time, the social and cultural diversity both of the nine selected individuals and of the hundred-plus applicants suggest that, as ever, the further one zooms in to the picture, the more detailed and complex it becomes.

At any rate, electivity as the fundamental basis of instrumental participation – actively wanting to be in the room, at the party – has to be present for the theatrical encounter to be fully alive, for its actors (on both sides of that radiant dividing line) to be alive to themselves. "Decisions are made by those who show up," says President Bartlet in *The West Wing*, more than once.[40] Just as to make art is to want to place in the world something that isn't already present (even if that 'thing' is a certain quality of attention towards the familiar or the mundane), so to be an audience is to want to see something else, to want more, to want different; to bear witness to change, and to change with it; to show up in search of a decisive act. Street theatre and guerrilla performance and 'outreach' and the interventions of cutting-edge social practice may startle latent desire into consequential palpitations, or they may confuse and alienate and repel, especially when they take the form of impositions without consent or dialogue. On the whole, I don't think I want to persuade anyone to be present in a theatrical encounter, or bribe them, or even minimise the risk they take; on the contrary, in a sense it's the risk, more than anything, that they have to want. More often than we want to acknowledge, actors and audience alike may be bodily present in a theatre event without in any meaningful sense "showing up". Only electivity – even in the form of the vaguest hunch, the blurriest sense of frustration and anomie and the wish for everything to be somehow 'better' – will hold audience and makers alike in a position of availability to the kinds of movement that theatre can initiate. In a sense, theatre is simply a name for a certain kind of speculative arrangement within a particular community of interest – that interest being not literature or leisure or edification or entertainment, but the registration and experience of difference and the imagining and enaction of personal and social change.

Where theatre institutions, especially building-based organizations, undertake 'outreach' projects, often in response to the observation that the profile of their audiences does not match the demographics of the locale in which that theatre is situated, it is crucial that these enterprises are not undertaken in a spirit of advertisement: "Did you know this facility was here? Did you know the invitation is extended to you, and that you are welcome? Did you know that we think the price of admission represents reasonable value for money?", and so on. These enquiries, however subtly or tactfully framed, simply ask a new constituency to consent to being sold to. The imperative is to engage people in conversation about their lives, their expectations, their sense of the change they would seek and the barriers to that change. Only a theatre that can follow up its opening 'Hello' with a conversation about change, about what people want, will be seen to have meant that 'Hello' in the first place. And only a theatre that can respond to that conversation about change by constantly and gladly changing itself will earn the privilege of its site.

A couple of years ago, in an email exchange about the nature of theatre 'space' and its invitation to audiences, the writer and maker Andy Smith (who sometimes goes by the working name 'a smith') made the following observation:

> Every week my mum and dad and some other people get together in a big room in the middle of the village where they live. They say hello to each other and catch up on how they are doing informally. Then some other things happen. A designated person talks about some stuff. They sing a few songs together. There is also a section called "the notices" where they hear information about stuff that is happening. Then they sometimes have a cup of tea and carry on the chat.[41]

It is not necessarily obvious straight away that Andy's talking about a church. But on seeing that he was, I was instantly transported in thought back to the late summer of 2001. I was working as an administrator for a theatre charity that happened to be based in an office upstairs at St Paul's, a beautiful Inigo Jones church in Covent Garden which, by dint of its location and its historic association with West End theatre, has long been known as the Actors' Church. It was whilst listening to the radio in that small office that I heard the first reports of the September 11th attacks. Over the subsequent fortnight or so, the church was very often considerably busier than usual, especially at lunchtimes: people were dropping in to the church on their break, to sit quietly, perhaps to pray or to light a candle, sometimes to cry, sometimes to have a sandwich and a think. My sense was that these were not, by any means, exclusively habitual churchgoers, accustomed to visiting or using this church (or any other church) as a place for reflection or simply for acts of attendance. The doors were open; people came in. They were able to identify St Paul's as a place of hospitality to thought, and silence, and confusion, and remembrance; a place that would admit strangers, including themselves. A place, perhaps, to sit together with others, without necessarily contacting those others except in emotional and vaguely psychic ways. For myself, trying to conceal a flickery agnosticism while undertaking a job that assumed a stable and competent religious faith, it was not easy to sit still in such a place, or be thoughtful, except along lines that doubted or even rejected outright the kinds of religious structures and narratives that seemed at least partially to characterise the context in which the attacks took place. Nonetheless, I found it impossible not to be touched, and very struck, by the civic meaning of the church (I mean that particular church, rather than the Church in general) and its open invitation to access during those exceptionally difficult days.

Different people, for various more-or-less legitimate reasons, will react quite differently to Andy Smith's description of a church (or church-like) space that, viewed secularly in formal terms at least, could serve simply as a site for community gathering, the circulating of information, the celebratory enaction of lives shared (not unintelligibly refracted or totally obscured by privacy). For me, despite my ambivalence about churches and the rituals they contain, Andy's portrait is of an ideal theatre space: at least, as far as it goes. In some ways, Andy's (or his parents') church is quite unlike St Paul's, Covent Garden in September 2001: in particular, in the former there is a "designated person" in a focal role, while the latter exhibits a kind of strength which derives from the lack, in fact the palpable absence, of any such person (unless the altar, or some of the artwork, represents such a person to that *ad hoc* congregation: but I'm not quite sure that that would be exactly true); more complicatedly, there is a gregariousness in the first picture and a matrix of multiple insularities in the second, which is perhaps circumstantial, though those two contrasting snapshots of social valency also seem to be deeply about each other and about the capacity of language to act as a carrier of social information. But both these church spaces, in their divergent ways, clearly represent what I take to be an instrinsically theatrical tendency towards the constructive force of electivity: that is, their meaning is defined in practice not by their appointed custodians but by their users, and not in abstraction but in the enaction of – and the patterns of want and desire that are expressed through – that usage.

Perhaps to really discern the precise imperative of this wanting we need to return to, and replace, the image of the "wide open … door" at Jarman's party or at CG&Co's *Open House*, imbuing it more vitally with the importance of 'knowing about the party'.

In one sense this is merely about being 'in the know'. In the years since I started making theatre, the processes by which we experience our own electivity have become greatly curtailed and dissipated, and this may be problematic to us as political thinkers. One example: in the mid/late 90s, when I was beginning to develop an interest in small-press experimental poetry, finding information on the work, or even finding out how to find out, was a steep task, requiring sustained effort, gestures of personal contact, and a degree of ingenuity; someone in the same position now could access in thirty minutes online a vastly bigger store of data and resources than I was able to piece together for myself in three years of spare-time detective work. The advantages of this probably outweigh massively the disadvantages: but my experience of that period of discovery certainly informed and enriched the relationship I built with that work, and I wouldn't swap that richness, that sense of value, that experience of wanting and of (sometimes) finding what I wanted, for any measure of convenience or rapidity. Electivity, the capacity to want, to choose, must be consciously experienced in order to register productively – to fit attained knowledge to the need to know.

And it is *this* knowledge – knowing that one does not know (yet), that one needs to know – that is present in those actors and audiences who will be able to speak formatively to each other. Those who stumble across, or are imposed upon by, unsought theatrical experiences that pop up or are parachuted in, may or may not find in them a transformative proposition; some of the seed, after all, will fall on fertile ground. But something more interesting, more radical, happens when an audience member's (or an artist's) wanting meets a timely invitation to come into a new room. The most exciting picture shows us not a wide open door, but one that seems to be closed, until, out of your need for another room, a 'something else' to enter, you try the handle.

In 1960, Paul Goodman published *Growing Up Absurd* – a celebrated book in its time, now little-known, in which he attempts to think sympathetically through the emergence (and the social construction) of what was at that time a new, or newly identified, phenomenon: the 'juvenile delinquent'. Goodman's thesis in a nutshell is that the American capitalism of the 1950s fails to provide an adequate society for young men to grow up *into*. (His focus, for reasons to do equally perhaps with an excruciatingly dogged chauvinism and his romantic and erotic attachments, is entirely on young men.)

In one chapter of the book, entitled 'An Apparently Closed Room', Goodman describes a kind of analogue for the society he wishes to critique:

... [I]magine as a model of our Organized Society:
An apparently closed room in which there is a large rat race as the
dominant center of attention. And let us consider the human relations possible in such a place. This will give us a fair survey of
what disturbed youth is indeed doing: some running that race,
some disqualified from running it and hanging around because
there is nowhere else, some balking in the race, some attacking
the machine, etc.[42] [Goodman's emphasis.]

Goodman systematically identifies some of the various tribes of
young men whose relationship with this actualized 'rat race' can be made
out: the young strivers who are afraid to reject it though they know it is
meaningless; the 'Corner Boys', perhaps equivalent to today's 'hoodies';
the delinquents, the drop-outs, the Beats, the hipsters, the French
'existentialists', the British 'Angry Young Men'[43]. All of these groups
have worked out their position in relation to the 'rat race': but all are
so mesmerised by that machine, in its central position in the room, that
none has bothered to try the door to the room. If they did, Goodman
implies, they would find it open, and themselves free to leave.

Goodman's model somewhat recalls the idea we find in the writings
of the seventeenth-century philosopher John Locke, concerning liberty
and power:

... [S]uppose a man be carried, whilst fast asleep, into a room
where is a person he longs to see and speak with; and be there
locked fast in, beyond his power to get out: he awakes, and is
glad to find himself in so desirable company, which he stays
willingly in, i.e. prefers his stay to going away. I ask, is not
this stay voluntary? I think nobody will doubt it: and yet, being locked fast in, it is evident he is not at liberty not to stay,
he has not freedom to be gone. So that liberty is not an idea
belonging to volition, or preferring; but to the person having
the power of doing, or forbearing to do, according as the
mind shall choose or direct.[44]

Goodman extends Locke's idea towards a corollary which seems to
describe very acutely the patriarchal capitalist system of 1950s America,
and indeed global capitalism now. Suppose the same imprisoned man, in
trying to leave the room, discovers that he is captive; but that, the man
eventually having become reconciled to his imprisonment, the door is

then silently unlocked again: is he then free to leave? Nothing is stopping him, except his now incorrect beliefs regarding the limits of his own movement.

This, then, is, in essence, the door that I want audiences – and artists – to notice and to try, in response to a conviction that the 'something else' they are seeking in their lives and their work is present, and proximal, and they need only want it enough to go looking for it. Where Jeremy Hardingham's vision for his early work was of "theatre rushing out of its own emergency exit", I wanted a Möbius twist on that image: audiences and makers alike rushing in to the theatre through its own 'emergency entrance': a completely reclaimed escapism – the offer of an escape into a more creative social reality.

My own interest in the (still relevant – perhaps increasingly relevant) thesis of *Growing Up Absurd*, and in Goodman's life and work more broadly, led me to conceive a piece with the working title *An Apparently Closed Room*, which subsequently became *Hey Mathew*, my first collaboration with Jonny Liron. I was extremely interested in trying to suggest some parallels between Goodman's anarchist philosophy and life-practice – including his personal sexual libertarianism (not least as an openly and assertively gay man in public life at a time when this was wildly unusual and incredibly risky) – and various unexamined and largely untested conventional limits on what the theatre might feasibly contain or present.

One image that we played with in the making of that show, and particularly in the development of its physical language, was derived from the idea of the 'kinesphere'. The conception of pioneering choreographer Rudolf Laban, the kinesphere is the area within which the body is moving at any moment, defined by the furthest extent of the body's reach in that moment, and often depicted as a sphere or as a cage-like cube around the body. The kinesphere could be imagined, then, as a kind of invisible cubicle within which the body travels, everywhere at all times: and considered in this way – as an apparently closed room the body can never hope to exit, because the kinesphere always moves exactly with the body – a certain claustrophobia quickly sets in.

I remembered, however, a highly suggestive essay by Patricia Baudoin and Heidi Gilpin on the work of the choreographer William Forsythe – a very important influence on my own making and thinking (though in ways that are admittedly hard to track). Baudoin and Gilpin observe that, whereas Laban's kinesphere implies one fixed centre of the body, the single point through which the various axes of the cube or the sphere all travel, Forsythe's work reimagines the kinesphere by "reassigning its centers infinitely throughout the body":[45]

> Forsythe assumes a whole array of kinespheres, as it were; each is entirely collapsible and expandable. [...] [A]ny point our line in the body or in space can become the kinespheric center of a particular movement. [... Forsythe] searches precisely for those superkinespheric moments when the limits are transgressed, when falling is imminent: he offers the failure to maintain balance as an essential project.[46]

And so for six weeks, Jonny spent much of his time trying to hurl himself eccentrically out of his own kinesphere, as part of a project that also involved attempting to leap over some of the normative boundaries of propriety in public performance: culminating in a monumentally unbalanced sequence where he both tried physically to escape the cube of the theatre auditorium and danced ecstatically with, as it were, the impossibility of doing so, while a video projected on one of the walls showed multiple cut-up sequences of him masturbating to orgasm.

As *The Hitchhiker's Guide to the Galaxy* instructs us, there is: "...a knack to flying. The knack lies in learning how to throw yourself at the ground and miss."[47]

> Since the new direction has no directions, this is an opportune place to recall that speed is basically undirected energy. New approaches call for new mediums. Concrete topographies severely hamper the spontaneity of a given movement because ground contours guide the flow. What is needed is a multidirectional framework to improvise upon. Air offers the consummate natural medium – it's totally unrestricting, has a low frictional coefficient, and is free for the taking. Gravity and centrifugal forces are the new dynamics for aerial attacks.[48]
>
> — C.R. Stecyk III, 'Fear of Flying' (1975),
> from *Dogtown – the Legend of the Z-Boys*

> Stand in the place where you live
> Now face North
> Think about direction
> Wonder why you haven't before[49]

— R.E.M., 'Stand'

It is possible to think a great deal about direction in theatre – about what it means to be (or at any rate to work as) a theatre director – without really "think[ing] about direction" at all. That is, as a director one's focus is often on the possible relations between different kinds of object – between an actor and a written text, say, or between two design elements on stage, or between one scene and the next – in ways that call for pragmatic, situational thought, or perhaps for a more intuitive reaction. It is quite possible, by working methodically through a career's worth of such decisions, to become an established director, without

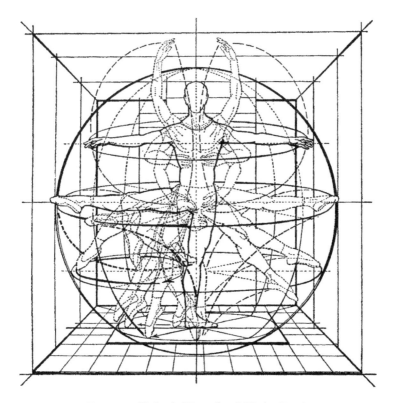

Diagram of Laban's 'Kinesphere' (Carlus Dyer)

ever giving deep consideration to what the work of 'direction' actually entails, or what the word itself proposes. How is 'giving direction' in a theatre process like, or unlike, giving directions to a lost tourist in the street? What, if anything, connects the task of directing actors with that of the political activist whose mode of engagement with injustice is 'direct action'? What is the nature of a director's 'directness'? Many directors, for example, will immediately recognize the vital importance of being *indirect* in their negotiations with actors, of creating a space in which the actor can find for herself (or as though for herself) a course of action which the director had in mind for her all along; but equally, less cynically, that indirectness or obliqueness may give rise to a quality of collaboration in which outcomes unexpected by actor and director alike are acknowledged to be more successful than either of them individually could produce. Directors more often have to be cajolers, ticklers, seducers, ponderers, supposers, wonderers-out-loud: sometimes because they don't know what they're doing, but often because they know exactly what they want.

As critic Sara Ahmed has noted (writing on phenomenology rather than theatre): "Within the concept of direction is a concept of 'straightness'. To follow a line might be a way of becoming straight, by not deviating at any point."[50] The '-rect' of 'direct' is the '-rect' of 'correct', and of 'rectitude': non-deviation from the straight path is essential, for example, in describing the perfectly orthogonal form of a 'rectangle'. And so it's hard not to hear, for instance, some resonance with that rectilinearity in the term 'blocking', which is used in mainstream theatre to refer to the process by which the director establishes the score of actors' positions and movements on stage, in order to ensure a clear, workable picture with decent sightlines, and to make legible to some extent the dynamics of a scene. Though recorded use of the term 'blocking' only dates back to the 1960s, it refers to a much older process in which blocking – originally, moving around a set of small blocks of wood, each standing for an actor – was part of a director's *preparation* for rehearsal, rather than part of rehearsal itself. Peter Brook, for example, describes preparing for the first day of rehearsals on his 1945 *Love's Labour's Lost*: "fingering folded pieces of cardboard – forty pieces representing the forty actors to whom the following morning I would have to give orders, definite and clear."[51] He goes on to recount how badly his prepared blocking translated into the rehearsal room, the individual actors unpredictably exceeding or mis-fitting their assigned moves: and in reflecting on this experience he sees that his quandary – whether to stick to and enforce his prepared choreographies, or to abandon them and deal directly with the actors in a more spontaneous exploratory way – was crucially formative: "I think, looking back, that my whole future work hung in the balance."[52]

In practice, then, directors are no more the custodians of the 'straight and narrow' that their job title implies, than actors are uniform blocks of wood. But Brook's crisis speaks to the heart of any practical consideration of theatrical space, how it is used and what it can be expected to do.

In her final book, *I Remember Nothing: and Other Reflections*, published shortly before her death from leukaemia, the screenwriter Nora Ephron wrote a list of things she wouldn't miss and things she would. Under the heading 'What I Will Miss', among such items as "My kids", "Waffles", "Reading in bed", and "Fireworks", she posits the following sequence:

A walk in the park

The idea of a walk in the park

The park

Shakespeare in the Park[53]

This list seems to me to be a miniature but suggestive essay on theatricality, even before Ephron comes to mention the venerable New York institution of 'Shakespeare in the Park', originated by Joseph Papp in 1954. Perhaps it's easier to see if we swap the first two elements. In its present order, a poignant micro-narrative is set up: in saying that she'll miss "A walk in the park", Ephron observes that the *idea* of a walk in the park, that has come in to her mind at this point, is in itself pleasurable, in a way that seems not subordinate to but quite independent of the physical experience of walking in the park. Reversing this ordering, a simple theatrical process is proposed: "The idea of a walk in the park" is followed, and perhaps in some sense replaced or fulfilled by, "A walk in the park": idea gives way to action, and, in a sense – to return to Bollnow's language – 'mathematical' space is supplanted by 'experienced' space. Or, to use the terms we began with, space is realized as place.

Except that "A walk in the park" is not a place, but a placed action.

The place itself is named third by Ephron: "The park." The sequence, then, suggests a phenomenological conception of theatre in which it is the active (or material) realization (in 'space') of the idea – or, we might say, of the desire – that produces the site in which the action is undertaken: not an objective 'park' which precedes and outlasts "A walk in the park", but a deeply subjective location which comes to be known through its activation as a site for walking, and which in turn generates further 'ideas' for use, such as "Shakespeare in the Park". This noted, the ordering of the first two elements – the walk, and the idea of the walk – becomes more ambiguous. "A walk in the park" may produce "The idea of a walk in the park" in the way that a theatre maker visiting a disused milk bottling plant may find herself responding to it, physically and imaginatively, by creating "The idea of a disused milk bottling plant" which, if it is the right idea – or even if it is not – may give rise to an idea for "Shakespeare in the disused milk bottling plant". (She's going to need a snappier name for it.) In practice, of course – at least in terms of our theatrical co-option of Ephron's list – the ordering of "A walk in the park" and "The idea of a walk in the park" is much more complex: each flickers with promise in relation to the other, each forms and continually re-forms the other imperfectly in its own image.

What I'm describing here is the process by which a theatre event – to return to a phrase we have already used – 'takes place': in other words, the transition by which something imagined or speculative comes through the acts of its realization to be placed, and by which the site of that placing makes a similar transition. The ingenu Peter Brook with his useless folded cardboard provides us with a very distinct image of the problematic nature of that transition; but all theatre makers are constantly faced with the same problem – to the extent that we might almost call that problem 'theatre' itself.

However, it is the array of possible approaches to that problem with which I am most interested in drawing this chapter to its close.

Brook's crisis, that "hanging in the balance" of which he writes, might seem to suggest that the problem that inheres in the direction of a movement from mathematical to experienced space is one that sets an inert, anti-'live', anticipatory management style, which seeks forcibly to adapt lived experience to the deficiencies of the model that has been prepared in advance at too low a resolution to represent it adequately, against a fluent, spontaneous, improvisatory choreography that wishes rather to learn from experience and to reflect that experience in its determinations. And certainly it is clear that the latter mode is generally more effective than the former as a working methodology for the director on her feet in the rehearsal room. But in fact, all that's at stake in preferring the second approach over the first is the matter of when in the timeline closure is enacted. Blocking is blocking, finally, and the question of when it happens – of how long to defer the point at which directorial power stakes its claim to a definitive staging – is one that speaks to efficiency, to what produces the best, clearest, most dynamic arrangements in performance. Neither of the propositions on either side in Brook's quandary actually sits in any critical relationship with the premises of that 'efficiency'.

With the tracing-paper pages of *The Dust Archive* in mind, we might visualize the director's task as one of overlaying two translucent images of the same ground-plan: one, the top sheet, which represents the envisaged production as it is conceived in mathematical space; the other, below, the site-as-place, the experiential frame by which the piece will be contained. For example, in a relatively traditional arrangement, the top sheet would be the playwright's script, or more generally 'the writer's vision' (which, in literary theatres, it is often taken to be the director's job to 'serve'), and the bottom sheet would be the set of material and cultural conditions that taken together constitute the real-world location of the presented work. In this situation, the director's task would normally be seen to be to align, as perfectly as possible, the top and bottom sheets: to map the vision congruently and *directly* (i.e. correctly, in as straight a way as possible) on to the available reality.

My contention is that this quality of alignment is lethally unproductive: it creates a stability within the encounter that is profoundly untheatrical because of its wholeness. It completes a movement that ought never to reach its end. On the contrary, it is in the misalignments between these two plans that theatre shows itself; these dissonances produce a radical instability which prohibits the theatrical event from ever becoming complete. The essential task is not direction, but misdirection – the vigilant disavowal of the 'straight and narrow'.

It's no accident of language, or of conceptual integrity, that 'misdirection' is a skill associated with conjuring and magicianship. In that context, the word can sometimes resonate with ideas around confidence tricks, even of a quasi-criminal fraudulence. But what well-deployed misdirection can produce in an audience exposed to a fluent, elegantly crafted routine, is a sublime sense of disorientation, which delights as it confounds, offering up events and behaviours which a normative (recti-) linear reading will insist are out-of-bounds of the possible.

And so we approach the grounds for an assertion about the inherent queerness of theatre. If 'straightness' registers as an orientation in phenomenology – walking in a straight line, for example – just as it does in sexuality, then a refusal of or resistance to 'straightness', a prioritising of instability and disorientation and misdirection of a kind that maximizes the possibility of theatre – that is, the state of action in which all relations are at least temporarily (re-)negotiatable, is a strategy by which theatre makers necessarily associate themselves not only with a certain set of formal and aesthetic commitments but also, by the same token, with a particular vantage in the culture. (This depends, of course, on a construction of 'queerness' that has to do with readings and positionings and identifications rather than personal sexual behaviour or inclination, though it's hardly revelatory to suggest that theatre has historically provided a hospitable environment to queers of all stripes; perhaps this present argument might begin to suggest why that is so.)

If, then, *Hey Mathew*, my collaboration with Jonny Liron, was an example of queer theatre (and I think we concertedly made it so), that queerness was embodied not only in its candid – even militant – homoeroticism, but also in its approach to inscribing itself onto the 'apparently [but not actually] closed room' of its theatrical situation: in spoken texts that were re-written every night, during (and in response to) each performance; in a movement score which prescribed tasks but not parameters, leaving Jonny sometimes scaling the walls of the studio, or hanging ill-advisedly from lighting bars; in a degree of spontaneity and unpredictability that led on one occasion to a pretty gruesome injury and a post-show visit to A&E; in long periods of stillness or very little action, during which the audience was hopefully encouraged to consider itself in motion, its relationship with the still or the slow or the unforthcoming object continually shifting over a period of some minutes; and perhaps above all, especially in the later stages of the piece as its argument started to pressurize its movements, in Jonny's extreme physical rejection of balance, centredness, orientation, a composed and collected 'straightness': his shucking-off of the 'correct' use of stage space as a ground for the body, in favour of a hurling, hurtling, restlessly unstable flight out of the emergency exit of his own kinesphere.

In developing this material we were particularly inspired by William Forsythe's CD-Rom, *Improvisation Technologies*,[54] which is perhaps the most accessible resource through which to discover a kind of evidence in support of Baudoin and Gilpin's claims about Forsythe's use of multicentredness and the 'superkinespheric' impulse. *Improvisation Technologies* comprises several dozen video clips, ranging from a few seconds' to a few minutes' duration, and each featuring either Forsythe introducing and explaining one of the fundamental elements of the movement vocabulary he had been originating with his dancers at Ballett Frankfurt over the previous decade, or one of those dancers demonstrating the same principles in the context of more fully developed improvisational dance sequences. One especially compelling feature of the video is that in post-production, the trajectories of particular movements have been tracked, and the presences of imaginary forms (lines, planes, three-dimensional shapes and objects) captured and preserved, as line-drawings: as if, say, a finger or elbow or coccyx really could be used as a crayon, or the mind/body could project into space a rudimentary wireframe of a form in relation to which it's positioning and experiencing itself.

One of the chapters of *Improvisation Technologies* is concerned with what Forsythe calls 'Reorganizing': that is, the set of conceptual processes or speculative readings that permit dancers – and, by implication, any body – to rearrange the material of a movement or to reimagine or redistribute or re-read the space in which a movement occurs. The first subset of Forsythe's 'reorganizing' technologies concerns 'spatial reorientation', and it addresses the possibilities that open up in reconfiguring the relationship between a movement, or a part of the body, and the space in which that movement is initially made or that body part oriented. As the body turns, an imaginary room turns with it (an extension of its kinesphere, essentially) which is no longer aligned with the physical room where the dancer finds herself: "And there is my right side," says Forsythe as he demonstrates: "but according to the original room, my right side is back there."[55] And so a movement can be translated into this new orientation. Likewise, the room can be 'reoriented', re-labelled: with a shift of perception, the ceiling can 'become' the left wall, say, and in that shift, movement conceived relative to the actual left wall of the room will have to be translated into this new orientation.

If this is hard to capture vividly in plain text, we might consider as a near analogue the experience of skateboarders, as reflected in the quotation above from Craig Stecyk's writing on the pioneering Zephyr skate team (the legendary Z-Boys). The whole grammar of skateboarding changed fundamentally and irrevocably when, during the Californian drought of 1976, the Z-Boys and their allies started to skate in drained backyard swimming pools: in those spaces – and particularly when one is travelling around them at some velocity – the floor and the wall are not distinct, but exist in one continuous uninterrupted curve: suddenly, the floor beneath you is also perpendicular to the ground you started on. Thus, in the passage above, Stecyk is making the case for a proto-Forsythian strategy of radical reorientation in which the sky is treated as the ground.

The Dogtown style that Stecyk monitors in the mid 70s and helps to create a critical language for is one that harnesses the energy of misdirection and reorientation within an unhampered spontaneous flow of high-speed navigation and instinctive phenomenological analysis. Indeed, footage of skaters such as Jay Adams and Stacy Peralta can make the reorientations of Forsythe's Ballett Frankfurt dancers in relation to a perfectly flat floor seem positively hidebound. Certainly, it hardly seems fanciful to suggest that the relationship between Forsythe and the classical tradition with which he remains in sometimes furiously antagonistic dialogue is in some ways similar to the relationship between skilled skaters such as the Z-Boys and the concrete urban architecture they ecstatically repurpose. Both can be seen as projects of queering, using the critical body to create states of dissidence and destabilization; as such, I would contend, these are also projects of theatricalization – the holding in productive and irreconcilable tension of a constantly refreshed mathematical space and a continually updating experienced space.

The theatre maker's task, then, or perhaps rather her responsibility, is to develop a mode of creation which uses both the permissiveness of space and the hospitality of place, but does not seek to match the first completely and perfectly to the second. At the same time, in the same movement, the director gratefully surrenders her authority. The movement happens not once, but constantly, endlessly: and it is this movement, not its resolution, that produces meaning for an audience, through a deep negotiation that has little or nothing to do with the surface operations of written language or composed image or pre-arranged choreography (though all of these can potentiate it under the right conditions). When an audience is moved by a piece, this is the movement with which they are in sympathy.

Here's a final image on the topic of space and place. In 2008 the conceptual artist Michael Asher had a show at the Santa Monica Museum of Art, for which he simply rebuilt all forty-four of the temporary walls that had been erected for every exhibition in the gallery since its opening on that site a decade earlier. The appreciative Los Angeles Times review of Asher's installation describes how "[a]n array of unfinished and intersecting walls, permeable volumes, apparent passageways and occasional dead ends unfolds in the piece, which creates a dense and fantastical maze of light and shadow."[56] It sounds a little like a more emphatically material take on *The Dust Archive*, a superimposition of multiple layers of history and memory and reverberation and erasure, and a realization of that composite with all its contradictions and competing logics. Wholly existing neither in conceptual space nor in inhabitable space, Asher's piece – which I did not experience for myself, and can only (begin to) imagine – seems to me to be highly theatrical, as a puzzle, as a labyrinth, as a provocation, as a poem: the array of possibilities it offers to its visitors cannot be internally reconciled, except incompletely, partially, in the singular experience of each curious, searching, sublimely disoriented attendee.

Some varieties of immersive or participatory theatre might seek to establish relations with their audiences which are structurally quite similar to Asher's invitation to visitors to his installation: though quite

Jay Adams, 1976 © Glen E. Friedman.

often they will layer over some kind of narrative, or simulation of a narrative, in order to encourage those who prefer their befuddlement a little more mediated. Even less happily, they tend to be inclined to create labyrinthine play-spaces, rather than creating argumentative propositions of which the labyrinth may be an emergent property: again, the direct versus the indirect.

More often, though, we have a capable proxy (allowing us not least to keep our seats): the actor, whose acting-on-our-behalf allows us to find our own place within the motile system of the work, and in relation to whom we attempt and re-attempt our own self-orientation in the sited event. Notwithstanding Forsythe's multicentric construction of the body and its kinesphere(s), we know where we are with the actor, even if where we are is hopelessly lost. It's only in the actor's acting – in their movement (which includes their stillness), and in the movement that surrounds them – that we can understand through experience the orientation of our own attention.

In her brilliant book *Queer Phenomenology* – a book which could easily be read as being secretly about theatre all the way through – Sara Ahmed powerfully quotes from Maurice Merleau-Ponty's *Phenomenology of Perception* a passage which I later deployed as a kind of slightly out-of-line epigraph to *Where You Stand*, my 2010 collaboration with Jonny Liron in which we tried to investigate the ways in which rural, and especially forested or wooded, areas might or might not be as hospitable to concertedly queer activity as are metropolitan centres. This is a passage in which Merleau-Ponty could well be thinking through the implications of vert skating, though we assume he is not:

> What counts for the orientation of the spectacle is not my body as it in fact is, as a thing in objective space, but as a system of possible actions, a virtual body with its phenomenal 'place' defined by its task and situation. My body is wherever there is something to be done.[57]

Standing, or sitting, in the place where we are, we await the presence of the actor. We think about direction, and its opposites. Suddenly, the actor arrives. He is naked, which is only to be expected.

"My body is wherever there is something to be done," he announces, sounding a bit like a superhero.

2. The naked and the nude

We must see, we must know
What's the name of that star?
How that ship got inside the bottle
Is it true your father was a swan?
What do you look like without any clothes?[1]

— Philip Whalen, from 'The Slop Barrel:
Slices of the Paideuma for All Sentient Beings'

L'action décisive est la mise à nu.
[Getting naked is the decisive act.][2]

— Georges Bataille

Some years ago I took part in a workshop run by James Yarker, the brilliant artistic director of the Birmingham-based company Stan's Cafe. For one exercise, James asked us all to consider what were the clichés of our work, the tropes and tics that seemed to keep turning up in everything we made. Any number of things might have occurred to me, but what came most quickly and forcibly to mind was this: if you come and watch a show of mine, sooner or later – probably sooner – someone on stage is going to get naked.

In fact, by no means all of my theatre work includes nudity. But much of it does: and certainly, I've thought a great deal about what it means to invite an audience to look at a naked actor on stage, or to ask that actor to be looked at naked; and what it is about nudity in performance, and in the social environment of the theatre, that I find not just interesting or appealing or compelling but actually crucial – and abundantly, indicatively problematic in lots of useful ways.

There was what we might quaintly call 'a nude scene' in the first play I ever wrote. I was eight years old and I'd just been given an Olivetti typewriter for my birthday. Following a prodigious initial burst of concrete poetry, I set about bashing out an adaptation of a children's novel I'd been reading. There can't possibly have been any justification within the source text for my interpolating a scene in which the actors I intended to co-opt – friends from junior school and the neighbours' kids – would strip off; nor can I remember any narrative turn that warranted it. I suppose I was simply ventriloquizing the insistently curious voice of Philip Whalen's extraordinary poem 'The Slop Barrel': "What do you look like without any clothes?"

I must say straight away that the play was never performed, with or without nudity. I never dared show it to anyone. In fact, it was never even finished. In writing the 'nude scene' I had reached the end of my own longing, and there was no impulse to continue. Nevertheless, describing this episode now, I feel a strange prickling sensation which recalls even after thirty-plus years the intense excitement of writing that breathtakingly exploitative scene; of course my current physical reaction probably has to do with the profound difficulty at this time of writing about the erotic fixation of a child on the bodies of other children, even though – perhaps especially because – the child in question is me. Perhaps the feeling is complicated further by that element of exploitation: I'm not sure whether to be ashamed or amused that my first reaction to experiencing the licence of my own authorship was to use it to try to undress my friends. Certainly I seem to have picked up right from the start, rather precociously, a sense that playwrighting was a way of inscribing scenarios directly into the world – I could write down in the zone of fiction what I wanted to see happen in reality, and never quite have to take responsibility for it: I already saw that, by the time I came to 'direct' my play – to put it on, as I imagined it, in the living room at home – most of the authority would be vested in the paper text. I was already hip to the idea that I could get to see whatever I wanted, provided I made it clear that my negotiation with my actors was not about what *I* wanted – perish the thought – but about what *the script* required.

There was surely something deeply formative about the experience of enjoying – and agonizing over – the incendiary presence of my own secret desires at the heart of my writerliness. And some recollection of that excited terror still remains present every time I experience my authority as a grown-up and somehow legitimate maker of theatre, the capacity I have for being able to ask to see the thing I want: not just, but not least, the unclothed bodies of people I like and find – in whatever way – beautiful.

It feels very important, in setting out to essay a serious consideration of stage nudity, straight away to uncouple the components of the sense of illicitness I've just described. The dodgy element isn't, or isn't necessarily, about nakedness itself, but about coercion, and power exercised in the absence of engaged and thoughtful discussion. When we think about nudity on stage, we are very often thinking about something happening in an industrial context, in which a range of economic and cultural pressures have some complex bearing, and with regard to which it is not only possible but terribly easy for profoundly exploitative and essentially violent relationships to be exercised. These are structural problems which are to some degree inherent in the single-author model of theatre-making wherever it occurs, even when an eight-year-old boy is seated at his birthday typewriter; nor are they dependably absent or negligible in any other kind of theatrical process, no matter how groovily consensus-based and non-hierarchical it might be.

But I don't want those important problems entirely to overwhelm us or prohibit our careful thought as we notice our own experience of desire in relation to each other within the theatrical encounter. If I wince at my juvenile nude scene – or at any of my professional involvements, both in mathematical and in real space, with naked bodies – I don't want it to be because of the genuine desire I was feeling in the moments and movements of that work. Invariably, that desire is a kind of curiosity, about the lives of other people and about the nature of the distance between us and the possibility of our closeness in spite of that distance. It's clear that by the time I was eight, I already had a sense that some very potent and dynamic information could be revealed by dint of the special permission of theatre, which the rest of the world was conspiring to conceal.

The voice or voices at the beginning of 'The Slop Barrel' ask four questions, one after the other, with an insistence that seems child-like: especially that fourth, "What do you look like without any clothes?", seems to capture a distinctly infantile quality of intellectual curiosity which is suffused with an unselfconscious erotic urgency. Whalen's opening line – "We must see, we must know" – is a version of the unspoken mission statement that sometimes seems to propel little children – to an almost alarming extent – as they start to orient themselves within an adult-owned world that appears to them to be keeping itself almost entirely out of reach, hidden away, on a too-high shelf, or after bedtime, or wrapped up in a remote conversation conducted somewhere in incomprehensible airspace. But that same inquisitive line is also a very serviceable *modus operandi* for the actor.

The attainment being sought through the explorations both of young children and of intrepid actors is, more than anything, one of intimacy. Intimacy is a relational quality that is prized in theatre, and in particular theatre on a small scale: when a space, or a performance, is described as 'intimate', it is invariably meant as a compliment, even though many of the most culturally prestigious spaces tend to be so large that a workable sense of intimacy is all but impossible to establish. In a sense, intimacy is almost an opposite of spectacle: not many productions or events can do both, and certainly not at the same time. If we accept that, at root, 'theatre' fundamentally refers to a place where spectators gather to watch spectacles, then the making of intimacy within theatre speaks to a kind of adaptation in the medium that is historically comparatively recent. The language of 'intimate' theatre is a response to cultural changes in how we see and read; it is a product of photography, and the new syntagmata of cinema and television, and of the technologies of electric light and amplified sound; it arises out of changing attitudes to representation and the 'realistic', and social and cultural movement around some of the ideas that we presently take the notion of intimacy to connote: tensions between privacy and exposure, possibilities of social informality and sexual candour.

Certainly, the theatre I find most interesting is often predicated on and potentiated by kinds of intimacy. Likewise, of course, boring or otherwise bad theatre may be hobbled by a lethal lack of intimacy, or, even more likely, from its signalling an intimacy that is manifestly pretended or unachieved. The etymology of 'intimacy' may help us to understand why. For a long time I was under the casual misapprehension that 'intimacy' must have something to do with fearlessness – the 'tim' of 'timid' and 'timorous'. But in fact, the 'tim' of 'intimate' is the same as the 'tim' of 'ultimate': it signifies a superlative. Just as 'ultimate' is about going as far *beyond* (L. 'ulter') as you can, 'intimate' is about being as far as possible *in*. In a truly intimate experience, you go all the way in. Whatever it is, you're really, really in it.

Intimacy, then, is deeply collaborative, a kind of embodied reading in which an offer of an intimate encounter is recognized for what it is and accepted, and that recognition and acceptance then feed back, affirming and perhaps extending the scope of what's intimately possible in the relationship. This is as true in theatre as it is in (some kinds of) sex, or chamber music, say, or palliative care. My sense is that in theatre – unlike in some other kinds of personal relationship – intimacy is not, quite, an emergent quality, but one that has to be consciously initiated. Intimacy is not an accident; it does not happen while no one is looking.

This might be a good time to return to our actor, who arrived in the space at the end of the last chapter, ready to go to work. Why is he naked? What kind of signal of intent is that? (We might also want to ask, at this point, why he's a male actor; we'll come back to that.)

An important moment early on in my critical thinking (as opposed to my romantic daydreaming) about nudity in theatre occurred in around 2005 during a period when Theron Schmidt and I were working together under the duo name Exit Strategy. Together we wrote and submitted a proposal for a funding opportunity – I no longer remember what, exactly – which included an artists' statement about the questions we were pursuing in our practice at that time. As part of that statement, I wrote something about being interested in "the limits of the body", as they might be represented in exhibited states such as stillness, sleep, exhaustion and nakedness. (We had already made a show in 2003, called *his horses*, which set to the gentlest work the intimacy of my personal friendship with and closeness to Theron; it was the first piece I worked on in which nudity became a tonal carrier in itself, rather than an instrumental feature helping to deliver some consequent effect. As such, I found it very beautiful and heartening, and I wanted to see what else that kind of application of nudity could do.)

On writing that proposal, I caught myself noticing the apparent oddity of describing nakedness as some kind of limit state. In one way, of course it's the end of a line (in the act of undressing); but there is something bothersome in the perception or presentation of nakedness as an extreme, when in fact it's exactly – and, in a phenomenological sense, *literally* – central to our human experience. Nakedness is our base state, from which everything else is a departure. Only the interference of various extraneous dynamics around private property and public propriety estrange us from the basic familiarity of nakedness as a state, to such a remarkable extent that, generally, when theatre performances feature naked bodies, warnings have to be posted and disclaimers issued (in this country, at least, and at this time), and some spectators may well be expected to flip out.

Interestingly, this is one unusually clearcut distinction between even the most nominally experimental 'theatre' and what we currently call 'live art', in which nudity is very often present and more-or-less unremarked. Partly this is to do with the lineage and inheritance of performance art, which was initially – and, to a considerable degree, still is – formed and shaped by the codes and languages of visual art, in which the nude is valued and in some sense profoundly comprehended. Somewhat aside from this, though, the focus in live art and related performance modes is quite often on the artist's body, or on the body in general. Certainly it is more often true in live art than it is in theatre, even in solo theatrical performance, that the maker of the work both conceives and performs it, frequently on a wholly individual basis, meaning that anxieties about power relations are less proximately engaged than they are in theatre: the artist decides to present herself naked in front of an audience, or not to do so. For my part, when I have wanted to place a naked body – often a solo performer – before an audience, it has never (yet) been my own, meaning that the presence of the actor instantly gives rise to questions about the premises of the relationship, in its power structure(s) and its intimations.

For all that different attitudes to staging nakedness may pertain either side of the (otherwise often smudgy) line between theatre and live art, there is such a compellingly radical integrity to live art's relationship with the body that it poses a question that theatre cannot simply ignore. Clothing is not part of the body: it is not intrinsic to it, nor immediately implied by it. Rather, clothing is part of *the place that the body is in*: and a practice which determines to focus the attention of audiences and/or makers principally or substantially on the body of the actor must surely account for the ways in which our cultural defaults tend to require of the actor's body that it occupies a place which partly or wholly conceals or distorts the very entity to which we are invited to attend. (This is not a matter of preferring one type of clothing over another – of supposing, for example, that a 'flesh-coloured' dance leotard which reveals with some fidelity the lines of the body and may more-or-less plausibly approximate the wearer's skin tone is a better solution than a vivid floral muumuu. The problem is only secondarily practical or aesthetic, and primarily ideological.)

So when the actor arrives, whose body is "wherever there is something to be done", my imaginary relationship with him – visually, sensually, communicatively, socially – begins, at least in theory, with his unclothed body. And in fact, this is where work has sometimes begun, both in the rehearsal room and in public performance. One exercise I have often found useful is to invite an actor, starting naked (and, as it were, acclimatised to his nakedness), to choose single items of clothing to work with, investigating the ways in which they change his perception of his body, the way he moves, the sense he may have of a small shift of persona; working with a mirror – or, sometimes, an imaginary mirror defined along a visible line taped on the floor of the room – can help. To begin to see the unclothed body not as extreme but as essential, not as a temporary destination (as in a "nude scene") but as a reliable point of departure, is a shift of perspective that, in my experience, has only ever proved effectual and energising. And where the actor becomes accustomed to this shift, it can translate to the stage most productively. For example, working with Jonny Liron on a movement-driven piece, *O Vienna*[3], at Toynbee Studios in 2009, we found that the logic of the work simply didn't require that he wore clothes, and so he didn't: except for a sequence near the end for which he put on shoes, only because this seemed to be a logical response to the implications of the text we were staging. That piece did not 'contain nudity' in the way that, say, *his horses* had; but a similar intimacy seemed to be produced in respect of the attentiveness of the audience.

"Nudity," cautions the choreographer Jonathan Burrows, "is no more neutral than a large hat."[4] But in wanting to invite actors to experience the primacy of their presence as bodies in a theatrical encounter, and to ask audiences to see and accept that primacy, I don't seek to advance the case that a body without clothes is in any sense 'neutral' – as if that were anyway a desirable condition. Partly, in respect of Burrows's axiom, there's a problem of language, which we will turn to shortly: 'nudity' and 'nakedness' both have their particular connotations, and the drastic faultline that runs beneath the surface of their apparent casual synonymity has, I will suggest, much to tell us about how audiences look at actors, and how actors see themselves. But using the word 'unclothed', as I sometimes do, also presents a problem: the word, unlike the body it describes, implies that we start clothed – which in a practical sense is true, in that actors seldom arrive at the theatre already naked, but in a conceptual sense returns us to a particular place (the place of clothing) in relation to which we are forced first to define and orient ourselves, when our practice asks for something else. Perhaps the best we can do is to take seriously the challenge we set ourselves, and our audiences, when we speak or write of "the body".

The anxiety that to talk of "the body" is problematic in turn starts to be felt when we read Peter Brook, in *The Empty Space*, aptly exhorting theatre makers to avoid 'deadliness':

> Deadliness always brings us back to repetition: the deadly
> director uses old formulae, old methods, old jokes, old ef-
> fects; stock beginnings to scenes, stock ends; and this applies
> equally to his partners, the designers and composers, if they
> do not start each time afresh from the void, the desert and the
> true question – why clothes at all, why music, what for?[5]

"[W]hy clothes at all?" would seem to be exactly the question I've been wanting to frame in these pages. But I am troubled, as ever with Brook, that this question is exposed against a backdrop of "the void, the desert". Perhaps Jonathan Burrows is troubled too by the same idea – his other statement on the unclothed body in performance, in his valuable *A Choreographer's Handbook*, is: "Silence is no more neutral than nudity."[6] What, then, is the trade-off that allows the apparent freedom of Brook's question, "Why clothes at all?", to ramify in the presence of the actor? What silences, what neutralities, what voids and deserts must be imposed on the scene before Brook's actor will come to us unclothed?

In the light of Brook's deceptively airy provocation, we can see that our reference to "the body" will not quite do. It is one thing to suggest that an actor in mathematical space may usefully be naked *a priori*; it is quite another to ask an actor in a lived place to take off their clothes in front of others. We may see the actor in mathematical space as "the body"; but the actor in our experiment who has come to where there is work to be done refers instead, quite properly, to "*my* body". There is a certain violence in the abstractive reference to "the body", as if the actor were merely a grounded representative of a Platonic ideal. When I think about the performance afterwards, I will not – I hope – think about 'the bodies' I have seen, but about *his* body and *her* body, *this* body and *that* body, perhaps the cat's body (if she's there), and about *my* body in relation to each of theirs: so that, if I end up thinking about *every*body, it will be an everybody that really looks like everybody, in all the infinite variety of shapes and sizes and forms that we see in the inhabited world.

A body – I mean all bodies, everywhere, but I'm thinking of any particular body – has a context, a history, a political meaning, a life story; and of course in fact it has not one of each, but many. What does the body disclose about itself, straight away, or over time? It may or may not match or resemble the images we create for ourselves, for whatever reasons, of 'able-bodied' or 'disabled' persons. It may invite us to read a narrative of race or ethnicity that might or might not be, in itself, a whole story. It may or may not indicate an apparently clearcut, definitive biological sex; we will probably see also that it is gendered, though that gender may be multiple, transitional, provisional, contested, unnameable, resistant, et cetera; and that gender is also partly constituted by the expectations and impositions of the cultures that are being inhabited and moved through by the person whose body we are thinking about. There may be times when it is productive to *not* 'see' sex and gender, but on the whole I am interested, as a maker whose instinct is to try and create theatrical situations in which we can see each other in the highest possible resolution, to handle with care these arcs and fragments of personal identity and to try to be sensitive to the forces at work within and around them. Even taking a fairly crude view of gender and other social coordinates, it should be obvious that not all bodies are culturally identical and that the differences between them register in complex and various ways in the interactions those persons have with labour, capital and value – all of which are as intensely present in a theatrical encounter as they are presumably absent in the unbreathable empty space of Peter Brook's "void".

So: the reason why I chose to make our actor male (and, tacitly, cisgendered) when he showed up naked at the end of the last chapter is that, in working quite often with nudity in the projects I've undertaken over the past twenty years, I've had to negotiate frequently and openly (and sometimes, God knows, awkwardly) with many actors – male, female, trans – around this topic: and in general (with a few exceptions) I haven't felt, and don't feel, OK as a cis male director asking female or trans actors to consider getting naked in the work room as a matter of course; and I've seldom put female nudity on stage. The industry in which we work is still heavily and oppressively biased, both in terms of who is most often asked to appear nude on stage and who is most often the person doing the asking, and what the power structures are that connect them and keep them apart. Sometimes I have collaborated with female actors who have their own interest in working with nudity or whose response to a particular theatrical situation will not necessarily exclude offering or negotiating around nudity where they can see the merit of such a decision. I'm grateful to them for opening up those conversations, and for the images and events we have been able to create together as a consequence. But broadly I maintain, for the moment and fairly undogmatically, a personal conscientious objection to *asking* women to be naked either in rehearsal or on-stage. Hence I have preferred to invoke a male actor in our present demo mode.

This shouldn't be taken to imply that I take the nakedness of cis male actors lightly either; nor am I insensitive to the accusation that as a gay male director, and as someone who speaks openly about liking concertedly erotic work – and, it follows, values queer or homoerotic work in particular, the labour relations I have with (often young) male actors are necessarily densely complicated and tangly and may take us to the brink of exploitation. The only answer to this that I have ever been able to trust, practically at least, is transparency on all sides, the constant presence of scrupulous and careful dialogue. One thing's for sure: the daunting complexity of what happens when actors get naked is not a reason for not doing it. On the contrary, creating supportive environments in which that nakedness is possible, compelling, celebrated even, is of profound importance.

In part, a properly rigorous examination of the meaning and practice of nakedness in theatre, in all its complexity, needs to be understood in relation to the equal and opposite complexity of clothing. It is not as if by choosing to avert our attention from the naked body we let ourselves off the hook. The dressed body can be cacophonous: clothes increasingly are commercial adverts for themselves or their makers, not only where there are prominent logos, say, or where t-shirts bear slogans or loaded images, but even in the case of plain or apparently 'generic' garments, which nevertheless are often semiotically noisy and assertive and ideologically skewed. Moreover, wearing shop-bought clothes will very often place the user at the end of a supply chain which cannot easily be tracked but may well include instances of exploitation and the abuse of power that, in their programmatic cruelty and cynicism, greatly outweigh the potentially difficult negotiations that may sometimes quite properly characterise the experience of working with nakedness in theatre. Nudity may not be neutral, but no clothing is innocent either. Even the most blameless granny-knitted sweater is caught up in a conspiracy not of its making: the cultural prohibition of nakedness is one of the most fundamental drivers of the privacy agenda that keeps us in what any dispassionate observer would surely concede is an extraordinary pickle: a state in which extreme curbs are placed on the display of the unclothed body, in which the sight of our friends and neighbours and even (or especially) our children without their clothes in a public zone is presumed to be liable to cause alarm and offence and disorder. This overbearing constraint, serving as it does the valorization of the largely unspoken idea that we are, first and foremost, private individuals with an interest in the protection and promotion of privatized activity, rather than social beings whose chief concern is our communal and collective well-being, makes the civic position of theatre as a place in which our nakedness might be shared and harboured an exceedingly valuable and deeply important condition of its existence. The peerless and pioneering US performance artist Tim Miller, whose intimate theatrical work very frequently uses his own nudity as a way of activating the angry and joyous political agenda that runs through his storytelling, puts it beautifully:

> I think theater has always been a place where the presence
> of the body is allowed… In our fucked-up American culture
> right now, the theater is virtually the only place (other than
> the occasional, remote nude beach!) where the naked body is
> allowed a public presence in real time.[7]

Tim Miller in *US*. © John Aigner.

Certainly, one of the aspects of stage nudity that audiences find challenging in fact (rather than merely in anticipation) is that they are so unaccustomed to really looking at unmediated, unclothed bodies. Some viewers may by now be very used to seeing moving pictures of naked people on screens, but their learned experience has forced them into positions of furtiveness and embarrassment in relation to real naked humans inhabiting a constructed space with them. It is as if they cannot believe it's all right to look – not just to glance, but to look, extendedly and critically, and perhaps even with pleasure – at an actor's body.

Notwithstanding the license that theatre affords (albeit accompanied with disclaimers and sometimes greeted with reductive, trivializing critical reaction), the presentation of naked bodies – perhaps especially one's own – in a context that fosters thoughtful and unhistrionic companionship of a kind that seems genuinely intimate, can definitely feel like, and read like, a gentle act of resistance, in which irrelevant social mores can be suspended for a while, and perhaps everyone can breathe more easily. Audience members responding to my own work when it has included the extensive use of nudity have sometimes reported feeling not the anxiety that they might have expected, but rather a sense of relief. It is not, or not only, fanciful to suggest that the dissident public function of theatre somehow supplants Whalen's question, "What do you look like without any clothes?", with another: "What do you look like underneath all that capitalism?" Which is not to suggest that capitalism doesn't somehow quite reach the body – we know the opposite to be true, that capitalism and patriarchy shape and contort the body in myriad ways – but rather that theatre, in taking on to itself the function of shelter with which our relationship with clothing originates, holds open a space in which our nakedness can become the beginning of something else: a particular kind of testimony, perhaps, which seeks to elicit a special quality of witness.

Of course an actor may deeply comprehend all of this and still find himself inhibited or doubtful in relation to his own nakedness. Partly I suspect this has to do with the difficulty of inhabiting a contradiction, in which to be naked on stage, or within the unfolding of a theatrical process, may be seen on the one hand to be an act of resistance, of anticapitalist affirmation or questioning, whilst on the other hand stage nudity is widely seen as a kind of premium offer within the labour compact, something somehow prestigious which ought to be commensurately expensive.

For example, the online service Casting Call Pro, on which actors can advertise themselves to prospective employers, asks them to specify if they are willing to "perform nude": to which the three possible answers are: 'Yes', 'No', and 'Only professionally'[8]. Perhaps unsurprisingly, it's the last of these boxes that most actors using the site seem to tick.[9] It's an expression of the terms in which nudity is often discussed in the industry. Here, as in countless other instances, the negotiation is usually terribly flawed because its participants are mesmerized by the *content* of the work as the sole repository of value and, by extension, the site of exchange. So the questions that arise are generally along these lines: Is the nudity artistically merited (or 'justified')? What function does it play in the narrative? Is it crucial, rather than ornamental? Is it 'tasteful'? What does it say about the character concerned?, and so on. In these terms, the worst that can be said about an incidence of stage nudity is that it is 'gratuitous' – that its justification within the narrative structure, the textual source, the character arc cannot be dependably ascertained, or perhaps that any such justification is undermined in production because the moment is, say, overextended or too starkly lit.

However, because nudity communicates with us principally at the level of form rather than content, these surface-level questions do not necessarily speak to the consideration we have shown the naked actor so far; certainly they do not resolve the contradictions inherent in the industrial structures of established theatre (which may reach into many more leftfield endeavours, just as devising structures often replicate exactly the hierarchies and orthodoxies they are designed to evade). Ultimately, these contradictions are not specific to theatre, but apply to all the ways in which individuals under capitalism do and don't (and can and can't) understand their value. For that reason, when I work with actors on nudity I am partly concerned gently to challenge or disturb their learned inclination to create a kind of economic system around nakedness. To some extent I am seeking to suspend or destabilize the pressures around 'professionalism': I don't want anyone to take off their clothes only because they are being paid to show up to work in the morning, and because I am the one who is doing the paying, or I represent that person in the rehearsal room, and their nudity (or their cooperation in general) seems to them to be something that I am hoping to purchase as part and parcel of that transaction. But also I want to stop them searching for a sense of return, except perhaps in so far as a benefit registers in a more-or-less comprehensible ethical system around the work. Instead, I want them to feel able to give their nakedness away – in other words, my suggestion to them is that 'gratuitousness', a nudity that is self-justifying within its own implicit argument amid the terms and conditions of a theatrical situation, is the most reliable guarantee of a significant and non-superficial transaction in the event. It is time, and not nakedness, that is a limited resource in the theatrical encounter; it is the experience of time (and maybe the concomitant sensation of urgency) that shapes our experience of nakedness, both as witnesses and as actors.

I can't think of the idea of 'gratuitousness' in relation to nudity without recalling John Berger's celebrated speech on winning the Booker Prize in 1972 for his novel G. Berger was pleased to be awarded the prize, and did not want to refuse it, but he was deeply uncomfortable about the long involvement of the award's sponsor, Booker McConnell, in chronically exploitative trading activity in the Caribbean, using indentured labour in the sugar industry it dominated for over a century. Berger's response was not to turn the prize down, but, as he said, to "turn [it] against itself."[10] This he achieved by donating half of the £5000 award money to the Black Panthers, the radical leftist party that was at that time spearheading advances in political organization and resistance specifically in the interests of America's black populations, as well as creating links with African and Caribbean activist groups who sought to work to overturn the baleful legacy of companies such as Booker McConnell. Berger explained his decision with a typically clear and potent phrase: "The half I give away will change the half I keep."[11]

The repressive, individualistic morality deeply embedded in and promulgated through capitalism seeks to keep people at a watchful distance from each other; to occlude their capacity for intimacy by aggressively commoditizing and misrepresenting the sexualized body; to estrange them from their own desires by enforcing across the board a category error that definitively assigns every body (beneath its commercially exploitative clothing) to the paranoid territory of private property and bombards that space with messages fostering insecurity and shame. Theatre – whether as a building or as a type of action – provides a public space for a refusal of these authoritarian perversions. That is the context in which the decisive invitation is conferred on the actor: not just to place their body wherever there is work to be done, but to give away the nakedness of that body gratuitously, without expectation of recompense or an answering justification other than the grateful attention of a thoughtful, witnessing audience, in whose own bodies we can imagine a profoundly sympathetic and perhaps inarticulable response being detonated.

In the special intimacy of theatre, what you give away changes what you keep.

––––––––––

'They': we do not know who they are.[12]

— J.H.Prynne

It hardly needs saying that working with actors on the technologies of nakedness is abundantly revealing, in more ways than one. An exercise I have often found extremely fruitful has two sections – both briefed at the beginning – and the actor's task in part is to try and run as smoothly as possible from the first into the second, creating the sense of one single unbroken arc. In the first phase, the actor is simply asked to get naked, in his own time and at his own pace, retaining an awareness of any shifts in his own feelings or perceptions as he does so; in the second, once he has taken off his clothes, he is asked to continue, at the same pace, to get *more* naked. The transition is, in a sense, an interpretive one, as a task to be executed literally gives way to one which can only be responded to through association: nakedness may be a kind of limit case in respect of clothing, but it also has a whole spectrum of personal and cultural connotations which need to be understood and encountered practically, in so far as the actor is freely willing.

Sometimes, the actor's pursuit of the naked-beyond-naked begins with an additional pass, in which items worn on the body but which do not feel like clothing and have initially been overlooked are taken off – a wristwatch, perhaps, or a bracelet, or a necklace, or even a wedding ring: it's interesting that these final accessories often carry intimate associations with particular people and events, and that removing them can produce a much bigger emotional jolt in the actor than taking off the last of their clothes; sometimes the language we have used around this moment, talking about it afterwards, has pointed towards a working difference between being 'naked' and being what we think of as 'stark naked', the state in which our nakedness has a kind of unfamiliar austerity about it.

From that point onwards, responses become deeply subjective and often, for actor and spectator alike, quite unpredictable. Inherited cultural constructions of nakedness may vie for priority with very personal associations; as different lines of inquiry start to suggest themselves, the task becomes almost collaborative, in that the actor's work is formed and limited in part by the nature and tonal quality of his relationship with the director whose invitation has initiated the exercise and whose attention now helps to hold open the space in which some 'authentic' response is possible, as well as with any others who may be present. (I have mostly used this exercise in one-to-one formats, which creates its own freedoms and pressures, all of which need to be discussed before any work like this can happen safely.) The actor's relationship with the room around him will likely inform his work, consciously or otherwise, and the extent to which he feels comfortable in the task – or content with his level of discomfort – may also depend on ambient temperature, or sound travelling in from elsewhere, or lighting levels; it will be a different exercise near the start of the day than it is near the end; and so on.

We might also note that in one very interesting and productive set of responses I've seen to the second half of the brief, the actor, in order to feel more naked, may start putting clothes on again, but in ways that somehow disturb the normative, culturally and socially endorsed hierarchies of the body. Putting his underwear back on will not (usually) help him feel more naked, but a transition out of being totally unclothed into wearing, say, just trainers, or an open shirt, or the beanie hat he wore when he cycled into work that morning, may create a greater sense of exposure or of a more arrestingly blatant variety of nakedness than wearing nothing at all. This seems to be at least partly to do with the erotic language of clothing versus nudity, a language with which we often discover a surprising facility and certainly a familiarity, whether we recognize it from highbrow art or low-rent pornography – Helmut Newton's wildly misogynistic images of otherwise nude women in stockings and stilettos, for example, or the splendid accessories and wisps that adorn Delacroix's *Woman with a Parrot*, or the familiar cliché of contemporary gay porn in which young twinks perform cheerfully permutating varieties of congress wearing only baseball caps and white socks. The unmistakably fetishy edge to these strategies of clothing serves to intensify the signalling of nakedness, not to soften it.

We can see, then, that, far from being a single or stable state of being with an objectively verifiable structure, nakedness is a profoundly subjective and contingent condition, which not only has degrees and variations and inflexions, but cannot even be assumed to preclude, in practice, the wearing of clothes. It's important to bear this in mind in starting to think through the ways in which we might want to consider distinguishing between 'nakedness' and 'nudity'.

Casual observation would suggest that the two words 'naked' and 'nude', and their variants, are for the most part used more or less synonymously and interchangeably: and in many contexts, this is so. Without recourse to slightly awkward or pedantic words (such as 'unclothed', which I've used above), or slang that conveys either a euphemistic or a prurient attitude (or both), the writer or speaker may tend to bounce between 'naked' and 'nude' simply to avoid repetitiousness. Any closer or more serious consideration, however, quickly uncovers differences in usage and connotation that have been substantial enough to support some close critical attention. As I am already beginning to suggest, the establishment of a tenable binary – 'naked' : 'nude' – is problematic, but a brief review of the territory may be worthwhile.

Discussion of the language and possible contradistinction of 'nakedness' and 'nudity' often starts with the setting-out of the ground as seen by the revered art critic Kenneth Clark, in his 1956 book *The Nude: a study in ideal form*. For Clark, the naked figure is in a state of deprivation, "huddled without clothes",[13] and as such is compromised by the force of its loss and social anxiety. (It can be seen straight away that part of my own work with the unclothed actor aims concertedly to challenge the ordering of this picture, even to the point of exactly inverting it, wanting theatre to be a place in which the actor need not be deprived of his nakedness.) The nude, at least as represented in the classical tradition of Western art around which Clark orients his thesis, is not deprived, partly because the nude figure is *not* unclothed, but shows us the body clothed in art. The nude is "balanced",[14] he says – it is composed, at ease; the sociality in which it participates is not under threat from its presence.

The most prominent critique of Clark's analysis of the nude has perhaps been John Berger's, in *Ways of Seeing* (1972). One might expect a vigorous Marxist critic such as Berger to attack many of the premises of Clark's analysis, as well as his conclusions; but in fact Berger accepts the dynamics of Clark's binary and aims rather to restate it in such a way as to ameliorate its reductiveness somewhat, by helping us to begin to discern the figure of the spectator – "the principal protagonist",[15] and the currents of economic and sexual politics that run through the situation:

> To be naked is to be oneself.
> To be nude is to be seen naked by others and yet not recog-
> nized for oneself. A naked body has to be seen as an object in
> order to become a nude... Nakedness reveals itself. Nudity is
> placed on display.
> To be naked is to be without disguise... The nude is con-
> demned to never being naked. Nudity is a form of dress.[16]

For Berger, then, it is not nakedness that is a state of deprivation, but nudity, in which the self is abstracted and objectified and finally "condemned"; the quality of elevation interpreted as prestige by Clark is seen by Berger as a kind of estrangement.

If Berger does not seek to refuse Clark's binary – merely to reverse its polarity – he does at least complicate it somewhat. Initially he limns, much as Clark does, a sketch in which, essentially, the naked belongs to life and the nude belongs to art; but he goes on to suggest that there can be exceptions to this rule – that in some paintings we see the subject for herself, as naked. We might infer, in Clark's terms, that there is an element of imbalance in such portrayals, a sense of naturalism rather than conventionality in the composition. (The exemplary image that accompanies this passage, though Berger does not refer to it explicitly in the text, is Rembrandt's *Danaë*; it's interesting to note, given his implication that we might see this figure as naked rather than nude – and, it follows, as no longer elevated in some uncontactable art-realm but rather somehow with us, on our level – that since Berger wrote about *Danaë*, the painting has been vandalised, in an acid and knife attack in 1985; it was restored and returned to public view in 1997.)

What makes the difference, for Berger, between the nude and the anomalously naked in these portraits? The crux seems to have to do with the presence of a real and undisguisable intimacy in the relationship between painter and subject, so that the nude figure seems to refer not to us as spectators, for our pleasure, but to the artist, for his. What we as 'audience' have, in other words, is privileged access to an otherwise private occasion. For Berger, this private space evades the political pressure of public scrutiny, and allows something more genuinely human, more trustworthy perhaps in its lack of performative self-consciousness, to come through. The ideal, the formulaic, is supplanted by the particular.

So now we are touching on some questions that will bring us back to theatre. Nakedness, we might say, has a specificity, and therefore some appearance of spontaneity; nudity is generic, conventional, and in its sense of balance and of rehearsed composition it may seem to exhibit a kind of 'wholeness'. Berger goes on to propose that nakedness – strictly, sexual nakedness – resists capture in static images, because it is relational (we might say collaborative, even), something in motion between people: "a process rather than a state."[17] This sense of movement, of negotiation, of nakedness as something that is endlessly *becoming* ('endlessly' because, as we have seen, in experience it refuses its own limit status, so it has no point of arrival, only perhaps a horizon), would seem to place it, rather than nudity, within the practice of theatre.

Yet, for Berger, the registration of nakedness in art is dependent not only on movement, but also on the realization of private intimacies. This raises a difficult question about theatre, and the extent to which it is and isn't a public space. Public intimacy, we know, need not be a contradiction-in-terms: the scope of codes and regulations for public conduct will not necessarily prevent us from being 'all the way in' in our experience of an event or a relationship. And yet even the most decidedly public theatres will often aspire after the conditions of privacy, or at least its signs – a sense of enclosure, of seclusion, of shelter; when a public theatre wishes to flatter its audience, it often does so in the language of secrecy or exclusivity. Avowedly demotic space is thus suffused with intimations of privilege, which acutely inform the readings that are offered in that place.

That there is a class element to nudity that mirrors the class basis of the theatrical establishment is starkly illustrated by the following description, in a recent newspaper article, of Walter Sickert's remarkable painting *La Hollandaise*:

> As Chris Stephens, curator of modern British art and head of displays at Tate Britain, explains, "it is probably of a prostitute in a seedy bed in Camden Town. She is naked, not nude. It's classic modernist English impressionism: lowly subject; dirty; urban; everyday."[18]

Not everyone, it seems clear, has access to nudity. Some are staged, lit, raised; some sit huddled in the dark. For John Berger, meanwhile, as we have seen, nakedness is not a depleted but an exalted state, one in which intimacy – specifically erotic intimacy – breaks through the fourth wall behind which nudity imprisons its subjects. In Berger's construction,

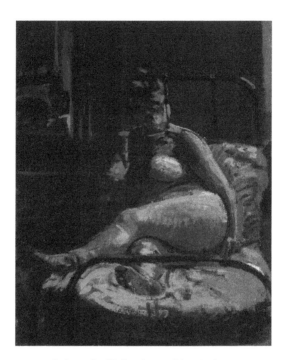

Sickert, *La Hollandaise* © Tate Archive.

however, this radically liberating movement depends on a kind of privacy with which a comparably radical theatre should have no truck. It is a paradox which churns away in the core of much contemporary treatment of the body on stage.

For instance, a striking if rudimentary manifestation of the private/ public tension as it shows through the naked/nude binary can be found in the matter of signage. Whenever my work features actors without clothes, I certainly see those actors in those moments as being naked, rather than nude: that's the reading that the other elements in my theatrical language are setting up – and anyway, as Berger says, "to be naked is to be [recognized as] oneself", and I have nothing to offer as a director if I can't recognize my own actors for being who they really are. But most theatres will wish to put up warning notices, so that punters know what they're in for: and the phrasing of those notices is invariably that the work in question "contains nudity". (This of course is an odd phrase in itself, borrowed – via the 'scenes of mild peril' advisory notes on adverts for movies – from legally exculpatory admonitions about allergens in food products. Maybe this linguistic styling is telling us – and I wouldn't necessarily disagree – that nudity is, or can be, 'contained', whilst nakedness is perhaps, in its resistance to resolution, uncontainable?)

Imagine this: our exemplary actor has showed up to work, on stage, and he is not wearing any clothes. Perhaps some audience members will be able just to see a body – *his* body. But it seems likely that many more, who have taken account of the notices on the way in, will see him as nude, as the carrier of the 'nudity' that the signage has caused them to anticipate – and perhaps, by extension, as signalling a kind of prestige, and with it a sort of permission: it must be all right to look: this is not a naked body, but a body-in-art. And so a relationship is created that speaks, albeit in a muffled or less-than-candid way, about relative value, about the special permissive seclusion of theatrical space, about the kind of cultural affirmation that is conferred by having the price (and thus the right) of admission; and let's imagine that relationship settles into a stable position.

Let us next imagine that the actor steps off the stage and starts to walk towards the exit – maybe the journey takes him through the auditorium, maybe not. He leaves – but if we could follow him, we would see him walk out through the foyer, past the bar, past the box office, past where they sell the Maltesers, out through the main doors of the theatre building, and into the street. Down the street he goes and off into the distance. (Don't worry, he'll be back.)

Out in the street, there's little doubt that our actor is seen as naked. Public 'nudity' seems to depend upon an order of composure just as much as nudity in art: in our imagining of her (or in numerous contemporary re-enactments), Lady Godiva riding naked through the streets of Coventry is naked only in so far as she is unwilling, but iconically elevated on horseback with her long hair carefully arranged to cover her breasts and protect some vestige of her modesty, she is certainly nude in a way that she would never be were she found skating the concrete ramps in St Margaret's Park. Conversely, a more topical icon, ex-Royal Marine Stephen Gough, whose heroically persistent opposition to the state's prohibition on publicly going without clothes has caused him to spend most of the last decade in prison in Scotland and England – he is again in jail as I write this – is better known to the public via his media-bestowed appellation, the Naked Rambler. The idea of a Nude Rambler seems almost self-evidently a contradiction-in-terms.

To return to our actor, then, as he disappears out of view, we might ask the question: at what point does he finally shuck off his nudity and appear before us naked, seen at last for himself? When does he divest himself of that last piece of clothing that we recognize as art? Does it happen the moment he steps off stage? As he leaves the auditorium? Or the theatre building? Is there some persistence of vision to be taken into account? Will an audience member who accompanies him out on to the street continue to see him as nude, as an emissary from the art-house, while an unsuspecting bystander waiting at the bus stop perceives only nakedness?

What we see when we look at a body in theatre is a question that lodges at the heart – or sticks in the throat – of many of these untenable binaries: not just naked/nude, but private/public, and intimate/ spectacular – and indeed it reaches back towards space/place. One particularly useful viewing device is an idea introduced by the American performance scholar Michael Kirby through an even more problematic antinomy: that contained in the title of his seminal 1972 essay 'On Acting and Not-Acting'.[19]

In this text, Kirby develops a line of thought that he had previously set out in a piece published seven years earlier, which aims to introduce readers to movements and tendencies within what he describes, in titling the essay, as 'The New Theatre'.[20] The survey takes in and attempts to situate John Cage, Allan Kaprow, Claes Oldenberg and Jackson Mac Low, among others: and it is interesting – and I find it heartening too – that although Kirby rightly states that "In discussing this new theatre, new terms are needed,"[21] he does not discard the word 'theatre'; what he (and others) are at this point calling 'Events', 'Happenings', 'Environments', etc., enlarge the territory of theatre rather than representing a breach with it. (He concludes that, with its emphasis on stasis and repetition, Kaprow's *Eat* is, on balance, "not quite theatre":[22] but the predominant sense is still that these works point towards future directions for theatre even from marginally outside its purview.)

The particularly suggestive terminology that Kirby introduces in this 1965 piece, and explores more fully in the later essay, is the dyad 'matrixed' : 'nonmatrixed'. The actor, says Kirby, "functions within subjective or objective person-place matrices":[23] in other words, when we look at actors they are overlaid by a matrix of fictionality, a 'who' and a 'where' that re-places them within a fictional construct. The non-actor – Kirby uses the word 'performer' – is not perceived as working within that matrix: the musician, the athlete, the priest are all performers, but we don't think of them as portraying characters or as being anywhere else in the world than where they really are in the moment of our watching.

At this stage, Kirby is cautious about translating 'matrix' : 'nonmatrix' into 'acting' : 'nonacting', because, as he says, "a person may be matrixed without acting. Acting is something that a performer does; matrix can be externally imposed upon his behaviour."[24] Matrix, then, is not a mode of acting but of watching: a play may through the interrelation of a whole array of signs seek to compel a matrixed reading, but, as we have already seen in our consideration of 'liveness', countless potential sources of interference may undermine the audience's ability to sustain the matrix that the performance requires.

It will be evident that the sense in which Kirby uses the words 'actor' and 'acting' to imply an ineradicable association with matrix is somewhat out of alignment with my own employment of those terms. Certainly by the time of his writing 'On Acting and Not-Acting', not only has Kirby's squeamishness around the idea of nonacting apparently abated somewhat, but, perhaps in the service of the distinction between acting and not, he sets out at the very beginning a definition of acting that may seem to contemporary eyes almost militant: "Acting means to feign, to simulate, to represent, to impersonate."[25] Kirby insists that no value judgement is intended, but it's probably fair to say that even actors whose work has mostly been in highly orthodox fourth-wall drama might feel that this summary of their job description is at best partial and at worst so reductive as to amount to a distortion.

We can usefully compare Kirby's model of 'matrix' : 'nonmatrix', and his association of matrixed performance with feigning and simulation, with the attitude of the great French film director Robert Bresson, as expressed in his invaluable *Notes on the Cinematographer*. Though tiny, it's a hugely rich and provocative book in which any thoughtful theatre artist will find much to chew on: but it can be a difficult read for those who are devoted to the stage, as Bresson emphatically and sometimes quite furiously sets cinematography against what he calls "the terrible habit of theatre",[26] and pursues the antagonism particularly through his categorical contrasting of the 'actor' – who belongs to theatre – and the 'model' – his preferred (and self-evidently loaded) term for the performer on camera. "No actors," he says early on: "But the use of working models, taken from life. BEING (models) intead of SEEMING (actors)."[27]

Perhaps partly because of their sharply concise and axiomatic form, these notes can be dispiriting to the theatre maker (I always find it particularly painful to read "No possible relations between an actor and a tree. The two belong to different worlds."[28]), but I find Bresson's thoughts on the figure of the 'model' highly suggestive – not only for themselves, but because they tend also to undermine the absoluteness of the binary on which he insists.

For Bresson – and for me – actors are defined by their agency: they're always up to something. To Bresson this perpetual state of over-solicitous offering, this ostentatious craftiness, this endless *doing* is a function of the actor's effortful manufacturing of the make-believe world in which they do their 'seeming'. (For instance, this is pretty much exactly the attitude of Dušan Makavejev towards Simon Callow, as recounted in *Shooting the Actor*.) Models, on the other hand, are "capable of eluding their own vigilance":[29] though this construction, in which the model is at least the author of his or her own response to the director's needs, seems quite at odds with other notes in which Bresson locates the authority in the relationship squarely within the director and not the model: "The cause which makes him say this sentence or make that movement is not in him, it is in you."[30]

At times, then, the ideal Bressonian 'model' seems to be not much more than a mannequin, to be manipulated, shaped to the director's will, and content to "be led… by the words and gestures you make them say and do."[31] But it is not quite this absorptive blankness that Bresson, finally, is looking for: the state of not-knowing in which he wants to hold his models is not ignorance but rather a kind of active and legible noncomprehension which seems to register not just within the system of the artwork but more existentially: "Against actors' assurance, set the charm of models who do not know what they are."[32]

What is the nature of this 'charm'? It seems initially as if it might sit closely with Brecht's famous pronouncement that "There is nothing so interesting on stage than a man trying to get a knot out of his shoelaces":[33] except that for the model, the nature of the task is disorientingly undefined: there are no shoelaces, only thin air and time, and the knotty problem is an inarticulable one to do with being and existence. But we can't ignore the magical connotations of what Bresson calls "charm".

Maybe we are coming near to the Christian theological concept of 'kenosis', of the emptying-out of the individual will in order to be closer to Christ and more open to the fulfilling presence of God. The idea of kenosis responds to the Biblical description of Jesus's transition from the wholly divine to the human: "[He] made himself of no reputation, and took upon him the form of a servant, and was made in the likeness of men" (King James Bible: Phillippians 2:7), where "made himself of no reputation" translates the Greek ἑαυτόν ἐκένωσε – literally, 'he emptied himself': an act undertaken, we might not wholly speciously say, in preparation for an uncommonly demanding piece of performance; it certainly makes most actors' warm-up routines seem pretty cursory.

In the sixteenth-century poem 'On A Dark Night' (usually referred to as 'Dark Night of the Soul') by St John of the Cross – often cited as a literary representation of kenosis and its aftermath – the darkness surrounding the narrating figure is illuminated by the light "which burned within my heart"[34] and which guides the narrator to his (male) lover, whom we are to read as Jesus. The startling erotic fervour of the poem draws out into a narrative line the intensely sexual freight of kenosis, which perhaps indicatively resembles the psychic and emotional modulations of what we may understand of 'subspace', the altered state of consciousness sometimes reported by submissive participants at the heavier end of S&M.

If 'subspace' feels too absurdly remote from 'charm', consider Bresson's note on the model: "Reduce to the minimum the share his consciousness has."[35] This directed kenosis, however, is enabling in ways which Bresson, like St John of the Cross, expresses in terms of both light and a kind of numinously eroticised reciprocity: "You illumine him and he illumines you. The light you receive from him is added to the light he receives from you."[36] It is curiously metaphoric language from someone with such an aversion to theatrical pretension, but we can at least infer that Bresson is attempting to describe something very 'real' of which he has direct experience.

The figure that seems to glow from within, like the narrator of 'On A Dark Night', is a pop-culture trope which helps us establish quasi-religious relationships with visitor / saviour / superhero characters ranging from Steven Spielberg's E.T. to Dr Manhattan of the *Watchmen*. But perhaps the most iconically potent rendition of the idea in recent times – and certainly the most erotically activated – is in the artwork of Keith Haring, whose trademark graffiti-style dancers and babies and canines, in all their friendly polychromatic diversity, often emanate lines to indicate a kind of radiance – part of the basic vocabulary of the cartoon. (Imagine a gold ingot, say, in a comic strip.) Sometimes these marks are hard to distinguish from lines indicating motion, which Haring also frequently employs; this in itself is instructive: whatever's going on inside these figures is a kind of movement in itself, even though their bodies may be stationary.

The most significant of Haring's glowing icons is perhaps what's come to be known as the 'radiant baby', or – as in the title of Rene Ricard's seminal 1981 essay on Haring and his confrere Jean-Michel Basquiat, among others, for *Artforum* – 'The Radiant Child'[37] (a sobriquet occasionally now applied to Basquiat himself). Ricard's piece aims to introduce these emerging bodies of work, and to think through the cultural currents that are fostering them. It is interesting to read Ricard on Haring, whose iconography has become so familiar over the past thirty years that it now almost resists careful attention, and whose pictures teem so abundantly with the demotic variegation and interaction of city life that they can only seem cheerfully suffused with positive energies. For Ricard, writing at the start of the eighties, in the early days of Reagan and with the Cold War ratcheting back up, something rather different comes through:

> These poor little characters wigging out from the radioac-
> tive communications they are bombarded with are superslick
> icons of turmoil and confusion. They are without will,
> without protection from impulses of mysterious source. We
> can laugh at their involuntary couplings and tiny horrified
> runnings around because we see them as we cannot see, as the
> fish cannot see the water, ourselves.[38]

For Ricard, then, those radiance lines are ambiguous: they might as well signify the 'bombardment' of the figure by invisible waves and rays from the outside, as a glow coming from the inside; or perhaps that glow is itself the toxic radiation leaking out of the saturated body. (As the critic Henry Geldzahler has helpfully pointed out,[39] Haring was raised in Kutztown, Pennsylvania, just fifty miles from the site of the nuclear accident at Three Mile Island in 1979; Haring had moved to New York by then, but the global anxiety to which the incident gave rise must have felt particularly acute to someone whose hometown was so directly impacted.)

Through this lens, Haring's 'radiant child' icon is not simply aglow with life-force, pulsating with the communicative and erotic possibilities consequent upon being born in a major American city in the late twentieth century; at the same time, it has already been zapped full of fallout of one kind or another, the invisible detritus of postmodern high-capitalist airspace: microwaves and AM radio, advertising messages and UFO tractor beams. Without actually *doing* anything, the baby is in motion, a jerked-around participant in a culture it cannot see or comprehend. And so we might productively link its "turmoil and confusion", via the ambiguous "radiance" it emits, to the "charm" of Bresson's models "who do not know what they are" but who can nonetheless give as well as receive 'light'.

We might prefer Ricard's word "radiance" over Bresson's "charm" not least because it is not satisfied with a language of magical ineffability, but seeks to attest to a describable social and cultural predicament whose effects are so excessively complex as to outstrip analysis. And this in turn makes sense of the collaborative reciprocity, the working balance, between director and model that Bresson idealises. The model is not possessed of some special supernatural quality which separates him from us; he is, if anything, an expert in being with us and breathing the same air, whose expertise is released in the act of his volunteering to suspend his individually distinct authority. What the 'actor' (in Bresson's terms) offers as assertion, the model conversely opens out as a kind of self-denial, a temporary and conditional kenosis in which self-will is traded against the possibility of real intimacy.

Thinking then of the 'radiant model', we come to a moment in the company of Jerzy Grotowski – much of whose career can be seen as a pressurizing of the crisis of spectacular assertion versus the offer of intimacy – talking to Richard Schechner about risk-taking in an interview in 1967:

> The first time we take a route there is a penetration into
> the unknown, a solemn process of searching, studying and
> confronting which evokes a special 'radiation' resulting from
> contradiction.[40]

So, this is a 'radiation' with which we are now familiar. The model is radically "unknown", even to himself: the emptying-out required in the Bressonian compact leaves a sort of glowing absence, which might bring to mind the comic-book convention for depicting something that's not there, that's surprisingly disappeared or not where it ought to be: an empty space surrounded by Haring-like radiance lines, perhaps captioned

'GONE!'. What, though, is the "contradiction" which Grotowski identifies as the light-source? His own explanation concerns the process of developing techniques for the attainment of self-knowledge – that 'wholeness' agenda again; I prefer to locate the contradiction elsewhere.

The key to interpreting the model's radiance is that it appears to greatly problematize Bresson's 'actor' : 'model' binary – and, by extension, Kirby's 'acting' : 'not-acting'. The reasons for this may be clearer if we nudge our vocabulary a little: a better word for the "charm" and "radiance" we are trying to describe and locate, in the context of performance, might be 'charisma' – a notoriously ticklish quality to define, tricky not least because we seem to identify it so readily and instinctively in individual actors, without recourse to reflection or critique. 'Charisma' carries with it a little after-note of the magical tenor of "charm": it is, after all, at root, a divinely bestowed gift; but beneath its basic meaning – something like 'grace' – is the etymological seed of 'desire'. Can we then imagine the desire which inheres in charisma as being akin to the radiation in Haring, or the illumination in Bresson: a forcefield of signals travelling in both directions simultaneously, and producing in that reciprocal relationship a special intensity of intimate attentivity?

If this is so, then the model (to employ one last time, for the sake of consistency, Bresson's distinctive terminology, though what he seeks in his 'models' is in some respects not far from what I personally want in actors) is not this charming man we've had described to us, the clueless, unvigilant, not-knowing, vessel-like figure whose role is as a semi-conscious receiver for the director's signals of intent. On the contrary, he or she is an active collaborator, a participant in the co-production of a desiring interrelation. The contrast of 'seeming' versus 'being' collapses in the heat of this *acting* (and now let us never say 'model' again, if we can help it), which places into a generative, luminous tension the equally positive actions of wanting-as-desire and wanting-as-lack. In Kirby's terms, this fits neither with 'acting' (with its connotations of 'feigning' and 'simulation') and 'matrix' (which is substantially irrelevant, or not necessarily relevant, to the matter of charisma), nor with the activity of the nonmatrixed performer who is seen wholly for herself: for charisma certainly makes the figure strange in her grace and her radiance, in her expertise at being at once intimately with us and intensely apart from us.

Charisma, then, disturbs and disrupts the processing of what we might call 'matrix data' – the cues and codes that tell us how to situate an actor in our reading of them. What we see and respond to in a charismatic actor is not their activation of matrix nor their lack of it, but the impossibility of tracking them in relation to matrix. No amount of information – either about any fictional construct within which they might be signalling, or about their real life outside the theatre or their task within it – can resolve the disturbance we experience in encountering them. We do not know who they are: and the more intimately we come into relation with them, the more we do not, and cannot, know. As Grotowski suggests, though, we perceive "'radiation' resulting from contradiction", and not the other way around: which is useful in that it may provide a key for talking about charisma, which otherwise tends to elude analysis (beyond "we know it when we see it"). Instead of saying that charisma resists matrix, we might rather suggest that the resistance of matrix – the refusal of its premises, the deliberate disruption of its syntax – in conditions of collaborative attentivity produces the effect of charisma.

To some extent, Kirby allows for the 'problem' of charisma (though he does not discuss it in these terms) by himself dialling down the binaries of acting and matrix. In practice, he suggests, performance is seldom clearly 'matrixed' or 'nonmatrixed', but rather takes place somewhere on a continuum: the legibility of matrix in any performative frame may be stronger or weaker. So: we might consider two actors playing Cordelia, one of whom is a recent drama school graduate making her first professional appearance, while the other is well-known from various television roles and occasional appearances in gossip columns and colour supplements. For most audience members, it will obviously be easier for the first actor to read straight away 'in matrix' as 'Cordelia', while the second may, at least initially, signal more strongly 'out of matrix', as a familiar celebrity with a household name: in fact, the degree to which the second actor's performance as Cordelia is judged to be successful may depend on the extent to which she is able to become more matrixed in the audience's reading as the performance unfolds and we 'lose' ourselves (and, by extension, her) in the story and the show. When the recent graduate's mother attends her daughter's press night performance, however, her perception of 'who' she is watching – her receptivity to the matrix data of the production – may be very different from the people sitting around her.

As Kirby allows, then, matrix is in practice unstable: it ebbs and flows, flares and subsides, as part of a complex ecosystem of signs and conditions within a constructed theatrical event, even before the multiple individual reading preferences and competences of a live audience are taken into account. At times it may flicker almost stroboscopically. It is also, as we have already noted, deeply susceptible to sudden unforeseen lapses and breakdowns: in fact it is obvious that the stronger the matrix, the more fragile it is likely to be. If a young performance artist – of no reputation, we might say – tries to light a cigarette as part of his performance, and the lighter won't work, then this becomes an interesting problem, of the order of Brecht's shoelace-knot; perhaps after a while someone in the audience will offer her own lighter, and the cigarette will be lit and the performance can continue, enriched if anything by the diversion. But if a famous young actor playing the lead in a fourth-wall production of *Hamlet* set in, say, Los Angeles in the 1940s tries to light a cigarette and has the same problem – in a situation where even the lighter is matrixed – we can more or less feel the matrix draining out of him: and a helpful offer from the audience will be the last nail in that particular coffin.

Nakedness, then, is toxically inimical to matrix: to see the actor for who he really is (in Berger's formulation) must necessarily be a syntax error in a theatrical encounter that has any designs on strong matrix – which is perhaps why those whose appointed duty it is to protect the play and the audience from each other invariably use the word 'nudity' in their warning notices. This should not be taken to imply that actors cannot be seen naked in shows where they play characters and speak scripted words: only that those productions need to be careful to establish a territory of weak or flickery matrix, which will be better able to withstand the infraction. The essential situation remains unambiguously clear: clothing belongs not to the body, but to the place that the body is in; place is part of what is constructed in the event, and the body, radically, is not. (Or, as one distinguished director put it to me when we talked about his own views on this topic: "The trouble is, once you've seen the actor's knob, he's not playing a character any more."[41])

However – to see the thought through – the undermining of matrix by the exposed body is only catastrophic if we choose not to be interested in it. Just as clothing can be used to potentiate nakedness by disrupting the cultural hierarchy of the body, nakedness in turn can throw our attention towards the grammar of matrix and the politics of hierarchy within the theatrical construct. In 2009 the director Natalie Abrahami wrote a blog piece explaining her decision to eschew nudity in staging Alexandra Wood's play *Unbroken* at the Gate Theatre in London:

> When a performer undresses on stage, I often feel like the
> child in The Emperor's New Clothes, my recurring thought
> being: "He has nothing on!" I don't believe I'm the only audi-
> ence member thinking this, nor do I believe I am the only
> one who has stopped listening to the text when this hap-
> pens… I tend not to want to create situations for audience
> members where they must decide between following the dia-
> logue or following an actor's paraphernalia around the stage.[42]

For all that the jocular coyness of that "paraphernalia" speaks volumes,
Abrahami's honesty is hugely important here and most people will
recognize the truth in what she says about how an actor's naked body,
in all its particularity, can be an almost tyrannically compelling presence
on stage. But her argument depends on a particular conjunction –
unexplored in her short piece – between aesthetic value and the codes
of propriety. For her, the exposure of the naked body is to be avoided
specifically because it tends to interfere with the priority act of "listening
to the text" and "following the dialogue". But even if I really can't look
at an actor's genitals and process what that actor is saying at the same
time, who's to say my preoccupation with their nakedness at the expense
of a close attention to "the text" isn't creating a richer and more deeply
engaging artistic experience for me? Why should the text condemn every
other element on stage to a secondary or supporting role? If the most
beautiful and rewarding presence before me is the body of an actor, and
I can't take my eyes off him or her, that sounds like a pretty good night at
the theatre in and of itself. Why would we devalue that experience, why
think of it as lesser? There is of course a deeply embedded feeling that to
gaze at a stranger's junk – or even a friend's – is unseemly, regardless of
their invitation to you to do so. But as Jonny Liron told me early on in our
working relationship, when I checked in with him about his experience of
appearing naked on stage: "If I'm going to go to the trouble of getting
my cock out, the least you can do is look at it." (A certainly unwitting echo
of Liberace's famous exhortation to his audience: "Well, look me over. I
didn't get dressed like this to go unnoticed."[43])

There is no doubt, notwithstanding the confidence and generosity of
Liron and Liberace, that many people, for various reasons, are deeply
uncomfortable with nudity on stage; as a maker, my preference – and, to
some extent, my responsibility, as someone who uses nudity quite a bit
– is to work to establish the conditions in which that discomfort can be

alleviated. I have no interest in shocking an audience: in itself, it's about the least creative thing you can do in a theatre. So, my task is to think about how the work I make signals to those who are bearing with it the premises, the values, the contracts on which our temporary cohabitation depends. Just as, in my work, narrative drama is often substituted by a palpable tension between two or more formal or tonal ideas that are working against each other, so the nature of exposition changes: what needs establishing in the opening moments of the piece – or, as far as possible, before the piece even begins – is not the matrix data of 'where' we are and 'who' we are about to meet, but rather some gentle indication of how to look, how to listen, and how to want, as we orient ourselves together in the unmatrixed system of here-as-here and now-as-now.

––––––––––

> The mystery which inflames him and at night in bed stiffens his penis leads the boy to ask a number of questions. But the questions are asked in a mixed language of half-words, images, movements of the hands and gestural diagrams which he makes with his own body. Thus the following are the crudest translations:
> Why do I stop at my skin?
> How do I get nearer to the pleasure I am feeling?
> What is in me that I know so well and nobody else yet knows?
> How do I let somebody else know it?
> In what am I – what is this thing in the middle of which I have found myself and which I can't get out of?[44]
>
> — John Berger, *G*.

Perhaps, in order to really understand what we are looking at when we look at an actor – at his body, at his nakedness – we have first to dare to look at ourselves looking, and to look at ourselves being looked at. We have to understand the ways in which we are the principal protagonists in the vital erotic life of the theatre.

I want to begin with a picture of two men sitting either side of a table, and to work towards a different picture, of two women who find themselves unable to sit either side of a table that is anyway no longer there, though it remains somehow radiantly 'GONE!'.

The men at their table, sitting opposite each other, are John Berger and the distinguished literary broadcaster Michael Silverblatt; the table is Berger's kitchen table, at his farmhouse in the hamlet of Quincy in the French Alps, where the writer has lived and worked since the early 1970s. In this video interview, from 2002,[45] their conversation is wide-ranging and warm, only stalling on occasion when Berger is too discomfited by Silverblatt's evidently genuine respect for his work and the superlatively glowing terms in which he expresses it. They drink, they smoke, they talk and play and think: Berger, in particular, thinks, through long silences in which he seems both excruciated and deeply submersed, untying perhaps some knot in the lace of his argument. It is a picture of friendship, of companionship, framed for the viewer by an extract placed by the editor at the start of the document, to function as both trailer and epigraph: Berger is talking about tenderness:

> It seems to me that one of the essential elements in tender-
> ness is that it is a free act, *a gratuitous act*. It has an enormous
> amount to do with liberty, with freedom: because one chooses
> to be tender. And in a certain sense, in face of, so often, what
> is surrounding us, I mean it is an almost defiant act of free-
> dom.[46] [my emphasis]

After that flash-forward, the conversation then begins with Silverblatt and Berger discussing the uses that they have made of literature, particularly as adolescents – turning to books in order to understand how others have lived, or how one might "behave".[47] When Silverblatt demurs at Berger's use of the word "behave", inferring from it something like 'act in accordance with etiquette', Berger attempts to clarify:

> You know, when you are eleven, or even when you're seven-
> teen, OK, and, suddenly you find yourself maybe for the first
> time in face of a woman who has just lost her man, he's just
> died ten minutes before... How to behave? It's not a question
> then of manners. Or maybe you find yourself alone with a
> dead animal... Or maybe...you find yourself frightened on a
> river or something.[48]

These two tiny extracts from a long and rigorous conversation are already busily alive with ethical questions that might properly belong to any discussion around the construction of the theatrical encounter: but

I simply want to draw attention to one tiny detail common to these two passages, which is Berger's distinctive use of the phrase "in face of". As someone who has lived in France for so long, Berger's English is now by habituation his second language, and here he uses a phrase which is not quite idiomatic (we might say "in the face of" or perhaps "faced with") but which seems directly to translate the French 'en face de', meaning 'opposite', and feels like it retains its phenomenological value.

On first hearing Berger use this construction, I was transported back to the process of creating *The Consolations*, an ambitious ensemble project I directed in 1999, for which the performers – many of whom went on to pursue their own brilliant practices as makers – were asked to develop characters in isolation from each other. One evening I taped Rajni Shah improvising a monologue in her persona as a bilingual, bisexual French photographer; as Rajni spoke, she slipped easily between French and English, sometimes translating herself as she went along, and an indicative moment for me in the aesthetic language of the piece as a whole was her saying: "Here, yes, in face with you – *en face de toi.*"

There is something immediately suggestive, I think, in this slightly unfamiliar and yet wholly meaningful construction of "in face of" or "in face with": and, in the present context, for me it immediately brings to mind a piece of prose that has been important to me ever since I first met it as an undergraduate student – and which, coincidentally, Bresson records approvingly in one of the occasional moments where he uses his *Notes* as a commonplace book: that is, Montaigne's essay 'Of The Custom Of Wearing Clothes', written around 1572-74, and this anecdote in particular:

> Someone or other was asking one of our beggars whom he saw in the depth of winter as cheery in his shirt as someone muffled to the ears in sables, how he could endure it.
> "And you, sir," he answered, "you have your face uncovered; now, I am all face."[49]

That someone who is naked or nearly naked could be perceived as being "all face" might work even better as a reassurance to those for whom visible nudity is anathema than for someone who's simply worried that the under-dressed person must be cold. But it might further suggest something about the special dispensation that applies (with the many caveats and frailties that we've noted) to theatre as a 'container' of public nudity: that in permitting and even fostering nakedness, theatre allows us to be 'all face' when we find ourselves 'in face of' or 'in face with' the other. Nakedness then becomes a more copious strategy in our coming to know "how to behave", our means of knowing what Berger goes on to describe as "what stance to take".[50] When we stand opposite the one who stands opposite us, our nakedness in that relationship can have an active ethical dimension – as we begin to uncover in the not-only-theoretical question "How can I become more naked?"; our defiantly gratuitous nakedness becomes part and (unwrapped) parcel of the greater 'defiance' of what Berger sees as our capacity for "gratuitous ... tenderness."

Marco Anelli, portraits of visitors to Marina Abramović,
The Artist is Present © Marco Anelli.

What's more, the enaction of such defiance can sometimes have a disclosing effect – which is to say, it's not always clear whose authority is being resisted until its custodians swing into repressive action. Take, for example, an intervention by Josephine Decker, a young filmmaker and performance artist who, on 31st May 2010, became briefly notorious (within an admittedly small community of interest) when she visited the closing day of *The Artist is Present*, Marina Abramović's blockbuster retrospective show at the Museum of Modern Art in New York.

The core of the MoMA exhibition was the new durational work from which the show took its name. For 'The Artist is Present', Abramović sat in a wooden chair, opposite a nearly identical chair, with a matching table separating the pair; she remained almost motionlessly present in the chair during the entirety of the museum's opening hours for the whole eleven week span of the exhibition. Visitors were invited to sit in the chair opposite Abramović for as long as they wished, looking silently at the artist and being looked at by her (as well as by horrendously long queues of those waiting their turn), and becoming in the process – according to the official MoMA blurb – "participants in the artwork." A second, less heralded but no less remarkable, output from the performance is that each sitter was photographed by Marco Anelli, creating a corpus of over fifteen-hundred portraits of people looking at, and being looked at by, Marina Abramović. (Two unofficial Tumblr blogs, still existent at the time of writing, collate subsets of Anelli's photographs under the titles 'Marina Abramović Made Me Cry' and 'Marina Abramović Hotties'.)

Although it was discussed in some quarters as though it were a wholly unprecedented event, 'The Artist is Present' in fact upscaled and opened out an earlier project undertaken by Abramović and her erstwhile collaborator and life-partner Ulay. In 'Nightsea Crossing', which was performed twenty-two times between 1981-87 in a variety of locations and contexts, Abramović and Ulay sat opposite each other, immobile, looking at each other, for seven hours a day: pictorially, then, the relationship is exactly as was seen in 'The Artist is Present'; aside from the 'participatory' element, the other significant change in the adaptation across to the MoMA piece is that the artists described 'Nightsea Crossing' as being undertaken "in a state of tranquility": a provision, and perhaps a kind of guarantee, that is inoperable in a participatory artwork, though the obligation of stillness and silence imposes some of the outward conditions of tranquility. Perhaps it is these constraints, and the resultant tension between emotional 'movement' and physical immobility, that produce – or, one might cynically suggest, are *designed* to produce – tearful responses in so many participating visitors.

There is no doubt that the strong reactions of some of those who sat opposite Abramović, whether for a few minutes or – as some did – for more than an hour, are a genuine and presumably spontaneous response to the encounter as it plays out in reality. Equally, it is clear that the construction of the event is designed to pressurize that encounter in quite extreme ways. The theatre maker and play-thinker Tassos Stevens has helpfully posited one of the more perception-shifting memes in current performance practice: "The experience of an event begins for its audience when they first hear about it and only finishes when they stop thinking and talking about it."[51] Seldom can this have been more persuasively demonstrated than in the case of *The Artist is Present*: Matthew Akers's documentary on Abramović and the MoMA exhibition[52] includes, for example, one visitor who has travelled from Australia just to sit opposite Abramović for a few minutes, and it is revealed that, towards the end of the show's run, some attendees who have queued forlornly all day in hope of taking part simply sleep outside the museum overnight so that they can be further up the line when the performance resumes the following day. The weight of expectation and investment that bears on the moment of encounter, the multiple gaze of other visitors and of however-many documentary lenses of various kinds, the presence of formidable uniformed guards marshalling the process, the strictness and rigidity of the contract: all of these mean that the signalled equipoise of the confrontation – apparently identical chairs (Abramović's is actually slightly adapted), balanced lighting and so on – is in practice heavily freighted in support of the designated artist. The opportunity to sit across from Abramović is both a gift bestowed and a weighty and massively overdetermined responsibility conferred by her and by the apparatus of the gallery.

And all of these factors are of course multiplied by the idiosyncratic celebrity of Abramović herself. As an artist she stands before an almost matchlessly significant body of performance work, documentary images of which have become iconic (not least in the standard texts with which students of performance will engage): partly because those that are not captures from video works are records of events that have otherwise vanished, and partly because many of Abramović's best-known works involve actions and processes that read to many viewers as 'extreme', including the extensive use of 'nudity'. Her Serbian provenance may register as exotic to American and Western European fans; the self-image she presents is of a beautiful and highly composed person with the taste and resources to clothe herself in high-end fashions, and these signs argue intriguingly with the spartan and self-denying or even self-harming appearance of many of her performed actions. She is, in many ways, exemplary of exactly that set of intersecting ambiguities with regard to matrix and 'authenticity' that, we have noted, produce an experience of charisma. This might then be another way of explaining the contradictory and confounding interferent patterns that contribute to the upset that can arise in people whose only task is to sit opposite her for a while and look her in the eye.

It is worth noting that, for Abramović, 'charisma' is a consciously manipulable instrument, one that is not merely innate, an accident of catching the light a certain way, but a constructive, constitutive technology, through which she generates what Akers and others have referred to as "charismatic space".[53] Visitors sitting across the table from Abramović are not merely in the presence of charisma, but are, by design, 'participants' or temporary cohabitants in a charismatic space, as if charisma itself had become a matrix. In this space, the radiance of Haring's babies and spaceships perhaps becomes the glow of Iain Sinclair's description of television: "where the act of stardom is to make the anonymous glitter. To spray anonymity in gold light…".[54]

More than any of these problematizing or vaguely alchemical factors, though, 'The Artist is Present' asks something difficult and exacting of its 'participants', which all of the other complicating elements tend to mask somewhat. It requires that, as well as looking at Marina (with whom, we hardly need Tassos Stevens's formulation to remind us, they already have some kind of relationship), they submit to being looked at by her, for as long as they are willing: and that for the duration of this transaction of gaze, they surrender also their access to spoken language. Whatever they may be thinking, they are prohibited from articulating, except in so far as they are able to express it non-verbally. (For example in the documentary we see a few sitters place their hand on their heart; though they are obliged to be still, this gesture is apparently non-threatening enough to escape censure.) To what extent, we might wonder, does this create a feedback loop, in which an emotional reaction becomes more intense precisely because it can't be spoken? Does their response deepen consequently to a point where they wouldn't be able to express it verbally anyway?

An instructive side-step, before we move on, might be to consider the extraordinary work of the Croatian 'gaze healer' Josip Grbavac, better-known by his trading name Braco. In a typical Braco healing, he comes out (after an ardent introduction) and stands on a raised stage or platform in front of a large audience, also standing; over the course of the next few minutes, he looks silently at the audience, attempting to create through his gaze a sense of eye contact which, according to his web site, "embraces the whole group";[55] and then he leaves. And that's it. The web is awash with testimony to the healing powers of Braco's gaze – minor ailments are cured, life-threatening conditions are reversed; those unfortunate enough not to be unwell nonetheless report that a sense of peace and tranquility is conferred. Footage from healing sessions shows audience members in tears. A descriptive language of 'light' (including "pure divine light"[56]), 'glow', 'beams', 'golden sparks', emerges in witness statements, echoing the title of one of Braco's many official promotional videos: 'The Gaze of Light'. In another video, a young man states plainly: "I think he's the most important person in the world today."[57]

All of Braco's public appearances – including those scheduled livestreaming events where he gazes directly to camera – come garlanded with sensible disclaimers regarding what can and can't be expected, especially in terms of medical outcomes. Nonetheless it is clear that, despite all the elements in Braco's self-presentation that make a sceptical observer like me giggle and squirm, some – perhaps many – of those who attend his events or visit his 'healing centre' in Zagreb are profoundly moved by the encounter. Undeniably, he has a remarkable gift for creating 'charismatic space'. Along with the trope of 'light' – it's notable that Braco's mentor Ivica Prokić described a decisive boyhood experience of "feeling a piece of the sun enter him",[58] like a living embodiment of Ricard's 'radiant child' – Braco's promoters also trail a language of 'lightness' (and, by extension, relevance): in other words, he evidently generates for his admirers a sense that his gaze, his elevated presence, at once with them and distant from them, is *about them*: the individually distinct them, and also the communal them. That relational positioning is certainly calculated (or intuited, maybe) to produce both in real space and in the audience's felt experience a high-functioning model of Walter Benjamin's concept of 'aura' – the radiance of the intimately unreachable, of what he called "distance as close as it can be."[59] (A formulation which may appear obliquely to prefigure the strapline of Akers's documentary on Abramović: "The hardest thing to do is something which is close to nothing.")

Perhaps, then, we see in Braco a pursuit to its furthest extent of the formal hypervalency of matrix: standing absolutely still and completely silent on stage in front of an absolutely still and completely silent audience, he proposes a highly orthodox theatrical relationship made potent by being completely evacuated of content: and in so far as only the gaze remains, what is fundamentally critical to his performative practice is not the active gaze of his looking at his audience (though this is the aspect that the discourse around him – including witness testimony – emphasizes); rather, it is his apparently uninhibited capacity for being looked at. Everything about the stage presentation of Braco facilitates his being the *object* of gaze, as well as its active and perhaps virtuosic exponent. He is almost infinitely relevant to the lives and needs of his visitors because he is not only superhero but also projection screen. (Inevitably, he invariably wears white on his upper body for his gaze events.) In standing before his audience, signalling as little as possible other than his apparent attentiveness and his Benjaminian aura – the matrix-confounding ambiguity of his transcendent accessibility, Braco *stands for* almost any content that an individual may wish to import into the encounter.

And again, as with the 'gaze event' of Abramović's 'The Artist is Present' (which, as we have seen, simply by dint of being a one-to-one rather than one-to-many confrontation, is able to disguise its structural inequity in a picture of balance-of-power), Braco's fecundity as a source of readings which have the ability to speak with uncommon directness to individual circumstances – precisely because the same individual brings the circumstance and the reading – is partly secured by his own spectacular non-speaking. Not only is he silent 'in performance', he also refuses interviews and other sites of public utterance – partly as an enaction of the raft of vigilant caveats that surround his work: no 'claims' are made about what effects he is capable of producing, and so another space is opened into which rush the testimonies of satisfied customers. It is true that disciples who visit his healing centre when the man himself is away on tour are invited to listen to recordings of his voice, for which the same healing capacities are advanced as for his gaze; but it is notable that in these recordings he speaks in Croatian, a language not in everyone's repertoire. Braco's website marvels that: "even in Germany or other countries, where people cannot understand what Braco is speaking, the reactions of the visitors during the session with his voice are exactly the same as with those people who understand Braco´s words": but again, of course, it is not the content of Braco's speech that his followers are responding to, but the remoteness of that content and the gap that's opened up in the absence of direct comprehension. Those who understand his words are, if anything, at a disadvantage.

To some degree, then, 'charismatic space' depends for the breathability of its air on the affective resonance of the radically unintelligible. When John Berger proposes as an ethical question the "stance" we might take "in face of…a dead animal", he is asking in part that we consider the ways in which our intelligibility to ourselves depends on our ability to see ourselves being seen by others. Joseph Beuys's iconic 1965 performance 'How to Explain Pictures to a Dead Hare' (recreated, not altogether successfully, by Marina Abramović as part of her *Seven Easy Pieces* series of re-enactions at the Guggenheim Museum, New York in 2005) dramatized this crisis doubly: in the piece, Beuys, his head covered in gold leaf and honey, and cradling in his arms a dead hare, whispers to the animal 'explanations' of the artworks exhibited in the gallery; but also, the gallery is locked and visitors to the performance are able to experience it only by peering through the windows of the building. Beuys's own highly developed private mythologies go some way to explaining his selection of elements within the system of the piece, but the performance also signals more broadly in relation to the ways in which expository communications based in language – and the failure of those communications – shape the often problematic experiences of intimacy and proximity by which we orient ourselves.

In his wonderful essay 'Why Look at Animals?', John Berger describes people and animals as looking at each other across "a narrow abyss of non-comprehension"[60] which is not mitigated, as it might be in an encounter between two people, by the existence of language: not necessarily a common language, but in the shared human fact of the possibility of language. Even in the case of a domesticated animal, says Berger, "always its lack of common language, its silence, guarantees its distance, its distinctness, its exclusion, from and of man."[61] This describes very exactly the distance, or at least the most fundamental of the many distances, explored by Joseph Beuys in his later performance, 'I Like America and America Likes Me' (1974), in which he spent three days in a room in New York alone with a wild coyote. It's a piece in which we see Beuys trying to discover what can be shared between himself and the animal, what non-verbal languages – "a language of primary sound",[62] he proposes – might bridge the gap of "non-comprehension",[63] alleviate the "exclusion"[64] of each from the other. Again, what Beuys in fact produces is an almost unassailably "charismatic space" in which the intractable non-comprehension that characterises the relationship between artist and animal becomes, again, a provocation about stance. Similarly, my own long fascination with the artist Peter Hujar's daunting 1978 photograph 'Goat, Westown, NY', in which a tethered goat stares out of its monochrome field – seeming, to me, not to heal with its gaze but, like the anti-Braco, to wound – led me to introduce that goat as a 'character' into a one-off performance at the National Theatre Studio of the Jacobean play *The Witch of Edmonton*, interpolating into the text a scene in which 'the goat' – played by a naked, crouching Jonny Liron – confronted our dramaturg, Sam Ladkin, who responded by reading to the goat Mark Hyatt's profoundly incompatible poem 'True Homosexual Love'. Given that the play already includes, in its authorized version, a (hind-leg-)walking talking Dog – the familiar of the eponymous witch – who interacts freely and personably, if disruptively, with the human community of Edmonton, there seemed to be something genuinely upsetting about the interposition of an encounter in which, at a literal level, two heterosexual men, one clothed, one naked, faced each other in a moment of (largely) pretended non-comprehension, in which the effort to bridge the "abyss" between them centred on the throwing-out of a quietly frictive homoerotic love poem. Here was the queerness of 'endless becoming' flipped to the queerness of radical inassimilability.

That the absence of a common ground of language in which to take one's stance is in itself not only an ethical problem, but a problem *within* charisma and thus within the 'charismatic space' of some performance, is clear in considering the difficulties around consent in performative structures, and especially those involving animals. For humans, the giving or withholding of consent is considered above all an event in language. Consequently we routinely kill and torture animals, abuse and exploit them, on the basis of a model of human supremacy that is ultimately authorized not principally by species discrimination or degrees of genetic difference, but by the failure of animals to withhold their consent formally by manipulating language formats that are comprehensible to us. The recourse to verbal language underwrites much of our self-exposure to risk – for example in the highly charismatic space of BDSM, with its potent adjacency to the realm of kenosis: a sadomasochistic scene that has gone 'too far' may be ended with the utterance of a 'safeword', a return to a contract of language-as-signal that an intense sexual or parasexual experience may otherwise disrupt or exceed. Notwithstanding the regulations that are designed to protect

Peter Hujar, *Goat, Westown, NY* © The Peter Hujar Archive.

animals in performance – and the force of cultural opprobrium and retaliatory threat that greets artists who transgress generally accepted boundaries, as in the case of Jan Fabre's filmed performance[65] throwing cats up a staircase at Antwerp City Hall in hommage to Philippe Halsman's famous (and evidently uncontroversial) 1948 photograph 'Dali Atomicus' – the predicament of animals within the theatrical situation nearly approximates the philosopher Giorgio Agamben's use of the concept, borrowed from Walter Benjamin, of 'bare life':[66] a kind of limit case for nakedness, in which the body is not even clothed in the protection (or the oppression) of the rule of law or the scope of civil intelligibility.

The 'bare' nakedness (in this sense) of animals is interestingly framed in the work of Wittgenstein: we might immediately recall his well-known maxim, in *Philosophical Investigations*, that "If a lion could talk, we would not understand him."[67] This somewhat resituates Berger's "narrow abyss" primarily as a fault not in language but in culture. Nonetheless, Wittgenstein repeatedly shows us the motility of culture through language, creating turbulence in the social spaces of negotiation and communality. In seeking to arrive at a particular 'stance', then, our reliance on verbal language may not help us capture thought as it moves, but rather confine or obscure it:

> Language disguises the thought; so that from the external form of the clothes one cannot infer the form of the thought they clothe, because the external form of the clothes is constructed with quite another object than to let the form of the body be recognized.[68]

Language, then, is to thought as clothing is to the body: and it follows that the nakedness of our stance "in face of" the other may depend upon the provisional construction of a negotiative space in which non-verbal elements – not just Beuys's "primary sound" but a whole array of technologies of presence and attentivity, including gaze, receptivity, gratuity, and, of course, literal nakedness – take precedence over the speech act. In other words, our distractedness in the theatrical situation described by Natalie Abrahami, where we become fixated on the nude actor to the detriment of our concentration on the "text", should be seen not as a lapse of focus, but rather as a reorientation of the spectator's active engagement around a complex relational signal in the face of which that individual can more effectively and dynamically think for herself.

At this point, let's return to the final day of Marina Abramović's advertised presence in the Marron Atrium at MoMA, and the moment at which Josephine Decker reaches the head of the queue. Four weeks earlier, at Abramović's request, the table that had previously separated the two chairs was removed: nothing now comes between the two figures, Abramović and her opposite. Smiling, Decker walks out into the centre of the space, halts by the empty chair, and pulls off her floral print dress, which leaves her wearing only her shoes – *naked, and then more naked*. Before the movement of her undressing is even complete, five gallery guards have completely surrounded her; she is cheered by the watching crowd. They watch her putting her dress back on, mumbling apologies, trying to control her breathing. The guards are booed as Decker is led away in some distress. A little later, in Akers's documentary, we see Decker tearfully waiting downstairs, unsure if she will be allowed another opportunity to sit with Abramović, and explaining her action in these terms:

I would love to just sit across from her. I mean I didn't know it was a rule. I didn't realise, and I would have obeyed the rule if I had known. But I wanted it to be spontaneous, I didn't want anybody to know. You know? I wanted it to be like my own thing and special with her. And I thought in that space, in that square, like you get your own... You know, it's like the audience is part of the art, you know, and you bring to it... And I just wanted to be as vulnerable to her as she makes herself to everyone else.[69]

Subsequently, Decker tells the Gothamist blog that her motivation in getting naked in front of Abramović – whose gaze is averted (not in response, but as part of the structure of the piece) during the whole episode – was a desire to "thank her".[70] Again she says that she had hoped "I could be, for a moment, as vulnerable to her as she constantly makes herself to us."[71]

What we see in the 'official' response to Decker's action is obviously first and foremost the gallery moving to protect its own authority, and the apparel of regulation in which Abramović's performance is clothed – and tight, revealing clothes these are too. For a participatory art work, the terms and conditions are hardly liberatory: sit absolutely still, don't speak, don't touch. (Those New York art-lovers who want that sort of experience would be better off going to a Broadway play, surely?) But more interestingly, what the gallery is policing in this moment, and what the rules of engagement require to be aggressively closed down, is an attempt to take seriously and draw active strength from the picture of balance that both the spatial arrangement and the relational offer of the piece appear to be promising. Decker's language is one of recompense: the equalling-out of 'vulnerability', but also the gesture of 'thanks'. Both of these well-intentioned movements, though, risk the 'charisma' of the space by introducing an *im*balance of matrix – doubled by Decker's unambiguous nakedness – which discloses the extent to which Abramović is located as the 'specialist', the designated artist whose power is vulnerability and for whom gratuitousness – the willingness to give things away at least nominally without the expectation of thanks – is an index of her designation.

Perhaps most tellingly of all, Akers smartly sets up the brief episode of Decker's intervention with a sequence in which an earlier visitor, also female, is being briefed by an invigilator. In running through the rules he can be heard saying: "You're going to sit across from the artist in silence. There are no distractions, distractions of any sort."[72] It's an uncanny echo of Natalie Abrahami's expression of anxiety around stage nudity, in which the naked body constantly threatens to distract from the primacy of the text. We might then ask: what is the – necessarily silent, unspoken – 'text' from which Decker's nakedness distracts so drastically that she has to be escorted from the gallery and threatened with arrest?

In order to consider that question, I want to think about one more piece by Abramović – perhaps my favourite of her works, and one in which the artist is not (physically) present. 'Wounded Geode' (1994) made a deep impression on me when I first encountered it at the Fruitmarket Gallery in Edinburgh in 1995. It is another piece which begins with two chairs separated by a table, set lengthwise; in this case, the furniture is not wood but iron. Viewers of the piece are invited to sit on the chairs, the seats of which are raised so that the spectator's feet will not touch the ground. The object of their gaze is a large, long, horn-like amethyst geode, which has broken open, revealing a coruscating interior of multiple reflective facets. Through a notice, Abramović briefs the visitor:

> Instruction for the public: Sit on the chair with feet not touching the ground. Observe the wounded geode, for a limitless duration of time.[73]

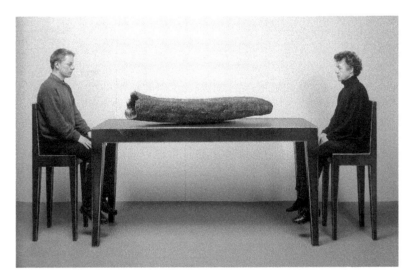

Marina Abramović, *Wounded Geode* © Sean Kelly Gallery.

This is a fascinating, slightly elliptical invitation, for at least two reasons. Firstly, there is the weirdly anthropomorphic framing of the broken geode as "wounded", as if it were a person – or rather, an animal, given that human language will be of no help or consolation to the mineral before us. Secondly, there's the invocation of "a limitless duration of time". Does this mean, as I initially read it, simply that the artist invites us to gaze upon the geode for as long as we want, just as visitors to 'The Artist is Present' can choose how long to sit opposite her? Or does she mean not merely that our temporal experience of this work is not delimited by her, but that we might aspire to sit here for an *infinite* duration? That our task in taking part in the work is ideally to remain there for ever and ever? This is not the fanciful reading it may seem: for a start it makes sense of the high-chairs, which elevate us out of a position of contact with the floor, implicitly suspending our participation in the diurnal, the temporary, the 'grounded'. But it also creates an almost narrative frame around the zoomorphic gesture. The "wounded" geode is poignant at least in part because this is a wound that will never heal. A wound normally implies a timescale, stretching either towards repair or death; but the 'wound' of the geode matches in its irresolution the potential limitlessness of our gaze. For as long as we look, it will not get better. Not even Braco can help us here.

This impasse becomes more resonant the more we can bring ourselves to take it seriously as an encounter with a kind of animal – or at least, to experience ourselves seeing inside a 'body' (from one end of the table, at any rate – the other end of the geode remains closed off). As so often with wounds, a sense of obscenity is present, a kind of turned-out explicitness that goes beyond the privileged 'in-ness' of intimacy. And yet, though there is a revelatory quality to 'Wounded Geode', of being able to see inside something that's normally closed off, there is also a built-in futility, the weird sensation of an aesthetic experience that will never attain the fully relational ramification that it's gesturing towards.

In his novel *Small World*, David Lodge gives his fictional American literary scholar Morris Zapp a lecture to deliver called 'Textuality as Striptease', in which he uses a heterosexually-oriented account of female stripping as an analogy for the futility of reading in pursuit of stable critical meaning:

The dancer teases the audience, as the text teases its readers, with the promise of an ultimate revelation that is infinitely postponed. Veil after veil, garment after garment, is removed, but it is the *delay* in the stripping that makes it exciting, not the stripping itself; because no sooner has one secret been revealed than we lose interest in it and crave another. When we have seen the girl's underwear we want to see her body, when we have seen her breasts we want to see her buttocks, and when we have seen her buttocks we want to see her pubis, and when we see her pubis, the dance ends – but is our curiosity and desire satisfied? Of course not. The vagina remains hidden within the girl's body, shaded by her pubic hair, and even if she were to spread her legs before us…it would still not satisfy the curiosity and desire set in motion by the stripping. Staring into that orifice we find that we have somehow overshot the goal of our quest, gone beyond pleasure in contemplated beauty…[74]

In a sense, the Wounded Geode skips straight to that unsatisfactory ending. A special, captivating orifice opens to us – within the construct of the installation, only one person at a time sees inside the geode – and, between its mute, terminal openness and the clear directions of Abramović's instructional signage, we are compelled to stare and stare. But in Lodge/Zapp's terms, this is an event which not only has no end but also no beginning: our "curiosity and desire" has not been engaged by an act built around "delay": everything in the piece is already present (meaning that the site of the geode's wound is not 'for' us or 'about' us: it is relevant only in so far as we can project into it), and will continue to be present after us, and any sense of gradual divulgence as we come into a relationship with the geode – as we come into a relationship with any art object – is instantly overwhelmed by the sense of "an ultimate revelation that is infinitely [or, we might say, 'limitlessly'] postponed."

Similarly, 'The Artist is Present' is both immobilizing, in its strict controls, and moving, in that both parties in the gaze relationship seek to find some internal negotiability. For visitors, this is predominantly an emotional response (we don't always really see the presence of 'motion' in the word 'emotion', but it's fundamental); for Abramović – to whom the durational nature of the exercise is very precisely limited, down to the minute, and who has largely ceded control of how long each relationship will last – the movement is more physical, and pertains directly to the strenuousness of the long periods of immobility: as she tells the MoMA blog after the end of the project: "I learned that in your body you have so much space and you can actually move inside that. There is space between organs, there is space between bones, there is space between atom and cell, so you can actually start training yourself to breathe a kind of air into that space."[75] What there is, however, is a beginning: Abramović looks up, in a gesture that hits 'refresh' on the scene, that offers (the sign of) a new start with each visitor. So, a steady state is created, held in check by regulation and secured by an absence of language that zoomorphizes both parties just as the wound zoomorphizes the geode: and in this self-imposed paralysis, the only things really moving are time, and the "curiosity and desire" response activated by the separateness of each gaze relationship that comes before and after it.

What this arrangement heavily (and perhaps, for some, euphorically) pressurizes is Berger's "narrow abyss" – a gap which becomes all the more palpable several weeks into the performance when Abramović asks for the table to be taken away. It is clear by then, in practice as well as theory, that the table is purely ornamental, and, worse, a hindrance: it is, in a sense, the worst possible metaphor for there being no table there. The work is about the gap, and the obstacle occludes the gap. Akers's documentary shows the gallery's security guards fretting about the removal of the table: nothing now separates the visitor from Abramović; but of course the fascinating gulf that remains, fixed in place by a crude objectifying syntax no less inflationary than Braco's and considerably more dissembling, is more radiant, more charismatic, than ever.

To the French writer Georges Bataille, the name of this "narrow abyss" – at its most basic, its least matrixed – is *discontinuity*:

> Each being is distinct from all others. His birth, his death, the events of his life may have an interest for others, but he alone is directly concerned in them. He is born alone. He dies alone. Between one being and another, there is a gulf, a discontinuity.
>
> This gulf exists, for instance, between you, listening to me, and me, speaking to you. We are attempting to communicate, but no communication between us can abolish our fundamental difference. If you die, it is not my death. You and I are discontinuous beings.[76]

And it is against – radically and furiously against – the lived experience of this gulf of discontinuity that Bataille locates eroticism. Erotic desire, he suggests, is essentially the desire to abolish the gap between us, or at least to alleviate it. It requires an effort of "dissolution"[77] – a word Bataille (or his translator) explicitly uses both as a way of describing the dissolving of the perceived barrier around the individually-distinct person, and as a carrier of the connotations of 'dissolute' behaviour, in which moral rigidities are loosened. Thus, eroticism works "to destroy the self-contained character of the participators as they are in their normal lives."[78] And Bataille is absolutely clear about what is at the crux in the commissioning of that erotic decontainment:

> Stripping naked is the decisive action. Nakedness offers a contrast to self-possession, to discontinuous existence, in other words. It is a state of communication revealing a quest for a possible continuance of being beyond the confines of the self.[79]

Or, as John Berger's young hero in *G.* asks in response to his own ineffable arousal: "Why do I stop at my skin?"

This, then, is the "decisive action" carried out by Josephine Decker. It is manifestly a response to the picture of discontinuity into which visitors to 'The Artist is Present' were asked to walk. It is an acknowledgement of the gulf that the technologies of Abramović as artist and MoMA as gallery conspire to render charismatic: but it is also a refusal of that gulf. It demands an order of intimacy that Abramović's gaze invokes in order to prohibit. We saw that Decker's language around her action was a vocabulary of equality and balance, of reciprocity and recompense, of being "as vulnerable to [Abramović] as she constantly makes herself to us": and in her sudden nakedness – no tease, no "delay" – Decker achieved exactly that: for Abramović, of course, almost uniquely adept at creating situations of charismatic authority, is extraordinarily powerful (and, surrounded by the vigilant gallery apparatus and a phalanx of uniformed guards, is probably the least vulnerable person in the entire museum); for about a second, Decker seizes an equivalent amount of power: her nakedness shuts down the highly individuating logic of the piece, and the conceptions of time and movement on which it depends. As she pulls off her dress, it is as if the Wounded Geode starts to heal. Decker's offer of dissolution, of erotic continuity, of the kind of real relationship that can only be negotiated in the absence of rigid authority structures, is, unwittingly perhaps on her part, a kind of putsch. It is the clearest example I've ever seen of theatre vanquishing performance. No wonder it's all over so quickly.

It is important for theatre makers wishing to achieve a similar quality of dissolution to understand the ways in which the 'gap' of discontinuity both is and isn't physical or spatial. As I have suggested above, the relations that Abramović and Braco seek to establish with those who elect to return their gaze are hardly unusual in the orthodox structures of theatrical presentation. Braco, dressed in white, standing in his light on a raised stage (and sometimes on a podium on that stage), looking out over a silent adoring audience most of whom profoundly believe that this experience will be good for them; Abramović requiring of her 'participants' that they are still, are silent, make no gestures, create no "distractions": these are simply two rather clearcut examples of a kind of relationship that, to a greater or lesser extent, is re-authored in most theatres much of the time. It is vital, though, that we do not locate the 'problem' of these structures only in the signs and codes of their spatiality. As we have noted, 'The Artist is Present' is able to marshall its power partly because it appears to be the picture of equity. Likewise, much 'immersive' theatre which appears to devolve to its audience unprecedented degrees of authorial freedom and active self-determination is actually enabled by power structures that in their inequality and rigidity outdo anything seen on a West End stage: it's just that (a) they often resemble the rules of a game, with which we readily comply for the sake of the entertainment; and (b) we only really come up against the might of that authority when, by accident or design, we find ourselves seeking to transgress its limits. And the same is potentially true of even the grooviest fringe shows, where audience and actors share the same physical space and the same light, say. It's a question not of spatial design (though this does signal to us pretty compellingly, to the extent that, for example, I now try wherever possible to avoid performing on a raised stage where many of the audience are looking up at me) but of the openness of the system it describes.

If the questions of space and place in the previous chapter turned out to be substantially to do with 'liveness', I want to suggest that our present concern with nakedness and eroticism is to a great extent a question of what I'd call 'life-sizeness'. Briefly put, the idea is a simple one. When we go to the cinema, we sit and watch people who are, on the whole, much bigger than us: we zoom into their faces and are dwarfed by them. When we watch television, the people are tiny: you could hold them in your hand. A sense perception I depend on in theatre, by which I orient myself in my understanding of where I am and what I'm doing, is that there may be a gap (or many kinds of gap) between myself and the people I'm watching, but that – even if the production requires, as it may reasonably do, that I sit still and quietly in the dark and do my best to pay attention as actively as I can – my capacity for that *active* attention is partly held open by my knowledge that, were I to lay all considerations of propriety and convention aside for a moment, get out of my seat and walk through the auditorium and on to the stage, I'd be standing next to people who are roughly the same size as me, and who are recognizable as intelligent humans beneath whatever matrix they're deploying. There must be that sense of continuity. All kinds of things can interfere with it: not only the obvious things like the integration of video screens and by extension the grammar of film or TV into the stage world, but elements like amplification and/or voice projection, or a large and commanding set, or virtuosity, or the register of the spoken text, or the way an actor handles objects. It is fun, sometimes, to be a little disoriented by such interference: but by and large, I not only prefer theatre to feel life-size, but need it to be so.

That's not to say, of course, that other media can't produce a feeling of life-sizeness. Perhaps the most effective piece of theatre I've mentioned in this chapter, to my mind, is the conversation between Michael Silverblatt and John Berger, at Berger's kitchen table. I feel, in a sense, not that I am viewing something that has been made for video, but that I am watching documentation of a theatrical encounter. At this point, the last vestiges of our idea of 'theatricality' as something flamboyant or hobbled by artifice must surely fall away. As we have already noted, Marina Abramović famously shares Bresson's distrust of theatre: "Theatre is fake," she says: "The knife is not real, the blood is not real, and the emotions are not real."[79] (It's so interesting, in the light of her long involvement with very real knives and blades, to consider the etymological connotation of cutting in Bataille's word "decisive" – compare, for example, 'incision' – when the nakedness of Josephine Decker's "decisive act" proved so inimical to the local power structure of Abramović's performance.) But a theatre that is truly live and properly lifesize fosters movement without the obligation of constraint or the desolation of assertive control: all is negotiable, all is becoming, all is constructive. Berger and Silverblatt, sitting at a table, talk like people in the process of becoming better friends. Berger is careful to insist early on that the dialogue is not, in the terms in which it has presumably been initiated, an interview, but rather "this conversation we're having, as equals."[80] The physicality of the two men is engrossing; their argumentation is not straightforward, but digressive, generously and playfully so. Their pace ebbs and flows without apparent force. They have their moments of complicite, and moments of non-comprehension where that simpatico briefly deserts them. I deeply feel that I am watching not just friendship, but an experimental sounding of intimacy. There is a palpable eroticism to the encounter that I cannot locate in their faces or bodies, in their speech, their cadences, their ideas, not even in their sharing a joke or a cigarette: I can locate it only in myself, and in my wanting to be with them *more*: more intensely, more intimately, more bravely. I want to uncover them in myself.

"Model," writes Bresson. "Don't just reduce or abolish the gap between you and him. Deep exploration."[81]

> I was in the congressional gym, and I went down and I worked out and I went into the showers… I'm sitting there showering, naked as a jaybird and here comes Rahm Emanuel not even with a towel wrapped around his tush, poking his finger in my chest, yelling at me because I wasn't going to vote for the president's budget. Do you know how awkward it is to have a political argument with a naked man?[82]
>
> — Eric Massa (US Congressman 2009-10)

> I danced because I fell in love with my sweat.[83]
>
> — Bill T. Jones

Nakedness, then, might be seen – in both its literal and its metaphorical senses – as a stance which the relationality of theatre activates into an erotic impetus. It signals our extension towards each other, our resistance to individual discontinuity, as the defining vector within the fluent promise of sociality. But in order for the nakedness of the actor's body to do that work, it is crucial that it is seen – and presented – as moving in itself. We need always to bear in mind Berger's contrast of nakedness as a process in motion with nudity as a state of privileged composition: just as Bataille's "decisive act" is, necessarily, a verbal rather than nounal phrase, the movement of becoming-naked (a movement which, I have suggested, is not limited by the actor being completely unclothed) rather than the wholeness of an achieved stasis. But the staged action of undressing is not the only way in which that motion can be captured: there are many ways of generating for an audience an experience of reorientation or parallax or disclosure in relation to the erotic body, and such movement can often feel outstandingly theatrical. Let me share two examples that have proved helpful in developing my own thinking in this territory.

For the first, we have to return, briefly, to Marina Abramović, and more precisely to *The Life and Death of Marina Abramović*, Robert Wilson's sumptuous and deliriously hagiographic stage portrait of the artist, which I saw during its run at the Manchester International Festival in 2011. One scene features a small ensemble of other performance artists whose own works are 'quoted' in miniature: including Kira O'Reilly, who performs a scaled-down version of her *Stair Falling* (2009), a piece in which the artist 'falls' in highly controlled slow-motion down a flight of stairs, across a duration of anything up to six hours. It is, when seen on its own terms, a beautiful, compelling, thoughtful work, and one in which O'Reilly's unclothed body usually seems to me to register as neither naked or nude but simply as a body, moving, negotiating, persisting. In the much-reduced *Life and Death* version, however, something very different occurs. In order to be aligned with the dominant aesthetic of Wilson's production, O'Reilly performs in full grey-white body make-up, as she painstakingly descends a barebones staircase. Instantly she reads not just as a body but as a nude: not, perhaps, inaptly, given O'Reilly's explicit location of the piece's origins in reference to Duchamp's painting 'Nude Descending A Staircase, No. 2', which seems to anticipate Berger's view of the nude by presenting the motion of the body in descent as a series of as-it-were superimposed stills. However, something more syntactically complex happens in O'Reilly's piece, because due to the physical contortions demanded by the performance, her buttocks are inevitably somewhat splayed at points, so that – at least from my seat in the auditorium – it's possible to see (and hard to look away from) the edge of her make-up, as far as it reaches, and the line of her un-made-up skin meeting it. The sign is no less clear for being inadvertent: this is the frontier of O'Reilly's nudity, and the rebellion of her nakedness in the contest of difference at that border. Bluntly, we can see Kira O'Reilly's asshole, and it's in a completely different show. We do not see her undress, that is not part of the drama here, but we nonetheless experience the brilliant 'distraction' of her anus as an erotic divulgence, a sudden 'decisive' irruption of militant intimacy, a refusal of the body to be tyrannized by Wilson's insistence on the pristine discontinuity of the stage. (Wilson has always asserted, for example – partly reflecting the formative influence of choreographer Jerome Robbins, whom he assisted in the mid-1960s – that it is necessary for the actor to re-learn how to walk, how to stand, how to sit, on stage.)

A similar sense of the body escaping or exceeding in intimacy its performative context marked my experience of Sean Holmes's acclaimed production of Sarah Kane's *Cleansed* for the then Oxford Stage Company (now Headlong) in 2005. I admire Holmes as a director but struggled with his approach to Kane's formidably challenging play: it seemed to me that his response to the intensely theatrical requirements of the text was, perhaps understandably, one that attempted to dominate and control the movements of the play and to try and resolve some of its quintessentially problematic demands in advance of the moment of showing the work to its witnesses; as a result, to my mind – though not to most critics' – the production was on the whole a bit stultified. The notable exception was in scene five, in which Grace and her dead brother Graham "stand naked and look at each other's bodies"[84] before making love, after which, in one of Kane's most celebrated stage directions, "A sunflower bursts through the floor and grows above their heads."[85] On the night I saw the show, as Garry Collins, the actor playing Graham, undressed in this scene, he (surprisingly and unmistakeably) had a hard-on. The effect was of what we might, not only jocularly, call an uprising: a kind of erotic insurgency against the closed system of the production: in the midst of so much carefully controlled simulation, a moment of genuine noncontrol, of real and present desire, of matrix overthrown, of truly live theatre bursting like a sunflower through the floor of Holmes's production.

Moments like these are exciting – and, in a sense, charismatic – because they disturb the gap between the performed and the real, the matrixed and the nonmatrixed, the stage and the audience, the actor and the spectator; between text and event, between mathematical space and the inhabited place. The taboos that are touched on in both these

examples – even in a show that 'contains nudity', you wouldn't normally
expect to see an exposed anus or an erect penis on a 'legitimate' British
stage – seem to invoke, in relation to those different kinds of gap or
abyss, a sense of the 'transgressive'. But the key elements in those
turbulent exchanges need not be so symbolically potent as to merit
that description. Any moment of (what reads as) 'real' tenderness, or
spontaneity, or understanding, or desire, or unselfconscious joy, can have
the same kind of effect. Perhaps the most indelibly affecting enaction
of nakedness I've ever seen in performance was one of the simplest: a
brilliant student production on the Edinburgh fringe in 1997, *The Day
of the 43 Sunsets*, included a scene in which, surrounded by the rest of
the performing ensemble who were miming dressing and undressing as
part of the busy routine of our everyday lives, one actor, in the centre
of the stage, quietly and undemonstratively undressed for real, stood
naked before us for the briefest moment, and then picked up his clothes
and walked off. It was – if it's possible to say this without innuendo in
the present context – a moment of real softness: partly because this
nakedness wasn't really *about* anything other than itself. It wasn't being
set to work in service of anything other than the negotiated reality of
the theatrical encounter.

"No costumes!" says Paul Goodman in his 'Art of the Theatre':
"– unless it is just the costume, or wearing the costume, that is the deed,
the thing to watch."[86] And ultimately I prefer over the language of
'transgression' a phrase which Goodman uses frequently across the span
of his writings: the idea of 'coming across'. This is pretty much exactly
the literal meaning of 'transgress' but its connotations and tone feel very
different. For Goodman, it's an idiom with multiple affordances: it might
mean treating someone compassionately, or stepping up, or changing
one's mind, or bestowing a gift, including the gift of intimate friendship;
it might mean 'putting out' sexually (especially in the case of a straight
boy consenting to queer sex), or flirting in a similar vein. The world
itself 'comes across' to those to whom it extends good fortune or an
occasional happy accident, or simply the means to go on. "For a starving
person," Goodman writes in 'The Politics of Being Queer', "the world
has got to come across in kind."[87] And in an essay on Wordsworth:
"My way of being in the world is writing something, to remain with my
only world when, as is usual, she doesn't come across for me; or if by
exception she does come across, I accept also that event by celebrating
it in verses."[88] In *Growing Up Absurd*, he "contrast[s] how people usually

hang around with how people come across in emergencies, or when they are enthusiastic, or when they are calmly absorbed."[89] And in his published diaries for 1956-57 he comments fractiously (and a bit uncomfortably, perhaps, for present-day readers) on:

> Young persons who can't make up their minds whether or not to have sex with you because afterwards the "truth" will be revealed, that they are not "really" interesting. Yet (to me at least) it is just coming across and taking a chance that is truly interesting.[90]

It sometimes seems that the agility of Goodman's rhetoric and the ardour and plangency of his lyrical prose is all marshalled in the service of getting others to "come across": to get naked, in other words; to close the gap.

The contemporary artist who, for me, most excitingly embodies Goodman's sense of 'coming across', with none of the lame 'shock value' of more concertedly 'transgressive' figures – and whose work feels more pertinent to the erotics of theatre than, certainly, anyone I know who's currently actually working in theatre – is the American photographer Ryan McGinley.[91] Like Goodman, McGinley's work is instantly recognizable as being produced by a queer artist: though, as filmmaker Larry Clark noted in a joint interview with McGinley in 2003: "I never think of Ryan as being gay, and I would go so far as to say that if I saw Ryan sucking a dick, I still wouldn't think he was gay."[92] What Clark seems to be picking up on, in his heavy-handed way, is that McGinley's queerness is – as Goodman's was, to some extent – focused not, or not only, on the homoerotic: he captures bodies and meetings and attentions that seem suffused with a desire that's specific not to the gender of the subject, the nature of the coupling, or even the orientation of the viewer, but rather is particular to the moment of the event. The nakedness on which he trains his camera is wide open to erotic response but does not turn itself towards, or away from, anything so inert as a categorical stability of sexual preference, except in so far as his subjects are generally young – recalling, perhaps, the 2003 exhibition curated by Francesco Bonami and Raf Simons under the aegis of the Fondazione Pitti Immagine Discovery in Florence which proposed in its title the idea that adolescence constitutes in itself a 'Fourth Sex'.[93] McGinley's models – and his most perceptive viewers – are too interesting to be boys or girls, gay or straight: they are simply (and far from simply) "coming across and taking a chance."

McGinley's early work documents the activity of what we might see as an at least partly constructed milieu: in other words, it responds vividly to being read in the lineage of Larry Clark or Nan Goldin, Mark Morrisroe perhaps, Collier Schorr or Ed Templeton, as a body of work that captures with unmistakeable intimacy a specific social scene or community of interest that in fact it's also quite consciously staging, if not quite fabricating: the artist's attention is both revelatory and formative – and the spectator's gaze is too. It follows then that McGinley's interest in the unclothed bodies of the young people we easily assume to be his friends plays with an abundantly charismatic tension between the naked and the nude. Often in those early images he captures his subjects in moments of apparently freewheeling spontaneity – rollerskating naked, skinny-dipping, leaping (trampoline not pictured), dancing through fireworks, sharing a bath or a joke; and yet as his work moves inexorably towards the manifestly fictional (particularly in the extraordinary left-turn of his 'Moonmilk' series in 2009), it becomes easier to see the degree of composition and authority that was always present, especially but not exclusively in the post-shoot edit. The logic of his move out of his favoured domestic and rural territories into the studio in 2010 for the nuanced but resilient monochrome portraits collected under the title 'Everybody Knows This Is Nowhere' appears as serenely predictable in retrospect as it was awesomely surprising at the time. But those pictures now, in turn, look like McGinley getting ready for the work he started showing the following year.

With those studio portraits, wonderfully successful though they are, it feels like something is slightly lost: they are, unambiguously, nudes: that earlier youthful energy and flirtation with disorientation (of all kinds) recedes in favour of a kind of poise and evidence of deliberation. If anything these portraits are even more intimate than the foregoing work, and the best of them are extremely beautiful, but they are performative where the earlier work was theatrical: that is, they lack incompleteness. The element McGinley brilliantly brings into the mix in order to achieve that dissolution is the presence of animals. In these sequences, nude young women and men are individually paired with live animals, often in playful, even punning compositions which seem both impeccably authored and highly serendipitous (the quality which we know animals are, at their best, almost uniquely placed to release into the studio); at times, a genuine collaboration seems to occur, while at others, the human body becomes no more than landscape. A perturbed-looking owl stares out, perching on a dune-like buttock; a giant albino snake insinuates

its way between a male model's legs; a lemur surveys the expanse of
a woman's breast with a palpable mad-scientist glint in its eye; a tiny
marmoset clings, apparently appalled, to a young man's genitals; a boy
and a white donkey cuddle together; some sort of rodent looks about to
disappear into a bearded guy's mouth.

What's most striking about these animal images, as they counterpoise
the human capacity for nudity with the non-human animal's radical
incapacity to be anything other than naked, is the sense of movement that
pervades even the most still-life-like of the pictures. What is captured
in these moments is exactly what I take Bresson to mean by "deep
exploration" of what I take Berger to mean by the "narrow abyss": and in
the trans-species negotiations of that quality of exploration, something
very dynamic is happening, which perhaps shows up most startlingly in
the scratches that are evident on some of the human models' bodies as
a result of their interactions with their animal collaborators. At one level
this is simply a good way of reminding us that, contrary to appearances
in some cases, these animals are real, and to varying degrees are wild, and
their consent to participate in this project is nowhere secured. But I also
find myself reminded by these scratches of Lucio Fontana's (still thrilling)
Concetto spaziale paintings, in which he slashes or punctures his canvases
– still, perhaps, the closest that painting has ever come to destroying its
fourth wall: we read those gashes as apertures through which the painting
and its viewer are both, at last, in the same space, breathing the same air.
Fontana's famous *Teresita*, like Abramović's broken amethyst geode, draws
us into an encounter with a wound that will never heal, that insists rather
on our nakedly ethical stance before an intimacy that will never resolve, a
state of remembrance that will always be raw.

I find I want to look at all of Ryan McGinley's work at the same time: I
want not just one image in isolation, or even one series with its fascinating
internal monologue, but this whole moving body of work. Perhaps it is
this that makes me want to claim him, somehow, as a theatre maker. It
is how he looks at people that moves me: even in the animal pictures, in
which he insists the animals are the subjects and their human partners
merely backdrops – or in the 'Moonmilk' pictures where he dwarfs them in
colour-saturated landscapes: I love that he knows that people are beautiful
when they recede like that. Somehow his people are always lifesize, no
matter what scale we encounter them in, so that in his measuring human
bodies against tiny creatures or vast rock formations he seems to re-
energise what seemed in the postmodern era like a lost idea: the notion

of the sublime, that which overwhelms us with its giddying enormousness or its irrecuperable ineffability. But more importantly, that lifesizeness is achieved through a kind of perpetual motion, in which the nudity of composition is constantly, limitlessly stripping naked (and getting more naked) in the heat of our attention. The late folk-singer and storyteller U. Utah Phillips used to credit the anarchist activist Ammon Hennacy with telling him, on the subject of pacifism:

> You came into the world armed to the teeth. With an arsenal of weapons, weapons of privilege, economic privilege, sexual privilege, racial privilege. You want to be a pacifist, you're not just going to have to give up guns, knives, clubs, hard, angry words, you are going to have lay down the weapons of privilege and go into the world completely disarmed.[94]

Ryan McGinley's work (with the exception I guess of his commercial and fashion photography) speaks to me exhilaratingly about that disarmament, about the laying down of the weapons of privilege as a decisive act. And if it seems difficult to reconcile that decisiveness with the perpetual motion I'm describing, the constant hitting of 'refresh' that keeps the wound from ever healing, it's only because the refusal of discontinuity is not a one-time action, any more than capitalism is a single baleful lapse in our social reality. Those weapons continually replenish themselves and in our name they're turned on distant strangers while we sleep or fuck or go to the theatre.

Of that perpetually moving nakedness, let's describe one final image. It's one of the most familiar pictures of naked people in recent culture: from 1972 (the year of *Ways of Seeing* and the death of Paul Goodman), the illustration of a naked man and woman etched onto a gold-anodized plaque and attached to the Pioneer 10 space probe, which after some eleven years' travel would become the first human-made object to leave the solar system. The plaque places the two human figures against a number of visual aids to help extra-terrestrial readers locate the origin of the spacecraft, and a diagram of the probe itself, against which those same recipients would be able to extrapolate the size of those human bodies. That is, we sent lifesizeness into space: an inherently theatrical, incredibly heroic act of wilful anti-discontinuity. Now that's what I call coming across.

These naked figures caused no little controversy at the time, with some conservative commentators complaining that, by dint of the illustrated nudity, we were pretty much introducing ourselves to distant alien civilisations via the medium of pornography. More progressive observers were unhappy that the woman was positioned somewhat behind the man, and that while he actively waved hello, she meekly and inertly stood by.

But a more interesting set of objections arose in relation to the cultural assumptions encoded in the engraving. Would E.T. understand the conventions of perspective? Would they be able to 'read' the arrow in the part of the diagram that traced Pioneer 10's trajectory through the solar system, or is an arrow symbol only comprehensible to the inheritors of a hunter-gatherer mindset? And how would the human figures be interpreted? Might the man's raised hand look aggressive? Moreover, Carl Sagan, who designed the plaque with his then wife Linda Salzman and SETI pioneer Frank Drake, had initially wanted the figures to be depicted holding hands, but then became concerned that the two humans would be interpreted as one single organism rather than a couple.

Towards the beginning of her still unparalleled performative deconstruction of contemporary Western semiologies, *United States* (1983), Laurie Anderson briefly alludes to the Pioneer plaque – and in particular the man's waving arm – using her pitch-downshifted 'voice of authority' to give her remarks a quizzically ironic edge:

> In our country, we send pictures of people speaking our sign language into outer space. We are speaking our sign language in these pictures. Do you think that they will think his arm is permanently attached in this position? Or do you think that they will read our signs? In our country, goodbye looks just like hello. Say hello.[95]

The intention behind the nudity and the friendly waving hand of the plaque is clear to us. The man and the woman have laid down their weapons, their clothing, their privilege; they come in peace. Like us, they stand totally naked 'in face with' an unknown other, at the edge of an abyss across which they long to be able to extend themselves. But the anxiety of interpretation might well threaten to overwhelm them: and how well we know the shape of that anxiety. Will 'they' see us as we really are? Will they project their own hopes and fears onto us? How shall we communicate with beings whose lives we can't begin to imagine, with whom we might have no common ground at all? Do you think that they will read our signs? Will they understand us when we say hello?

Don't be scared. It's time to talk about audiences.

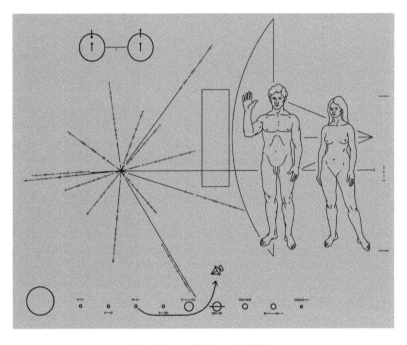

The Pioneer 10 plaque © NASA.

3. Signal and noise

> Whatever it may have been in the past, the idea of content is today mainly a hindrance, a nuisance, a subtle or not so subtle philistinism.[1]
>
> — Susan Sontag, 'Against Interpretation'

> Well, content is never more than an extension of form and form is never more than an extension of content. They sort of go together is the absolute point. It's really hard to think of one without the other; in fact, I don't think it's possible.[2]
>
> — Robert Creeley

> …form is rarely read until it is broken…[3]
>
> — Marie-Anne Mancio, *An A-Z of The Ting: Theatre of Mistakes*

Audience members responding to my theatre work have sometimes offered me variations on: "I liked it – but I'm not sure I got it." I always reply (or want to): "Hey, if you liked it, you got it." But their remarks contain in miniature a rich and complex set of ideas about what it's like to be part of an audience; and lying beneath my glibly reassuring comeback is a considered statement about what I hope to do as an artist. So: to those audience members – not only of my work but of any theatre they felt they liked but maybe didn't 'get' – I should like to dedicate this chapter: which opens with a scene from near the beginning of *Enter the Dragon*.[4]

Bruce Lee is in the garden with a student, and he says to the student: "Kick me." So the student tries to kick him, and Bruce Lee says: "What was that? An exhibition? We need emotional content! Try again." The student has another go, but Bruce is unimpressed: "I said emotional content, not anger! Try again." A third time the student kicks his master, and this time Bruce is pleased. "How did it feel to you?", he asks, and the student replies: "Let me think…"

"Don't think!" says Bruce Lee, slapping his pupil. "Feel!"

And he goes on to explain: "It is like a finger pointing away to the moon. Don't concentrate on the finger or you will miss all that heavenly glory."

This is an idea that originates in the Surangama Sutra, a key text in Mahayana Buddhism. The Buddha tells Ananda, his disciple:

> You…still listen to the Dharma with the conditioned mind, and so the Dharma becomes conditioned as well, and you do not obtain the Dharma-nature. This is similar to a person pointing his finger at the moon to show it to someone else. Guided by the finger, the other person should see the moon. If he looks at the finger instead and mistakes it for the moon, he loses not only the moon but the finger also. Why, because he mistakes the pointing finger for the bright moon.[5]

My own first encounter with this parable of the finger and the moon, however, was in a rather different context: the educationalist Sir Ken Robinson, in a 2011 talk on the topic of 'passion', used it as a way of distinguishing the human capacity for acts of imagining:

> I'm convinced that the most distinctive feature of human life is [the] power of imagination. If you take a small baby into the garden…at night, and point at the moon, the baby will look at the moon. If you take your dog into the garden and point at the moon, the dog will look at your finger… Human beings are born with expansive imaginations, and a sense of reference and possibility.[6]

So, Robinson and the Buddha are slightly at odds here. What Robinson calls "imagination", we might more accurately (if less romantically) think of as a propensity for *interpretation*. To the dog – if indeed Robinson is correct about this – a finger is just a finger, exactly as, to Gertrude Stein, "Rose is a rose is a rose is a rose"; but to a baby, a pointing finger is already a sign: it sees not merely a finger, but an instruction to be followed, a moment of choreography in which to participate. Robinson's description of the experience of the animal (non-human) reader who does not speak the language in which the pointing finger is a legible sign,

obviously recalls the critics of the Pioneer plaque who sensibly think it
unwise to assume that an extra-terrestrial (non-human) reader of that
image will understand correctly that the naked man is waving hello, and
not that his arm is permanently bent like that.

The point being made by the Buddha (and implicitly by Bruce Lee)
is a more specific one: the student is foolish if he or she mistakes the
teaching itself for the enlightenment it points towards. But there is still a
broader theme here about the transactional nature of perception within
particular cultures: the present thing we actually see in front of us is
quickly traded for the absent or removed thing to which it is taken to
refer. If we only see the finger, we do not see the moon; but unless we
see the finger for what it actually is, as well as for what it may signify
within this system of "reference and possibility", then we lose our
sense of both finger and moon: the finger is too quickly traded for its
exchange value.

Susan Sontag's seminal essay 'Against Interpretation' treats of our
unwillingness to, as it were, see the finger. For complex historical reasons
that she quickly limns, we frequently struggle now to see art for what it *is*,
hoping only to come into what feels like a meaningful relationship with
what it is 'about', with what the artist is 'trying to say'. (This formulation
is often particularly frustrating to artists, as it immediately demeans
their work by embedding in the critical response a sense of failure or
underachievement. As the novelist Julian Barnes says, for example,
during his appearance on the radio programme *Desert Island Discs*: "The
question that you're often asked is: What were you trying to say in such-
and-such a novel? To which the answer is: What I was trying to say was
what I did say… What you are – too often perhaps – invited to do is…
reduce a sort of complex novelistic structure to some Christmas cracker
motto, some little piece of wisdom which is what you were really 'trying
to say' all along."[7]) The determination of audiences of different kinds to
'unlock' the work of art, to exchange it for a concise and disambiguated
summary of its operations and of the artist's motivation in making it,
repels Sontag because – just as the inattentive disciple misses the 'point'
of the finger and thus destroys both the finger and the moon – the
seeker after the 'latent' content lurking Freudianly beneath the 'manifest'
content of an artwork both diminishes and vandalizes it. Poignantly to
later readers, she suggests from her vantage in 1964 that both abstract
art and Pop art are "in flight"[8] from interpretation – not an ideal state of
affairs, she thinks, since art should not be condemned to such a fugitive

position, but at least one way of resisting the reductive 'deciphering' approach; fifty years on, we see how the paintings of key figures like Pollock and Rothko are almost unavoidably overlaid with biographical readings of their work – indeed, it could be argued that such artists become key figures partly *because* their biographies are most susceptible to these interpretive manoeuvres; meanwhile the iconic images of Warhol and Lichtenstein, so "blatant"[9] (to borrow Sontag's word) as to seem to defy the interpretive impulse, are nonetheless everywhere co-opted into narratives both grand and inert about consumer capitalism and the performances of the art market itself, to the extent that these excursive interpretations become what the work is indelibly 'about'.

Theatre – which generally tends away from pure abstraction, not least because it mostly draws our attention continually towards the human figure and invites us to enter into a human relationship with that figure by means of recognition and perhaps empathy – is hugely open to interpretation, partly because the critical culture around it remains desperately underdeveloped: everybody wants to say what a play or performance is 'about', to draw out what the writer or director is 'trying to say', to demonstrate an acuity of insight in relation to what's *behind* or *beyond* the work, in the hope that these skills will divert us from the poverty of the language and the paucity of attention which is being applied to the task of saying what's there, what's actually been seen and heard and how those things relate to each other, how they move, and what is made in those movements – a language of form, in other words, a way of seeing form.

But if content is wildly overemphasized (because it can be traded for interpretation in the marketplace of saleable readings) and form disastrously underacknowledged, it is not simply the fault of a critical culture that is not sufficiently attuned to what theatre really is. It's also because as artists in theatre we are faced with a continual problem. The semiotics, the sign-language, of theatre is so extremely fragile, and so unstable, that it is of limited use as a tool for authoring. This is, in a sense, a flaw – perhaps *the* flaw – in theatre: but it's also what creates theatre's capacity for effecting powerfully moving experiences in people's lives.

The fundamental question that opens up with this radical faultline is simply: *What can you see?*

In a sense, this is merely an extension of the sometimes ambiguous viewing structure we explored in the last chapter, for which we used Michael Kirby's language of 'matrix' and 'nonmatrix'. Is the actor 'in character'? And if so, what happens when something occurs – like a nude scene – to cause us to 'see' the actor as somehow *opposed to* or existing in a divergent or contradictory relationship to their character? Likewise, are we to locate ourselves imaginatively in a place other than the theatre? And if so, what happens when we find ourselves noticing that one of the stage lights seems to be buzzing loudly all of a sudden? Do we notice the stage hands, if there are any? Do we notice them less because they're dressed in black, or does that only make them more present? Do we notice the four puppeteers animating a broken schooldesk that 'becomes' an elderly man walking tentatively across the stage? Is our immersion in that moment undermined by seeing them? Or is it somehow enhanced? How do we see through the frame of a proscenium arch differently to the way we see a performance in the round, or a flashmob on the concourse of a train station?

What, we might go on to ask, do I think I'm doing when, as has often been my practice, I try to make certain elements of my theatre works visible that might not be otherwise? When I place the lighting operator on stage with me? When I invite the actors to have printed scripts to hand? When I describe what's going to happen before it happens? When I ask actors to make real choices in front of the audience by tossing coins or drawing straws? When costume changes happen in full view? When the running order of the show is written in marker on a piece of flipchart paper stuck to the wall at the side of the stage? When I interrupt myself to talk about the sound coming into the theatre from the street outside? (Hopefully it's clear too that the equal and opposite questions could be asked of situations where all these things are concealed rather than revealed: what *then* is at stake?)

For my part, the formal and aesthetic decisions implied in this litany of questions are about not wanting certain kinds of power – the spectacular power that comes with the prestige of the stage and the authority of the artist. In part, for sure, there is a double edge to this apparent transparency: if I appear to be so strenuously honest, I can also, from time to time, afford to be a little sneaky. But the basic impulse is genuine. It just isn't *quite* about the visibility of those elements as an end in itself. To make something visible is not, in practice, to know that it is seen. The basic reason why I wish to divest myself of so much of my authority as a maker is not because it is politically unsound or ungroovy, but because it is untenable. This is what I mean by the sign-language of the theatre being flawed as an instrument of authorship. Everything on stage, every element that contributes to an individual audience member's experience of a constructed event in the theatre, is potentially a finger pointing to something else, either within or outside that system. It's also potentially just a finger. Sometimes that individual audience member is a baby; sometimes she's a dog; sometimes she's some weird flickering mutant dog-baby. Sometimes she's a good disciple, sometimes a bad inattentive student. Crucially, she and I are either side of a gap, and from our respective situations on either side, there's only so much I can do to make sure she doesn't miss the moon – especially if she's really enjoying looking at the finger.

Hotei pointing at the moon © Fūgai Ekun.

Here's the poet Andrew Motion talking about that gap between us:

> Public readings are floating worlds – there's a strange disparity between what you're saying and how it's understood, because

people come with their own preconceptions and prejudices…
[I] have felt puzzlement bordering on dismay and disappointment at discovering that several of the things I have said have
been massively misunderstood. You must grow another layer
of skin, or become accepting.[10]

This chapter is, essentially, a study of the nature of that 'acceptance',
conceived in a desire to reposition it as a more progressive, a more
energised, a more creative 'becoming' than the somewhat tired defeatist
shrug in Motion's analysis.

Sontag – who wrote admiringly about both Bataille and (with some
reservations) Paul Goodman – ends 'Against Interpretation' with a
statement that has become well-known: "In place of a hermeneutics,"
she says, "we need an erotics of art."[11] That is: hermeneutics, the
philosophy of interpretation, has, for Sontag, ceased to be viable as a
way of bridging the gap between art and its audience through negotiated
transactions in which contextualisation promotes comprehensibility.
(And if this was true for Sontag in 1964, how much more might we
suppose it to be accurate now, when the life-experience we bring to bear
on our reading activities as audiences is so much more atomised, and
when so many of the previously dependable narratives of social and
cultural intercourse no longer obtain. The person we happen to sit next
to in the theatre is likelier than at any previous time to have a life and a
world-view vastly divergent from our own, and to be viewing the work
on stage through very different eyes.)

When Bruce Lee slaps his student and crossly says "Don't think! Feel!",
what he's really saying to the lad is: "In place of a hermeneutics, we need
an erotics of art." Sontag, of course, is not advocating – any more than
I would – a policy of privileging affect at the expense of intellection: if
anything, she's asking for a bolder, more intimate thoughtfulness, one
that confronts head-on the object of desire, without – to use her word
– 'taming' it: "Real art has the capacity to make us nervous,"[12] she notes.
We cannot do enough, we cannot be enough in relation to ourselves and
each other, in the face of what Bruce Lee calls "an exhibition". We need
emotional content: by which I take Lee to be referring not to 'content'
at all, but to form – that motile armature which requires of us not our
strenuous interpretive dancing, but only our human nervousness: our
thoughtful inhabiting of the ambiguous region between the finger and
the moon.

To know the universe, one must examine its garbage.[13]

— Kazuo Ohno

...Rubbish is
pertinent; essential; the
most intricate presence in
our entire culture; the
ultimate sexual point of the whole place turned
    into a model question.[14]

— J.H. Prynne, 'L'Extase de M. Poher'

In 1997, something rather significant happened to American poetry: something that went largely unnoticed and unremarked, even by those poets on whose writing a markedly different light was suddenly shone.

In that year, the Standard Industrial Classification (SIC) system, which for the past sixty years had been used by the US government as a taxonomy for tracking and analyzing data relating to industrial activity, was largely replaced by the comprehensively updated North American Industry Classification System (NAICS). The reboot was intended to reflect important changes in the structures underlying and the perceptions surrounding commerce and the economy. In that shift between systems, many industrial sectors were reclassified, none perhaps more radically than that relating to publishing and the arts. At the beginning of 1997, poetry was classified as a branch of manufacture; by the end of that year, it had been definitively redescribed as belonging to the sector of American industry called 'information'.

In a sense, this change did no more than its useful face-value work of bringing the classification system used by government and other agencies into line with the emerging reality on the ground – or in the air – of what was by then quite widely being referred to, in line with Marc Porat's coinage of 1977, as the 'information economy'[15]. In particular, it was clear by the mid-nineties that the world wide web, and other corners of the internet such as Usenet, were profoundly and irreversibly changing and extending the means by which literary and artistic productions were disseminated and the forms in which they may be encountered or might need to be protected: and so the transition to NAICS, and numerous subsequent updates of the newer system, sought simply to respond to this. But it is not a simple manoeuvre, not merely an administrative procedure, to assert such a modification of the 'place' of, for example, poetry: to shift the focus away from the manufactured object of the book to the essential data of the poem itself. As the US Census Bureau plainly states: "The value of these products to the consumer lies in their informational, educational, cultural, or entertainment *content*, not in the *form* in which they are distributed."[16] [my emphases]

Poetry, then, is positioned as a species of information which can be moved between formats without there being any substantial alteration to that information in the course of its moving. This ought, perhaps, to be recognizably true: that, for example, a poem by Wallace Stevens is not essentially different if encountered as part of a blog post on a tablet, or in a flogged-off water-damaged library book, or letterpressed on artisan paper. But we also know that it is not *completely* true, because while Wallace Stevens (in this case) has produced a poem, it is we as readers, in dialogue with Stevens, who produce the meanings of that poem. I can buy a chef's apron with Philip Larkin's 'This Be The Verse' printed on it; I can use part of Gertrude Stein's 1935 recording of her own 'A Valentine to Sherwood Anderson' as my ringtone; I can arrange to have Paul Celan's 'Todesfuge' iced onto a birthday cake: I cannot really accept that my experience of each of those poems in those renderings is the same as it would be reading them in some nicely-produced anthology of twentieth-century poetry. But then: I also cannot really accept that reading those poems in such an anthology is quite the same experience if the book is set in Palatino as opposed to Garamond (let alone Comic Sans).

What's crucial about the material form of the poem in our encounter with it is not, or not merely, that it may enhance or enrich or helpfully complicate our relationship with the 'information' of the poem itself, but that it is, to the reader at least, *an extension of* the formal activity of the poem-as-information. NAICS chooses to treat that materiality as irrelevant, presuming that only the content of the poem is of 'value', but part of that content *is* form, and the point at which form supposedly tips over into being of no or negligible value is impossible to discern. In other words, NAICS is apparently blind to the 'form' embedded within 'in-form-ation'. The shape of the poem shapes the reader: if information changes us, form is the shape of that change.

It is interesting, in the light of the reclassification of poetry as information, to wonder what Wittgenstein would have made of the transition. As he writes in *Zettel*: "Do not forget that a poem, even though it is composed in the language of information, is not used in the language-game of giving information."[17] This remark serves as a point of departure for the poet and critic Veronica Forrest-Thomson in her influential study *Poetic Artifice* – which she was writing at the same time as Marc Porat was completing his thesis on *The Information Economy*:

> We must try and describe the language-game in which poetic language is used, and here the initial difficulty is the relationship between the language-game of poetry and what Wittgenstein calls the language-game of giving information.[18]

With the introduction of NAICS, the task of distinguishing between poetry and information has completely flipped its polarity: we are no longer seeking to describe what is self-evident to Wittgenstein, and axiomatic but problematic to Forrest-Thomson; instead we occupy a position of dissidence, a conviction that to classify poetry as a kind of information whose form is immaterial is not merely to reduce it but to abandon it, to render it terminally incomprehensible.

I have started here with poetry, rather than theatre, because the material nature of most of our encounters with poems – the fact that we meet them, not exclusively but most often, as objects rather than processes – makes the poem's status as informational artefact *and* formal entity more legible. With theatre, there is no such object: the target is not only moving but, in a sense, self-destructing – disappearing, and anyway appearing only provisionally; there may be objects before or after the fact – a play script on the desk, a body of documentation in the archive – but the audience's task is to establish relations with an event, and to perceive the movements within that relationship: and as such, it is less difficult to accept that the staged event is essentially a source of streaming information – especially if we are careful to preserve and attend to the sense of 'form' within that information.

What, then, are the kinds of information that theatre moves around? This is a question that often matters in particular, and in a fairly rudimentary way, to some makers whose intentions – responding to the collective, the communal and the civic affordances that certainly seem to be present in the theatrical situation – are avowedly political. Agitprop, in its various guises, has often been despised not (only) for the explicitness of its ideology or the raggedness of its materials but for the crudity of its impulse towards information-sharing; some echo of the same attitude perhaps informs the reception in some regions of the contemporary scene of verbatim documentary works, especially those that aim towards a scrupulous accuracy of rendition, such as Richard Norton-Taylor's *The Colour of Justice* (which drew on the transcripts of the Stephen Lawrence inquiry) and *Bloody Sunday: Scenes from the Saville Inquiry*, or those which present a body of research in a more pedagogical way, like David Hare's *Stuff Happens* and *The Power of Yes*. (I was struck, watching the latter during its run at the Lyttelton, by how much more theatrical vitality was to be found in the programme, which included a spread presenting certain statistics regarding the financial crisis with which the play was concerned, and doing so in an attractive and immediately compelling way through the graphic designs of David McCandless, author of *Information is Beautiful*.)

In this context, however, information is not just a set of facts to be imparted or ideas to pass on. Narrative is a kind of information; so too is colour; and so are gesture, and clothing, and metre, and perspective, and kissing, and sound design, and the movement of eyebrows, and the fading of lights. It is not a stretch to think of Shakespeare's plays as being packed with information – historical narrative, philosophical testimony, social portraiture; easy, too, in a way, to see live art as informative, in so far as it often stages actions which are presented as nonmatrixed fact-like events: here, say, is Ron Athey's blood, for real, dripping from his head, and here he is fisting himself, and this is in a sense quite pure information: it does not require (though it may not preclude) interpretation: those actions may speak to a political situation, say, but their ritual quality does not prevent them from being actions that are here with us now, that inform us, that invite us to admit them into our experience and somehow take their shape into ourselves.

What kind of information, though, is coming through in a piece such as Robert Wilson and Philip Glass's *Einstein on the Beach*? It is not, for example, all that functional as a biographical sketch of Einstein – though those who go in knowing Einstein's biography will find numerous fragments of his life refracted through the stage world as images and in-jokes. There are patterns of repetition and variance that suggest a basic narrative grammar, but not enough corollary information to populate such a narrative. There are texts which seem to report from a real world – the "prematurely air-conditioned supermarket"[19] of Lucinda Childs's composition, or the AM radio disc jockeys celebrated in the strange, dazzlingly beautiful writing of Wilson's autistic collaborator Christopher Knowles: but most of these texts seem to obey only an independent interior logic, pivoting endlessly on unresolved ambiguities – never wholly incomprehensible but never quite arriving in the territory of the understood. There is stillness, slowness, recursion, but also ineffable speed, especially in Glass's relentlessly permutating, often hurtling score: music which sounds like raw information, like data spilling endlessly from a broken pipe. Despite appearances, despite a sense that what we see in *Einstein* is some kind of poetry, there is little in it that responds to interpretation: its systems are not lubricated by the permissiveness of metaphor or fixed-gauge symbology. (Small wonder that Wilson was one of Sontag's favourite theatre makers.) Perhaps the most useful information in watching *Einstein on the Beach* across its five-hour duration is that which is imparted directly to the spectator before the show begins: you are free to exit and enter the auditorium at will. This, of course, doesn't just define the etiquette of choosing (if one wants) one's own interval; it changes how you watch what you're watching, how you listen to what you hear. It fundamentally alters your sense of the formal relationships that will shape your experience.

In contemporary theatre – which, for all its ravishing pleasures and excitements, the 2012 revival of *Einstein on the Beach* (1976) did not quite seem to be – it is those makers who, consciously or otherwise, are particularly adept at manipulating the technologies of information (not information technology) who most successfully create what feels like culturally urgent work. Kieran Hurley's solo play *Beats* is a terrific example of a smart, hugely popular show that derives much of its dynamism from the interplay between different registers, different frequencies, of information. At one level, Hurley's story simply plays through the tensions between three characters: Johnno, a teenage Scottish lad launching himself nervously into the mid-nineties free party scene for the first time; his mother; and a police officer nearing retirement, who ends up beating Johnno with his baton as the rave is broken up. There's a layer of highly detailed, magic-tinted social realism in the storytelling. But there's also a documentary element, with Hurley keen to situate his tale against the backdrop of the framing and passage of the Criminal Justice Act of 1994, including a brilliant account of the response of dance music duo Autechre to the provisions of the Bill. Near the very top of the show, after a brief montage of some of the voices that the piece will go on to feature, Hurley addresses his audience, introducing himself and the collaborating on-stage DJ and setting up what's to come:

> Hi
>
> In 1994 the Criminal Justice and Public Order Act made it illegal to have certain gatherings of people around, and this is a quote; 'music wholly or predominantly characterised by the emission of a succession of repetitive beats.'
>
> I'm Kieran. This is Johnny Whoop. And none of this is real.
>
> In a minute I'm going to tell you a story.[20]

There is a huge amount of information in this short passage, beginning with the greeting, "Hi": which tells us, as an audience, that this will not be one of those plays where we supposedly can't see each other or acknowledge each other's presence; that we're starting in a demotic register, a place where we can relax. The statement of fact that follows then sets up the whole piece – not just the context of the story itself, but the context that places us within the constructed space in which a young man called Kieran introduces himself: "I'm Kieran." Already, saying who you are becomes framed as an act with a political valency and, somehow, a backstory. But just a few seconds later, the same man who said "Hi" to us, who refused the protection of the 'fourth wall', will have said: "None of this is real." And the move *en passant* is to introduce us to the DJ "Johnny Whoop", whom we will feel pretty certain is not named 'Johnny Whoop' on his birth certificate: and the extent to which the act of saying who you are is already a performative act, an act with the capacity to unsettle, to align and to separate, will be coming into focus as we are told "none of this is real": which we will know, or will want to know, is both a plausible statement to be made by an actor on stage, and also a terrible lie that seems to reject the factual currency of everything that Hurley's told us so far. Reality, we seem to be being reminded – and so early on!, is not a given, not necessarily something we hold in common, not necessarily something uncontested. So that when he finally says: "In a minute I'm going to tell you a story," there is something quite unnerving about the quiet implication that "I'm not telling you a story yet."

Not all of the information in *Beats* is told to us by Hurley. The two performances of it that I've been fortunate to see are shaped partly by the presence not only of the on-stage DJ but also the unseen VJ, whose video manipulations are projected on a screen above Hurley's head, as well as someone operating a rig of club lights. The interplay of these elements, particularly at their most full-on as the party builds to its climax and Johnno comes up on MDMA for the first time, feels like an essential source of information, especially for those (like me) who may not have first-hand experience of what's being described in the story. At the same time, I think back to my first taste of *Beats* – of sitting on the bare concrete floor of The Situation Room, Jonny Liron's live/work studio in Tottenham, with a few other leftist theatre folks, listening to Kieran read a short extract from the then-unfinished piece, with no music, no club lighting, no visuals: just a circle of friends, leaning in to keep faith with a nervous, unadorned voice. This too was thrilling, in a very different way.

The published script of *Beats* has a clear prefatory note regarding those light and sound elements that make such a difference in performance – not least the importance of the DJ, who performs the show just as much as Hurley does, on an equal footing; this is carefully framed as a note "on the original production",[21] but there is a clear implication that these strands of information are seen by the author as crucial rather than in any sense extraneous. But this opens up a fascinating question, about what kinds of information can be captured, scored, translated – and what can't. What is the information that comes through in that brief bare-bones Situation Room reading, that doesn't come through in a full production; and what happens to it, where does it go? How do we use it? Where does it live in the work? How can a script tell you what a piece was like before it was finished? Before it was started, even?

These are all, in their different ways, questions about discontinuity: about the times when we are not together, or when we are fleetingly together but about to become separate again. But they all also speak, inarticulately perhaps, to a basic set of questions about the nature of information as it relates to the discontinuity, the apartness, described so dismally in Andrew Motion's picture above, of "floating worlds" and the choice that is forced: "to grow another layer of skin, or become accepting": the nature of information as it relates to the published play text, to stage directions and introductory notes, to promotional interviews and whatever remains in the archive. It's clear that the evanescence of the theatre event creates a paradox at the level of information: a whole raft of ancillary documents whose purpose is, in a sense, to protect the show, as a time-limited relational activity, from exactly the disappearing act that most distinctively and valuably characterises the maker's chosen medium.

The absence of a persistent object at the heart of the theatrical enterprise, then, makes it weirdly easier to conceive of the theatre event, rather than poetry, as a kind of information: not because the apparatus of theatre, taken as a whole, amounts to an efficient transmitter of information, but because it is so disorientingly inefficient that it makes the very category of 'information' critically, and abundantly, problematic, to the extent that the activity of theatre is always somewhat *about* information as an ethical construct.

A useful adjacent way of approaching this is through the terminology of 'signal' and 'noise', and the concept of signal-to-noise ratio. I should say straight away that although this is a language that has been of tremendous formative importance to me, I'm definitely a lay-person when it comes to the applications of this idea: electrical engineers, statisticians, optical scientists, sound technicians and so on will all have their various uses for it; mine has none of the precision of theirs – it's simply an idea that's useful for thinking with: perhaps those who are offended will oblige me by averting their gaze. Fellow general users will probably recognize the basic idea. With most signals – the signal here being the stuff we want to communicate – comes a certain amount of unwanted noise. Thomas Edison's tinfoil cylinder phonograph rendition of 'Mary Had A Little Lamb' in 1877 has a very considerably lower signal-to-noise ratio than Paul McCartney's version of the same ditty on the digitally remastered compact disc of Wings's *Wild Life* album released in 1993.

In fact, of course, it's necessary only to track the development of audio recording and playback technologies since Edison to observe that the quest for 'better' – that is, higher – signal-to-noise ratios has consistently been among the drivers for innovation in this sector, and, by extension, that noise is generally seen as a problem, as something to be reduced and ideally eliminated – just as it is for, say, astronomers trying to capture CCD images of faint stars, or political forecasters trying to disregard unhelpful or misleading data in order to predict polling outcomes. (The celebrity psephologist Nate Silver's best-selling first book was called *The Signal and the Noise*.) In these contexts, noise is, by definition, that which is undesired, and which we consequently seek to minimize.

In his published diary for 1995, however, the musician Brian Eno suggestively reconstrues 'noise' – as it relates to information – from a different perspective:

A signal sent through a medium interacts with it in complex
ways and some of the information breaks up into – noise...
In music, noise is the signature of unpredictability, outsideness,
uncontrolledness...
   Distortion and complexity are the sources of noise.
Rock music is built on distortion: on the idea that things are
enriched, not degraded, by noise. To allow something to become
noisy is to allow it to support multiple readings.
It is a way of multiplying resonances.
   It is also a way of 'making the medium fail' – thus giving the
impression that what you are doing is bursting out of the material: 'I'm too big for this medium.'[22]

Reading for the first time Eno's paean to noise, I instinctively
understood that there was something here with which a budding theatre
maker might seek to come to terms. This was not simply a kind of
envy, that rock music, with its noisiness and richness and complexity
and 'bursting out', could be seen to be having all the fun. It was also an
intuition that theatre was ineluctably noisy, in the terms that Eno was
describing, and that the crucial question that needed to be addressed
was about how we who made things in the theatre might respond to that
noisiness. Was it our task, as so many writers and directors seemed to
think, to work – almost as engineers – to find ways to minimize noise;
or was it to work more like rock gods, to accept and foster and revel in
noise, and to discover what it might make possible?

It is not, I think, fanciful to see theatre (as we currently know it, or its
rudimentary western models) as a medium with an inherently low signal-
to-noise ratio: in fact, this is, to a great degree, simply another way of
describing the complex of conditions we normally identify as 'liveness'.
Compare, again, the theatre event with the poetic text. The reader
establishes her own relation with the text by reading 'in her own time',
perhaps re-reading, perhaps speed-reading and then refining, perhaps
starting in the middle and working outwards, perhaps returning to the
same text an hour or a week or forty years later; the audience member at
a stage event has no control over the time axis – the show burns up like
a slow fuse, vanishing in every moment; whatever is replayed later in the
mind, re-evaluated, 're-read', is already a subjective, unreliable reading,
and it already has more in common with the archive than with the event
itself. The encounter with the poem is most probably one-on-one, in a

book opened (or on a screen angled) towards the reader; theatre is, even on the fringe, still most usually seen in the company of others, and so a collective (or, at least, aggregate) reaction is produced which may or may not be aligned with one's own, and which feeds back into and potentially interferes with the personal experience of the event. Importantly, the ambiguities of a poetic text at least reside (most often) within a stable material construction, an object-like composition which will not itself move, though it may contain or suggest movement; the ambiguities of a theatre event are, at one level, immersive, and as such they place the spectator inside a fundamentally unstable construct, in which the turbulent interplay of real and non-real elements is itself productive.

At the same time, because the theatre-goer, unlike the poem-reader, has so little control over what is unfolding, the sense of the gap between stage and audience – even when it's physically suspended – is greater. The difference between being lit and sitting in the dark, between moving around and staying still, between the permission to speak and the invitation to listen, is not constitutive of the gap, but symbolic of it: the real abyss is an imbalance of power, which can be every bit as present (and is often even more strongly policed) in performance structures where the audience is nominally lit and mobile and interacting. The live event makes not only manifest but actively crucial the element of "disparity" to which Andrew Motion refers: if a home reader, curled up – perhaps due to illness or bereavement – with one of his books, "massively misunderstands" Motion's poetry, the misalignment has no further ramification. The reader may come back to the poem later and adjust her response, or she may think it a lousy poem forever, or she may be perfectly satisfied with the reading she's made of it and learn it by heart. In the live public event, however – in the dance of "floating worlds" – Motion, or whoever occupies the author's place on-stage, may be upset by the extent to which meaning and value in the transaction are co-produced. "You must grow another layer of skin, or become accepting," says Motion, and the tinge of resignation in his conclusion may perhaps be forgiven: his act, in reading his work publicly, has been, in a sense, to adapt for – or to haul onto – the stage an array of literary artefacts, written principally for the page; perhaps the public reading is not much more than a commercial advertisement for those pages. For the theatre maker, though, whose work is conceived and created first and foremost for the stage, any such disappointment is an expression of their own deep misunderstanding of their form. To "become accepting" is exactly the least one can do, except for nothing.

Here's a story about what comes after acceptance.

For a while, I enjoyed the company of an imaginary friend – an extra collaborator in the rehearsal room, a companion at my writing desk, a figure only ever glimpsed in my peripheral vision. I called him the Invisible Lunatic, and he became a kind of mascot for the work I was doing towards the end of the last millennium. There was, I remember, a class I taught at the Actors Centre: 'The Theatre of Invisible Lunatics'; a paper I gave at the Cambridge Conference of Contemporary Poetry: 'Towards a Poetry of Invisible Lunatics'.

The Invisible Lunatic was – being an imaginary friend – no more than an idea with a name attached, and the name and the idea were one and the same. As you may already have recognized or deduced, "invisible lunatic" is the output phrase generated (perhaps apocryphally) in an automated translation of the English idiom "out of sight, out of mind" into, say, Hungarian and back again. His presence was a constant reminder of the law that underscores all theatrical activity: as information travels, it is changed in transit by the medium it moves through. A simple signal sent through a loop arrives back where it started, transmogrified into a poetic misunderstanding of itself.

At the time that the Invisible Lunatic and I were going everywhere together, I had just set up my first professional company under the name Signal to Noise. The name never really caught on because no one understood what we were doing with it. (From one organization into whose database we'd been inadvertently absorbed, we used to receive items of correspondence addressed to 'Signal to the Nose': which at least had an ironic touch of invisible lunacy to it.) At a time when British theatre felt meagre to us, hemmed in by irony and the first intimations of what became – and remains – a fetishization of failure *as the opposite of success*, it seemed adamantly generous, romantic even, to invoke in our company name the overwhelming rush of noise that we hoped would kaleidoscope even our strongest signals into a beautiful chaos of unexpected colours and patterns, formed by failure *as an engine of proliferation*. But to those who hadn't yet seen our work, it wasn't clear we weren't a small company of performance boffins who carried an oscilloscope everywhere we went.

Particularly in our first show, the surprisingly mid-scale ensemble piece *The Consolations*, we brought to a kind of apotheosis some of the tendencies that had been shaping my work over the previous three or four years before the company came into being. A fragmentary narrative, driven by what seemed to be a sort of dream logic; the use of multiple spoken languages, and quite often no speaking at all, but rather gesture, image, dance, and, when in doubt, a mirrorball; bodies, stark or illegible, meeting and separating, coming and going, coming and sometimes staying, dressing and undressing; layers and layers of sound, woozily shifting in and out of comprehensibility; a UFO fly-past and a man greeting it in a best attempt at dolphin language; lists and love songs and lines from Shakespeare and rough sex and an erratically freeform trombone solo, and, as a kind of apogee at the end of the first half, a stage filled with several dozen de-tuned radios blaring their indignant static. Most of the characters – there were, at least, characters – seemed to have wandered in from a bunch of completely different shows: from the worlds of Russian clown and Austrian performance art and Belgian dance-theatre and American po-mo storytelling. Maybe some people who saw it told each other the story afterwards, or in the interval even; maybe they argued over plot-points that were radiantly obvious to them and which had never passed through our collective minds, not even slightly. But I think we hoped they would feel that they had been moved by something that resisted decoding or interpretation, something that placed its resources just out of that intellectual reach and invited its audience to be moved instead by its formal score: its shifts, its cadences, its rapid cuts and strategic longeurs, its slips and slides and glances, its will to surprise and to seduce. I can't claim that all of this was immaculately composed – in fact, as we began the first performance for a paying audience, I still hadn't finished script-writing the second act (but, ah, what's an interval for?), and the climactic scene five minutes from the end of the show existed as nothing more than a couple of loose unrehearsed ideas around which the actors were obliged to improvise: but what I think we did reliably know, even in the midst of such mayhem, was that this all required a curious bravery on everyone's part, that would communicate itself more vividly and appealingly than any slickness or easy facility could; that a truly noisy environment in which our desires could be excitingly and authentically signalled required of us an unstinting faith in our noncontrol and in the integrity of not-knowing.

More than anything else, *The Consolations* was the show in which I started understanding the vital importance of what I've come to call 'scuffing'. Perhaps the closest analogue to this practice outside of theatre is what's known as 'greebling': the adding of detail and texture to (usually, these days) a computer-generated surface, so as to make it look more real. The origin of the term is in sci-fi, where it was more about adding 'cool stuff that doesn't do anything but looks as if it does' to spaceships or robots or costumes. Much of our perception of the world we live in has to do with an apprehension of or engagement with texture; when simulated or synthetic worlds fail to convince, it is often because they do not have the level of high-resolution detail to pass as real. This visual, quasi-tactile information – and sound designers often do the same in their medium – is a kind of useful noise. We can recognise similar procedures in popular music: the scratchy vinyl samples that make some digital hip-hop feel warmer and more 'authentic'; the whole nineties genre of 'lo-fi', where low signal-to-noise ratios become an aesthetic which is taken to connote a kind of truthfulness in the face of commercial mendacity; or the lengths to which a contemporary act like Boards of Canada will go to imbue their recordings with the characteristic distortions of worn cassette tape – borrowing the limits of an obsolete medium, just so they can inhabit the precariousness, the inverted prestige, of those limits. (See also My Bloody Valentine, whose extraordinary album *Loveless* I bought on cassette in 1992 and listened to over and over again, only to have a college friend suggest to me that I should take the tape back as it was obviously damaged; imagine my relief a couple of years later when I picked up a copy on CD and found that what had sounded to my friend like damage was part of the design.) My own interest in 'scuffing' is essentially a subtle application of these processes to theatre: I'd use such techniques to warm up and open out a sequence that has perhaps been made with particular care and precision, or too artful a degree of control, by gently harming it: in other words, by letting it be a little inflected by the noise it will anyway yield to as soon as it really starts to meet its audience. What scuffing and greebling and lo-fi and Eno's musings all share is an understanding that noise – like rubbish – can be information-rich provided its presentation is comprehensible and attaches somewhere to a larger narrative of value or meaning-production; it may be that in these circumstances, as the critic John Hall puts it, "you find yourself treating the noise as the signal."[23]

The Consolations – even the title was partly a deliberate mishearing (of 'constellations'), another glitch in the data stream – was warmly received by almost all of the hardly-anyone who saw it: but one cast-member's parent confessed to a certain sadness. It had seemed to him that our commitment to noise was a melancholy one, a worldview in which all the signals were lost, and humans were endlessly thwarted in their forlorn, inevitably obliterated attempts to communicate with each other.

Chris Goode / Signal to Noise, *The Consolations*. The Place, 1999 © Sarah V. York.

That there is a certain appeal to such a vision of the world – or to such a view of theatre as a space for telling stories about the world – is hard to deny, especially if we aim at least partly to critique the ways in which capitalist societies aim systematically to inhibit and crowd out attentive communication between persons as a quite deliberate strategy; and it follows that not much in my body of work is wholly free of exactly that order of melancholy. But the theatre of Signal to Noise, and the work that I've continued to do since that company fell quietly into desuetude, did not set out to downcast its audience or dampen their ardour. We wanted it to sing with the optimism of a kind of sincerity that, at that stage, did not feel as dishonourable as it does now; we wanted to insist that storytelling was still possible, was in fact necessary; it just needed to look, and feel, like something else now: something truer to our experience at the end of one century and the beginning of the next. A mode of storytelling that welcomed misunderstanding and disorientation and the collision of floating worlds; that contained and exemplified and harnessed to its own ends the impulses of transition and revolution; that was faithful not to the deadly rollercoaster formulae of playwriting classes but to the lived shapes of love and anger and sex and hope and to the contours of the city that hurt us and protected us, then as now.

Still, the question deserves pursuing a little further. What is the virtue of a noisy theatre? Its aesthetics may or may not appeal, but on what basis can a claim be made for its radicalism, and for the imperatives that follow? If noise obliterates signal as paper covers rock – or as bushel smothers light – how will we ever get anything *built*, beyond a giant beautiful heap of fragmented cultural detritus? What, and where, and where above all within theatre, is the ethical index of information?

———

Failure: accident, mistake, weakness, inability, incorrect method, uselessness, incompatibility, embarrassment, confusion, redundancy, incoherence, unrecognizability, absurdity, invisibility, impermanence, decay, instability, forgetability, disappearance.[24]

— Matthew Goulish, 'Failure: an elegy',
in *39 Microlectures in proximity of performance*

Honour thy error as a hidden intention.[25]

— Brian Eno & Peter Schmidt, from the 'Oblique Strategies'

As we know from John Cage's frustrated anechoic adventures, noise goes with us: wherever we are alive and kicking, wherever blood hums and neurons squeal, noise is as much a marker of human presence as the hindbrain rhythms of breathing and blinking. But as much as it is pervasive, noise is also specific, contingent and political: it is always framed subjectively, it is always defined against its plausible opposites (signal, sound, 'silence'), and it always has to do with what is and isn't wanted.

A helpful territory in which to study the politics of that wanting is the genre – or, rather, the order – of Noise music. Even the appellation 'Noise music' signals a kind of paradox, albeit one we have already rejected in this chapter: if noise is fundamentally undesirable, then for it to attain the condition of music seems, at least, perverse. But we have seen how noise as a presence within organized music can be enriching and resonant: and everything else is a question of degree, and of circumstance, and of personal taste; perhaps capital-N 'Noise' is a bit like the BDSM of music: everyone will draw the line somewhere, and what makes some users recoil will be barely sufficient to keep others awake.

Noise as a vector within modernism has a distinguished, or at least a

distinct, history, which can be traced back at least as far as Futurist and
Dadaist agents such as the Russolo brothers and Kurt Schwitters, and to
the maverick sonic experiments of Satie, Varèse and Antheil. For all of
them, in various ways, the story of culture in the twentieth century is of
a tendency always towards increasing complexity: away from the simple,
the consonant, the resolved, towards the dissonant, the ambiguous, the
fractional: towards a contested aural bricolage heavily inflected by the
sounds of heavy industry and city traffic and the experience of war: the
noise-life of modernity. There is a drive towards an expanded lexis of
sound art, which does not posit an escape from noise, but rather seeks
to accommodate and direct the energy of noise's vandalizing, liberating
proliferation. Continual, desirous nudging at the edges of what can (just
about) be tolerated – the excitement of noise's challenge to the settled
integrity of the 'cultured' individual – eventually permits work whose
only material is noise, somewhat composed perhaps as in Lou Reed's
notorious (and, to these ears, pretty ravishing) *Metal Machine Music* (1975),
or aggressive and not wholly controlled, as in the live work especially of
groups like Throbbing Gristle or Whitehouse.

At the present time, the artist who perhaps appears above all others
to have pursued Noise into its most compelling and vivacious territories
is the Japanese artist Masami Akita, a.k.a. Merzbow (with an explicit
nod to the precedent of Schwitters, whose *Merzbau* project renders in
architectural space many of the defining gestures of Noise). Though
others, following Merzbow's lead, have arguably gone further – I have a
particularly soft spot for the hysterically extreme recordings and often
abortive performances of Masonna (briefly Akita's bandmate in the
shortlived supergroup Flying Testicle) – it is Merzbow who, due partly
to the giddying size of his discography and his evident determination
to continue to pursue new directions and ideas, seems to exemplify
almost iconically the tendentious cultural position and meaning of
Noise.

In 1994, the small Swedish record label The Releasing Eskimo put
out as its first disc Merzbow's album *Noisembryo*. As well as the regular
CD, there was a limited edition of fifty copies with a specially numbered
cloth cover, packaged in a carton which also contained a 'noise-shirt'
and a can of mushrooms relabelled 'Merzbow noiserooms'.[26] Famously,
however, there was also an even more limited edition available: a single
copy of the disc came sealed in a used Mercedes 230. The car's CD
player was rigged so that playback began when the car was started, and

was then impossible to turn off.

The punchline to the story of the Merzbow Car is that it was never sold. Is that surprising? There's normally at least someone – isn't there? – to whom any extremely limited-edition artwork is desirable. Perhaps this mischievous offering ended up too close to the plight of Schrödinger's Cat: as soon as the car's USP was put to the test (even for authentication purposes), its resale value would have collapsed. In a way, the bathos of the story only reflects the unsaleability of the merchandise in such a way as to endorse the implicit argument of the proposition, the prank edge of the gesture: the Merzbow Car is simply a material realisation of what is often taken to be a conceptual truism: that noise (especially in so far as it's pursued and desired in Noise music) is intrinsically inimical to the operations of commodity capitalism. After all, as we have seen, except within certain quite narrow and oppositional cultural parameters noise is merely a problem to be solved, an unwanted presence that efficient systems need to minimize.

In his essay 'Noise as Weakness', Paul Hegarty offers a useful typology of Noise and the ways in which it's viewed and discussed: noise as ecstatic, noise as extreme, noise as "physically threatening", as proliferant, as irrational, as "the culture industry's last gasp"[27]: and so on. Against these theoretical encapsulations he posits noise as a kind of weakness, trapped in a permanent state of short-fall and ambiguity. It is a weakness that inheres in the category: Noise when it is sought-after ceases to be noise; likewise when it becomes familiar, when we come to an accommodation with it. Noise can never achieve the total 'extremity' towards which it is oriented; it never quite succeeds but nor can it ever altogether fail because it always includes and anticipates its own failure. Interestingly, Hegarty describes noise as a "material that is emission, not presence",[28] and as such unfeasible "in either commercial, artistic or communal circuits".[29] As soon as we study it, value it, crave it, we also elevate it to a position where its own category is desolated. The weakness of Noise, then, is in its fragile, radical unviability: it has no place to be and nowhere to go. But we can, nonetheless, see ourselves encountering noise: we can consider our relationship with noise, our own desire for what is noisy, and the pleasure we may take in somehow becoming more susceptible to noise ourselves.

Let's get into this through the work of two quite different artists, both American, both called Basinski. They are Michael Basinski, poet and librarian; and William Basinski, composer and sound artist. Neither would identify 'Noise' as their medium as Masonna might, but both have made profound engagements as artists with the power (and the weakness) of the noisy, in ways that might well appeal to theatre makers.

William Basinski's best-known work to date is a set of four albums known collectively as *The Disintegration Loops*; the project sits in an interesting space, presenting work that is both sonically and conceptually rich without depending on a listener's cognizance of the full context of the work to appreciate it. Each album comprises two or three long pieces (between roughly ten and sixty minutes in duration) created by transferring to digital format a set of old reel-to-reel tape loops, recorded in the 1980s and capturing processed extracts from easy-listening radio broadcasts. Basinski's discovery – at once forlorn and serendipitous – was that as the old magnetic tape passed over the playback head, it was physically disintegrating with each repetition. This process of decay is compellingly audible in the digital capture, as more and more of the 'information' from the source tape is gradually lost: and though each of the *Disintegration Loops* pieces has its own character and tone, they all share in common this sense of jeopardy, of a live and unrepeatable performance being enacted. The circular nature of the original material is crucial in establishing a pattern through which the temporal movement of the slow dilapidation can be tracked, and an engrossing tension arises between the decorative stasis of the music and the perilous quality of its constant erosion.

If ever an artwork produced richness out of noise, it is *The Disintegration Loops*. There is inevitably a quite open metaphoricity to the work: it is immediately 'about' life cycles, about diurnality and ageing and death, bereavement and loss and the persistence that runs underneath them – which means that it is also 'about' history and narrative, memory and forgetting, legacy and the archive, and about the human contest between 'signal' and 'noise', wherever it may be found. All of these glosses – at once vague and yet uncannily apropos, like horoscopes – have been (one might say tyranically) activated in particular by the close association of *The Disintegration Loops* with the World Trade Center attacks of September 11th 2001, which coincided with the composer's completion of the first of the recordings, such that he was videotaping the smoky aftermath of the attacks from the window of his Brooklyn apartment as he and his friends listened back to the crumbling music for the first time. Images of 9/11 feature on the cover art of successive commercial issuances of the recordings, and Basinski dedicates the work to the victims of those attacks; it will be for individual listeners to consider for themselves whether the insistence on this connection enhances or inhibits the emotional and intellectual resonance of the works themselves.

For me, *The Disintegration Loops* is also a work about theatre: about its disappearances and its residues, and about the drama that inheres in the directionality of our perception of time. The predicament of the loop that audibly degrades brings to mind my experience of watching (especially the first time) Complicite's *The Street of Crocodiles*, at the Cottesloe in 1992. Wanting to understand how it had moved me so much, and thinking obsessively about that question in the days that followed, I realised above all that the decisive underpinning factor in my experience was the way in which the piece made me unusually aware of the passing of time, most rudimentarily by placing an ominous event at the beginning of the show and then playing everything else essentially in a kind of flashback mode: as the narrative flowed inexorably towards what looked like being a tragic conclusion, the evanescence of every moment on the timeline became painfully beautiful, not least because it was subjected to the pressure of an unstoppable process – the passage of time – which belonged not only to the stage world but to the audience's world too: right from the start, the piece is very palpably moving towards its end. It is exactly the logic of any of the *Disintegration Loops*: we love it for its disappearance – its mortality, we might even say ("The music was dying,"[30] Basinski writes in his liner notes) – even though its disappearance is what takes it away from us, is what will eventually confiscate it from our lived experience of the present. (This sense of 'confiscation' is an essential part of what I take to be my toolkit now as a maker: to give an audience something beautiful and then to snatch it away from them is perhaps the most dependable instance in my practice of being cruel to be kind.)

The loop itself as generative – or, more pertinently, degenerative – is a rich resource. (Even my beloved 'Invisible Lunatic' owes his existence to a very simple one-twist Möbius loop.) One key scene in *The Consolations*, inspired by a field recording we made during rehearsal of the mechanical 'song' of a slightly knackered photocopier at Chisenhale Dance Space, described a subtitled dream that "kept repeating, in a loop":

And when it repeated, down at the bottom, it said:

This is a copy.

This is a copy of a c-c-copy.

Th-th-s is a c-c- a -opy f a ccop yoff f a c opy y-.

Thhxhs ss..sc a xxop;cy ff ac coppp/ y yf acc c cpcpy yy !fff a cx.xxppy xxy.[31]

– and so on, until, as the narrator of this episode, my speech had almost completely given way to a vocal performance of indecipherable noise. It is a small, two-minute sequence that simulates the presence of both mechanical and assertive noise (i.e. distortions arising both through a repeated copying process and through authorial intervention) in collaborative productions such as Harmony Korine and Christopher Wool's gorgeous monograph *Pass the Bitch Chicken* (2002), in which the two artists trade images to be passed back and forth, re-copying and assaulting or further obliterating at each stage "until the images are reduced to ghostly shadows"; or Bob Cobbing and Lawrence Upton's vast *Domestic Ambient Noise* project, in which a visual poem by one of the two makers would form the basis for a set of six 'variations' by the other, with one of these variations then being selected by the first as the source for *his* next set of variations: and this procedure is sustained across what eventually became a series of no less than three hundred published booklets between 1994-2000, using photocopying as a fundamental creative technology, and featuring "the injection of unpoetic materials... [including] packaging, clipart, Marmite smears. ..."[32]: in other words, various quintessences of the 'domestic ambient noise' we mundanely inhabit. The poet cris cheek comments on how the series implicitly critiques:

> Forms of information storage, inscribing value to information that other writers might rightly or wrongly discard, thereby challenging conventions of usage and retrieval in the pool of meaning making. [*Domestic Ambient Noise*] is beligerently [*sic*] inclusive, to the point of overload. Features are made of distending through enlargement and reduction, of 'poor qual-ity' copying, of faulty computer print outs, of high quality reproductions of what might conventionally [be] considered to be unreadable and so on. Through knowledge of such pos-sibilities, they become integrated into the 'performance' of the writing, at every stage of production and reproduction.[33]

How writing – or, for that matter, acting – might 'perform' the noise

of 'overload' or 'faultiness' is an interesting and suggestive question, in
that it starts to approach the complex presence of failure within theatre
and performance. One fascinating execution of the 'disintegration loop'
can be seen in Dan Rebellato's 2009 piece *Theatremorphosis*, created for
Suspect Culture's installation *Stage Fright* at the Centre for Contemporary
Arts in Glasgow. Rebellato succinctly describes the basis of his piece:

> My part of the installation placed an actor in a cage in the
> centre of a gallery space. The particular actor has received,
> the previous day, a short script (usually less than a minute in
> length) which they have learned. As the gallery opens, they
> begin performing it and when they finish, they immediately
> perform it again, trying to reproduce what they did the previ-
> ous time. And again. And again. With each iteration, small
> errors, new inflections, changes, stumbles, hesitations are
> folded into the performance and the piece transforms – or
> virally degrades – over the course of the day.[34]

It sounds, of course, like an actor's nightmare: to be trapped not only
in a cage but also in a looping text, and required not only to observe one's
errors but to replicate them; and yet the transformational movement
that Rebellato has in his sights speaks to a generous impulse – the wish
to acknowledge and accommodate the noise of failure which always
(though usually tacitly) accompanies any live staging of a text: there is
always some falling-short of the ideal, even if, in a sense, that strand of
failure is an essential part of that ideal, an ingredient that we interpret as
a strongly characteristic aspect of liveness.

It is interesting, though, to compare *Theatremorphosis* with a non-live
performance that makes use of noise-versus-signal with an equal but
opposite generosity: Alvin Lucier's 1969 composition *I Am Sitting In A
Room*. In this classic piece of American minimalism, a recorded text,
spoken by Lucier, is played from tape into a room, and that playback is
itself recorded on tape, slightly inflected by the sound of the room itself
as certain frequencies in the playback activate sympathetic resonances
in its material structure; as the process repeats, and each new playback
is re-recorded, the original signal of Lucier's speaking voice gradually
recedes, and the sounds of the resonant frequencies of the room
become dominant, until the text finally is unintelligible. It's an absorbing
acoustic experiment in itself, but Lucier's recorded speech deepens the
listener's relationship with the work by describing an ulterior motivation

for it: Lucier has a mild speech impediment, a stutter which is detectable at a couple of points in his reading of the text:

> I am sitting in a room different from the one you are in now. I am recording the sound of my speaking voice and I am going to play it back into the room again and again until the resonant frequencies of the room reinforce themselves so that any semblance of my speech, with perhaps the exception of rhythm, is destroyed. What you will hear, then, are the natural resonant frequencies of the room articulated by speech. I regard this activity not so much as a demonstration of a physical fact, but more as a way to smooth out any irregularities my speech might have.[35]

In Lucier's piece, the cumulative effect of the 'noise' element of the process is akin to a kind of forgiveness, a gradual blurring which moderates the 'error' embedded in the source. Where Rebellato's piece uses its liveness to some degree *against* its actors, feeding their own failure back to themselves brilliantly but (to say the least) uncomfortably, Lucier creates an event in which the mechanics of the process act out the drama of noise without the jeopardy of performance anxiety. It might reasonably be pointed out that the comparison is unfair – that Rebellato is working in theatre and Lucier in sound art or musical composition; but I'm not sure it's as simple as that. Given its essentially task-based nature, *Theatremorphosis* sits more directly in a performance or live art context (and was, after all, conceived for a gallery situation), while the mediated process of *I Am Sitting In A Room* seems in its design to anticipate the specifities of its setting – the fact that one room will have very different resonant characteristics from another, and that Lucier is content for any recorded text to be used in performance – such that the voice and the room seem to become (at least in Makavejev's sense) the actors in an unfolding relational encounter which depends on a similar 'liveness' to Basinski's *Disintegration Loops*; I don't think it's fanciful to suggest that *I Am Sitting In A Room* is first and foremost a piece of theatre.

More significantly, though, the drama of *I Am Sitting In A Room* – in its original version, at least – is played out between two contesting varieties of noise, or of 'failure': the process harnesses a noise-generating operation – a simple loop structure – and applies it to the human noise of Lucier's stammer; the drama may be predictable, but as it plays out, the utility, the productivity, of noise as a presence in human interaction is unmistakeably, and perhaps inspiringly, salient. What Lucier's piece does is to invite us to consider the possible relationships between two different (if necessarily entangled) strains of noise: systematic noise, the failure inherent in any system that involves the movement of information; and performative noise, which exists in the discrepancy between ideal and enaction (or, we might say, between mathematical space and liveable place). The noise generated by a disintegration loop is systematic: whether that's William Basinski's metal tape falling apart, or a repeatedly photocopied image becoming increasingly murky, or an online translation engine sending linguistic data on a turbulent circular journey, the limitations of the medium and the vulnerability of the material are revealed and amplified, and the outputs from that system may or may not be interesting. The cumulative 'degradations' of the texts in Dan Rebellato's *Theatremorphosis* arise out of pressurizing the gap – in this instance, an authorized gap – between intention and execution; in a sense, this too is a disclosure of the limits of a medium (human performance), but this noise is not the disinterested material entropy of data in transit – "The channel does not know the difference",[36] as one dictionary entry on 'noise' has it – but an unpredictable variance in the efficacy of targeted action. If 'noise' is always ultimately a value judgement, then systematic noise has no stake in that judgement: it proceeds at the level of fact: whereas performative noise embeds within its own production some acknowledgement of what it may indicate or connote.

Beyond this distinction, it is important to note an interest among many contemporary theatre and performance makers in failure as one species of noise to be not merely accommodated or even fostered, but actually to be deliberately staged – with that degree of deliberation even extending as far as a paradoxical retreat into comfort-zone instincts of control and high-fidelity. For example, during a 2007 conversation curated by Jonathan Burrows under the rubric 'The Imperfect Body', Tim Etchells makes a point of distinguishing between the work his company Forced Entertainment does in the format of the ninety-minute standalone studio theatre show, and their durational performance works which may last up to 24 hours, and the ways in which the idea of staging failure manifests in each. Etchells's long association with work that challenges or collapses conventional models of prestige and valuation in performance – perhaps most particularly evidenced by his project The Institute of Failure,[37] co-curated with Matthew Goulish (formerly of Goat Island) – turns out, in his own account, to harbour what seem like two quite contradictory impulses.

Etchells describes to Burrows the ways in which the long-form pieces, like the midnight-to-midnight versions of *Who Will Sing A Song To Unfrighten Me?* or subsequently *Quizoola!*, are conceived and constructed as fixed-duration systems for incubating failure:

> where there's a kind of rule structure that's pretty simple… This structure is allowed to play itself out, and in that, nothing's fixed… We contrive to set up a structure in which we are sure to fuck up, to fail. Um, we know that's going to happen, but what we don't know, what we haven't rehearsed endlessly, is the moment where we're gonna [fail]… We've set up the circumstances under which that will happen, but we haven't rehearsed the whole thing.[38]

So, for example, the duration of the work is not only one of its frames but part of its drama: as situations become unsustainable and the actors start to be affected by fatigue, failure in turn becomes inevitable, in a way that is at once broadly predictable – "we know that's going to happen" – and specifically unpredictable – "we don't know…the moment" (or the exact nature of the failure). It is a situation fraught with palpable liveness, but not with the anxiety of precariousness: the event is constructed in such a way that it is enhanced, enriched by the welcome noise of failure.

Contrast that with Etchells's description of how the company stages failure in its shorter pieces, where the material making up the work is developed in rehearsal over a long period and gradually ordered and set:

> We're working a lot with improvisation and, um, very often what you see in terms of the finished work is a kind of very scored, very highly rehearsed, very precise reconstruction of improvisation that happened sometime in the last several months or year… You know, we use the idea that it's all falling apart or that 'this is going wrong now' as a kind of dramaturgical tool. I mean it's a structuring device… In the theatre work, that's incredibly sort of, in the end, very manipulated, I think, and fixed.[39]

This, then, is not failure as a potentially disruptive factor in a live relational event, but as an appearance, a carefully controlled simulation, which may or may not be interesting to an audience at a narrative level, but is no more radically engaged with the social meaning of failure within theatre than, say, Chekhov's Chebutykin smashing the clock in *Three Sisters*, a moment which reads as sitting ambiguously between accident and purpose; Forced Entertainment may double this ambiguity by causing the weak matrix of their performance personas to flicker and warp, but their hosting of failure in this instance is enacted through gestures of control and closure. Near the end of 'The Radiant Child', Rene Ricard, writing on Haring and Basquiat, comments that: "This article is about work that is information, not work that is about information."[40] Likewise, Etchells here describes a breach in the performances of Forced Entertainment, between work that *incorporates* failure and work that is *about* failure; between work that is noisy and work that is about noise. The difference is exactly the same tension that underscores Sontag's 'Against Interpretation': as Andy Lavender has written of Robert Wilson's work, "The first question is not, 'What is it about?'…but, 'What does it do with me?'"[41]

It's revealing that Etchells freely points towards this distinction himself, because often the line is harder to read. A clear precedent for this aspect of Forced Entertainment's practice can be seen in the work of The Ting: Theatre of Mistakes, the UK-based performance company founded in 1974 by Anthony Howell and involving key figures such as Fiona Templeton and Julian Maynard-Smith (later of Station House Opera) during its seven-year existence. The company's score-based works were often rehearsed across periods of up to a year, and Maynard-Smith has said of the work that it was "extremely tightly ruled",[42] notwithstanding the company's evident interest in the category of the mistake – the error, the deviation, the lapse – as a strategy for revealing or exposing the forms and structures it was working within. Critic Marie-Anne Mancio suggests that the position of the (accidental or deliberate) mistake within the company's work changes across the lifespan of the group, essentially starting as an obvious surface feature, then becoming more embedded in the making of the work (and "fully rehearsed"[43]), and finally inflecting the thinking that precedes the devising process. Again, the company's work is both noisy and *about* noise; it wishes to draw attention to itself *through* noise and suggest readings that are shaped *by* noise. This apparent multiplicity and multilocality of error suggests at least that the 'ruling' figures in the company had much to keep them busy – that the tension between control and resistance in the Theatre of Mistakes never fully settles into a purely aesthetic programme to do with failure (noise, error) as a cherished dramaturgical agent or narrative instrument, as it is in Forced Entertainment (or, for that matter, in a typical bedroom farce).

Essentially, though, while the two concerns may overlap or each may occasionally express itself in terms of the other, it is the acceptance of noise, rather than the representation of failure, that is the radical task in theatre: the will to harness the generative fecundity of noise not by seeking to control it and determine authoritatively its parameters, but by wishing to collaborate with it, by seeing it as conducive; by treating the Invisible Lunatic as a companion, a friendly colleague, rather than as a spy or hooligan or a rival in love.

A formative influence on my own relationship with noise has been the practice of Goat Island, the performance company who operated out of Chicago between 1987 and 2009 and built strong relationships with UK audiences through crucial venues such as Arnolfini in Bristol, the CCA in Glasgow, and Dartington College of Arts. I owe much to Goat Island, and especially to their generosity in publishing a series of workbooks and other documentary materials alongside their performances, detailing their making processes and offering multiple routes into the often oblique character of their work. From these publications I soon became aware that noise was deeply embedded in the company's methodologies, above all in the form of the productive lossiness of translation: often material is devised through processes that begin in recall of or reflection on personal experience, or response to external stimulus that the individual maker has found resonant for whatever reason; but the outputs from these initial activities are usually then edited, rearranged, shared, modified, remixed, resampled. The company's performance language was always vividly alive with the energy and friction of these translations: actions and relationships show up as polysemous, unstable, arcane – and yet some trace of the initial emotion or subjectivity is preserved, so that what may be puzzling or inscrutable in performance never appears wholly hermetic or arbitrary.

One way I have often introduced the idea of noise into workshops and classrooms is through the beginning of a creative process outlined in Goat Island's *Schoolbook*, the 'textbook' documentation of their 1996 Summer School at the CCA. The exercise begins with a simple instruction: "1. Write an impossible task on a piece of paper. / 2. Pass the paper to the person next to you."[44] Some examples of such impossible tasks are then given:

> Tie a knot in a rope of water.

> Walk along a silk wire.

> Watch the back of your head.

> Jump in the air with both feet off the ground and stay suspended for 5 minutes.

> Lick your eyes without pulling them out.[45]

– and so on. The exercise then proceeds through seven further stages, with the 'information' of the impossible tasks travelling across a number of different kinds of gaps, being degraded and reconsolidated at each step until finally a performable output is reached which bears little obvious relation to its starting point. The only overt commissioning of failure here – *pace* Forced Entertainment or the Theatre of Mistakes – is in the creating and enaction of the impossible tasks: yet even these are about a kind of noise not wholly to do with failure. Indeed, in a sense, when faced with an impossible task, failure is not an option, because the stated impossibility releases the action from the possibility of success: and so – as my frequent use with students of just the very beginning of this chain of events ardently attests – there is a very liberated feeling in the room: freed from a performance task – a definable target to be competently achieved – the actors tend to apply themselves to the *theatrical* event of their inevitable short-fall with gusto: and this pleasure is only amplified by the element of noise – the utter unpredictability of individual responses to those theatre tasks.

In the light of this observation, we begin to approach a possible description of the role of noise within theatrical form: if performance sets a target – a script to be enacted, a score to be interpreted, a task to be accomplished – and noise refers to the complex of additional patterns and occurrences that permeate the event context within which the performance takes place, then theatre is the totality of the performance plus its attendant noise. Or, to rearrange the equation:

noise is the difference between performance and theatre.

For example, we might consider Alison Knowles's celebrated Fluxus event score from 1962, called 'Proposition', in which the performer's task is simply: "Make a salad."[46] This is a score that I've seen performed a number of times, sometimes at my instigation; in the performance of the score, the performer makes a salad. Here he is, sitting at a table, with a sharp knife, a chopping board, a metal bowl, some salad vegetables; patiently, he chops the ingredients, assembles them in the bowl, maybe adds a little dressing if he's brought some, mixes the salad; once the salad is made, the performance is over, the task is fulfilled.

While this is going on, a number of other microevents emerge from or arise alongside the enaction of the performance. The table is slightly wobbly, and the perfomer wonders briefly whether to stop and find a piece of paper to fold and stick in the gap that's causing the wobble, but decides that he'll ignore it. The sound of glass bottles being emptied into a recycling bin can be heard faintly coming from the foyer. The aroma of fresh salad permeates the air in the auditorium and one middle-aged woman in the audience is reminded of a picnic with an ex-lover, and suddenly this superficially banal piece of performance art means something quite different. The man sitting behind this woman is annoyed because he can't quite see properly, and even though he knows what's going on, he'd like to be able to see it. The lighting operator, noticing the agitated man, slightly adjusts the balance of the lighting in the hope that it will help the audience to 'tune in' to the performance. The performer's knife is not as sharp as it might have been, and the slicing of the cucumber seems to the performer to be taking a very long time. A teenage girl in the front row thinks the performer is very beautiful, with his kind face and his untidy beard, and for a while her attention shifts to a private fantasy of marrying the performer, or someone like him, who will calmly make salad while the children play in the garden, and coming out of her reverie she notices that she is obviously lonelier than she thought she was. Meanwhile the fiancé she came with is not watching the salad-making at all, though he is contentedly aware of the sound of it as his visual attention is trained on the lint dancing in the face of one of the stage lights and he is captivated by its movements. The performer worries he is being boring, and becomes a bit more flamboyant as he sets about tearing lettuce leaves and throwing them into the bowl. The usher looks at her watch, at the second hand, at how the second hand never quite lines up exactly with the 12. A student takes copious notes; another student a few seats away can't imagine what could possibly be worth writing down. It is a little bit too chilly in the theatre to be comfortable; some people keep on their coats and jackets, others don't. The performer starts to chop a stick of celery; someone in the audience is very allergic to celery; suddenly this is, to them, a scene of mild peril. The green emergency light over the fire exit flickers slightly, and two or three people catch it in their peripheral vision; this tiny shift in concentration is enough to cause one of those people to notice that they have toothache. The note-taking student is more and more sure this piece is a critique of commodity capitalism and private ownership; his boyfriend, who is studying fine art, sees something a bit like a still life, only it's moving. The performer, nearing the end of the task, starts to think it would have been better to make a fruit salad, and wonders if that's allowed. The performance will have taken six minutes all together; by the end of it, out in the world about 1600 babies have been born.

Well, this is a fun game. And in a way I'm concentrating on much smaller events and variations than the situation might hold. I can think of the time when Jamie Wood and I performed together in Cambridge in 2006, and during Jamie's rendering of 'Proposition', a member of the audience stepped up into the stage area and relieved himself into Jamie's salad bowl – an intervention which even Jamie blithely assumed I had pre-arranged without his knowledge: in the entire room, only the perpetrator and I knew different. Or I recall the occasion in an east London gallery in 2012 when I sprung 'Proposition' on another collaborator, a young man who, it turned out, had never made a salad, and was so confounded by the bag of supposedly commonplace ingredients with which I had supplied him that eventually he had to abandon his performance altogether, clearing away into the same carrier bag an array of sorry-looking vegetables mutilated by guesswork and blind panic.

If even such a very clearly targeted performance instruction as "Make a salad" can be the source of and occasion for such variant and unforeseeable secondary events and conditions, it is easy to see how a performance with a much lower signal-to-noise ratio is so subsumed by noise that a control reflex is rapidly triggered in any maker who hopes to express or articulate something in particular. We might accept that theatre is no more or less than a constructed space in which the emergent life of a performance "falls into place" (as Etchells smartly puts it in his conversation with Burrows); what's harder to reconcile is that the text of that performance – whether such a thing exists in a literally textual format or not – may be more or less invisible to or occluded or remote from the present audience. Quite often I perform for audiences the work of Michael Basinski. *This* Basinski is a poet, whose writing sometimes uses only that set of linguistic resources that we tend to associate most immediately with poets: that is, words, of the kind you might find in a dictionary. But more characteristically he seeks to extend his lexis – and his alphabet – through what, enlarging a term originated by visual theorist Edward Tufte, he refers to as 'chartjunk': the ever-increasing arsenal of symbols and signs with which most readers and writers are now familiar from dingbat fonts: extra-alphanumerical glyphs such as emoticons, bullets, arrows, stars, astrological symbols, musical notation, and so on. Beyond this pivotal chartjunk – most of it close to the threshold of readability (we know how to 'read' a smiley face but not necessarily how to read it aloud; we understand the function of a bullet in a list, but again, would normally feel reticent about pronouncing it; only the context, and a bit of intrepidity, will – or won't – tell us how to 'read' a playing-card diamond symbol, or whether the difference between two snowflake dingbats is or isn't strongly meaningful) – Basinski's material opens out into a realm of visual poetry: in his case, a cartoonish language in which hand-lettered text, often weirdly distended or warping or melting, meets (im)purely graphical elements including found drawings and other bric-a-brac, while the page territories these occupy are overgrown with pictograms and hieroglyphs, spores and spirals, quasi-doodled hooks and fungi.

For Basinski, unreadability is a tactic with a hardly-hidden libertarian agenda, as he notes in a short, pungent text called 'UNREADADABABLELITY':

> If there were an other recognized tradition in poetry, besides our frozen, antique, ego-centric, arrogant, frozen reading of the page, ego intoxicated, refined white flour precious poodle poet tradition it would be da tradation *[sic]* of UNREAD-ADABABLELITY or composition by improvisational render-ing of a poetry. Improvisational poetry depends upon a poem that can't be rendered comfortably with our too many current conventions, like the book, page, poem, poet... Hence all the old is vomited away into the dust bin of poetics and a most pleasant and extreme poetry of the unreadable using UNREADADABABLELITY manifests like an ectoplasm of worbs. *[sic]* ... Pure poetry process imagination where all

things written (if at all) act as signals or cues for instantaneous interpretation, like rune reading, calls to the pagan and subverts the parochial. One can hope. The poet that calls upon unreadability in any fashion extends the limits that poetry sadly constantly endures.[47]

Here, the poet speaks – of course – with forked tongue: our knowledge that there certainly is just such an 'other' parallel tradition in poetry is prodded by the embedding of 'DADA' within 'UNREADADABABLELITY' (and perhaps by the reverberations of 'BABLE' as 'Babel' or 'babble'); what's more, even as Basinski describes the predicament of unreadability he offers plenty of hints on how one might approach the 'unreadable' poem. Certainly, he and I have both given public readings of his work, though perhaps these are more often referred to as 'performances', in the particular sense that, in common with much visual poetry, the sounding of his work involves processes of analysis, interpretation and imaginative response that (weirdly, in a way) are perceived somehow to exceed the terms and conditions of plaintext reading. Above all, there is a call to spontaneity – "instantaneous interpretation" – which in itself speaks to the carrot-and-stick nature of the performance of visual poetry: in the absence of those "current conventions" to which Basinski refers, there is no agreed 'correct' way of enterting a performative relationship with the text: which makes the confrontation both intimidating and exhilarating. The formidably resistant nature of the poem requires the application of an inventive, intrepid, acutely responsive attentivity, and a willingness to find ways to express (not necessarily articulately) in sound, and/or with the body, the readings that are being produced; but the little shot of adrenalin that goes along with being 'on the spot' can sometimes open up an exciting sense of latitude and energy. Beneath that agreeable sense of spontaneity, however, lie two main challenges, both of which relate to the noisiness – semantic, optical, even ethical perhaps – of the visual poem: firstly, disorientation; secondly, doubt. These two ideas, in this context, merit a little further consideration.

A productive paradox in the far-from-straightfoward process of translating the field of a visual poem (perhaps including many extraverbal elements) into a vocal/sounded performance is that, in some ways, a visual poem like Basinski's has more in common with an aural than a literary construction. Among the conventions that this work eschews is the top-to-bottom left-to-right reading pattern that is the default setting for Western text; almost anything might feasibly be an entry point, or an exit route, or both. (Even if one wanted to force a reading in that orderly fashion, it may not always be clear which is the top of the visual field, which its left hand side, and so on.) The path of the eye across the visual field has more in common with parkour, say, than with standard methodical reading practices – especially in performance, when the pressure of the live event compels motion and rewards momentum; but what may seem radical in this mode of ocular reading – to the extent that the object can pass as 'unreadable' – is commonplace in aurality.

"All sound is queer,"[48] writes Drew Daniel of the electronic music duo Matmos, pointing us back towards Sara Ahmed's thinking-through of the politics of disorientation. We are constantly immersed in the sound of the world, we cannot close our ears at will and so we are are constantly making adjustments to tune into or out of specific sounds in the mix, the sounds and noises that will help us navigate and interpret our environment. Sound, according to Daniel, "queers the self/world boundary, all day, every day."[49] The hierarchies by which we organize our visual environment – including information on the page and the screen – and which help to make that information legible, comprehensible, are not present in the sound world. The predictable regimented linearity of alphabetic language culture, where words are put together in lines, and lines are stacked, now dominates our thinking and shapes what has become normative. Marshall McLuhan describes this shift thus:

> Until writing was invented, men lived in acoustic space: bound-less, directionless, horizonless, in the dark of the mind, in the world of emotion, by primordial intuition, by terror. Speech is a social chart of this bog.
>   The goose quill put an end to talk. It abolished mystery; it gave architecture and towns; it brought roads and armies, bureaucracy. It was the basic metaphor with which the cycle of civilization began, the step from the dark into the light of the mind. The hand that filled the parchment page built a city.[50]

For McLuhan, the really decisive shift comes with printing – for with the printed page, the printed book, come structures of privacy, of individual isolation, of the fixed point of view. For Drew Daniel, meanwhile, words are "seductive cottonballs which stuff the ears and dull the edge of what sound offers."[51]

Visual poetry, then, disorients, disrupts, offers a playful experience of 'unreadability' that reaches away from the linear rigidity and orderly rectitude of normative language use, and back towards the 'bog' of priomordial acoustic space; or, as Basinski prefers, it "calls to the pagan and subverts the parochial." But the deeper corollary of this playfulness is the doubt that comes with the suspension of normative language operations, the impossibility of *knowing* how to proceed, except by some negotiation between intuition and etiquette. Noise in most of its guises, both in theory and in practice, tends away from certainty and towards doubt: and this may be especially true of those noisy situations where language breaks down, or is broken apart: for example, when we experience pain.

In her seminal *The Body in Pain*, Elaine Scarry describes, in discussing our experience of our own pain versus the pain of others, an "absolute split between one's sense of one's own reality and the reality of other persons."[52] Because verbal language is so unequal to the conveying to other people of our experience of pain, and because pain may anyway destroy or degrade our access to language, a situation arises in which, as Scarry puts it:

> for the person in pain, so incontestably and unnegotiably pre-
> sent is it that 'having pain' may come to be thought of as the
> most vibrant example of what it is to 'have certainty', while
> for the other person it is so elusive that 'hearing about pain'
> may exist as the primary model of what it is 'to have doubt'.[53]

Furthermore, of course, there is a potential feedback loop here, in which the experience of pain is intensified by the incommunicability of that pain, by the way in which it reinscribes our discontinuity from each other.

What, then, do we see – and hear – happening in vocal performances of visual poetry, in which performers volunteer to admit themselves to the same noisy sublinguistic territories that pain occupies? To hear Lawrence Upton perform his nonverbal work, or to listen to recordings of Bob Cobbing, is often to be confronted with the sounds we know from occasions when language fails us: the sounds not only of pain and distress, but of shock and anxiety; the animalistic and the infantile; gasps and sighs and snores, and the whole battery of noises of sex and violence and imitations of the sounds of industry and war. (Much sound poetry today still stands in direct lineage with the Dadaist impulse to abandon contaminated discursive language and to use bolder paralinguistic modes to approach or reckon with the atrocious noise of the First World War.)

In a sense, then, the performance of such work has a self-harming aspect to it – and not only in the degree to which it may hurt a person's throat (to which I can attest). It might even be surmised to have a masochistic quality, surrendering one's access to language in favour of the pleasure of a more disoriented aggregation of vocal events outside the realm of normative communicative speech, on the understanding that the ambiguities and the sensational density of that subspace can be abruptly curtailed with recourse to a 'safeword': a precise single unit of verbal language that snaps off the dominance of the unutterable.

But this is just one instance of a wider tendency in which noise either acts out or gestures towards self-hurting or self-thwarting behaviours: after all, noise is still categorically 'undesirable', and so flipping it into functioning as a carrier of desire must reposition it in a functionally deleterious relationship with the information with which it is associated. Again, this is perhaps more easily perceived in relation to noisy music. Here's Michael Silverblatt talking to Dennis Cooper on Silverblatt's *Bookworm* podcast in 2012 about Cooper's avowed love for the rock band The Jesus and Mary Chain:

> It was you who said to me: you can't hear the words, they're buried in a thundering tide of music, and the creators of the song are trapped inside, trying to allow you to hear a message that their music will prevent you from hearing. And I thought: Wow! What an intention![54]

Which would seem to take us back to that post-show moment after *The Consolations* – a sad parent worrying that the signals all get lost in transmission. But once again, our task is not simply to read the battle between signal and noise, but to see ourselves and our own desires as we participate in and become amplifying instruments of that contest.

What never feels quite right – though it doesn't altogether stop me trying – is doing public readings of works by Michael Basinski or Bob Cobbing as their sole performer. Much more often, I have performed this material in consort with one or more others: for instance, as part of one event during *Lean Upstream*, a season of my work at Toynbee Studios in 2009, Jonny Liron, Keston Sutherland, Lawrence Upton and I all performed Basinski's 'The Germ of Creativity'[55] together. No rehearsal or prior discussion took place, except for an agreement to spend about a minute on each of the four pages of the text; consequently, each performer took their own improvisatory and idiosyncratic route through each section. Did this constitute one collective performance of that work, or four simultaneous renditions? It's hard to say, though it's also difficult in the end to say why that should matter; certainly the multivocality in itself communicated to our audience something about the nature of Basinski's work, and perhaps of visual poetry more generally.

Extract from *The Germ of Creativity* © Michael Basinski.

Bob Cobbing once described how his work with Lawrence Upton, for example in their *Domestic Ambient Noise* series, is often "far too complex on the page for one voice to do an adequate version of it. And therefore it's a good job to have a collaboration between the page and *two* voices."[56] It obviously makes sense that it should be so, that no one voice can contain the multiplicity of noise, that noise is intrinsically a social phenomenon; but what's particularly telling about Cobbing's remark is that it explicitly locates the page as, itself, a collaborator – just as I liked to think of my imaginary friend the Invisible Lunatic as an active contributor to the work. If noise generates proliferant alternative variants around the signal, it multiplies the possible sites at which the maker and the audience member can collaborate with that noise in the production of meaning, value, affect and response.

This is to say, then, that noise ultimately has to do not with fidelity but with access. To allow noise to be fostered and cherished is an act of hospitality: it clarifies and relaxes the problematic relationship between form and content, by encouraging the widest possible range of negotiations through which an audience can make its own sense of its experience, while simultaneously soliciting a non-interpretive response that downgrades the most heavily authored aspects of content and invites instead a direct (and hopefully less anxious) encounter with the material and formal, textural and tonal qualities of the work as it falls into place.

For some this will be too sentimental a construction, but I like the idea that, in confronting noise, we are given a picture (or a portrait in sound) of otherness. It's a way of unlocking the paradox of noise and desire: if noise is necessarily that which is unwanted, we can nonetheless want it *on behalf of others*. Somewhere in all that apparent chaos and disorder may be exactly the entry-point that someone else needs in order to make a productive relationship with an art work. (In saying this, an image comes to mind of my fascination as a kid with the static it used to be possible to watch on a detuned analogue television. In those swirling, dancing grey and white dots I seemed to see something that had to do with people, with how many of us there were and how we moved in patterns too apparently disordered to be tracked: and yet, I felt, if you could just slow it down enough, study it hard enough, stand in the right place to see it all, every bit of that white noise would make sense, like a tiny point of data being buffeted by all the other information.)

The fundamental beauty of a properly noisy theatre piece is that the question of 'getting it' becomes irrelevant. No one 'gets' the whole thing, because there is no one stable unified set of solutions to be directly downloaded from the experience. Even a simply staged, plain-text, concertedly narrative storytelling show, or a verbatim piece dependent for its efficacy on its accurate handling of factual information, will meet every member of its audience quite differently, and as makers this ineluctable condition needs to be among our first thoughts. A piece that cannot admit noise needs to go and live somewhere other than in theatre: in a leaflet, perhaps, or on military manoeuvres.

When we see our relationship with noise – in any transaction, not just in theatre – there is always an element of the Jesus and Mary Chain about it, that self-thwarting, self-denying aspect that comes through (for example) this *ad hoc* description by Lawrence Upton, for a radio audience, of one of his and Cobbing's – and the Invisible Lunatic's – collaborations on paper:

> It's terribly inky. It's quite varied. Heavily textured. There is some cross-hatching here. There is some total black areas with white spots in it here. There is a sort of obliterated X which is obliterating something else that's so obliterated you can't see.[57]

And yet when Tim Etchells talks to Jonathan Burrows about failure, he says:

> I'm kind of interested in the people that are doing the thing in front of me, and… I think work that allows…a kind of glimpse of failing, or a glimpse of the striving and a glimpse of the failing, is work that – I think it affords me a better view of the people that are doing this thing… I get to see better the people that are there in front of me.[58]

– which I certainly recognize from watching students hilariously and beautifully attempt Goat Island's impossible tasks, and which I fondly remember from *The Consolations*, with its blizzard of languages and broken signals, its scuffs and greebles, its animal impressions and ruined boyband gyrations and its unrehearsed seat-of-the-pants set pieces. In the company of noise we are at our most distinct, most uniquely ourselves: not least because at the same time we have the pleasurable satisfaction of knowing that, in the midst of such multiplicity, we are, in ourselves, countless unknowable others – all the others that all the others glimpse in us, in our striving and failing. The desire we are trying to communicate may be thwarted, but the desire behind the desire – the basic desire to communicate, to be somehow legible to each other despite everything – is a signal that no amount of noise will obliterate.

Failure: accident, mistake, weakness, inability, incorrect Noise
is a world where anything can happen,
including and especially itself.[59]

— Douglas Kahn

I have always been interested in animals, how they hear
with their entire body.[60]

— Robert Wilson

What, then, in the end, is going on in this picture: a stage world, lit and
populated, organized and authorized; an audience, dark and regimented
and mostly doing its best to suppress the noise of its own presence; and
a gap inbetween, a turbulent air-space across which information flows
and breaks apart and is complicated by its own movement? How now do
we understand that narrow abyss? Might noise, in its perpetual 'coming
across', heal the wound of discontinuity?

If noise begets doubt, and if discontinuity is a wound, then we might
first pause to consider Caravaggio's famous painting *The Incredulity of
Saint Thomas*: an image which has cropped up more than once in my
work, most directly in the play *Speed Death of the Radiant Child*. The
picture is one of an intensely Bataillean eroticism. Thomas, confronted

Caravaggio, *The Incredulity of Saint Thomas*

with the appearance before him of the risen Christ, can see the wound in his side, can see inside it even, but cannot assuage his own doubt in response to Christ's body-in-pain. Only the direct evidence of haptic intimacy is sufficient: Thomas needs not only to see, but to touch. He's putting his finger inside Jesus: because only the sensual experience of his body moving inside Christ's body will convince him that the other man is real. It's like a noise duet between a wounded body and a doubting body, behind which the signal of desire, the desire to close up the gap of discontinuity between those bodies of noise, remains sufficiently radiant and communicative that Caravaggio's rendering of it still has the capacity to disturb, to move, and to leave the viewer – empathetically – deeply and intimately touched.

In a statement wrought in the context of a 2013 trans-Atlantic poetry conference called *Poetry and/or Revolution*, Keston Sutherland concludes: "The living labour of poetry makes audible as music and makes count as longing the infinite distance between people that is locked inside even the smallest material distances between people."[61] In thinking this through, we need not stop to worry that his ostensible subject is poetry: 'poetry' is no more or less than 'making', and 'living labour' brings us palatably close to the liveness of the made event rather than the textual object, not least because, as he suggests, this is a making that sublimes or distills itself, that releases itself into its fractions of music and desire.

Cy Twombly, *Blue Room* © Cy Twombly Foundation.

So this is not poetry as opposed to theatre, but poetry aspiring towards theatre. Sutherland's proposition is a concise and potent account of discontinuity (in the sense that Bataille and Berger and Goodman mean it) as a generator of longing, and it is also a statement about how we become more aware of ourselves and others as discontinuous through the practice of making and our relations with the made. But this predicament, in Sutherland's construction, is also "locked" down: nothing in it moves apart from the labouring poet. What reads first like an ardent optimism comes quickly to seem like a position of resignation, albeit one decorated with the hollow promises of art and love. Is this where we get off? Or is there something still in play, something that allows for – or even compels – productive movement?

In a wonderful essay on the artist Cy Twombly, Roland Barthes remarks on the 'inimitability' of Twombly's line – the idea that no one makes marks quite like Twombly: an idea borne out, incidentally, by the editorial note in volume one of Twombly's Catalogue Raisonné which informs us that his 1957 canvas *Blue Room* "contains one drawn element, a looping line that is not by the artist":[62] a tiny vandalism which apparently stands out – to the educated eye – despite the painting being, in John Waters's (wholly respectful) words, an example of Twombly's "signature scratch and scribbles".[63] For Barthes, this inimitability, the *absolute* distinctiveness of that visual "signature", becomes an emblem of discontinuity, in that:

> …what is ultimately inimitable is the body; no discourse, whether verbal or plastic…can reduce one body to another body. [Twombly's] work reveals this fatality: my body will never be yours. From this fatality, in which a certain human affliction can be epitomized, there is only one means of escape: seduction: that my body (or its sensuous substitutes, art, writing) seduce, overwhelm, or disturb the other body.[64]

This is not far off Keston Sutherland's analysis, except that here the act of making (which in this construction would appear to include the act of making love) does not make us feel the discontinuity more keenly, and perhaps more vivaciously; it offers instead an "escape" route in which action – the making-practice of the actor, who is at once "[a] body" and the embodiment of the "sensuous substitute" – is possible, is necessary. And yet the abyss-like gap we commonly find structurally embedded in the power relations of theatrical performance is not so easily collapsed in practice.

Is there, though, an echo perhaps of Barthes's action plan – "seduce, overwhelm, or disturb" – in the immersive quality of our experience of sound, and especially when contrasted with the way in which visual reading tends to reinforce the problematic abyss? In considering theatre sound, for example, Patrice Pavis makes the distinction in this way: "We spend our lives faced with images: they stand in our way, they guide us, and they absorb us. But we live inside the world of sound: it encompasses us, mothers us…"[65]

Sound, then, and perhaps more exactly the noise/sound complex, refuses the structural gap, the spectacular face-off between audience and image; it seduces and overwhelms and disturbs us because it will not permit us to be separate from it: it is all around us, as irreducibly present to us as the kinesphere of our own body. Even the most distant sound is *with* us, in a way that even the most proximal image might not be. Which is not to say that the "strange disparity" identified by Andrew Motion as his spoken words are "massively misunderstood" by his audience is not real: only that that gap is suffused with noise, of which even he himself agrees it may be necessary to "become accepting."

It might well be objected that I am allowing these terms to shift in relation to each other – that 'sound' as an acoustic phenomenon and 'noise' as a conceptual model of a hermeneutic effect are categorically dissimilar. But in drawing attention to how we are, at once, oriented within sound and productively disoriented by noise, I am not at a fundamental level making a claim about our experience of the sonic. The distinction between the visual and the aural has a deeper function: it describes back to us an argument about power: about where power is concentrated, and where it is dispersed or shared; about control and about acceptance, or the will to surrender control (or to be thick-skinned); about insistent authority versus companiable collaboration.

"The spectacle," writes Guy Debord, "is not a collection of images; rather, it is a social relationship between people that is mediated by images."[66] And this is crucial in understanding the state of affairs he describes in his still-incendiary *The Society of the Spectacle*. The detachment, the separation Debord describes may take the form, for real or in our imagining of it, of a theatre-like situation in which spectators watch media images across a physical and symbolic gap; but the spectacular *per se* is not what is staged, but instead refers to the relations of power and authority that are enacted in that situation. "Separation," Debord says, "is the alpha and omega of the spectacle."[67] But that separation doesn't always show up as a type of spatial distribution; nor does a spatial arrangement in which separation is visible necessarily enact more fully the logic of the spectacle. The most immersive theatre now being made – or the most interactive, or that in which the audience is most mobile, or that in which actors and audience most concertedly share the same 'space' – may very well in the event replicate and even reinforce the power structures of 'conventional' theatre; it may offer carefully crafted simulations of freedom and power-sharing that, once tested at their borders, turn out to be the most disappointing apparitions. Indeed, it's these supposedly free-range experiences that often have to operate under conditions secured by extremely precise and accurate control mechanisms in order to achieve the audience's sense of fluency in movement and curiosity.

In any live theatre event we may attend – even a completely 'silent' performance or one staged wholly in the dark (it has certainly been possible to do both on the fringe in the past few years) – we are compelled to play two simultaneous roles: we are both spectator and audience, both the ones who came to see and the ones who came to hear: and thus we always embody, sometimes consciously and sometimes not, the tension between separation and commonality, between individual isolation and social valency. There is always signal and there is always noise, and there is always a negotiation taking place to do with where our activity as receivers of the work intersects with the makers' instincts as technicians of authority and control. And it is this negotiation that creates the dynamic basis of our reorientation in relation to the event. We need to feel the gap; we need to feel the desire to move across it; and we need to feel ourselves in motion – and specifically in *that* motion, in the motion of 'coming across'.

If, as we might infer from Paul Hegarty, the most radical property of noise – not only in its sonic form but as a constitutional property of theatre *in excess of performance* – is weakness, perhaps it can be seen as correspondent to the idea of the 'crack' in John Holloway's brilliant and influential *Crack Capitalism*:

> The opening of cracks is the opening of a world that presents itself as closed... The method of the crack is the method of crisis: we wish to understand the wall not from its solidity but from its cracks; we wish to understand capitalism not as domination, but from the perspective of its crisis, its contra-

dictions, its weaknesses, and we want to understand how we ourselves are those contradictions. This is crisis theory, critical theory…the theory of our own misfitting.[68]

Wherever noise intervenes, it creates a mesh of tiny errors in the system, which stimulate us and enrich our experience of theatre and of ourselves as collaborators in the production of theatre as a social action, and which allow us to really see ourselves – not more clearly, perhaps, but more fuzzily, more ambiguously, and in the end more truthfully: noisy, and misfitting, as we are. In the space of theatre, we come as audiences to attend to the queerness of sound and its structural analogues; to listen, like animals, with our whole bodies.

If noise, like everything cool, returns us finally to the body, then it makes sense that my favourite 'noise piece' is one in which bodies are present in a lucid and unabashedly sensual way. Dennis Oppenheim's *Two-Stage Transfer Drawing* (1971) comes to us as photographic and video documentation of an act of performance that gives rise to a ravishing instance of theatre. In the piece, Oppenheim draws with a marker on his son Erik's back; Erik's task is to replicate on the wall in front of him, moment-to-moment, the drawing that he senses being made on his own back, attempting to recreate it exactly; Dennis and Erik then swap roles, with Erik drawing on his father's back. The noise in the piece occurs visually, in the discrepancy between the original drawing and its tracking on the wall: it is, literally, an index of the noise inherent in the nervous system as one person – as Oppenheim puts it – draws "through"[69] another. As such it reads very clearly as an almost scientific experiment or demonstration: but it is also bountifully metaphorical. For Oppenheim, the trans-generationality is crucial (a subsequent version involved his daughter Chandra), and touches ideas of inheritance and ageing; but when I've on occasion given live performances of this piece myself, it's been with the collaboration of Jamie Wood or Jonny Liron, with whom I have no family connection, and I suspect that the sensuality of the piece, its homoerotic connotations (in a Bataillean sense), come through instead. A little crudely perhaps, rather than drawing freestyle on my collaborator's back, I've sometimes written a word in capital letters – composing it fragment by fragment so as to make its movements harder to track – such that the rendering on the wall of a completely distorted, probably illegible, version of the same word speaks to the fragility of language in the rough-and-tumble of communication, even (or especially) when the process is as intimate as the making of marks on bare skin. The hope, of course, would be that neither image harms or overloads the other: that we see the broken drawing, but we also see the reality of an intimate human contact that persists and remains obstinately significant despite that brokenness.

Can audiences ever feel that we are drawing through them, writing on their skin, inimitably marking their nakedness? Or that they in their reciprocal attentiveness are doing the same to us? In face of each other, in or out of the theatre, communicating across the noisy abyss from our respective floating islands, it is hard sometimes to feel that it might be so. Perhaps the great gift of noise, the benefit that it bestows on those makers courageous enough to admit its influence, is that it obliterates the basis on which we conceive our fear of audiences. Noise answers all the unanswerable questions with a resolute 'Don't know'.

Quite often I've played to actors in rehearsal rooms or students in university studios the sound of what I think is my favourite ever audience – not an audience of mine, but an audience remote in space and time that nonetheless tells me, here and now, not to be afraid of the dark. It's a recording of the audience in attendance at the beautifully intimate thousand-seat Sanders Theatre at Harvard University in Cambridge, Massachusetts, in 1980, where they've gathered to hear the near-legendary folk-singer Pete Seeger, already a shade past his sixtieth birthday. It's a remarkable document of a popular music artist at the zenith of his skill and confidence, his ease in front of an audience.

Kicking off with an exhilaratingly robust 'John Henry', right from the get-go Seeger uses his between-song commentary to make explicit the entanglement of his repertoire, his audience members' capacity for creativity, and the urgency of social and political change. Midway through the second half, he introduces 'The Water is Wide', an extremely old English folksong whose popularity in the twentieth century Seeger himself had done much to promote, whose lyrics are the plaint of a singer separated from her or his lover by a body of water – an image that gradually through the song releases its metaphoric reflection on the difficulties attendant on sustained love relationships. During this introduction, Seeger explains to the audience his own changing relations with the song:

> When my sister was going to Radcliff in the mid 50s, I visited
> Cambridge, and I learned this song from her. I'd seen it in a
> book and I'd passed it by; I said, hm, another sentimental song.
> It means an awful lot to me now, because I keep thinking of

the ocean of misunderstanding between human beings. And we can sing all sorts of militant songs, but if we can't bridge that ocean of misunderstanding we're not going to get this world together.[70]

It looks corny on the page, perhaps, but by this point in the concert, Seeger has consistently made plain his commitment to action, to thoughtful analysis and to a more than merely picturesque social unity. And so this statement becomes a call-to-action, not only in the broad general commissioning of 'bridging' acts and behaviours in everyday life, but in the here-and-now of artist and audience and the gap between them, fraught with the possibility – as Andrew Motion would have it – of being "massively misunderstood". Seeger makes plain that his audience – who have been singing along with the better-known songs in his set all night, though perhaps a bit too tepidly for Seeger's liking – are not just welcome to join in, but that it is pretty much their responsibility to expand the scope of this particular song with their own unguarded voices: "Now even if you've never heard this song, you can hum along with it. It's a nice song to harmonize on. Literally any note works, I've found."[71] (He even finishes up with a gently satirical nod to a not-quite-modish concept in art music: "I think they call it tone clusters."[72])

So, there's no excuse, Seeger implies, for anyone to feel reticent about singing or humming along with this song: if "literally any note works" then there is no possibility of dissonance, no exterior to the prospect of harmony. In other words, it's impossible not to 'get it': because in this instance, 'getting it' doesn't mean understanding the song well enough or with sufficient sophistication to be able to join in; it means understanding that no one is exempt from the invitation to immerse themselves actively in the communal queerness of this sound world. Not only by obliterating any grounds for resistance to this social action of singing together, but by calling out the lyrics ahead of each line in the manner of an old Baptist preacher, Seeger hurls his authorial power and prestige out of his arms like sweets at a pantomime, and the audience respond to this charismatic example of leadership without hierarchy by singing together, spontaneously, unrehearsed, in huge-sounding organic harmonies. They give themselves completely over to their tone clusters (a concept which is, after all, no more than the diatonic quantizing of complex noise), and Seeger sings not just with them but, in Dennis Oppenheim's sense, *through* them. Of course there may have been many in the audience who did not, despite everything, join in – it's impossible to tell from the recording; and yet, of course, in a way, we hear them too: not, on this occasion, seduced, but overwhelmed, and perhaps a little disturbed.

"What we desire," writes Georges Bataille in *Eroticism*, "is to bring into a world founded on discontinuity all the continuity such a world can sustain."[73] It is hard to imagine a better summary of Seeger's programme, his own desire. And this is why the hospitality of tone clusters, of the irresistible invitation to an audience to make some noise, is so vital to theatre as a collaborative public act – and why the concept of noise, which so often belongs to abstruse theoretical conversations and specialist discourses, is actually as mainstream as it gets. If Seeger's great and inspiring example, as he and his audience sing together

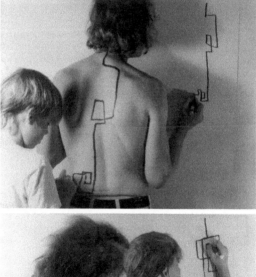

'Two Stage Transfer Drawing' © Dennis Oppenheim.

'The Water is Wide', is to hold together several hundred mutual strangers in one collective action of harmony and noise and silent opposition, then we might remember that the idea of 'holding together' is what lies etymologically behind perhaps theatre's least controversial promise: that it will strive to 'entertain' (Fr. *entre* + *tenir*).

In an increasingly atomised society, in which common experiences and grand narratives are ever less prevalent, the possibility of 'entertainment' in theatre has for the last thirty-odd years started to seem intrinsically problematic – *vide* Forced Entertainment, of course – and perhaps a crass or ignoble aim in itself. As we now move on to think about how the theatre – space plus place, actors and audience, all the signals and all the noise – sits in face with the world that surrounds it, we'll consider how this shift has taken place, and how it fundamentally changes what we need to imagine theatre being able to do. How, now, shall we be misfits?

4. The forest and the field

FERDINAND: … O you wonder![1]

— William Shakespeare, *The Tempest*

A culture is no better than its woods.[2]

— W.H. Auden, from 'Bucolics, II: Woods'

From time to time I've run workshops for actors who find that their relationship with text – and particularly with Shakespearean language – is not as comfortable as they'd like it to be. The school system and much of what passes for 'drama' training, were they designed specifically to inculcate fear and dread around the written word, could scarcely be more intimidating to some otherwise assured performers: and it's always pleasurable to try and create an environment in which some of that baggage can be put down.

There's one Shakespeare passage that I've often asked my students to try and take on, and though most of them come to enjoy performing this speech, there's one word in particular which they tend to struggle to pronounce correctly. You might like to read this passage aloud to yourself, or to your cat or whomever's to hand, and see if you can spot which word presents that especial difficulty:

> O for a Muse of fire, that would ascend
> The brightest heaven of invention,
> A kingdom for a stage, princes to act
> And monarchs to behold the swelling scene!
> Then should the warlike Harry, like himself,
> Assume the port of Mars; and at his heels,
> Leash'd in like hounds, should famine, sword, and fire,
> Crouch for employment.[3]

The most troublesome word for an actor in this, the famous prologue to *Henry V*, is, as you may have guessed, "O". Where longer words can be moulded to a more nuanced intention, "O" is an intractably stark and daunting syllable to vocalize. As an actor, your mouth just opens – and (if you're giving "O" its full weight and substance) stays open. It's exposing, intimately so, almost embarrassing. As soon as it starts, we would like it to be over. And so, quite often – especially in those classes – it is. I have to remind my poor students that there is a significant difference between the "O" of "O for a muse of fire" and the "Oh" of "Oh I've forgotten to get milk." Properly confronted, "O" is testing because the more its presence registers, the more too does its absentness. In a way, "O" isn't really a word at all, but the lack of a word, a gap in the language. Spoken, it's a half-sung siren, the sound of an alarm going off, an emergency arising; on the page, a diagram of a rabbit-hole big enough to topple into; a hieroglyph representing the aperture of the wide-open mouth. The nakedness of yet more actorly self-exposure. Watch out, Hal, we can nearly see your fillings.

"O" is a quintessentially theatrical utterance in that it is a radiantly expressive noise, emitted in a moment when suave, blasé, competent language fails us, and fails *through* us. It comes to us when language leaves, when our experience is too intense to be articulated any other way, when we have something to sing or signal or say that exceeds or eludes or maybe even precedes language and our facility with it: which is disturbing for an actor, whose access to the prestigious stage most likely depends at least partly on precisely that facility. "O" is language's ground zero, from which the grand edifices of poetry have been razed – not even a consonant remains, unlike such other comparably confounding Shakespearean particles as "Fie!" or "Pah!" All that remains is the territory of visual poetry: impure sound denoting pain or despair, shock or awe, longing or wonder, the sublime and the disorienting. (Say "O" for half a second too long, you may feel, and Doubting Thomas might well be along to stick his finger in the hole.) When not even Shakespeare can find words adequate to the magnitude of your emotions or the scale of your perceptions, all you can do is open your mouth and say "O".

In his essay 'English Poetry and Emphatical Language',[4] J.H. Prynne suggests that in our encounters with interjections such as "O" we must as a matter of course take into account their dual function both as carriers of these excessive sentiments which defy articulate expression and as markers of apostrophic use in addressing, for example, deities, or places: there is, then, an ineffability embedded at the heart of "O", a magnitude, a sense of reaching, in both its vocative – "O Superman" – and its interjectional – "O woe is me" – senses.

But not much later in *Henry V* we hear "O" again, meaning something else, and, if my students are anything to go by, far easier to say:

> Can this cockpit hold
> The vasty fields of France? Or may we cram
> Within this wooden O the very casques
> That did affright the air at Agincourt?[5]

Not an elevated or excessive 'O', this time, but one whose basic adequacy, even, is being openly questioned. Because this, now, is not the 'O' of wonder, of the imagination, but an 'O' of material reality: not an airy wishful-thinking 'O' but a "wooden O": the almost-round Globe Theatre, where in 1599 *Henry V* had its first performance – and which was itself inaugurated as a theatre with that same premiere. Thus, the first utterance ever heard by the audience of the Globe was 'O'; and then just a few seconds later, that audience heard the building at which they had gathered described to them as *an* 'O'. This, it is implied, is a building made in the image of longing: the 'O' of desire and astonishment, the 'O' of Gods and Muses, translated into architecture. So, the Prologue

The Globe Theatre © Getty Images.

asks, can this material 'O', this man-made 'O', possibly be big enough, can it possibly be anywhere near sufficient, to contain the vastness of the wanting 'O'? With this flip, from the conceptual 'O' to the real 'O' – from space, in other words, to place – the echo creates a useful pun: that first "O" in the speech becomes (also) vocative: "O, O!" declaims the Prologue. This is about you.

It would seem, then, that for Shakespeare, 'O' is, itself, a theatrical space, a locus of expression for the wondering imagination, the anguished mind, the desiring body – and that the vocal "O" is like an avatar for the 'O' that establishes itself in topographic space, either in the reality of the Globe or in the fiction of, for example, *The Tempest*.

> O, wonder!
> How many goodly creatures are there here!
> How beauteous mankind is! O brave new world
> That has such people in't![6]

This is Miranda, suddenly confronted for the first time with a diversity of human presence: not one (Prospero, her father), not two (Ferdinand, her newly encountered first love), but an apparently uncountable many, the royal party, shipwrecked on the island and now in Prospero's thrall. And the 'O' of her own wonder quickly becomes a pictorial 'O', a dingbat of the island that Caliban has already described to us as "full of noises":[7] 'O' is both the noisy unstable song of her surprise and astonishment, and a tiny map of this new world.

Islands, of course, and particularly desert islands, have always been interesting laboratory spaces for writers, dramatists and broadcasters. Stranding a character or a small group on an island allows for a particularly clear and controlled thought-experiment to be enacted in examining the most fundamental structures that shape and determine human social relations: the 'O' of the island is the 'O' of the petri dish in the laboratory, wherein a culture may be incubated with a particular question or set of questions in mind. We see it in *Robinson Crusoe* and *Lord of the Flies*, in numerous iterations of *The Blue Lagoon*, in TV shows like *Lost* and *Survivor*, in the long-running radio series *Desert Island Discs*. Cast away from social norms, brought sharply up against the imperatives of survival, do we replicate the old orders, is injustice hardwired in us, or do we have the capacity to start over? It's worth noting how many reality television formats, though they may not be set on islands, aim to simulate exactly those conditions: so not just in the island-based *Survivor* but in the jungle of *I'm A Celebrity*...and the fake suburbia of *Big Brother*, contestants are cut off from the usual outside, the networks of communication and value on which they customarily depend, in the hope that conflict and entertainingly anomalous behaviours will arise in the collaborative project of redesigning – amid deprivation and the various quasi-arbitrary contortions of the game structure – a way of life fit to be inhabited.

And it is these questions which prey, too, on the mind of Gonzalo, aged counsellor to the (not actually) bereaved King in *The Tempest*. Ostensibly to distract the King from his grief, Gonzalo fills the awkward silence with what starts out as a game of pretend, a daydream shared for the sake of having something to say:

> Had I plantation of this isle, my lord –
> [...] And were the king on't, what would I do?
> [...] I'th' commonwealth I would by contraries
> Execute all things, for no kind of traffic
> Would I admit; no name of magistrate;
> Letters should not be known; riches, poverty,
> And use of service, none; contract, succession,
> Bourn, bound of land, tilth, vineyard, none;
> No use of metal, corn, or wine, or oil;
> No occupation, all men idle, all,
> And women too, but innocent and pure;
> No sovereignty...[8]

This really is a picture of a "brave new world" emerging out of the laboratory 'O' of an apparently deserted island: a "commonwealth" of Utopian anarcho-communist character – a just and equitable social arrangement markedly out of step with the day-to-day reality of island life for Prospero, his daughter Miranda, his servant Ariel, and Caliban his slave.

As it unfolds, Gonzalo's thinking-aloud seems to become more radical the more it accumulates detail; it shifts from being a playful speculative fiction to finding itself more in the mode of a political manifesto, especially as it reaches its rousing and marvellously sentimental conclusion:

> All things in common nature should produce
> Without sweat or endeavour. Treason, felony,
> Sword, pike, knife, gun, or need of any engine
> Would I not have, but nature should bring forth
> Of its own kind all foison, all abundance
> To feed my innocent people.[9]

And yet it is treated as a game – not least by those others in the party who heckle throughout; but also by the King himself, Alonso, who allows the (admittedly gentle) *lèse majesté* of the exercise to go unchecked. Gonzalo's is a revolution in a think-bubble, which shudders and pops almost as quickly as it is formed.

It is this game-like quality that bolsters the sense that, just as in the opening of *Henry V*, Shakespeare is using the idea of the 'O' – the island, the experiment, the daydream – as a way of thinking about the nature of theatre space and its radical potential: a potential that is always threatened by the speculative energy that gives life to it in the first place. If we come to the theatre to play a game, then our permission to reimagine, to reconfigure, is secured in part by the knowledge that sooner or later the game will be over. After all, as Prospero reminds us at the end of the wedding masque – another theatrical space embedded in the contested and unstable power structures of *The Tempest*:

> Our revels now are ended. These our actors,
> As I foretold you, were all spirits, and
> Are melted into air, into thin air,
> And, like the baseless fabric of this vision,
> The cloud-capped towers, the gorgeous palaces,
> The solemn temples, the great globe itself,
> Yea, all which it inherit, shall dissolve,
> And, like this insubstantial pageant faded,
> Leave not a rack behind.[10]

No matter how radical our imaginings, this seems to say, nothing lasts of them: and this may be what permits those anarchic thoughts free flight in the first place. In which light, it's poignant – and not a little eerie – to hear in Prospero's pronouncement that "the great globe itself, / ...shall dissolve" a premonition: within two years of the play's first performance, the Globe Theatre had burnt to the ground. (A bit of a cock-up with a cannon during a performance of *Henry VIII*.) The "wooden O", built in the shape of our desires and speculations, going up in flames.

This would appear to be a somewhat discouraging model of theatre as a space in which games are played that might toy with ideas of change, but can create no lasting or consequential transformation. At the end of the show, the dead stand up and bow alongside the living, and our applause conspires in the unmaking of what's just been made. But the O-shaped, theatre-like zones which Shakespeare builds into his plays suggest in themselves a more positive outcome: the potential, always, if not for revolution exactly, then for reorientation.

It's easier to perceive these spaces if we think of them structurally rather than topologically – as regions of temporary enchantment or festivity or magic or wonder or difference. So they are not only islands, but foreign realms, or festive celebrations, or storms, or masked balls, or theatrical performances: and, most signally, they are forests. We might immediately call to mind the Forest of Arden in *As You Like It*, or the woods outside Athens in *A Midsummer Night's Dream*, in both of which, identity is slippery, relationships are fluid, love is a delirium; to be present in these places is to be performing a profoundly unstable version of presence, in which nothing is fixed amidst the permissiveness of play. Even the forest itself may be far from static, as we see in the creepily peripatetic Birnam Wood in *Macbeth*, first implausibly invoked by a childish apparition conjured by the prophetic witches, and then chillingly enacted by the English army under Malcolm.

So, the island and the forest (or forest-like 'O'-space) are important – to narrative structure, and, by extension, to the formal operations of the play – because they allow the solidities of self and other, and the relations between them, to become liquid, or even nebulous; they permit certainties to be negotiable, customs to be suspended, givens to be taken back; they create a conducive space for movement that would otherwise be constrained, speech that would otherwise be stifled. And this of course is true not just of Shakespeare, but of almost all dramatic narrative. Every crisis that throws unlikely bedfellows together, every lift that ever got stuck between floors, every haunted house, every high-school prom is a forest.

But there's something else about the forest space that's crucially important: nobody gets to stay there. (Those who belong permanently to the forest never belong to the whole story.) The experience of the forest throws everything excitingly up in the air: but what goes up must comes down; the music stops, the carnival is over.

A word that often gets used in talking about the 'O'-ness of theatre and performance and the nature of the forest is 'liminality'. The forest, like the theatre that it so resembles, is a 'liminal' space. 'Liminal' was for a while – and to some extent remains – a performance studies buzzword, especially suited to critics and theorists who, for their various reasons, have grown squeamish of talking about 'postmodernism'. With its root in the idea of a *limen* or threshold, liminality is concerned with the idea of transition, the movement of things-becoming-other-things. In liminal spaces or periods or zones, divisions are blurred, categories collapse, states are disrupted and reoriented. In the last couple of decades, liminality has particularly been a way of talking about the absorption of increasingly sophisticated digital technologies into theatre and performance, and the ways in which that technology shows up in the treatment of images (and, to some extent, sound) – mirroring, morphing, multiplying. Liminality means hybridity, sampling, the mash-up; it means texts cannibalising other texts, language as virus, writing as performance, as improvisation, negotiation and (always) translation; it means fragmentation, the old unities in all their now-impossible coherence and integrity irrecuperably shattered, replaced with an endless shape-shifting fluency. It is the cavorting of noise at its most seductive.

But this accepted roster of telltale signs that your performance may be having a liminal affair with itself represents, to some extent, a hijacking of a concept with a very specific history and quite a tightly focused meaning. 'Liminality' enters the discipline of performance theory through the working friendship, in the 1970s, of the American theatre director Richard Schechner and the British anthropologist Victor Turner; but the dialogue between these two figures is premised wholly on the earlier work of Arnold van Gennep, the pioneering French ethnographer who in 1909 became the first person to identify and describe the 'rite of passage' – a common term in colloquial use, but one that at its origin refers to a specific grammar of personal and social change.

Van Gennep's analysis, which Turner and Schechner's dialogue investigates and expands, breaks down the rite of passage into three distinct stages: the pre-liminary, the liminal and the post-liminal: or, separation, transition, and incorporation. These stages might be clearly discerned in considering, for example, the passage in a tribal society of an adolescent male into adulthood, where such a movement is still formally marked by a ritual of initiation. The subject, perhaps in the company of a peer-group who are all undergoing the same process, is separated out from his home, and thus from his hitherto stable social existence; in this separate space he remains for a while, with none of the fixed orientations of status or identity that he previously had, but also not yet any of the new orientations he is about to assume; and then, finally, he returns home, to a new status as an adult.

The shape and quality of this tripartite structure is, of course, by no means particular to the rite of passage in small-scale tribal societies that van Gennep describes. For instance, on first encountering it I was struck by its similarity to Eugene Nida's model of the process of translation in language, in which the movement from source text to target language is broken down into three stages: analysis, transfer, and restructuring. As with van Gennep's rite of passage structure, the movement begins with an act (or acts) of discriminating isolation, a careful establishing of the frame around the subject; there is then a period of ambiguity and liquidity, in which multiple possibilities are both speculatively inhabited and at the same time held in abeyance; finally, there is an impulse (or a compulsion) towards consolidation, focus and, at least provisionally, a renewed stability.

For Victor Turner, drawing on van Gennep, it is the complex period of liminality (or, for Nida, 'transfer') that seems to be richest: his description of the lived experience of the liminal phase really captures the imagination:

> ...[I]n many societies the liminal initiands are often considered to be dark, invisible, like the sun or moon in eclipse or the moon between phases, at the "dark of the moon"; they are stripped of names and clothing, smeared with the common earth rendered indistinguishable from animals... [This] places them too in a close connection with non-social or asocial powers of life and death. Hence the frequent comparison of novices with, on the one hand, ghosts, gods, or ancestors, and, on the other, with animals or birds.[11]

The appeal of liminality to theatre makers is immediately obvious: especially so in Turner's extension of the idea of such liminal modalities into a new category of the 'liminoid', a register of social space in which the three-part rite-of-passage structure is absent but the qualities and behaviours of liminality are nonetheless present. So, even in contemporary Western societies, vestiges of liminality in the context of rites of passage can be seen in, for example, marriage ceremonies, or Baptism, or university graduation; but we more frequently experience 'liminoid' events, which are embedded into our lives in ways that are not necessarily perceived as once-in-a-lifetime occasions, but more as periods of special permissive license: Mardi Gras, or the office Christmas party, or stunts in aid of charity, or gap years spent inter-railing, say; the idea of the liminal/liminoid was also, understandably, catnip to theorists of the rave scene from the late 1980s onwards. To Schechner – who in 1967 was the founding director of The Performance Group, which later spawned The Wooster Group – not only was the idea of the 'liminoid' mode instantly applicable to performance, both in and out of theatre, but it also provided a new frame in which to think about, for example, the process of rehearsal, or warm-ups, or the ways in which actors 'come down' from performances.

For Schechner and Turner, the liminal or liminoid quality of performance (including but not limited to theatrical performance) is most usefully characterised as 'subjunctive': that is, it connotes a territory of 'as if'. Generally this subjunctivity has to do with the perception of two simultaneous readings of performance activity, which can be held together in the mind of the actor or spectator but not satisfactorily reconciled. A crude gloss of this tension might describe a 'fictional' layer of action, supported by a layer of 'reality' beneath; but in practice – as we saw earlier in considering the construction proposed by Schechner's friend and colleague Michael Kirby, the 'matrix' of performance, which is hardly ever 'on' or 'off' ('matrix' vs 'non-matrix') but most likely 'strong' or 'weak' – any such distinction is usually untenable: there is too much ambiguity, the tension is too flickery.

My own most educative immersion in the subjunctivity of theatre performance was during my period on tour as an actor with Tim Crouch's *The Author*, in 2010-11, following the play's highly acclaimed initial production at the Royal Court Jerwood Theatre Upstairs in September 2009. It is a play in which the characters have the same names as the actors: when I took over the role that had been played at the Royal Court by Adrian Howells, the character 'Adrian' was renamed 'Chris' and the published text was amended accordingly in its subsequent reprint; Crouch indicates in a prefatory 'Performance note' that: "If the actors change, then the character names change accordingly, with the exception of the author, whose character's name should always be Tim Crouch."[12]

This exemption in the case of the 'Tim Crouch' character – played at the Court and on tour by Tim Crouch – is mirrored in another note regarding the location of the play: "*The Author* is set in the Jerwood Theatre Upstairs at the Royal Court Theatre – even when it's performed elsewhere." Outside of the published text, an audience explicitly confronts this provision only once, when the character of 'Esther' (played by Esther Smith) says, with regard to the trajectory of her career as a young actor: "And look at me now – at the Royal Court Theatre!"[13] This manoeuvre was often questioned by audience members, for example in post-show discussions or more informal conversations, and mentioned in reviews; more than once I heard it described as "lazy" – as if, having gone to the trouble of taking the show on the road, Crouch and his team had fallen short at the last and couldn't quite be bothered to re-write and re-learn that line so that it would refer to the theatre in which the performance was actually taking place.

This construction is the clearest imaginable indicator of Crouch's passionate investment in the subjunctivity of theatrical space – though his perception is, in a sense, the inverse of Schechner's: where Schechner disavows all such identifications, applying to environment the same parsing with which he reads or understands performers – the idea that the performing individual sees herself as both "not me" and "not not me",[14] Crouch insists on the audience's capacity to be both 'here' and, imaginatively, 'somewhere else': and any loss of that conscious duality is deleterious to that audience's sense of what's happening, its grasp of what its role – and the responsibilities of that role – might be. Crouch would probably associate himself with Schechner's summary, which dispenses with the 'neither...nor' of his model of subjunctivity to describe in the affirmative the mode of theatricality that audience and actors share:

> The spectators do not "willingly suspend disbelief."
> They believe and disbelieve at the same time. This is theater's chief delight. The show is real and not real at the same time. This is true for performers as well as spectators and accounts for that special absorption the stage engenders in those who step onto it or gather around it.[15]

Crouch's work to date has typically dispensed with, or acutely defamiliarised, the apparatus of 'legitimate' theatrical presentation: set, costume, lights, sound are all either radically minimized or made strange.

For example, one sequence in the original Royal Court production of *The Author*, which could not usually be replicated on tour, invited the audience to experience as a kind of interlude a short choreographic display of moving lighting units, which is offered in and of itself, for its material pleasures (and as a cadence in the structure of the show), rather than throwing out some eye-catching lighting effects as a way of potentiating a moment in the narrative, say; often, lighting designers are – or say they are – pleased when their work is not noticed, but Crouch wants to draw attention to lights, to the lighting rig, to the complicated grid above our heads, to the technology that normally catches our attention only when something goes wrong. To some extent this recalls Paul Goodman's maxim, stated in his 'Art of the Theatre': "No costumes! – unless it is just the costume, or wearing the costume, that is the deed, the thing to watch."[16] But Crouch invites his audience not merely to see, to recognize, but to interrogate: or, in the words of Robert Wilson's famous statement of intent: "...to say, What is it? And not to say what something is."[17]

Esther Smith (standing) with the audience of *The Author*
© Stephen Cummiskey.

In *The Author*, Crouch pursues this line even further by abolishing the demarked stage. Audiences arriving for the performance find only two banks of seats, facing each other, with a narrow strip of floor space running between the two front rows. The four actors sit with, and among, the audience – the character of 'Chris' is, himself, no more than a member of the audience, just like them – and, to the uninitiated or unsuspecting, are likely to be indistinguishable from the rest of the audience: at least until 'Chris' starts speaking at the outset of the play. Even then, his words are directed to them, sometimes in the form of questions or invitations to speak, and I can certainly testify to having sat among audience members who still weren't sure that the play had begun by the time that first intervention by 'Chris' had ended, some minutes later. The one core element that Crouch does not care to dispense with is the script, which is as tightly written, carefully rehearsed, and (ideally) accurately delivered as one might expect of a Pinter play. But even when audience members may be clutching copies of the published script, which they've bought on the way in by way of programmes, the crucial presence of the *enacted* script can often elude them: and Crouch tests this faultline further by requiring 'Chris', the first character to speak, to elicit responses from those sitting around him or opposite him, in such a way that it is easy, and far from inexcusable, for audience members to conclude that the play is going to be rather more interactive in its form than it actually turns out to be. The rule of thumb in performance is that, with the particular exception perhaps of 'Chris''s first sequence, responses from the audience – and especially audience interjections: that is, responses whose expression has not been invited within the action of the script – are, ideally, not returned with improvised text, but perhaps simply with eye-contact, or, if appropriate, a smile. The audience is invited, in other words, to understand that their speaking is heard, and to that extent respected, but it won't initiate an exchange within the structure of the play, because the play-text is – as its publication suggests – essentially fixed, and the complete performance of the play is the contract on which the event is premised. But the resistance to a more freely responsive engagement has to do not only with the preservation of textual authority (though it seems to me that, as a play, *The Author* is very deeply inquisitive about the nature of that authority): or, at least, it needs to be seen as a productive resistance, not merely a negative constraint. At a symposium on *The Author* at the University of Leeds in November 2010, Tim Crouch describes one instance of this productivity:

> It's not a traditional picture of participation. Last night someone in the audience said to me, in response to one of my lines, 'What do you mean?' Fantastic question. *What do you mean?* What a beautiful question to have hanging over this play. And I think it would be reduced if I just said, 'OK, so

what I mean here is, dadadada!' How much more exciting it is if someone who is *not* the actor has broached that wall, and has placed that question. And I hope that the vibrations of that question will reverberate through the rest of the play…[18]

What Crouch requires of his audience is not merely a thoughtful and sensitive mode of engaging with his plays, but a kind of precision: he needs them to be alert to what's happening here-and-now, not in plays *like this* ("Oh, I get it, it's a Happening!", one audience member in Los Angeles told me delightedly, before the performance had even begun), but in *this* play, in this moment, with these people. As such, the degree to which Crouch creates conditions in which his audiences are apt to become critically disoriented as they attempt to navigate a path through their experience of the radical, shimmering, intensely problematic subjunctivity of the work, can give rise to situations of unusual volatility.

On the evening of Thursday 30th September 2010, *The Author* played the third performance of its run at Bristol Old Vic. About fifteen minutes in to the show, at a point where the lights slowly fade to a total blackout, one member of the audience started to feel unwell. (This is by no means an unprecedented occurrence at this stage in the proceedings.) This person happened to be sitting in the front row next to one of the ushers provided by the Old Vic, and told the usher that he needed to leave. He stood up to go, and the usher accompanied him; we watched him walk quite unsteadily for a few paces, and then, when he was out of my sight round the corner of the seating bank on the way to the exit, he seems to have fainted, possibly hitting his head against the wall at some point. He ended up lying on the floor, not unconscious, apparently awake, but perhaps a little concussed or confused.

The usher, seeing that the man had not passed out, evidently began to suspect that this was all part of the performance. It is perhaps not an unreasonable supposition: a plant has already walked out of the show some minutes prior to this – an important exemplary action, indicating to the audience that the option to leave is one that any of them may exercise at any time should they wish. So it was in this context that the usher made the decision to leave the man lying near the exit and resume his seat. The only people within the auditorium who could be absolutely certain that this sequence of events was not scripted were the four actors, of whom only one, Esther Smith, could see from her position in the audience what was going on. Esther – who had not yet spoken in the play, and who was therefore presumably not necessarily 'read' by many audience members as being an actor – got out of her seat and walked over towards the spot where the man still lay, saying in passing to the usher something like: "We need to do something about this, this isn't part of the show." The stage manager brought the lights up, and Tim Crouch left his seat and went over to assist, making an announcement to the audience after a few moments, explaining what was happening, asking for quiet while we waited for paramedics to attend, and reiterating that this was not part of the play.

It was, however, clearly evident from the reactions of the audience – which was dominated on this occasion by a large group of students whose response to the whole evening so far had been characterised by a good-humoured, noisy, fairground-ride excitement – that on the whole they did not believe Tim's assurance that this turn of events was outside the play; nor did they necessarily disbelieve it: in a perfect illustration of Schechner's 'not x / not not x' construction of subjunctivity, it was more that they didn't know what not to believe. What followed was an extraordinary sequence of manifestations of an unusual kind of confirmation bias, in which whatever evidence emerged simply deepened the audience's experience of doubt and of not-knowing.

For example: it had been established during the play's opening passage of interactive dialogue with the audience that the woman sitting to my left was a doctor; when she eventually asked me: "Do you think they need assistance?", my reply was: "I imagine they may do": an inadvertently ambiguous response which reflected my uncertainty in the moment, but which she may have interpreted as intentionally ludic. After a while she did go over to help, but on returning to her seat she still didn't seem convinced; she mentioned a mark on the injured man's forehead, but plainly wasn't certain that it was genuine bruising rather than make-up. At the same time it occurred to me that other audience members may well have thought this woman, too, was a plant: wasn't it just too neat for me to be sitting next to a doctor?

After a few minutes, the man who had been unwell recovered himself sufficiently to be able to stand: whereupon he quite cheerily announced to the audience that he was all right, before leaving the auditorium: a well-intentioned act that apparently confirmed to some dubious spectators that this had all been a hoax. And so, when the play finally resumed, it was palpably clear that the audience was still deeply unsettled: not just by the interruption to the play, but to the detriment of their willingness to trust the play as a containing structure. The rest of the evening was played out in an atmosphere of curious overdetermination. One woman later (improbably but sincerely) reported having heard Esther's first line, immediately after the resumption – "Has anyone here ever marched against the war?" – as "Has anyone here ever marched into a wall?" And there was, inevitably, a weird colouration to the passage in the play where it's revealed that, crucially to the plot, my character 'Chris' has on a previous occasion had to be escorted disruptively from a theatre audience having suffered some kind of fit induced by flashing lights. It seemed there was no way out of the self-sustaining (and quite understandable) paranoia to which this audience's experience of its own unusually explicit inhabitation of theatrical subjunctivity had given rise. Several of the people we spoke to post-show who were still insistent that the whole episode had been a put-up job were carrying copies of the published script, in which, of course, none of these events occurred: but obviously, for the fiction to work, we would *have* to misdirect them with phony play-texts, wouldn't we?

Needless to say, the weird jagged uncertainty of that performance soon crystallized into a smooth set of anecdotes and in-jokes: but to experience as a live emergency that enveloping ambiguity, as one of the very few inside the event who confidently knew the 'reality' of it, was disconcerting and upsetting (and only then, and only spasmodically, exciting). Incredibly, the whole kerfuffle was rounded off with a sort-of pleasing postscript: the following night's performance also had to be briefly suspended, when an audience member interrupted my speech towards the end of the play to object strongly to the content of a scene some minutes earlier in which one character, the young actress 'Esther', is subjected to a profoundly abusive 'hotseating' exercise by the character of the writer 'Tim Crouch'. The play, it is fair to say, is entirely in agreement with the spectator's furious discomfort: but she was demanding some acknowledgement of that position by us as actors: which, even in the performance of a play whose 'participation quotient' and responsive latitude can easily be misapprehended by spectators who have not *precisely* understood the rules of engagement in *this* structure, is an indicative (that is, non-subjunctive) gesture best avoided. But it was, and is, interesting to see these two unscripted events in relation to each other: on Thursday, there is within the audience a refusal to accept that something real is happening; on Friday, a refusal to accept that it is participating in a fiction. Crouch's insistence on the capacity for irony –

the willingness to be (and, more exactly, to be paying attention) in two places at once – as fundamentally constitutive of the critical proposition of theatre can quickly confound and even hurt the audience that falls short of its urgent invitation.

To disturb and unsettle an audience may, of course, be a highly ethically vigilant function of the theatre maker. But there is an important question beyond this, which has to do with the condition of subjunctivity, and the dangers attendant upon it, or the risks that are harboured by it: and ultimately, it is this question, more than any other, that locates and distinguishes theatre as a social practice and as a potential site of political significance.

> DARKLY: Someone told me you can only walk halfway into a forest. After that…you're walking out.
> CALLIE: Well, whoever told you that was wrong. You can walk as far into the woods as you have a mind to. It can go on forever sometimes.[19]

> — Philip Ridley, *The Passion of Darkly Noon*

> [I]t wasn't a dream. It was a place. And you – and you – and you – and you were there. […T]his was a real, truly live place. And I remember that some of it wasn't very nice. But most of it was beautiful.[20]

> — Dorothy in *The Wizard of Oz*

> Back to life, back to reality
> Back to the here and now, yeah[21]

> — Soul II Soul, 'Back To Life'

Sometimes the liminal 'O', where words fail us, is neither forest nor island, but merry-go-round:

> If I loved you,
> Time and again I would try to say
> All I'd want you to know.

If I loved you,
Words wouldn't come in an easy way.
Round in circles I'd go![22]

So sings Julie Jordan, "afraid and shy",[23] to Billy Bigelow, the fairground barker, in Rodgers and Hammerstein's *Carousel*. It's one of the great love songs in the canon of American musical theatre. And yet: is it, actually, a love song at all? It emerges out of an exchange in the dialogue in which Julie and Billy have just reassured themselves that they don't love each other – and, whether or not we believe these protestations, it's undeniable that the lyrics of the song are carefully framed in the subjunctive world of 'as if'.

Rodgers and Hammerstein's great invention in this, their second musical together (following *Oklahoma!*) – and one of their most celebrated legacies as a songwriting partnership – is this mode of the 'conditional love song'. It's an elegant solution to a nagging structural problem with the classic musical: for the sake of the narrative, the central love relationship can't be forged too quickly or easily; but equally, the audience doesn't want to have to wait too long for a big swoonsome romantic number. The conditional love song – another example would be 'I'll Know' from Frank Loesser's *Guys and Dolls* – amply satisfies both requirements: this is *not* a love song: but if it were, it would sound like this.

The conditional love song is an interesting case of theatre modelling and harnessing its own subjunctivity: after all, the whole of *Carousel* is a magical-realist fantasy, but it is strengthened by the creation and protection of an embedded play-space in which the dangerous idea of romantic love can be flirted with; there is necessarily more drama in the speculative exploration of unspoken desire than in the culminatory triumph of requited love: and this is true also of the larger structure of the piece. Subjunctivity is an essentially permissive state, and, by extension, propulsive: it releases energy by training attention on desire and the emotional and intellectual potency of movement.

It's apt that in setting out the territory of the subjunctive, Richard Schechner at one point uses the example of Olivier playing Hamlet – "Olivier is not Hamlet, but he is also not not Hamlet…[and] Hamlet is not Olivier, but he is also not not Olivier"[24] – because perhaps the most explicit reflection on the permissive energy of theatrical subjunctivity that we have is indeed in *Hamlet*. At the end of Act II, Hamlet conceives the plan of asking a visiting troupe of travelling players to perform a particular play – *The Murder of Gonzago* – with the inclusion of an interpolated speech, penned by Hamlet himself; for Claudius, whom Hamlet suspects to be responsible for the murder of his father, the content of this play will be too close to the bone:

> … I'll have these players
> Play something like the murder of my father
> Before mine uncle. I'll observe his looks;
> I'll tent him to the quick… The play's the thing
> Wherein I'll catch the conscience of the king.[25]

Claudius is indeed discomfited – "frighted with false fire",[26] says Hamlet – and asks: "Have you heard the argument? Is there no / Offense in't?"[27] To which Hamlet, performing the sidestep that the subjunctivity of the theatrical scene permits, can more-or-less legitimately reply: "No, no. They do but jest, poison in jest – / No offense i' the world."[28]

And so Hamlet can accuse Claudius of murder, and at the same time not actually have said anything at all: just as audiences for *The Author* are invited to watch a play that's set at London's Royal Court Theatre while seated themselves in the auditorium of, say, the Kirk Douglas Theatre in Culver City, California, and to hold both places in a productively tense balance. The permissiveness of subjunctivity is traded against consequence, and for some users, such as Hamlet, this is nothing but positive: it opens up an additional, commodious space in which the unspeakable can be spoken without catastrophic risk. It's surely significant that Hamlet's most famous soliloquy is spoken between his conceiving of the performance that he nicknames "The Mouse-trap" and its playing; Schechner would perhaps suggest that subjunctivity is the key to Hamlet's existential conundrum: to the options, "To be, or not to be,"[29] he might well add a triangulating third: "or not not to be…": is that the answer?

The exploitation of the liminal, subjunctive, conditional modes of theatrical play can, however, have much darker applications. Consider this extraordinary passage:

> I'm going to tell you a story you've never heard before, because
> no one knows this story the way I know it. It takes place on
> the night of June 12, 1994, and it concerns the murder of my
> ex-wife, Nicole Brown Simpson, and her young friend, Ronald
> Goldman. I want you to forget everything you think you know
> about that night because I know the facts better than anyone.

I know the players. I've seen the evidence. I've heard the
theories. And, of course, I've read all the stories: That I did it.
That I did it but I don't know I did it. That I can no longer tell
fact from fiction. That I wake up in the middle of the night,
consumed by guilt, screaming.
    Man, they even had me wondering, *What if I did it?*[30]

One of the most striking things about this, the opening to a highly
controversial book published in 2007 and credited to its ostensible
narrator O.J. Simpson (but actually ghostwritten by Pablo F. Fenjves), is
how quickly and vividly it establishes a sense of the liminal: a space of
"forget[ting] everything you think you know"; of multiple contradictory
stories competing for airtime and supremacy; of a disjunct between
action and consciousness; of fact and fiction becoming indistinguishable;
of darkness and night terrors; of "wondering" and "What if...?".

The establishment of this liminal atmosphere is crucial to Simpson
and Fenjves's book not merely for aesthetic reasons but in respect of
the law, too. Despite Simpson's promising a "story" made credible by
his knowledge of the "facts" surrounding the murder of Nicole Brown
Simpson and Ronald Goldman, of which he was famously acquitted
in 1995 (though he was found liable for their wrongful deaths in a
later civil trial), the narrative content of the book is carefully posited
as counterfactual, with the title in particular – *If I Did It* – framing
the whole work as a hypothetical reflection on the events. This highly
theatrical subjunctivity confers a strange diaphanous amnesty on what is
clearly pitched as Simpson's confession. (Indeed, the rights in the work
are now owned by Goldman's family, and the version of the book now
in circulation has an appended subtitle: "Confessions of the Killer";
the attempt to drag the text into the realms of the indicative and the
manifestly consequential even extends to the cover design, in which the
'If' of *If I Did It* is shrunk to a fraction of the size of the other words,
and all but hidden inside the pronoun 'I'.)

Simpson and Fenjves's appallingly ingenious strategy serves a simple
aim: the phantom best-seller, O.J. Simpson's *OK Yes I Admit I Did It*,
is unpublishable, but the money it would make is irresistible. And so
this subjunctive confession emerges, the equal and opposite artefact to
Hamlet's incriminating 'The Mouse-trap': it is both said and not said
(or, in Schechner's terms, both not said and not not said). *If I Did It* is
Simpson's conditional love song to his own ego and his bank account.

So, again, with O.J. Simpson as with Hamlet, subjunctivity allows for – indeed, it insists on – an uncoupling of action from consequence, and, by those means, produces a surge of (as-if liberatory) permissive energy. And in this instance it's abundantly clear to what ends that energy is being harnessed. But there is an obvious problem in the subjunctive permissiveness of theatre in general, if it places the stage event – and the audience's apprehension of it – in a state of elevated seclusion, separated from the unfolding of indicative life around it as if surrounded by a moat. If the condition of subjunctivity inflects the perceptions of its inhabitants so powerfully and so comprehensively that a doctor watching a real bruise form on the face of an injured member of the public comes away convinced it's all being done with make-up and sleight-of-hand, then the problematic quality of that register radiates far beyond the rudimentary syntax of theatrical fiction, which allows the many 'dead' at the end of *Hamlet* to stand up and take their bows hand-in-hand with the living.

If, then, we turn from the conceptual space of 'If I Loved You' and *If I Did It* back towards Gonzalo's "Had I plantation of this isle, my Lord...", we now see (for the moment) a thought-experiment whose radicalism is apparently a function of its already-thwartedness. If this speculative bubble within the larger island zone is, like 'The Mouse-trap', a kind of play-within-a-play, this might be seen as Shakespeare's melancholy reflection on the political inefficacy of theatre; how differently it reads if we look forward to Caliban's eventual repentance for his part in the comically ramshackle seditionary adventure prosecuted in collaboration with Stephano and Trinculo: "How fine my master is! [...] I'll be wise hereafter / And seek for grace."[31] Trinculo has already coined one of the play's most picturesque images: if, as he believes, there are only five people on the island, and the two he's yet to meet are as daft as him and his drunken revolutionary comrades, then "the state totters".[32] It is a laugh line: but somewhere within Gonzalo's Utopian monologue, between the heckles and beneath its ludic carapace, we have unmistakably glimpsed the precariousness of the tottering state, and even heard a programme – strong on radical conviction if not on practical detail – for an alternative. And yet it is an equivalent theatrical space to the subsequent wedding masque: it is rich and vivid and absorbing, and then, in a moment, it vanishes "into thin air". In a sense, both Gonzalo and Caliban in their quite different ways open up spaces of protest, which the establishment tolerates and absorbs (or 'pardons'), knowing it is ultimately strengthened by its capacity to frame dissidence as either marginal eccentricity – the dream-antics of a 'lunatic fringe' – or as the antisocial behaviour of the "misshapen",[33] whose rebellion is deplorable not because it seriously threatens social order (which, in fact, it well might), but rather for its affronting lack of "manners".[34]

This, then, is the position that theatre occupies in relation to the political establishment – or at least, that species of theatre that refuses to align itself tacitly (let alone overtly) with the interests of that establishment. Its dissidence is bought by its subjunctivity – because, as Marina Abramović likes to put it, "the knife is not real, the blood is not real": and an unkind re-phrasing of Tim Crouch's asking his audiences "to be in two places at once, to hear two statements in one sentence, to see two identities in one actor"[35] would be about theatre wanting to have it both ways: seeking often to intervene virtuously in complex social realities but wishing also to remind angry or disturbed audiences who have forgotten what they're watching that this is 'only' a play. Lubricating all of this is a basic theatrical and artistic idea: that of 'metaphor', the technology by which ideas are (etymologically speaking) 'carried across' the threshold between the symbolic and the literal, just as, in one liminal rite that persists in some advanced Western societies, the groom will carry the bride across the threshold of their new home together.

How, then, is theatre of any consequence? At the point an audience starts to applaud (or to leave the performance space, if a director engaging with this very question has sought to disqualify them from applauding – as indeed happens, for example, quite rightly, at the end of *The Author*), that action terminates two highly intricated conditions: the play abandons the subjunctivity that has been its most fundamental premise and justification, and the audience relinquishes its implied contract, and, by extension, its complicity in the nature of the constructed event. ("As you from crimes would pardoned be, / Let your indulgence set me free,"[36] asks Prospero, channelling O.J.) There may well be some degree of after-effect: we may be emotionally shattered by *King Lear*, or newly informed by some verbatim piece, or inspired by a rabble-rousing participatory show; but will these sensations last beyond the first cup of tea back at home? Will they linger overnight and rose-tint the next morning's shower? Even a mad-keen theatre-goer or a professional maker might be hard-pressed to list more than half-a-dozen shows that have felt to them truly consequential.

One particularly forest-like theatre space – no longer operating, but buzzily prominent between 2003–10 – was Shunt Vaults, a 65,000 sq. ft complex of cavernous spaces underneath London Bridge rail station, curated and managed by the theatre company Shunt, and housing a multitude of variably provisional performance areas centred on an increasingly busy and popular bar. There is no doubt that a large audience who would not otherwise have attended theatre or live art were attracted to the Shunt Vaults initially by the stylish bar (and a certain word-of-mouth hip factor) and secondarily but not insignificantly by the novel and compelling performance events that infiltrated the bar or were arrayed throughout the rest of the venue. The company's commentary around the artwork that thrived in the context of the Shunt Lounge was often realistic about the nature of that engagement: the work had in a sense to be competitive, to be strong enough to capture some degree of attention in the first place, and to accept the parameters within which it could expect to operate: but, again, it's undeniable that that work could be – indeed, had to be – eye-catching and provocative, in ways that might be argued to have some political valency. But the Shunt Lounge was, *par excellence*, a liminal space: characterised by crowdedness and intoxication, by the surreal and the dreamlike; even the entry procedure – through an anonymous-looking door from a London Bridge ticket hall, and then down an extremely long passageway which was usually dark and tunnel-like, a horizontal rabbit-hole for tumbling along into a brash but carefully-confected wonderland – maximised the sense of liminality.

I had many happy and interesting experiences there during the years that Shunt had run of the Vaults, and there was much to like and enjoy in the slipperiness and colour-saturation of the performativity fostered in that space. But I often wondered a bit sceptically about the virtue it sought to make of exposing its audience to the unexpected – a currency that often becomes devalued even when a large amount of top-flight creativity is being invested in its success. Shunt, it was often suggested, would change the way you looked at things: which was true, I thought, to this extent: that it changed the way you looked at things while you were at Shunt – mostly because it changed the things you looked at. But that long tunnel, and the discontinuity it seemed to narrate, only reasserted the uniqueness of the Shunt brand. What remained of that experience once one was on the nightbus home? What persisted through the following day? If I – not myself, but one of those unwitting or part-witting Lounge visitors who wouldn't normally attend performance events, a stockbroker perhaps or a systems analyst – felt that Shunt really had made me see things differently, what would I do with that feeling?

If the permissive liminality of the Lounge spoke to me, could that speaking somehow be incorporated into the discursive competences of my day-to-day life? Or would I simply – or complicatedly – feel that the magical properties of Shunt specifically belonged to Shunt, to that out-of-the-ordinary space and those eccentric "misshapen" artists? What more could I do, than just go back again next week?

This brief thinking-through of the work of a company I admire is intended not to denigrate their activity (though admittedly I often found that, for me, the Shunt Lounge's problematics tended to overwhelm its pleasures) but to point up the basic syntactic difficulty of constructing sustainedly dissident theatrical event-space in a liminal-subjunctive mode. It is a difficulty reflected – at some remove, perhaps, at least at first sight – in this extraordinary critical passage by Keston Sutherland, at the climax of an essay on the work of J.H. Prynne and 'radical thinking':

> We all now rightly know enough not to be capable of radical love for ourselves and for the world grasped in one common bond together as the truth of intimacy and illimitability, and we are rightly eloquent enough not to be capable of speaking that bond as lyric poetry. Whoever might be the person capable of that act would be someone who did not live under capitalism, someone for whom the extension of economic ownership through imperial violence is not and cannot be the most radical form of self-extension; and as we know, since we know enough, and since we eat enough, living under capitalism is not itself an act anyone can desist from, terminate, or even pause in. Try doing it now.[37]

Like anyone who's used to following stage directions, I find I am haunted by that final imperative remark (borrowed from the end of Prynne's *To Pollen*) – 'Try doing it now' – and by the tautly ambiguous contradiction at work in its tone: it seems to me neither decisively an inspirational exhortation, nor wholly a wearily sarcastic shrug. To try, for a moment, not living under capitalism is self-evidently as impossible a task as those that form the Goat Island exercise we looked at briefly in the last chapter – "Jump in the air with both feet off the ground and stay suspended for 5 minutes,"[38] said one; and we can no more inhabit a sustained and consequential anticapitalist dissidence than we can defy gravity. Instinctively I tell myself that the hiatus-within-capitalism that Sutherland forlornly describes sounds very like an ideal theatre space – and perhaps it is: except that, as Sutherland himself was the first to remind me, people live in places, not spaces, and perhaps the difference between space and place can at one level be described in terms of the movement of capital and the rapacious prosecution of imperialist projects. So, we can, perhaps, make, through our art, a kind of shelter, in which the terrible grinding logics of capitalism can be temporarily suspended through the wilful and consensual application of the technologies of subjunctivity and metaphor and the other theatrical apparatus that permits us to examine and reimagine our social relations. Perhaps such a space of shelter can be imagined with such care and in such detail that it can be substantially realised, materially and relationally, and temporarily occupied. And perhaps there are ways in which the information that arises in that space can be transmitted beyond its boundaries, can be made to ramify somehow in the living quarters of the surrounding world. But always, still, the provisionality of that shelter, and the mode of subjunctivity that secures its permissiveness as a space, becomes an inhibiting discontinuity at the point of exit. In this model, art – and particularly theatre – becomes an act of jumping in the air and trying to make the period of elevation as extended and as action-packed as possible, before the inevitable return to the ground. We are all ballet dancers now.

So, it's plain to see the predicament which apparently makes theatre's participation in the engineering of prospects for political change a horizon for contemporary practice – an orientation to track, but not a substantially attainable goal. If theatre is able to distinguish itself as a form and practice, it seems to be able to do so only through a self-secluding inscription which isolates and privileges it within the fray. But I want to try and show that this model of theatrical dissidence is not the only one available to us: and that, actually, a more careful examination of the cultural contexts in which we currently make theatre – the "now" in which we "try doing it" – will open up the alternative space we really need.

Crucially, we first return to Victor Turner and, behind him, Arnold van Gennep, in whose work the problem of theatrical liminality appears to be dispelled with ease. Returning to these core texts, we are reminded that liminality is only comprehensible, as a mode of action, *because it ends*; because, having been temporarily inhabited, it is moved through: the initiand comes out the other side. A rite of passage – or any other

process which exploits a liminal phase – that does not complete itself
through the enaction of a post-liminal incorporative phase (the return
to the home after the period in the forest), that does not ensure its
consequentiality by embracing its capacity for consequence, makes no
more sense than an act of translation that is never finished, that remains
an inarticulable cloud of possibilities in the mind of a translator who
is reluctant ever to commit to one particular route through their task.
We might sympathise with the predicament, we might understand their
reticence – it seems a shame to close down ambiguities, to reduce nuance,
to assert one particular choice: but a translator who does not eventually
make that choice is not really a translator at all, but simply a thoughtful
person who knows more than one language and can't pay the rent.

It may fairly be argued that this incorporative return is an explicit part
of the structure of almost every constructed event within the genus of
theatre. The show ends, there is applause, everybody leaves the theatrical
forest and goes home. Sometimes, as in a durational performance, there is
no 'end', or there are many ends, each chosen by an individual spectator;
sometimes there is no applause because the presenter of the work has
chosen not to invite it (and the audience has read that sign accurately),
but this is unlikely to cause a radical instability in the ending of the piece
and the transit back to indicative reality, not least because the syntactic
function of the 'missing' applause will normally be fulfilled by some
other component in the system – a lighting or sound cue, the opening of
doors, an outbreak of conversation. But there is always a traversing of
the psychic boundary at the end of the artwork, whether the feeling of
that moment is bumpy or smooth, abrupt or gentle, whether it registers
consciously or not.

This analysis, though, however accurate, merely redescribes the
problem we began with: the necessary border, however permeable it
may be in practice, between theatre and its outside. Theatre's hard-won
discontinuity from the social landscape it interrupts could, in respect of
Keston Sutherland's invocation of the apparently impossible "pause"
in capitalism, seem its strongest and most plausibly effectual proviso.
But what we see within its operations – even action which may seem
exemplary – can only be exemplary in relation to its own terms and its
own subjunctivity. We can't simply carry it across into application to our
own lives outside the theatre, which are fraught with all the complex
and disastrous influences that the dissident theatre exists temporarily to
refuse.

But it is the wider context that presently surrounds the task of incorporation that begins to suggest, if not exactly a resolution to this paradox, then a reconfiguration of it. We might begin to approach an understanding of this if we were to think more laterally about the problem of leaving the theatre. What if we never left? What if we went to theatre and – well, we just stayed there?

What if we can imagine – and I often have imagined this, to the point of pitching it in pilot form to various producers and potential collaborators – a 24-hour rolling theatre, in which a pool of actors and other creatives improvised together a performance event that never ended, that kept pace with the 24-hour supermarket or the 24-hour drive-through fast food restaurant, allowing audiences to come and go as they please but also, in theory at least, permitting them to stay forever, to move in, to become not theatre's audience but its housemates? If nothing else this immediately points up the weakness, especially audience-side, of the matrix of subjunctivity (which, after all, is what Kirby's matrix basically is). When we go to the theatre, we are still living our lives – or, we are not not living them; and as Keston Sutherland reminds us – realistically, we might say – we do not in any meaningful sense "desist from" or "pause in" living under capitalism. We may collectively perceive the 24-hour theatre as an 'island' space, and we may even create a performance structure in which, through efforts of participatory collaboration (of a kind that I have tried to come close to in *Open House*, or in some of my work with Jonny Liron), we feel that 'we' together really do have "plantation of this isle". We could rip up the auditorium seats and create allotments in their place. We could rig any number of LED stars to sleep beneath. We could even declare ourselves an independent state. What would we be making together, in this most immersive of theatrical events? What might be the relationship between that genuinely anarchic, anticapitalist-minded, fully inhabited space, that island life in which we might finally approach living conditions in which – as Stephano sings – "Thought is free!",[39] and the world surrounding it?

In practice, of course, the answers to those questions would inevitably be heavily contingent on a number of factors that can hardly begin to show up in such a thought experiment; but in theory, that endless performance – appealing though it certainly sounds (to me), and valid in a myriad of ways – does not seem to me to create a consequentially anticapitalist space, but rather, a quintessentially late-capitalist one, embedded in a larger capitalist culture with which its relations would very likely be largely benign. The reason I argue this is not principally a reflection on the conceivable potency or saliency of such a performance, were it to be constructed and sustained. My problem with it is partly that it doesn't solve the problem of incorporation, but merely defers it indefinitely; more significantly, though – and this, I think, is the rub – by doing so, it replicates exactly the conditions through which capitalist culture sustains and advances itself.

Especially if we accept Victor Turner's category of the 'liminoid' – the social and cultural space that mimics the state of liminality without actually serving a liminal function (which, as we have seen, must necessarily include giving way to an incorporative phase) – then it is plain to see that the contemporary Western culture that has been aggressively rolled out more-or-less globally in recent decades can be quite adequately described in terms of the characteristics of the liminal. Particularly because of advances in communications technology – including a whole new species of liminality known as the 'virtual' – and vast changes in the routes and contours of trade and the movement of capital, the parameters by which our relationships and interactions are defined have almost all shifted radically since the 1980s. The speed at which information travels and the forms in which we encounter and harness it; the ways in which we now apprehend, and no longer apprehend, distance and time; our increasingly anxious relationship with borders and mobility, and, beneath that, with the idea of difference, proximity, intimacy; our developing, and sometimes bewildering, sense of ourselves as living performatively, especially in our daily interactions with people we might not 'know' in any sense that our recent ancestors would have recognized; the uncoupling of our patterns of consumption from natural cycles of season and rhythms of climate; our understanding of money, and wealth, and economic value, and the violently complex abstractions that now render large parts of that conceptual territory unintelligible to most people; the major shifts in the global distribution and operation of manufacturing industries, and the vertiginous growth of new sectors focused specifically on the leveraging and manipulation of intangible assets and the accelerated movement of personal data; a far greater acceptance of, but a commensurately amplified cultural disquiet around, the liquidity and multiplicity of personal and social identities and the blurring of boundaries around privacy and public currency, especially through surveillance and telematics; the collapse of the natural sublime in the terrible face of anthropogenic power: all of

these dynamics, and many more, characterise the ways we now live in
the West, and not only in the West: and each of them is in its way a
liminal reality – not so much moved through as endured (or enjoyed),
at least until such time as economic or environmental catastrophe, or
political revolution, ushers in a long-deferred and irresistible phase of
incorporation.

It may be interesting to consider in this light the strain that the working
relationship between Richard Schechner and Victor Turner underwent
with regard to their respective views of the highly fructile, distinctively
liminal turbulence of the late 1960s in the U.S. and Europe. Where did
all that social and cultural energy go? For Schechner, there was a tragic
loss and disappointment in the failure of the promised revolution to
materialise. That countercultural movement, it seemed to him (as indeed it
did to Paul Goodman), lost its way: a moment of rich promise unravelling
heartbreakingly in violence, stupor and disintegration. For Turner – much
more the disinterested anthropologist than the agitator *in media res* that
Schechner had been – there were obvious signs embedded throughout
the culture that the liminal ferment of 1968 had been incorporated into
the more settled mainstream of the subsequent decade, exactly as might
be expected: the legacy of the 'Summer of Love' was largely absorbed
within the ever-expanding territory of commodity capitalism: potentially
radical sexual permissiveness was translated into a means of advertising
more seductively to consumers; 'New Age' became a genre of music for
securing the functional sales-ambience of coffee-shops and elevators;
ecological consciousness was broken down into slogans the right size
for bumper stickers to adorn gas-guzzling air-polluting automobiles.
For Turner, this incorporative passage was all in order; for Schechner,
who had thought that the upheavals of that late sixties period presaged
genuine revolutionary change in the fundamentals of society and its
ideological subtexts, there was nothing but disenchantment. From this
distance, it is of course easier to see how both were, to a degree, right:
after all, the revolution that comes isn't always the one you want, or the
one you expect; it might not even be immediately recognizable as such.
The really radical change that arose from and resolved the social and
cultural liminality of that period was in the event a series of extensions
in the working apparatus of capitalism, made possible by a murderously
shrewd programmatic exploitation of the fluid permissiveness of the
liminal experience. The social reconfigurations that occurred in the late
'60s around personal freedom, sexual self-expression, the valorizing of

'peace', the pursuit of altered states of consciousness, the hard-won advances being made in relation to civil rights and the perception of minority identity politics: these all become translated into a fearsomely radical investigation into the capitalistic affordances of directionless velocity, deregulation, the positioning of choice as intrinsically morally virtuous, the distortion and dismantling of historic narratives of class and community, the aspirational privileging of leisure and recreational modes of individual behaviour. The characteristic liminality of 1968 is deeply embedded in the programmes of Thatcherism and Reagan-era conservatism, which in turn beget the sleek, supposedly frictionless manoeuvres of globalization, on which even the most refusenik city-dweller now depends at a basic structural level.

The liminal, or liminoid, has, then, become so embedded in the quotidian reality of our daily lives that its moving-through is now conceivable only in apocalyptic or revolutionary terms. And this creates an obvious – and a relatively new – problem in relation to the idea of dissidence, the idea of creating and inhabiting a space that's consequentially critical of and resistant to the dominant social reality: which is that the liminal, or liminoid, has generally been the mode of such dissident activity – and, as such, this current phase of late capitalism has essentially denatured the normative structures of protest and refusal, by aligning itself more-or-less identically with the sociocultural space of dissidence.

For example, in a video posted to YouTube by his publishers Routledge in December 2012, Richard Schechner, introducing students to the concept of the 'liminoid', makes enthusiastic reference to:

> ...even now, as we're talking, as I'm recording this, down in Zuccotti Park, where the Occupy Wall Street people are calling for a restructuring of American financial society, American social contract. So there they're existing in a liminal phase: they're neither continuing as ordinary citizens, nor have they emerged in the Utopian community. They're in this special isolated place, Zuccotti Park, which is part of down-town Manhattan, but really fenced off at the same time.[40]

Schechner evidently reads this isolation, this sense of being "fenced off", as an interruption in the fabric of "financial society", a material and topical rendering of the kind of "pause" that Keston Sutherland enjoins us (with a forked tongue that, in this context, seems much less ambiguous) to "try doing". But the details and co-ordinates by which Schechner decodes the Occupy camp's liminoid credentials – discontinuance, the temporary suspension of citizenship, non-emergence, pre-Utopian community structure, "special"-ness, isolation, being "fenced off" – are all also strategies that the liminoid state uses, in various configurations, to stifle and obstruct its "people" in their assertions of nonconformist political and social desire. The ramifications of Occupy Wall Street in its wider social context may be eye-catching, may be successfully media-baiting, may promote debate, may register strongly as social action and provocation: but they do not successfully locate that programme outside the structures that already contain it. This is not by any means to disparage the Occupy movement, but it perhaps begins to suggest why its spectacular energy has, at the time of writing, dissipated to such an extent: it is too easily and quickly absorbed by means of what we might see as a forcible or tyrannical incorporation, in which media interests, "financial society", and state power serve each other with surpassing fidelity.

The sustained liminoid character of late capitalist society has not (yet) been so widely remarked upon that the dominant narrative of liminality as constitutive of dissidence has been at all effectually displaced or superseded. But the eminent sociologist Arpad Szakolczai has commented frequently and suggestively on the condition of 'permanent liminality':

> Human life is not possible and worth living without some degree of stability, meaning and a sense of home. Liminality is indeed a source of renewal [but]… If everything is continuously changing, then things always remain the same. Liminality is a source of excitement and variety and a shakeup from the dull routines of everyday life, but nothing is more boring than a permanent state of liminality, where even the hope of escaping the routine is lost. Individuals are forced to invent more and more sophisticated and ultimately perverse forms of entertainment in a mad search after experience, in the wish to surpass in excitement the boredom of the hectic existence in a permanent state of liminality.[41]

Szakolczai's principal focus here is on the cultural production of liminality, and the assertion through action of individual freedom and identity as a refusal of that otherwise impenetrable liminoid dominance (though he rightly later cautions against reading a politics of identity as an effective tool for initiating incorporative movement). And though this obviously speaks to the predicament and potential of theatre within liminoid culture, it only by extension reaches the possibility of consequential dissidence and the capacity of cultural activity to effect meaningful political change, which is what I take to be most urgent in considering the place of theatre. (As three or four billion people on the planet will quickly tell you, there are worse things than boredom.) But it does at least place under valuable stress the critical question of how we create meaning for ourselves – and for each other – defiantly and joyously in the face of liminoid capitalism.

Szakolczai notes how the "frozen ritual"[42] in which permanent liminoid culture is produced causes liminal 'playfulness' to stultify into a mode of performance which is inhibiting and constrictive and leads to stasis. "In the end," he says, "the differences between 'life' and 'stage' disappear and it seems that life itself is nothing but performance on a stage."[43] This observation, which confirms the difficulty for theatre to position itself as a distinct and separate space within a dominant capitalist culture whose entire permissive momentum is ensured by liminoid subjunctivity, is of course familiar from Shakespeare, most famously Jaques's "All the world's a stage / And all the men and women merely players…".[44] But we might also turn to one last Shakespearean forest/island space to study a detailed picture of liminoid society as a specifically theatrical problem.

In fact, Illyria, the setting of *Twelfth Night: or, What You Will*, is neither forest nor, exactly, island, though we are shown, early on, its coastline: in common with *The Tempest*, *Twelfth Night* is, among other things, a shipwreck play, a depiction of a place where the washing-up on the shore of stranded outsiders has the potential to disturb a settled social order – indeed, to change everything. But in the distinctly island-like seclusion of Illyria, disruption is a tall order. This is a society in which the legitimate permissiveness of 'Twelfth Night', the purposefully disorienting brio of festivity and misrule, has stultified – or, per Szakolczai, "frozen" – into a joyless, dysfunctional inconsequentiality, more *Groundhog Day* than *Twelfth Night* in its neurotic repetitiousness. The tone is drearily established by the Duke, Orsino, trapped in not even the churning paralysis of unrequited love but actually in what feels very like a self-regarding performance of the same, and by the object of his obsession, Olivia, who is similarly resisting the natural movement of change and adaptation by clinging to the liminal phase of grief for her dead brother, and refusing the slow process of incorporation, in which 'life goes on'; not for nothing are both these character names spelt with a capital 'O': for here, the feelings of pain and longing and the tyranny of subjunctive performance are all-encompassing, and words – a resource in which Illyria appears to be comically rich – "are grown so false," says Feste, "I am loath to prove reason with them."[45] And so, ironically, the potentially catalysing introduction of two figures from outside this system – the shipwrecked siblings Viola and Sebastian – does nothing but deepen and complicate the malaise, not *despite* but precisely *because of* the liminal character of those identities: not least, the fact that they're (of course!) identical twins, which allows for the gender confusion and the blurring of the living/dead binary that animates the plot. Only the volatility of the pointedly queer (and dangerously sincere) desire of Antonio for Sebastian, and of Orsino for 'Cesario' (Viola's cross-dressed alter ego), in any way threatens the comfortable numbness of the status quo: whereas, even under cover, Viola will only express *her* wonkily reciprocal desire for Orsino by fictionalizing it and translating herself into an ironized figment:

> DUKE: And what's her history?
> VIOLA: A blank, my lord: she never told her love
> But let concealment like a worm i' th' bud
> Feed on her damask cheek: she pin'd in thought...[46]

We have seen how Thatcherism harnessed the permissiveness of the liminal: and what could be more Thatcherite than the blanking of history?

Suggestively, the figure who is most responsible for giving Illyria the shake-up it so direly needs is Feste, the clown, whose license to turn everything upside-down, in the manner of the classic Shakespearean fool, requires of him, in this culture, a contrary inversion. Where, for example, Lear's fool is a little portable liminal zone in his own right, whipping up the storm in Lear's battered mind by tearing apart the armatures of language and authority in favour of a bleakly ludic proliferation and disorienting multiplicity, it is a measure of how awry things have become in Illyria that it falls to Feste to try to nudge everyone out of their dreamworld and back to reality – even if sometimes he has to resort to the crude transpositional technology of sarcasm, as in this moment where he confronts Sebastian, mistaking him for the supposedly identical 'Cesario':

> Well held out, i'faith! No, I do not know you, nor am I sent
> to you by my lady, to bid you come speak with her; nor your
> name is not Master Cesario; nor this is not my nose neither.
> Nothing that is so, is so.[47]

This bitterly ironic outburst in some ways recalls O.J. Simpson's railing at the alternative narratives surrounding the murder of his ex-wife, in contradistinction to which he insists he knows the "facts", while all the time he is utterly dependent on the subjunctive frame around his writing. Here, Feste's disgusted frustration at the subjunctivity he has been forced to live within emerges in a clear statement which is, as he says it, both absolutely sarcastic and, in respect of the malaise it describes, completely accurate: "Nothing that is so, is so." (From which we can extrapolate the conclusion that Illyria has, somehow, become intrinsically sarcastic *as a place*.)

In seeking to insist that, actually, what is so is so – wanting, in other words, to assert the plainness of the nose on his face ("this is not my nose neither") – Feste has by no means abandoned his role as authorized clown: he is still the one whose job it is to create playful disruptions in the social fabric of Illyria. But the most disruptive thing he can do in this place and at this time is to serve as the mouthpiece for what is actual, what is fundamentally and incontrovertibly real.

And in Feste, then, we find the seed of a new model for a dissident theatre within a frozen liminoid culture. If theatre has a dissident – or even, less controversially, a critical – role now, a role that allows it – or compels it – to look thoughtfully at and speak cogently to its cultural and political moment – just as we see it doing in all the Shakespeare plays we have considered in this chapter, for instance – then this is how that dissident role becomes possible again: in its abandoning of subjunctivity as the final frontier of its discontinuity, its handling of the structures of 'as if' or 'what if?' which have traditionally been its default modality as no more than topical strategies within a larger indicative project in which we are invited to see 'as is', say 'what is'.

This is certainly not to suggest that theatre can no longer be a space of thought-experiment and speculative action, that it can no longer afford the luxury of fiction or subjunctivity or matrix; a theatre that could not admit those means would quickly become inhospitable to almost any kind of concerted performance, and performance probably remains theatre's most viable basis for activity. To say 'what is' does not invalidate

any of these lines of enquiry: it simply frames them so as to remind all
participants – makers and audience alike – of their basic indicativity and
their potential for real consequence outside the theatre space.

To give an example – what feels, in some ways, like quite a crude
example – from my own practice: at the beginning of my 2012
performance *GOD/HEAD*, after a brief, knowingly fictional dream-
sequence preface, there was a passage by way of introduction to the
show, which I spoke every night, allowing myself to deviate a little
from the script if it was productive to do so. Among the elements I
made use of during that introductory sequence were the following:
(i) saying hello and welcome, and saying my own name and the name
of the show; (ii) saying a little bit about the content of the show,
and addressing in advance in particular the presence in it of very
personal material that might cause audiences to be concerned about
my real-life wellbeing, regarding which it felt helpful to reassure them;
(iii) indicating and naming some of the apparatus in the room – the
furniture, the lights, bits of set dressing – so as to remind everyone of
the constructed nature of the event and the materiality of the situation;
(iv) introducing my collaborator James Lewis, who was operating lights
and sound from a desk within the performance space, and explaining
why we wanted him to be visible rather than hidden away; (v) finally,
introducing each night's guest performer, explaining to the audience
a little about how they and I would have worked together during the
afternoon in the run-up to the show, and then welcoming my guest
to the stage. It was always possible for me to interpolate into this
preamble, without disrupting or jeopardizing it in any way, references
to any other real-life elements that I might find it beneficial to
acknolwedge. For example, the first quarter-hour of one performance
was beset by a lot of noise coming from offstage, and it was useful to
release the pressure of any tension around that simply by naming it; on
another night, I was glad to be able to welcome into the small fifty-seat
auditorium my friends' baby, who was attending his first ever theatrical
event: by naming him and celebrating his presence, and voicing my
own expectation that he'd probably join in a bit, I hope I dispelled any
anxiety that other audience members might have been feeling around
the possibly unpredictable consequences of his presence – and I can't
help feeling that that in turn assisted in the creation of a sufficiently
relaxed environment that, in the end, that youngest audience member
was incredibly quiet and unintrusive.

There is, as I say, a rudimentary, gestural quality to this set-up – pointing at the lights, pointing at James, pointing at the structure of the show itself – which was partly attributable to the nature of that piece and its focus on transcendental experience (with which this explicit materiality felt like an important contrast), but also simply felt like an expeditious routine through which to establish the parameters and permissions of the event, much as the safety demonstration at the start of a flight helps to frame what follows, even if individual passengers may not find it worth attending to. What I have never felt this sort of introduction do is undermine what's ahead, or rob it of its capacity to move or transport or affect its audience. The diction may be rather different in a small London fringe theatre: but saying hello, opening up the space, setting up the concerns of the show from its makers' perspective, pointing to the materiality of the theatre space itself and the collectivity of the audience: these are exactly what Shakespeare asks of the Chorus right at the beginning of *Henry V*.

In that sense, suggesting that theatre might make good use of the indicative frame in order to help an audience (and its own makers, too) read more critically the movements between the subjunctive and the indicative, or between matrix and non-matrix, or between the nude and the naked, that take place within that frame, is not a response to a particular cultural moment, but simply a deduction from the logic structure of the theatrical event. It is in considering how theatre might specifically bring about its phases of *incorporation*, its post-liminal return to indicativity, that we find ourselves speaking much more particularly to our present condition. As we have seen, the frozen liminoid culture in which theatrical events are currently situated – whether that situation can be broadly characterised as either participating in or interrupting or problematizing or enhancing the liminoid hegemony – has fully emerged only really in the third millennium.

In thinking back over my own developing relationship with these ideas, I am struck by how different my perspective was at the time of the setting-up of my first professional company, Signal to Noise, in 1999. At that point, perhaps the strongest influence on my thinking around what else theatre might be and do – apart from the negative influence of much of the theatre that was being made and feted at that time – was a manifesto written by the French poet and essayist Pierre Joris, called 'The Millennium Will Be Nomadic Or It Will Not Be: Notes Towards A Nomadic Poetics'. Joris's brilliant piece – I still find it brilliant, for all that

I would no longer accept its propositions – is about poetry, and about the culture of poetry, and its superficial consonance with the concerns of theatre and performance is intermittent at best, but Joris's thinking still seemed to offer an interesting and productive lens for looking again at how theatre might refresh its position and its standing in the wider culture. Joris's manifesto starts like this:

> The days of anything static – form, content, state – are over. The past century has shown that anything not involved in continuous transformation hardens and dies. All revolutions have done just that: those that tried to deal with the state as much as those that tried to deal with the state of poetry.[48]

It is clear right from the start that Joris is angling to pick up from the legacy of thinkers like Debord and Deleuze: all is drift, all is endless becoming. (I was especially delighted at the time to find that this seemed to chime with the thinking of one figure by whom I was then – as now – particularly inspired, Martha Graham: "No artist is pleased.... There is only a queer divine dissatisfaction, a blessed unrest that keeps us marching and makes us more alive than the others."[49])

Joris's programme is almost extravagantly liminal, as he breezily and attractively asserts the importance of restless, homeless language; of language's constant engagements with otherness, in all its multifariousness, and impurity (which we might call 'noise'); and of its perpetual movement between different kinds of 'outside', including exile, and different renderings of 'between'-ness, including translation. This all felt right, at the time, in relation to a theatrical project that was urgently seeking new forms and methodologies, and hoping perhaps above all not to replace the orthodoxies with which we had become disenchanted with different orthodoxies that would be equally disdained in time. What's more, it was easy to see straight away the possible applications and executions of some of these ideas in a theatrical context: for example, I was interested in virtuality and celebrity as two intersecting species of exile, which produced some of the background and content for *The Consolations* (1999) and *Napoleon in Exile* (2002); and in the noisy textures of translation and polyphony, which were important to both those pieces and to *Past the Line, Between the Land* (2003). Most of what Joris located in his 'noetics' (nomadic poetics) manifesto also seemed to me promisingly queer: its promotion of a confounding slippery shape-shifting otherness might activate all kinds of interesting effects in language, but it also made for an adventurous, impure, unabashedly erotic space in which to play with bodies, with gender, polymorphousness and fluid sexuality. Which was all to the good, though in a sense it represented a distortion of Joris's nomadic poetics, in which language did not in any sense appear to belong to the body, but rather to move through and between bodies; he speaks in the manifesto of "free lines of erotic flight",[50] but in pursuit of an otherness that seems to transcend and evade gender and carnality altogether.

Though Joris has continued to extend and expand his concept of 'noetics', the manifesto seems increasingly to me to speak from, and to, the moment of its inception in 1996. There is one key idea that Joris makes use of in the manifesto – the 'mawqif' (to use Joris's spelling; more usually, 'mawaqif'), an idea I'll discuss below – which, distinctively, has become more timely in the new millennium; the rest feels as if it has been somewhat overtaken by events. (At worst, it has come to look quaint.) The appeal of his essay for me lay partly in a question that Joris does not make explicit but was hugely pertinent at the time, and continues to become ever more so: that is, how do we, as activists, as anarchists, as makers against-the-grain, apply ourselves to the nomadic nature of power in a globalized political terrain? The speed and fluency and borderlessness that now characterises the movement of information and capital, the permissive grid that we used back then to refer to as the 'superhighway', had already radically transformed the contours of financial, military, governmental, industrial and surveillance operations, long before cultural commentators like Joris were using those shapes to think with. In this respect, much cultural activity lagged behind the political reality; even as late as 2003, I remember it feeling like a new, or at any rate desperately under-explored, problem with the protests in the run-up to the invasion of Iraq, and particularly on the exceptionally large march organized by the Stop the War Coalition on February 15th of that year: as we trudged through the streets of London, buoyed by the extraordinary size of the turnout, it was hard not to feel that we were shouting at empty buildings, we were performing our fury to vacated monuments that had long since lost their precise ideological potency. I kept thinking, "There's nobody there." The real power was no longer anywhere to be seen in the city's streets, or even in its theme-park array of institutional spectacle. Like Pierre Joris's nomadic poetry, it was always somewhere else, endlessly moving between placeless forms. Not only mass protest but almost all dissident or resistant cultural action

was missing the beat now, distracted and slow and dragging its heels
through evacuated roads. Almost ten years earlier, Critical Art Ensemble
had published their essay on 'Nomadic Power and Cultural Resistance',
about the already-changing nature of art-as-activism as a means of
creating political and social disturbance through acts of "subversion":

> Knowing what to subvert assumes that forces of oppression
> are stable and can be identified and separated – an assump-
> tion that is just too fantastic in an age of dialectics in ruins.
> Knowing how to subvert presupposes an understanding of
> the opposition that rests in the realm of certitude, or (at least)
> high probability. The rate at which strategies of subversion are
> co-opted indicates that the adaptability of power is too often
> underestimated...[51]

The essay goes on to discuss the importance of resisting nomadic
power "in cyberspace rather than in physical space",[52] through a
programme of hacking, targeted viruses, data kidnapping and so on.
(And for a while I got quite interested in virus-writing as a potentially
interesting form for a 'political poetry' worthy of the name, but as a
dilettante artist rather than a serious coder, my engagement with the
notion quickly got stuck at the conceptual stage.) But even the bracingly
militant Critical Art Ensemble disappointingly conceded that "this
suggestion is but a science-fiction scenario".[53]

Of course, activist networks (with and without the frontline
participation of theatre makers and other artists) have over the past
decade learned how to turn to their advantage the emergent structures
of several generations of social media; in a small way, and as someone
who has largely shied away from the possibilities that digital culture
have made available, I will gladly testify to the transformative effect
that Twitter has had on my practice, and in particular on the sense
I have of working in dialogue and solidarity with other artists;
likewise, maintaining a blog on-and-off since 2006, and interacting
with its visitors and with other bloggers, has been an extensive and
productive activity. But I have mostly cherished these online spaces
and conversations for their real-world outcomes: any number of
discussions and collaborations that have taken place in rooms and
parks, accompanied by tea perhaps or pizza, or culminating in a warm
bearhug or the exchange of gifts.

And it is partly this sense of real-world activity being invigorated by concomitant movements online that I am thinking of in suggesting that Pierre Joris's 1996 manifesto has been 'overtaken by events': but of course the most crucial event – at once the most complicating and the most decisive – is the series of terrorist attacks on the U.S., most saliently the World Trade Center buildings in New York City, on September 11th 2001. Thinking about 9/11 now – having myself been living without a television at the time of those events, so that the archive of visual documentary and iconography with which many people are still saturated is not as strong or as immediate in my recall – I think almost entirely about the much less spectacular movements in the aftermath, both immediately and in the longer term, as friends and colleagues and distant witnesses began to think and talk together about how it might be possible, how it might be conceivable, to react; to rebuild, but also to reflect, to respond, before rebuilding, so as to not build on the same faultlines. I think about the care that was taken, the promises that were made in that moment and those that could not be made.

In particular, I think of a feature on the web-based journal PORES ('An Avant-Gardist Journal of Poetics Research',[54] as it then dubbed itself), linked with the Contemporary Poetics Research Centre at Birkbeck, University of London. For their second issue[55] – undated online, but I'm deducing a publication date in late 2002 – the editors invited a number of poets and critics to respond to three questions: firstly, "What is your understanding of the cultural and political moment you find yourself in?"; secondly, "What necessities have emerged for you as a writer/artist/scholar after 'September 11' and the events that have followed?"; thirdly, a more general enquiry about political concerns and action. Twenty-two responses, almost all from American and British writers, are published at the site.

For me, the most immediately interesting and provocative of those responses comes from the American poet Brian Kim Stefans, writing in August 2002. His answer to the first question is distinctively liminal in character: "My sense is that we're kind of hanging in-between, waiting for that world 'to be born' that, from this vantage, doesn't look very good though I have this feeling that, once it's here, we'll all know what to do."[56] It's notable that in Stefans's construction, that liminal 'in-between-ness' is an uncomfortable position, and that some incorporative resolution is desirable even if the prospect is a challenging one; and the rest of his response continues to bear out this position.

In turning to the editors' second question, regarding the artistic imperatives that have come to the fore in the aftermath of 9/11, Stefans plays down the effect of those events on his practice – "I don't think my life has changed all that much"[57] – before opening up a speculative line of thought that, in the context of the present chapter, may seem highly suggestive:

> The only large difference might involve my turn away from internet art and an attempt to move more into performance/ theater and, most recently, photography, possibly because I think these skills will be more useful in a period of civil unrest (such as I anticipate, in a way), but also because they have something to do with witness and spectacle which the web never really dealt with adequately or interestingly…
>
> … I do have this sense that I want to get out of my room (where I am chained to Flash and such things when working on the web) and into the daylight.
>
> I feel some need to get back 'in touch' with the world on a basic epistemological level, since it was that world in which I was dumped when the planes struck on 9/11.[58]

He goes on to remark, about the often eye-catching, media-friendly "gesture[s]" that have characterised public demonstrations since September 11th, that "the puppets are good, but I think we need bodies out there…imagining what can be done now, in a group and as a culture, on the streets [where] we live."[59]

The theatre that Stefans is describing is clearly quite distinctively post-liminal in character: the "bodies…on the streets" for which he hankers are functionally similar to the "nose" on Feste's face, in all its indicative and incontrovertible plainness. Vibrating through this imagined (but becoming-real) scenario of being "back 'in touch'" is the idea of the body as it registers within the action of *in-corpor-ation* – a corporeal substantiality which connotes and connects both the individual body and the body politic, the public body, the body as "a group and as a culture", taking its place wherever "we live" together, and where our lives – as well as our bodies – consequentially touch each other.

I find it extremely interesting that Stefans yokes theatre and performance so closely and immediately to photography, as another medium "hav[ing] something to do with witness". In my own work I also have tended to think of photography as being particularly akin to theatre, in a way that film and video tend not to be; I've often used the work of photographers looking intensely at bodies – Francesca Woodman, Ryan McGinley, Wolfgang Tillmans, Will McBride, Peter Hujar, Nan Goldin, Larry Clark, Bruce Weber, Greg Gorman, Jessica Yatrofsky, Ed Templeton, Mark Morrisroe, Slava Mogutin all come readily to mind – as a point of departure for theatrical experimentation, and still photography gradually displaced video as the favoured means of documentation for my research work with Jonny Liron precisely because it seems to exceed its documentary role, not only capturing images and moments but often quite abundantly yielding other possibilities. My sense – not highly developed, but consistent – is that the still photograph, especially one that captures the body either in movement or very pressurefully in a single moment, requires of the viewer seeking a relationship with the image that *they* move, so as to complete the work; it is this sense of movement within the viewer that clinches for me the *theatricality* of photography which takes the body as its principal subject, whether the impetus is portraiture, or documentary, or out-and-out pornography.

One particular (and acutely theatrical) photo-based work that Stefans's incorporative desire might recall is fellow American artist Allan Sekula's *Waiting for Tear Gas [white globe to black]*, an installation of photographic slides from 1999-2000, which at the time of writing is on display at Tate Modern, London. It ought to be noted first of all that *Waiting for Tear Gas* predates the September 11th attacks; the major questions around liminality and incorporation that Stefans raises are only circumstantially – and not specifically or intrinsically – connected with the impact of those particular events, and it is important not to think of 9/11 as being a definitive landmark in the timeline of these cultural tendencies. A popular movement against the dangerous liminoid permissiveness of global capitalism was already underway and gathering momentum, as Sekula's photo-installation evocatively demonstrates. In *Waiting for Tear Gas*, we are shown a sequence of 81 slides on a fourteen-minute loop: Sekula's images capture moments from mass protests against the World Trade Organization conference in Seattle in November 1999. We see individual bodies and a collective body, and we see a constant movement between the two, as subjects framed centrally in one image are glimpsed again in the background of another; by extension, we see acts of (and are invited to readings of) individuation, and acts of authored collectivity.

Wanting to report from *within* the protests – to be another body on the street – rather than commenting on them from a journalistic vantage, Sekula uses entry-level photographic equipment without special lighting or post-production techniques; even more importantly, he does not carry a press pass or import into the event a photojournalist's sense of seeking single images that will function definitively or iconically (and, to that extent, transcendentally) in rendering the unfolding and sometimes disorienting events as a narratively clear commodity format. (In a way, Sekula's pitching of his work in this context mirrors Grotowski's concern that specialist technique tends to distort and estrange, even when it is intended only to connect and inspire.)

The WTO protests that *Waiting for Tear Gas* both documents and participates in are in themselves a fluid, nervous choreography of "bodies…on the streets" (including the artist's own), and Sekula's own commentary on the work is, again, assertively post-liminal:

> [S]omething very simple is missed by descriptions of this as a [protest] movement founded in cyberspace: the human body asserts itself in the city streets, against the abstraction of global capital. There was a strong feminist dimension to this testimony, and there was also a dimension grounded in the experience of work. It was the men and women who work on the docks, after all, who shut down the flow of metal boxes from Asia, relying on individual knowledge that there is always another body on the other side of the sea doing the same work, that all this global trade is more than a matter of a mouse-click.[60]

Materiality, as it shows up in considerations of gender, class, and labour relations, and the fact that nomadic power has by no means displaced the lethal corporeal realities of globalized trade currents, is the matter of Sekula's art: and, as such, his work clarifies something about theatricality and the location of what we might call 'incorporative dissidence' – that is, that dissident action that is energised not by liminal subjunctivity but by concerted movement beyond that liminality, the reclaiming of a voice in which to say 'what is'. And it is the indicativity of that voice, rather than the site in which the utterance takes place, that is the crucial and consequential factor.

So, we should be cautious, for example, around Brian Kim Stefans's eventual call for "effective street theater"; though it appears sound, we would do well not to take it directly at face value. Street theatre would seem to be the almost ludicrously obvious response to a call for politically active performance that places "bodies…in the streets". But the strategies that street theatre commonly uses in order to make its mark and attract its audience are often focused on discontinuities: spectacle, virtuosity (of physical skill, say, or improvisatory agility), scale, assertive power / highly dominant matrix (especially with walkabout performance), and so on. Mitigating these factors, of course, is the removal both of barriers to 'entry' or access, of the kind often disastrously associated with fixed and designated theatre buildings, and of borders to protect or elevate the work (which is why the conceptual barriers around it often have to

Still from *Waiting for Tear Gas* © Allan Sekula.

be insistently signalled by the work itself). Street theatre is as diverse as any other performative niche and at its best – and in the right context – it can be almost uniquely successful in intervening in political realities in a productive way. But much street-based work is heavily invested in its liminoid character – albeit with a more developed sense, often, of what that means – and there is certainly always the risk that it merely creates an alfresco version of the Shunt Lounge problem: that the radical potential it blatantly indicates is the property of the work itself, rather than of the social relations it might initiate; that engaged spectators and casual passers-by alike are asked to see the performers, the skills, the novelty, but are not always explicitly asked to see themselves watching that work, to see themselves as co-creators of a negotiated space rather than lucky recipients of a topical burst of creative largesse.

By the same token, the theatre artist as an exemplary 'body in the street' is an ideal figure whose pertinence is defined by structure rather than locality. In other words, the body in the street is the body of an actor who may, in the moment of action, be standing on the well-lit stage of a prestigious and heavily-subsidised proscenium arch theatre, or drawing in a notebook on the top deck of the night-bus and engaging fellow passengers in a conversation about local fire station closures, or hanging nervously from a trapeze in a found site on the edge of a city in front of an audience of hundreds, or silently undressing in front of two other people in an unloved rehearsal room with no natural light, or dancing along a rural horizon as part of a community-organized torchlit procession in the dead of night, or sharing your bed with you and trading whispered secrets – or even performing in a street theatre show actually in the street outside the entrance to a shopping centre on a wet Saturday afternoon. It is not the *street* that enables or guarantees the mood of indicativity that Stefans is asking for when he writes of the present necessity of "shucking off the worn ironies of an age of relative 'prosperity'": it is the *actor*, the attentivity and intrepidity of the actor-at-work, that makes incorporative dissidence possible as an enacted commitment in resistance to a frozen liminoid culture. The actor must be capable of making her own street. (Being able to see the rehearsal room, or the shared bed, as no less a public space than the pros-arch stage or the area outside the shopping mall is a vitally important start.)

It is time, then – it is *timely* – to prepare to quit the island of liminal theatre, like Prospero announcing his retirement to Milan; to walk out of the forest and into the light, inferring, as Puck counsels, that the strange slipperiness of our time together was all a dream. But where these Shakespearean endings nudge us out of the theatre and back into our everyday lives, we want to be *more* at the theatre, not less; we want to be more deeply engaged in lives we can stand to call 'real', and in which we stand together, more consequentially ourselves, single bodies reaching towards other bodies to make a larger body, a queer-anarchic body politic. How shall we imagine the space of *that* theatre? We walk out of the forest towards what, exactly?

Perhaps, on the way there, we might pick up on a useful left-over idea from Pierre Joris's Nomadic Poetics manifesto: the 'mawaqif'. This Arabic word describes the temporary resting-place, or the act of resting, between periods of nomadic transit. It is not a place of settling, because it is defined by the phases of travel on either side of it, and the pause occurs in the full expectation of that continued journey; it is a resting place in the sense of 'rest' that we associate with music, perhaps – the flow-forward does not cease in that silence; Joris refers to "this moment of movement-in-rest"[61]. The term has its origins in classical Sufi poetry, where the mawaqif has a spiritual significance which Joris strips out but which may nonetheless enrich our sense of the structure: in the pause of the mawaqif, the poet enters into a dialogue with God, and indeed the mawaqif poem quickly becomes a genre in itself (as in Muhammad ibn Abd al-Jabbar Niffari's tenth-century *Kitab al-Mawâqif,* or *Book of Standings*). For me, this brings to mind Caroline Bergvall's strange and fascinating poem 'VIA: 48 Dante Variations', which collates forty-seven translations (plus the original) of the first three lines of Dante's *Inferno,* assembling them in alphabetical order and giving an absolute minimum of citatory detail:

1. Along the journey of our life half way
   I found myself again in a dark wood
   wherein the straight road no longer lay
   (Dale, 1996)

2. At the midpoint in the journey of our life
   I found myself astray in a dark wood
   For the straight path had vanished.
   (Creagh and Hollander, 1989)

3. HALF over the wayfaring of our life,
   Since missed the right way, through a night-dark wood
   Struggling, I found myself.
   (Musgrave, 1893)

4. Half way along the road we have to go,
   I found myself obscured in a great forest,
   Bewildered, and I knew I had lost the way.
   (Sisson, 1980)[62]

– and so on. As the piece continues, the tension between repetition and variation produces some interesting effects, not least the continual restatement, in slightly different terms each time, of the location of the poet's predicament: "half way" through the journey of life, or "at the midpoint", or "midway", or "in the middle". This sense of mid-life crisis shimmers nonetheless with the promise of the mawaqif, partly because the discrepancy between each of the translations creates a tremulous sense of (to borrow Joris's phrase) "movement-in-rest"; what undermines that promise is our being located in a "dark wood" or "great forest". Dante's, then, is a perfectly liminal midpoint, whereas the mawaqif might usefully be seen as liminality inverted: structurally, it is basically identical – a phase of hiatus or suspension between two periods of movement which frame that suspension and give it its cultural meaning; but where the liminal phase is one of wandering, fluency, restlessness, rootlessness, the mawaqif is more like a landing-stage in a purposeful journey, a brief period of (as it were) vertical rather than horizontal self-projection, with a sense of forward motion on either side. What mawaqif shares with liminality (but not with the liminoid), then, is a sense of structural discontinuity – in which respect, mawaqif perhaps resembles the theatre-as-'shelter' we described earlier in response to Keston Sutherland's commission ("Try doing it now"). But what we are seeking, in wishing to redescribe theatre to ourselves, is a model in which any such discontinuity is, one, minimized, and two, located not in the object but in the viewer: that is, a model in which theatre can be construed as a mode of perception at least as much as it is a medium of presentation. In this model, the audience first and foremost sees and understands what *it* is doing, by way of a dynamic premise for the negotiation of a consequent relationship with what it is being given.

We walk out of the forest together, and we come to stand at the edge of a field.

———

Everything comes to him
From the middle of his field. The odor
Of earth penetrates more deeply than any word.
There he touches his being. There as he is
He is.[63]

— Wallace Stevens, 'Yellow Afternoon'

"…you make a field and then you leave inside it what is happening."[64]

— Eric Mottram to Bob Cobbing

Here we stand, together, at the edge of a field. We're trespassing in an essay by John Berger, written in 1971, presumably during the preparation of his seminal television series *Ways of Seeing* which was broadcast for the first time the following January, as the liminal tumult of the late sixties tipped into its drab back-to-life reincorporation. The essay we've stepped into here, which is also about ways of seeing, is called, simply, 'Field'.

The idea of the 'field' is set to work in many different disciplines and practices. It is a concept in geometry, and in algebra; in physics, and in spatial analysis, and in the study of visual perception. For the philosopher Pierre Bourdieu, 'fields' are structures – networks, or sets of relationships – in which people interact, socially, culturally, institutionally, and in doing so establish their relative power and cultural capital within the context of that particular structure. The idea of the field as a frame for or container of interacting or interrelatable elements has been powerful also in art; as a key part of the conceptual apparatus of abstract expressionism (especially in the emergence of Color Field painting in the 1950s and '60s), and – partly by association – in the mid-century activity of John Cage and Merce Cunningham, whose 1963 *Field Dances* was a hugely significant work that, in turn, influenced figures like the poet Clark Coolidge. More recently, at the point that, prompted by discovering Berger's essay, I started thinking about the idea of the field in relation to theatre and performance, I was interested to learn about the project *Field* initiated by Matt Davis, an extremely fine musician I had first encountered on the London free improvisation scene, and who had begun to curate a series of events, mostly based around Chisenhale Dance Space between 2004-6, and bringing together musicians, dancers and live artists in shared transdisciplinary space, and in cohabitation perhaps more than collaboration as such. Davis introduces the project thus:

> Field is a live art project which looks at space and spaces.
> Field is a controvertible space: one that refuses to prioritise interpretation before experience. To ask "What is it? Is it this or that", is pointless. The answer could always be yes or no, so it is always nothing. Field does not exclude the possibility

of other times and other places. It is a story with no plot and
no resolution. There is no clarified gameplan or artefact, and
has no distinct ideas to validate it. Each Field event is unique,
running to no preconceived, overlying structure.[65]

The final *Field* event curated by Davis, in an actual field in Hastings
one windy day in October 2006, turned out to be directly inspired by
Berger's essay:

> ...which seemed to articulate a lot of what we were talking
> about in the work: about how to achieve an appreciation of
> space through being. How to not do too much, how to not
> scapegoat the audience. How to be more real than we would
> be otherwise. I can't really say things like more real I know,
> but there you go. I think that's why we make the work.[66]

In the terms in which the argument of this book has been set out,
my feeling is that Berger's 'Field' is not a 'space' as such – at least not
really leaning on the sense of abstraction that Cy Twombly or John Cage
would keenly have recognized. In our terms, Berger seems to be talking
about 'place': but Davis, retaining a language of space (or a language in
which space and place suggestively commingle), nonetheless captures
the same mood when he notes that: "The physical aspect is important.
Space is not purely about us and our 'crossing trajectories' through it. It's
made up of earth, rain, concrete, grass, buildings, flesh, blood, shit…it
feels important to reclaim that somehow."[67]

Berger's exemplary field, likewise, is a space in which the "physical
aspect" is of paramount importance: it is a fully inhabited, highly
detailed place, teemingly alive with contingency. The first paragraph of
the essay is almost entirely made up of a single sentence which seems
to grab at impressions: at elementary colours (a rudimentary palette
of "green…blue …yellow…green"[67]), simple metaphors ("shelf",
"paper", "curtain"), a basic account of other actors in the scene: the
sun, the sound of a cuckoo. Only latterly does the elliptical voice reveal
its first secret: that this apparently improvised poem starts out being
about the field but ends up directed apostrophically *to* it: there is no 'O'
to signal it, no clear indication at all in fact, but the phrase "field that I
have always known"[68] turns out to be a pivot, after which Berger refers
to the field as "you".

This half-obscured transition establishes from the start a version of the movement that this whole essay ultimately seeks to describe, if not quite to define: it is a vision of the artist, standing at the edge of the field, whose attentive gaze gives way to an ardent relationship, in which the field that was "it" becomes the field that is "you": it is an intensely erotic transition, a traversing in denial (or defiance) of discontinuity. At the beginning of the second paragraph, the 'voice' pulls back again – recomposes itself – and its "you" now addresses the reader: but that sense of romantic volatility, the feeling that "you" may be engulfed by the rush of passion, suffuses the rest of the essay; I read the whole thing, partly, as a seduction, or as a performance standing on the edge of seduction.

Starting with this rapturously close engagement with one particular field, Berger then shifts to a consideration of a generic field – "Any field, if perceived in a certain way,"[69] he says, echoing the subject of his TV series; or, rather, he wants to talk about the *experience* of a field – just as Matt Davis attributes to social geographer Doreen Massey the useful positing of "Place as an event".[70] Berger's aim then is to think about the properties of the field that is likeliest to give rise to the experience he hopes to describe; so: it should be a grass field with visible boundaries but a minimum of order (e.g. the lines of regular planting); it should be a field on a hillside, so that "the relation between what is distant and near is a more equal one";[71] it should *not* be a field in winter, when activity is reduced; and it should not be boundaried by hedges, so that the greatest possible number of entrances and exits is preserved. (Eye-catchingly, Berger in passing compares this "ideal" field with "a theatre-in-the-round stage":[72] though he quickly thinks better of it, noting that such a theatre space, in its designed cultural context, properly comes after the field, not before it – so the comparison is only really valid the other way about.)

So, then: we are standing, now, on the edge of our ideal field.

> You are before the field, although it seldom happens that your attention is drawn to the field before you have noticed an event within it. Usually the event draws your attention to the field, and, almost instantaneously, your own awareness of the field then gives a special significance to the event.
>
> The first event – since every other event is part of a process – invariably leads to other, or more precisely, invariably leads you to observe others in the field. The first event may be almost anything, provided that it is not in itself over-dramatic.[73]

In other words, something initially catches your attention, and because your attention has been caught, you then notice something else, perhaps some smaller event that you might otherwise have missed. Berger's list of possible 'events' makes for rather a nice poetic text in itself: it begins:

> Two horses grazing.
> A dog running in narrowing circles.
> An old woman looking for mushrooms.
> A hawk hovering above.[74]

– and so on. It may be interesting to readers coming to this essay with theatre in mind that Berger cautions against the "over-dramatic",[75] the event that causes the viewer to lose her sense of the whole field, the event that disrupts or overwhelms everything else, that leads to nothing beyond its own too-obvious repercussions. Berger is after the perceptual chain that draws the viewer gradually in, encouraging their seeing in higher and higher resolution: "Having noticed the dog, you notice a butterfly. Having noticed the horses, you hear a woodpecker…"[76]

"By this time," says Berger, "you are within the experience."[77] And this immediately transports me, in my memory, back to seeing *Gathering*, by the performance collective Rabbit, at London's Chelsea Theatre in January 2005. 'Seeing' *Gathering* was far from straightforward: this was a constructed event in which the audience became the (only) actors, finding their way through a meticulously choreographed series of prompts and cues and invitations. Although the piece's creators watched us remotely as we navigated this confected structure, our sense was that we had been left alone. At first, one watched, more than a little nervously; but before long, everyone had been, to varying degrees, drawn into the playing-out of the piece, and watching was just part of the complex of activities in which we participated from the inside of the structure. There was no sensation of a tipping-point between 'outside' and 'inside': just a gradual enveloping, a gentle absorption. An extant photograph captures me in the middle of playing 'wink murder'; I vividly remember listening to a friend struggle (with great grace) to read aloud a printed text; at some point, a real delivery guy showed up with pizza for us. As I write this, my recollections of the event feel like emanations from a liminal haze, but that's partly just the blurring of memory across a decade and partly an index of the difficulty of really 'seeing' *Gathering* from an interior vantage: in fact, despite the atmosphere of doubt and confusion and slight disbelief, the piece was not really liminal or liminoid at all, but strikingly indicative: nothing stood in for anything else: we were doing exactly what we were doing, and in doing those things we were also building a provisional micro-society that held our actions in a common place. I left feeling both that I'd been absorbed into something but also that I had somehow 'seen' – been invited to see – something very remarkable. *Gathering* is a show that continues to inform my thinking about what I do: I recall it often, especially when I tell people these days that, as a theatre artist, I don't make things, I make the space for things to happen in.

For Berger, this new 'within'-ness changes how we see the field:

> You relate the events which you have seen and are still seeing to the field. It is not only that the field frames them, it also *contains* them. The existence of the field is the precondition for their oc-curring in the way that they have done and for the way in which others are still occurring. [...] You have defined the events you have seen primarily...by relating them to the event of the field, which at the same time is literally and symbolically the *ground* of the events which are taking place within it.[78]

This movement feels like it may have something in common with a sensation familiar to me as a theatre-goer: especially in respect of work which is particularly disjunctive or especially inhospitable to narrative readings – a show like Goat Island's *The Sea and Poison*, say, or Jeremy Hardingham's *And yet but still just this*. Pieces like these depend upon the spectator's perception of the frame of theatre (or performance), which confers on the work a call to attention – just as Paul Goodman says how much he approves of the rising and falling curtain (even in 1964 a slightly old-fashioned bit of business), because "the curtain has nothing to do with illusion, but with watching. 'Look! this is worth watching. Now don't look, go home.'"[79] So we watch these deliberately non-dramatic events, which we might well walk past on the street or flip through on the TV: we give them our attention, because the theatre invites us to: and because we attend to them we may start to find them absorbing, engrossing, both in their own right and in their relations and their consequences; and then, at some point, perhaps not even perceptibly, there is a shift, and we find ourselves reflecting on theatre itself, as the enabling mechanism of this bountifully rewarded attention; we see ourselves, in the theatre, participating in the event: and we are no longer standing at the edge, because the frame has been silently redrawn around us, so that in this moment we are not separate from the work, but clasped within it.

"You may complain," continues Berger, "that I have now suddenly changed my use of the word 'event'. At first I referred to the field as a space awaiting events; now I refer to it as an event in itself."[80] And in this "inconsistency", as he describes it, is the movement of theatre. The space which awaits the event becomes the event: and this is true not only of the theatre building, the bare stage and the expectant auditorium in the designated theatre; it is true of whatever we frame as theatre. A few times I have taught at Queen Mary, University of London, in a black box rehearsal studio which happens to have a very large window in one wall, affording a view out on to the campus. By default the window is covered up with black drapes, for the sake of privacy and seclusion; but I have always felt compelled at some stage with each group of students to ask them to sit for a while in front of the exposed window, with the curtains pulled back. We sit and watch the world going by for ten or fifteen minutes – fellow students running or dawdling between classes, deliveries being made, minor building works, blackbirds hopping, cranes slowly twirling in the distance, the coming on of rain or of unexplained laughter. It's hardly a profound trick but it's worth doing for those few minutes – actually sitting and watching and responding, rather than enjoying the conceptual provocation and moving on. It is surprisingly easy to argue about the 'choreography' of what we see – the moments of serendipity, and of clunkiness; the patterns, the rhythms, the fluid dynamics; the snatches of dialogue we overhear; the moments when there are no human figures passing before us, and other things become the actors for a few seconds – a squirrel, a rubbish bin, an intense point of reflected light. I remember, one time, a furious disagreement in the class about the 'effectiveness' or not of moments when the fourth wall is broken, and some passer-by outside observes that she or he is being watched, and stares back for a few seconds, puzzled, perhaps defiant, just making out in the unlit room our lines of plastic chairs, our various attitudes of paying attention, our ways of seating.

It would be wrong to elide this window exercise too fully or quickly with the conditions of theatre. Though I take it to be a constructed event on the model of theatre, and though it is a rich experience every time we do it, and though it bolsters a useful sense that an agreed frame and a special quality of attention can in themselves be enough to create a genuinely theatrical experience, it's nonetheless true that most instances of theatre will, and should (for ethical reasons not least), be created out of relationships between conscious and consenting participants; and the difficulties attendant on that consciousness and on the legibility of that consent are, no doubt, necessary and disclosing impediments to the ease with which actors and audience might otherwise share a room.

Nonetheless, Berger's 'field' as theatrical space (or, more properly, place) seems to me an abundantly suggestive and enticing alternative to the no less seductive liminality of the forest. Especially the qualities of his "ideal" field contain much that seems positive and workable in the context of theatrical making.

He asks, across two separate points, that the boundary around the field should be discernible, but not inhibiting or excluding – a demarcation, but not a barrier. In this way, attention is focused on a single plane, a situation with edges. This allows us to read the place of our coming-together as special, but it does not require it to be discontinuous from the other places it abuts and reflects; more precisely, the specialness of this place has to do with how we, standing at the edge, will read it, will bestow on it our attention, our involvement, our desiring imagination. This reading act might be instigated and supported by some physical signs, but more than the minimum will tend not only to overwhelm but in fact to contradict – the invitation to engage may come from the work, but the willing acceptance must come from the audience. Any attentive maker will know that the special boundaried theatre space is almost always most excitingly and productively marked-out either by lines of LX tape on a rehearsal room floor, or by stage light. Anything heavier than that becomes an instrument of power. So, for example: more than many so-called experimental makers I am a fan of quite traditional audience/stage splits, in so far as they can be managed softly to support (rather than enforce) a deeply present and attentive engagement on both sides; but I am never at all happy for my work to play on a stage that is higher up than eye-level for the lowest spectators. A raised stage, all too often, is more about an asserted dominance than about clarity of sight-lines.

Secondly, Berger asks for the field to be on a hillside, "seen either from above like a table top, or from below when the incline of the hill appears to tilt the field towards you – like music on a music stand."[81] Interestingly, this is more often the experience of the actor, looking up at a tiered bank of seats: but the point holds totally. Berger's observation is about the unbroken singularity of 'here', a sense that the place we share is spatially and conceptually unified (for all that the experiences of an audience will be multiple and sometimes sharply individual); no part of 'this', or of 'us', is separated out from our intimate continuity. It is this commitment that lands me quite frequently in the fogeyish role of questioning the value of innovative structures that have the effect of dispersing or dissipating the sense of 'here' or atomising our experience of an 'us'.

One obvious mode of separation that undermines 'here' in mainstream theatre, for example – that refuses with almost comic literalness Berger's wish that "the relation between what is distant and near is a more equal one"[82] – is sending away to the margins of the auditorium those patrons who can't afford to pay as much for their tickets as those who are permitted to sit centrally; at the back of the second circle I am not in any meaningful sense 'here with' those who are sitting in the front stalls. Seeing Complicite's acclaimed *A Disappearing Number* from a long way back and a long way up at the Barbican, many of the key images in the piece simply didn't read, because my perspective on their composition was out of alignment. I still wonder if anyone associated with the production had ever attempted to watch it from those angles. As it was, beautiful though much of the stagecraft undoubtedly was (by extrapolation if not by immediate impression), that was, to my mind, a regressive piece of theatre, in that it was patently made specifically for the eyes of wealthy people. Interestingly, the trade-off from sitting in such 'bad' seats was that I got to see all the spike marks on the stage, and the crew creeping about behind the action, out of the line of sight of those in the more expensive regions of the auditorium: a clear reminder of the material realities beneath the magic, on both sides of the footlights. (We might, though, want to think about the ways in which other formats replicate the same issue in different configurations – for example, the immersive choose-your-own-adventure shows that penalise those with less confidence or less mobility or who simply aren't accustomed to a sense of access-all-areas entitlement.)

Finally, Berger cannot make much use of "a field in winter", the meagreness of "a season of inaction".[83] (Many of us have sat through one or more of those at a major subsidised theatre.) Here, the theatrical equivalent is plainly obvious: except it is not merely signs of life that we need, to feel theatre as a place we make and inhabit, but signs of liveness. The "field in winter" is something close to Peter Brook's 'Deadly Theatre', so overburdened with fantasies of authority and control, so flagging under the weight of heavy direction and constrained by artificial rigidities, that nothing can really live or grow there: no reviving kiss of contingency, no happy accident of serendipity, no invigorating glitch or burst of productive noise will make enough difference. Again, it would be a mistake to imagine that this moribundity is the sole preserve of the 'traditional' fourth-wall narrative play, drooping under hot lights and cumbersome costumes and blocked to death. The amount of executive control and hypernaturalistic detail required by some immersive theatre productions is not only deadly in itself but flashily deceitful in the simulation of liveness it sells (far from cheaply) to its flattered audiences, who are no more creatively or meaningfully exploring the syntax and parameters of their freedom than are bored frightened teenagers drinking themselves daft in a city centre precinct on a Friday night.

What Berger's field offers us, then, is a theatre of lightness: lightly framed, minimally controlled, openly accessible from every angle, encouraging of attention, cherishing of both togetherness (in one place) and multiplicity; a theatre in which content is a lightly sketched pretext for the conscious and consensual inhabiting of experimental social form.

Possibly the most radically extensive and potentially disruptive text for performance I've ever come across has exactly this lightness; it is exactly five words long. It consists of no more than a brace of (what read like) profoundly simple stage directions. This 'script' is a performance score by the artist Ken Friedman, one of the key figures in Fluxus since the mid-1960s, though this piece dates not from that liminal high-water mark, but from 2003 – post 9/11, then, and not too long after Brian Kim Stefans's call for "bodies…on the streets". Here is the score in its entirety:

CENTER PIECE

Imagine a life.

Live it.[84]

'Center Piece' is genuinely unnerving partly because, like so much Fluxus work, it feeds off its own seclusion as an artefact, yet it asks to be enacted as an event. In other words, it implicitly lifts itself out of the dirt and complexity of political reality, thriving in the pristine art-space of text on paper. "It's not that simple!", we might well want to shout at its addle-headed fantasy-activism. And yet, we know that we imagine lives, many lives, for ourselves and each other, all the time: wildly different lives, lives much the same as the ones we live in but a tiny bit better or a tiny bit easier; in the span of a Tuesday afternoon we may imagine a life in which everyone on the planet has enough to eat, and we may imagine a life in which the rollerblind in the bathroom is fixed. And we know that sometimes we endeavour to live a changed life that, by necessity, we first have imagined or envisaged for ourselves: a life in which, for the fortnight it lasts, we take the stairs rather than the lift, or in which we stop eating bread or reading the Daily Mail web site; and sometimes, an imagined life lurks tauntingly at the edge – or at the core – of our day-to-day reality: a life in which we quit the job that hurts us, or begin the journey of transition into inhabiting fully the gender we've always on the inside known was truly ours.

In fact, our day-to-day reality is a constant, more-or-less conscious negotiation between the lives we can imagine for ourselves, and the capacity that we may or may not have to allow those imaginings to shape our sense of what, for us, is liveable. In this context, two things in particular strike me as brilliant in Friedman's event score. Firstly, with astonishing economy of means, he draws attention (and a kind of dread, I would say) to the movement between 'Imagine' and 'Live' – that is, to the movement between subjunctive and indicative, between liminal and incorporative, between forest and field. Secondly, and even more provocatively: this is a score for performance, and it can be performed. I know this because I've seen it performed. Twice I've sprung it on my friend Jonny Liron, during a live event in front of an audience: he's opened an unmarked envelope to find Friedman's score inside, and he's had to produce a performative response to it within those particular contexts. To describe either of those memorable occasions in any detail, in terms of what actually happened, would be to risk an unwanted prescriptiveness in relation to a piece whose performance history, it seems to me, is better left unwritten – a blank slate for all who encounter it. But, especially the first time Jonny performed it, something truly extraordinary, and yet very human-sized, took place, in a way that I imagine may have permanently imprinted itself on the memories of many who were present, certainly including myself; bear in mind, as I say that, that Jonny and I were the only two people in the space who knew what the instruction in the envelope was, that produced such a remarkable event.

That invisible, unspoken – unspeakable? – pivot between 'imagine' and 'live' seems to be at work in Berger's shifting perception of his experience of the ideal field, and of the location of the "event". First,

standing on the edge, we look at the idea; and then, in a rush we may
hardly notice, we are absorbed into the idea, participating in it. The
phase of 'imagining' is not completed, nor is the phase of 'living' wholly
inhabited: but our experience is of arriving, constantly, in a place that is
congruent with our re-imagined, re-framed sense of the liveable.

The "inconsistency" that Berger admits in considering this shift
seems to have much in common with another inconsistency, one we have
already been close to but not looked at in detail: that is, the process of
absorption that seems to capture Gonzalo, as he narrates to the King his
Utopian vision for the island of *The Tempest*. "Had I plantation of this isle,
my lord," he begins, "…and were the king on't, what would I do?"[85] But
my ellipsis already conceals an interjection by the shipwrecked courtiers
Antonio and Sebastian, following a pattern established early in the scene
in which almost every utterance of Gonzalo's is heckled, derided or
undermined by this cynical pair. But their satirical commentary is, at
least, fair at this point, several lines into Gonzalo's speculative poem:

> GONZALO: No occupation; all men idle, all;
>   And women too, but innocent and pure;
>   No sovereignty; –
> SEBASTIAN: Yet he would be king on't.
> ANTONIO: The latter end of his commonwealth forgets
>   the beginning.[86]

This 'forgetting' seems strikingly like Berger's "inconsistency": just
as Berger is absorbed by the "event" of the field, so Gonzalo loses
himself in what feels like the beginning of an attempt to live the life
he's imagining: here he is, learning about it as he goes along, thinking
aloud. This is not some frozen liminoid dream-space that Gonzalo's
conjuring, not some "baseless fabric", but a critical engagement with the
affordances of a "brave new world" in which reality, rather than fantasy,
is truly up-for-grabs.

What begins to come into focus, then, is a set of possible movements,
all of which seem somehow to describe the same dynamic, the same
impulse. The space that lights up the imagination slowly, gradually,
imperfectly layers itself over a physical site to create a place that's fit
to be inhabited. An actor comes to life in that place by taking off his
clothes, and then his nudity: an act in which the weapons of privilege
and authorial power are decommissioned, an act of undressing and

unmatrixing as the laying-down of arms. A message of desire, encoded in pulses of light or language, in gestures of speech or movement, hurtles through the air between the people in this place, and breaks up as it goes, becoming incomprehensible, and at the same time more recognizably human, and more exactly true. A man stands at the edge of a field, alone, or with many others standing alongside him and consciously together, and as they are grounded there, the incidental life of the field becomes the life within which their togetherness is expressed.

And all of these movements, these incorporative movements – back to life, back to reality – are perpetual and endless. These are not one-shot gestures, like the lowering of house-lights before the start of the show, or the offering of applause at the end. Our lives continue in the theatre just as they did through breakfast or on the bus travelling in to town: we do not suspend them, we do not check them at the door. The escapism theatre offers us is now inverted: an escape into the real, into the indicative zone of incorporative dissidence. A window open onto the world as we might also imagine living there, and then live there. These acts of movement, of relational change, are never decisive beyond the moment of their making: they have to be perpetual, at least until the liminoid capitalist culture in which we live, the culture that wants to keep us stupid and fearful, is finally unfrozen, is finally thawed by the heat of our newly intelligible desire.

And so we are always taking our place. We are always getting naked, and then more naked. We are always yielding to noise, and letting it surround us. We are always letting what we imagine become what we live.

Perhaps the last word in the topological metaphors through which this chapter has advanced its argument might be given – or loaned, at any rate – to Nicolas Bourriaud, the art writer who in 2009 curated the second Tate Triennial. To generally sceptical reception, Bourriaud coined for the occasion the idea of the 'altermodern' – essentially, the 'something else' that comes after, or alongside as a set of alternatives to, the postmodern: in a sense, it's supposed to be what follows Brian Kim Stefans's sense of "waiting for that world 'to be born'", though I'm not sure it's quite what Brian was waiting for. There is, however, something interesting in Bourriaud's explanation of his term, and of the Tate exhibition that bore its name, in that he invites us to consider the idea of the archipelago, which he says has been inspirational with regard to his conception of the work in the show:

> The archipelago (and its kindred forms, the constellation
> and the cluster) functions here as a model representing the
> multiplicity of global cultures. An archipelago is an example
> of the relationship between the one and the many. It is an
> abstract identity; its unity proceeds from a decision without
> which nothing would be signified save a scattering of islands
> united by no common name. Our civilisation, which bears
> the imprints of a multicultural explosion and the prolifera-
> tion of cultural strata, resembles a structureless constellation,
> awaiting transformation into an archipelago.[87]

The sense of perpetual departure and endless (re-)incorporation is
nicely captured in Bourriaud's model of the archipelago: it is, essentially,
a field of islands: and a quasi-nomadic occupation of that field, moving
restlessly from island to island but always experiencing that travel within
the larger frame of the field, is perhaps the least paradoxical or the most
consistently imaginable way of thinking about the task of the theatre
artist in relation to these kinds of space.

That idea of endless incorporation finds a very different voice,
though one intimately close to Berger in some ways, in the climax of
Peter Handke's extraordinary play *The Long Way Round*, written in 1981
though not performed in English until the National Theatre production
of 1989. Nova, a character who describes herself as "someone from
another village, not very different from this one",[88] climbs a ladder to
make an oration she calls a "Dramatic Poem" in which, through a lengthy
monologue, she counsels and encourages the other characters whose
despair and chagrin has been the material of the whole play. At times
the speech reads like a *Desiderata* for the rural poor, and to contemporary
eyes it may perhaps teeter on the edge of a New Age platitudinousness.
("Yes, it is possible to bow down to a flower,"[89] she says at one point,
particularly annoyingly: though, to be fair, if Yoko Ono said that, I
probably wouldn't mind so much.) But the incorporative urge of her
speech – and, we might imagine, of Handke's authorial desire behind
it – is unmistakable:

> The one thing I can promise you is *nature* – the only reliable
> promise. In nature nothing is ever finished as in the world of
> games, where it must then be asked: 'And what now?' True, na-
> ture can neither be a refuge nor an escape. It provides a model
> and a measure; but the measure must be taken each day anew.[90]

Perhaps the most crucial distinction in a theatre of incorporative dissidence is exactly this: that it is never finished: its work is just carried on by other means, in the transmission of dissident action from place to place and from person to person. One framed, designated performance or event may come to an end, but the event is not a game and that moment is never 'GAME OVER'. Incorporative theatre extends itself not by means of games but through a sustainable state of play, of playfulness – a mode without an object; a way of seeing.

We might worry that there is a paradox here: that all we have done, by imagining (and seeking to realise, through material and event) a space of incorporative dissidence, is invert the problem we were trying to solve. First we were anxious that the liminal seclusion of theatre meant that what happened within its frame belonged so wholly to the authorised permissiveness of its space that it had no hope of exporting back out into the wider culture anything of consequence; then we were concerned that a liminal space embedded in a liminoid culture couldn't aspire to a critical function; now, if the polarity of the first situation is simply reversed, and theatre aims to create an incorporative structure that exists in a dissident relation to the liminoid freeze all around it – and if that dissidence can't anyway be the 'pause' in the operations of capitalism that it might wish to be – what ramifications can theatre actually have in wider society? We will think a little more about this question in the coda that follows, but an important perceptual starting-point is this: it is a strength of incorporative theatre as I have been describing it here, not a flaw in its design, that it occurs within, not outside, liminoid capitalism, and is not discontinuous from it. Theatre, as we have come to understand it here, is no more or less than the emergent property of a constructed event or set of events; likewise, capitalism is a construct: it is not the complex entanglement of unstoppable, unknowable natural forces, as it is so often sold to us; nor is it simply a map of the greedy, venal, competitive, violently unjust natural instincts that it asks us to believe are lurking within us all (or, at best, within those who are out to get us): it is a sublimely terrible network of interlocking systems all of which are no less or more authored constructions than is *King Lear*. It is daunting, but it is not unintelligible; we have resources, and if we believe that theatre is, or can be, among the most crucial – and the most bountifully renewable – of those resources, then we have at our disposal formidable means. We have an apparatus not of brute power, but of a thoughtful, humane, erotic weakness, in the face of a fundamentally malign system that requires our strength to hold it up.

"What we desire," says Bataille, "is to bring into a world founded on discontinuity all the continuity such a world can sustain."[91] And so we stand at the edge of a field, which adjoins another field, and another, and another; and there are enough of us to stand consciously together at every edge and pay careful and loving attention to what we see.

"The field that you are standing before," writes John Berger at the very end of his essay, "appears to have the same proportions as your own life."[92]

5. Coda: Changing the world

> I am here to change the world, and if I am not,
> I am probably wasting my time.[1]
>
> — U. Utah Phillips

> We need a futile gesture at this stage.
> It will raise the whole tone of the war. [2]
>
> — Peter Cook, in 'Aftermyth of War'
> (*Beyond the Fringe*, 1960)

"Theatre can't change the world,"[3] wrote Michael Billington, straight out just like that, in his glowing review of the original Royal Court production of *My Name is Rachel Corrie* in April 2005: and the show's producers were happy enough to display his words outside the theatre when the play transferred to the Playhouse the following year.

To some observers, the very idea that theatre might be (or imagine itself to be) able to change the world is inherently risible, an expression of fantastic hubris and pitiful delusion on the part of egotistical writers and vainglorious actors; even to those commentators, like Billington, who firmly believe that theatre has the capacity, and perhaps the responsibility, to reflect and comment on political realities, to provoke discussion and to foster debate, it is an acceptable unvarnished truism that theatre cannot itself effect change – at least not on a scale that could plausibly be thought of as "chang[ing] the world".

Yet to an artist like the late Utah Phillips – a singer and storyteller – and, to that extent, a theatre maker; and an activist and organizer – and, to that extent also, a theatre maker – to work with any lesser intent is, as he states, a waste of time. I tend to agree with Phillips, though I imagine I might choke a bit on so bald a piece of sloganeering (for which, let me say, I admire him and reproach myself); certainly, the degree of motivation that I feel for my work would be significantly diminished if

I ever believed for a moment that Billington's opinion was correct. But that's hardly a properly rigorous basis for interrogating the truth of his assertion. What I want to do in this brief coda, then, is think through some of the possible responses to Billington's axiom – which, I should emphasize, it is hardly fair to call Billington's alone, given that perhaps a majority of people (maybe including a majority of theatre makers, even) would share its view, many of them more categorically than perhaps Billington does – as a way of examining the premises of our work in theatre and the proportionate aims of our thought and our activity.

The most obviously facetious objection – though one not wholly without merit – is a methodological one. We can't know whether theatre changes the world, because we don't have a control world without theatre, against which to compare the fortunes of our own. There is a lot of theatre going on all the time, and maybe by the grace of some unseen mechanism it is this effort that's holding up the sky. This is, perhaps, flip, but it's not demonstrably untrue, and as such, we can be heartened by it; after all, even the most strenuous denier of anthropogenic climate change usually struggles to contradict a simple grandmotherly saw along the lines of 'better safe than sorry', and if theatre hasn't the capacity to change the world, either for good or ill, then no one is seriously harmed if we continue anyway. But, admittedly, as rallying cries go, this is hardly the Internationale.

A more developed version of the same thought is this: we don't know whether theatre can change the world because not all the results are in yet. We haven't made all the theatre yet. We've barely begun to make theatre that knows how to situate itself in relation to the brutal degrading tyrannies of liminoid capitalism. Too much of our work has counted for basically nothing, because we did not dare to value it highly enough ourselves, or value ourselves highly enough in making it; we are not always confident of the righteousness of our vision, and often we are more-or-less forced into positions of complicity or insipid superficiality or hidebound conservatism in order to try and get anything done at all. Not daring to want to change the world, or (understandably) not knowing how to begin when confronted with the gigantic systemic violence of capitalism – or even with the sometimes equally overwhelming systemic weirdness or inertia of many theatre institutions and organizations, we have probably sometimes (and even in the wretched sorrow of full self-knowledge) been guilty of wasting our time, and the time of others. We have to know we can do better; meanwhile, the world doesn't know where to look: but no, not all the results are in yet.

Another reasonable objection can be made on the basis of testimony. It depends, of course, what you mean by 'changing the world', but many – if not most – of us who work in and/or care about theatre would say, without hesitation, that we have been changed by theatre: that the worlds that we inhabit have been transformed, electrified, sometimes even magnificently ruined, by theatre. I think theatre has made me a better person. I think because I 'do' theatre, I see more thoughtfully, I think more feelingly, I listen more carefully than I otherwise would; I think I am politically and socially and sexually more radically curious because theatre has needed me to be so. I think I can be a better friend, and a better stranger, because of theatre – though often, I confess, I'm not, because theatre can also be a consuming and an interferent medium to inhabit, and an exhausting one. But above all I think theatre changes lives – and how else will we change the world, if not first by changing people and changing the relationships to which people are willing to risk exposing themselves? – because, as Tim Allen and Andrew Duncan say in relation to poetry (and to my mind this is ten times truer of the best theatre):

> Attention is a pure good. What brings states of high attention, is successful as art without further ado. [...] There is a circularity in the situation where someone perceives something vividly because they are in a high attentional state, and are in a highly attentive state because they perceive a cognitive object or set vividly.[4]

And if by 'changing the world', we want only to mean wholesale revolutionary change, and not merely our own narcissistic dabblings in the self-help section – though, again, how else will we change the world, if not first by changing ourselves and our capacity to reach others inspiringly and seductively and encouragingly? – nevertheless I would still be more than happy to begin that decisive surge towards global upheaval with nothing more in my pockets than: "Attention is a pure good."

Most of all, though, we can insist that the question of theatre changing the world is in some degree redundant, because we know these two other things to be true: that in theatre – more clearly in theatre that knows it is incorporative – we can act, consequentially; and the world is changing anyway. The world is changing anyway and that change is coming directly towards us. Baron Tuzenbach in *Three Sisters* already knows this, which is why I transposed his speech of ecstatic foreboding to the very beginning of *...SISTERS*, my naughty deconstruction of that play:

The times are changing, the shadows are closing in; and a
great storm is gathering that will shake us all up when it
finally breaks. It's almost here; you can smell it in the air.[5]

What you smell is the field: it's Matt Davis's list: "earth, rain, concrete,
grass, buildings, flesh, blood, shit": it's the smell by which you know
the difference between "puppets" and "bodies out there". That change
is coming directly towards us and the challenge that is already upon us
is about acting boldly in accordance with it. How can we change with
that change? How can we shape that change towards us and make it
ours?

A richly interesting development in the last few years has been the
emergence, via one particular research project centred on the Department
of Life and Environmental Sciences at the University of Exeter, of
a proposed new disciplinary praxis under the name of 'anticipatory
history'. The year-long project had as its key output a handsome and
engrossing book, *Anticipatory history*, which is introduced by its editors,
Caitlin DeSilvey and Simon Naylor, in these terms:

> We are told that we are facing the real prospect of an increase in
> the rate and scale of environmental change in our lifetimes. [...]
> But the range of available responses to these changes is limited –
> usually cast in terms of loss and guilt – and we often do not have
> the cultural resources to respond thoughtfully, to imagine our
> own futures in a tangibly altered world.
>
> From September 2010 to April 2011 we gathered people in
> a research network to explore the roles that history and story-
> telling play in helping us to apprehend and respond to changing
> landscapes, and to changes to the wildlife and plant populations
> they support.[6]

Noting the important role the humanities have to play in shaping
these debates, they frame the book, and its core idea, in this way:

> This volume poses the term 'anticipatory history' as a tool
> to help us connect past, present and future environmental
> change...[and] consider how the stories we tell about ecologi-
> cal and landscape histories can help shape our perceptions of
> plausible environmental futures.[7]

These objectives chime for me in relation to an anxiety I've had for many years about concertedly political theatre which seeks to 'raise awareness' around issues or 'share information' on certain topics. These tasks can certainly be important, and the pedagogical role of theatre is not necessarily to be disdained, though it needs handling with especial care; but my sense is that only seldom is the problem that we 'don't know' – or, at any rate, that we don't know enough. The real problem is that we don't have a living-space in which to fully know what we know, in which to confront that knowledge and respond to it emotionally without immediately becoming entrenched in a position of fear, denial and hopelessness. We know, for example, a good deal (at a lay-person's level) about climate change, and the threats that it poses to our ways of life, the rhythms and currents on which we believe we depend. It is irrational for us to continue to live as we mostly do. My suspicion is that very few people, now, are unaware of this, or genuinely sceptical about the base of evidence beneath it. I suspect the major stumbling block is that we most often receive news about these ideas – through TV and radio, online news and print media – while we're at home, in the very place where we most want to feel secure, and the place we're most frightened of loss, of risk, perhaps even of change in general. Don't we need a place which is neither entirely 'home' or entirely 'away', in which to come into a more rational, speakable, sensible relationship with our fear of what we know, or think we know? Doesn't there need to be a place in which an encounter with that knowledge can be supported? In which we can imagine change, in which we can tell the stories of the change that we anticipate lying ahead of us, and come to an understanding of those ideas in a way that makes them sites of living and breathing, not of panic, claustrophobia and denial?

I've been very inspired by what I've seen (admittedly not from close-up) in transition culture, which asks whole communities at a local level both to imagine change (in particular in relation to the challenges and opportunities of energy descent and the potential for rethinking money and economic systems) and to inhabit that change. Transition communities evidently become – have to become – very good at thinking together, at shifting the stories that get told, at creating local space in which collective change is plausibly conceivable, and in which the possibility of positive action helps to dispel the stifling atmosphere of individual fear. Recounting the events of a public meeting organized by Transition Town Totnes, transition activist Rob Hopkins writes:

... I felt very moved. There is a power here, I thought, which has remained largely untapped. Surely when we think about peak oil and climate change we should feel horrified, afraid, overwhelmed? Yet here was a room full of people who were positively elated, yet were also looking the twin challenges of peak oil and climate change in the face.

What might environmental campaigning look like if it strove to generate this sense of elation, rather than the guilt, anger and horror that most campaigning invokes?[8]

If there is a big idea with which to end this book, an idea which does not feel instantly unequal to the rubric of 'changing the world', it is, necessarily, at base a very small idea: an idea smaller in its immediate civic footprint than most theatre already is. It's simply this: theatre belongs to everybody; ideas belong to no one.

It seems to me probably true that most people, at some point in their lives, will write a poem: an adolescent nobody-understands-me poem; a roses-are-red Valentine's card poem; a song lyric, a scurrilous limerick, a shopping list that just happens to catch the light in a different way for a moment. Many people will bake a cake, or make a fantastic tarka daal, or knock up a mojito that earns a round of applause. Almost everyone, at some point, will start a band, or whistle a happy tune; or look after an allotment or a window-box; or design their dream kitchen, or crochet a hat for a baby in the family, or build a wall – if only out of Lego; or tell someone a scintillating joke that they're still laughing at two days later; or dance in the kitchen to Wet Wet Wet when they think no one's watching; or make a fancy-dress costume for the dog, or read a kid a bedtime story and do all the voices and really get into it, or sing with a choir, or give someone an awesome blowjob, or get roped into joining in with a community mural, or work on their keepy-uppy skills, or make a piece of jewellery, or go for a walk in the park and feel like it's more than just killing time. Almost everyone will do one or more of those things in their life and a few lucky people might do all of them. Almost no one will make a piece of theatre. And yet there is nothing categorical that should set theatre apart in its cultural or practical proximity by comparison with these other quotidian creative activities.

In other words, 'we' who make theatre, who draw its frames and assert its values, have done so in such a way as to make our friends and neighbours feel our ownership of it as prohibitive, so that that ownership does not seem to them a shareable condition, but rather a special one. Despite (or, maybe, because of) our widespread sense of professional precariousness, our own sense of exclusion and alienation within our industry and our art, we have made the territory of our active work feel strange and intractable. In particular – and perhaps this is, now, more an inherited problem than one of our own making; or perhaps not – we have signalled 'our' investment of an excess of cultural capital in buildings and in apparatus: in the 'trappings' for which, from the other side, live and visual artists despise us, or, worse, condescend to us: the plush, the velvet, the gilt, the swishy curtains (all of which, of course, have little to do in fact with the working lives of most theatre makers now); in the specialist equipment, the cliquey language, the overpriced drinks, the dark, the shushing. The associations that these elements have – of status, luxury, sumptuousness, poshness – also continue to assert themselves in situations where they're absent: uninitiated audiences coming to fringe theatres where I've been working are not uncommonly disappointed to see only rickety chairs and a makeshift design and lukewarm organic beer. What's wrong? Aren't we good enough, perhaps they think, for them to make the effort for the likes of us?

I do still believe that the civic function of theatre can be well-served by big (or small), accessible, exciting, multi-use buildings at the heart of their communities: by major metropolitan spaces hosting world-class events; by buzzing regional arts centres programming smallscale touring work alongside shows for family audiences alongside stand-up comedy or folk music or literary events; by the village halls and community centres served by rural touring networks, who might only have four theatre shows in a year but who manage to fold that work into the same story that brings local residents to that venue for political hustings or jumble sales. When a theatre building can genuinely serve as a centre of gravity for bringing people into encounters with new people and new ideas (or fresh relationships with old people and old ideas), and if it can do so in such a way that the people on the inside of the building look pretty much like the people in the street outside, I'm certain it still has a fundamentally important role to play.

But I've made enough shows for performance in people's homes – having struggled for years to raise any money at all for my work, and then, after a bit, finding I really liked doing those shows anyway – to know that theatre depends on absolutely nothing other than the generous attention of those who come together in a place to make something happen. Perhaps that attention can be shaped, choreographed a little: a table lamp here, a clutch of tea lights there; a bit of Vaughan Williams or Frank Ocean on the living room stereo, or the shipping forecast on the kitchen radio, or the window open to the street outside; a little food to share, maybe; a cat in the room, if nobody's allergic. Maybe someone tells a story, sings a song; maybe everybody does; maybe there's origami skills to pass on, or a conversation to have about some super-local issue that will never attract the attention of the council, or maybe everyone draws on everyone else's body with felt tip pens, or we all read *The Admirable Crichton* or Amiri Baraka's *Experimental Death Unit 1*. There might be a part called 'the notices'. We might just all ask each other, "How are you?", and then listen, really listen, to the answer. Maybe we all just admire the cat, try to be more like her.

What if going to the theatre meant going there, to that house down the road? Paying a couple of quid to cover the costs, or taking flowers, and being prepared for there to be hardly any difference between doing and watching? It might sound nice – or it might sound to you like an unconscionable nightmare. How, then, would you change it? What would be on offer if people came round to your place instead? Or what if, instead of changing your neighbour's event, you changed your mind about what you might want from an evening out?

And how, in the end, how on earth do we get from the changing of a mind in relation to some mild shenanigans three doors down, to changing the world? Well, how else: firstly, by adapting the events we make and the events we attend until they start to really change us, really change our week, our rhythms, our daydreams in the bath, our family outings, our fights with our lovers, the feel of our bodies when we get dressed in the mornings, what we think about time, what we think about voting, how we feel when someone asks us for money in the street. We make those events help to make that change. And then secondly, we make sure that, once a fortnight at least, there's someone on every street who's making their kitchen or their garage or the bit of common ground in front of their estate into a theatre for the evening. We make sure that everyone knows someone who does that, or who goes, and who swears by it. We let the relief show in our faces. We organise things so that the kids can play out more. We introduce the theatre-making people on every street to the people on the next street who are doing the same things, or really different things, and we share what we're finding out. And we let it change us, change how we are with each other: and maybe after a while there's someone on every street every night of the week, or in the morning, say, for the people who work nights or want to take their little kids along. And maybe once in a while, for a change, everyone goes to a professional theatre, to see if there's anything there that's worth copying or learning from or that makes us feel better about what we're doing instead.

And these front-room and bedroom and up-on-the-roof theatres become a network; then a mesh; then a fabric. And there are still some lucky people whose job it is to 'make theatre': and some of them will still work as they always have, doing plays and shows in the civic buildings; some of them will still work way upstream, in the studio laboratories and the institutional research spaces; and some of them will be the ones who help to make the domestic theatre happen, who have the craft skills to help everyone make their own events as brilliant as they can, and the organizational skills to help make connections across the neighbourhood and off into the distance.

In 2011, I made a participatory storytelling show called *Keep Breathing*, in which I invited members of the public to give me a message for the world that could be spoken in the length of a single breath. The piece made a quiet, unagitated case for activism, especially in relation to local issues: and instead of a programme, we made a little one-sheet pocket zine for everyone to take away, which was full of information (with corresponding web links and book lists) about how we'd made the show – where everything had come from, the stories, the music, the practical resources – and encouraged readers to think about making their own theatre piece, after the example of my own, which was exceedingly lo-fi and exhibited no specialist virtuosity really apart from the elegance of Naomi Dawson's set design and Kristina Hjelm's constellation-like lighting. The idea of the zine was inspired by reading in Simon Reynolds's excellent *Rip It Up and Start Again: Post-punk 1978-1984* about the sleeve of one of my favourite singles of that period, Scritti Politti's 'Skank Bloc Bologna':

> On the photocopied sleeve, they went one better than [The Desperate Bicycles] in the demystification stakes, itemizing the complete costs of recording, mastering, pressing, printing the labels and so on, along with contact numbers for companies who provided these services.[9]

I'm sure many upstart bands must have been not only inspired but practically aided by that sleeve. Whether anyone took my zine (and the show) seriously enough to make anything of their own, I don't know. In terms of the broader scenario of people everywhere making their own homegrown theatre, I seriously like the movement I'm describing; I have no idea how plausible it is – but perhaps that isn't the very first thing that matters. I like it because it is manifestly anticapitalist in its operations (and it's easy to imagine those who try to monetise it soon finding that they're talking to no one), but also, in a way, not really anti-anything. What I'm describing is an impulse to positive action – to doing rather than not-doing – simply because, when we allow ourselves to stop suppressing our desire and our anger and our hopes and fears, stop distracting ourselves from our pain and our doubt and our gladness (despite everything) to be alive and together, it is easier to do something with that impetus than to not do something. To get home after work and feel crushed and watch the TV and vaguely dislike everything and go to

How to make a one-sheet zine (as used in *Keep Breathing*) © Kevin White.

bed unhappy and unfulfilled is not easy; it is hard. To use theatre as a way of getting something done, getting something properly loved that is as big as the field you are standing before: that, given the chance, is easy. And it's a rush. John Holloway makes it plain:

> We are presented with a pre-existing capitalism that dictates that we must act in certain ways, and to this we reply 'no, there is no pre-existing capitalism, there is only the capitalism that we make today, or do not make'. And we choose not to make it. Our struggle is to open every moment and fill it with an activity that does not contribute to the reproduction of capital. Stop making capitalism and do something else, something sensible, something beautiful and enjoyable. Stop creating the system that is destroying us. We only live once: why use our time to destroy our own existence? Surely we can do something better with our lives. Revolution is not about destroying capitalism, but about refusing to create it.[10]

Keep Breathing. Drum Theatre, 2011 © Rob Ditcher.

As I re-type John Holloway's words, my heart beats a little faster: but also I feel in my body the doubt, the shortfall – not in response to this passage in particular, but in ending the making of this book. I have to tell you – I don't suppose you'll be surprised – that most of the theatre I make, on whatever scale, with whatever support, whichever partners, most of what I make is far from fulfilling the promise that I've tried to describe. It is not always, not even mostly, exemplary; it is (almost, but not quite, hopelessly) tangled up in all of the systems I came to this place to resist.

And I have to tell you also that I saw a show last night, at a major venue in London where the seats are expensive and the stage is somewhat raised, and I think it was probably the best thing I've ever seen. And it was partly field, and partly forest; it was by no means refusing liminality, but it was setting it to work; no one on stage got naked, but lots of people got half-naked; it was noisy but it was also intensely lucid and its signals feel imprinted on my life today. All of which tells me that some of what I've said here is probably right, and much is probably wrong, and when I'm next in a rehearsal room, in a few days' time, the questions will all still be unanswered.

Before that, I have a meeting with a longtime collaborator in a venue where I've spent some very happy and some very difficult times over the past few years; where I've been bold, and scared, and highly attentive, and never for a moment bored. It's a venue hardly anyone knows about; the work I've shown there, when it's been shown to anyone, has had audiences of a dozen, maybe, or half a dozen, or maybe just one man and a spider (for real): and some of that work, I count among the best work I've ever done, the most radical, the most changeful; the work of which I think I can be most proud.

Sometimes, walking in there, or walking out, I have thought of the words attributed to the anthropologist Margaret Mead (and quoted, needless to say, in an episode of *The West Wing*[11]). Never doubt, she said, that a small group of thoughtful, committed people can change the world. It's the only thing that ever has.[12]

Notes

1 Corrieri, Augusto. 'In Place of a Show (a lecture)'
(Unpublished performance text, 2013)

Introduction

1 Mitchell, Katie. *The Director's Craft: A Handbook for the Theatre*
(London and New York: Routledge, 2009)

2 Hytner, Nicholas. 'Foreword' to Mitchell, 2009, p.xi.

3 Ibid.

4 Redford, Paul & Aaron Sorkin. *The West Wing*, Episode 2.16
(Warner Bros. Television, 28 February 2001)

5 Prynne, J.H. 'A Quick Riposte to Handke's Dictum about War and
Language', *Quid*, 6 (Cambridge: Barque Press, 2000), pp.23-26
available online at: http://www.barquepress.com/media/31/pdf/quid6.pdf

6 Well, quite.

7 "Birmingham's what I think with." Fisher, Roy. *Birmingham River*
(Oxford: Oxford University Press, 1994), p.11

8 I have not been able to trace a primary source for this remark of
Campbell's, though he certainly said something like it to me in a private
conversation in 1999; but it is widely referenced, at various degrees of
separation: e.g. David Cairns, 'Skungpoomery, Part II' at *Shadowplay* (blog),
posted 25 May 2011, https://dcairns.wordpress.com/2011/05/25/
skungpoomery-part-ii/ [Accessed 2 April 2015]

9 "Reading difficult poetry in a swivel chair seems to help me to
understand it; the movement helps my brain to process and fly. Try it!",
https://twitter.com/IMcMillan/status/275565110083342337
[Accessed 2 April 2015]

10 Patterson, Ian. '"The medium itself, rabbit by proxy": some thoughts
about reading J.H. Prynne', in *Poets on Writing: Britain, 1970-1991*, ed. Denise
Riley (Basingstoke and London: Palgrave Macmillan, 1992), p.234

11 Bergvall, Caroline. 'More Pets', in *Fig* (Norfolk: Salt, 2005), pp.86-89

12 Upton, Andrew. 'The Resonating Space' (The 2012 Philip Parsons Memorial Lecture, delivered 2 December 2012), available online at: http://belvoir.com.au/news/the-resonating-space/ [Accessed 2 April 2015]

13 Gellatly, Andrew. 'It's a Curse, it's a burden', *Frieze* 45 (1999), available online at: http://www.frieze.com/issue/review/its_a_curse_its_a_burden/ [Accessed 2 April 2015]

14 Ayers, Robert. '"The knife is real, the blood is real, and the emotions are real." – Robert Ayers in conversation with Marina Abramović', at *A Sky Filled With Shooting Stars* (personal website), posted 10 March 2010, http://www.askyfilledwithshootingstars.com/wordpress/?p=1197 [Accessed 2 April 2015]

15 Higgins, Charlotte. 'Tino Sehgal's Turbine Hall commission: "Attention is what I work with"', *Guardian* (16 July 2012), available online at: http://www.theguardian.com/artanddesign/2012/jul/16/tino-sehgal-turbine-hall-tate [Accessed 2 April 2015]

16 *DC's*, http://denniscooper-theweaklings.blogspot.co.uk/

17 http://denniscooper-theweaklings.blogspot.co.uk/2008_02_16_archive.html [Accessed 2 April 2015; some elements are no longer functional]

18 Ibid.

19 See the discussion of 'matrix' in chapter 2.

20 Callow, Simon. *Shooting the Actor* (London: Vintage, 2004), p.288

21 Gardner, Lyn. 'All the flat's a stage', *Guardian* (8 August 2000), available online at: http://www.theguardian.com/culture/2000/aug/08/artsfeatures.edinburghfestival2000 [Accessed 2 April 2015]

22 My recollection – possibly unreliable – of a personal conversation some time in the summer of 1997.

23 Featherstone, Vicky. '"We have no theatrical tradition – just lots of good playwrights"', *Guardian* (1 November 2005), available online at: http://www.theguardian.com/stage/2005/nov/01/theatre.scotland [Accessed 2 April 2015]

24 Beck, Julian. 'Our mission' [n.d.], available online at: http://www.livingtheatre.org/about/ourmission [Accessed 2 April 2015]

25 Goodman, Paul. *Three Plays: The Young Disciple, Faustina, Jonah* (New York: Random House, 1965)

26 Goodman, Paul. 'Art of the Theatre', in *Three Plays*, pp.xvi-xvii

27 Ibid., p.xvii

Space and place

1 Brook, Peter. *The Empty Space* (Harmondsworth: Penguin, 1968), p.11.

2 Cage, John. 'Experimental Music', in *Silence: Lectures and Writings* (London: Marion Boyars, 1978), p.8

3 Bryars, Gavin. '*The Sinking of the Titanic* at Xebec' (1993), http://www.gavinbryars.com/Pages/titanic_xebec.html

4 Cage, 'Experimental Music', p.8

5 Brook, Peter. *The Shifting Point: Theatre, Film, Opera 1946-1987* (New York: Harper & Row, 1987), p.124

6 Leatherman, LeRoy. *Martha Graham: Portrait of the Lady as an Artist* (London: Faber and Faber, 1967), p.32

7 Clark, Thomas A. 'Some alternatives to the white cube', *The Little Critic*, 11 (London: Coracle, 1996), n.p.

8 Ibid.

9 Bollnow, O.F. *Human space* (1963), trans. Christine Shuttleworth, ed. Joseph Kohlmaier (London: Hyphen Press, 2011), pp.17-22

10 Ibid., p.20

11 Lefebvre, Henri. *The Production of Space*, trans. Donald Nicholson-Smith (Oxford: Blackwell, 1991), p.3

12 Ibid., p.6.

13 Ibid.

14 Greenaway, Peter. 'Just Place, Preferably Architectural Place', in *Movies*, ed. Gilbert Adair (Harmondsworth: Penguin, 1999), p.273

15 Kelly, Alexander & Lloyd, Annie. *The Dust Archive: A History of Leeds Met Studio Theatre* (Leeds: Leeds Metropolitan University Gallery, 2008)

16 *The Dust Archive*, p.1

17 Ibid., p.4

18 Ibid., p.6

19 Ibid., p.9

20 Ibid., p.17

21 Ibid., p.21

22 Beck, 'Our Mission'

23 Weir, Judith. 'Act I: A Traveller in the Desert: Look! There in the distance', from *The Consolations of Scholarship* (London: Novello & Co., 1985)

24 Beck, Julian. *The Life of the Theatre: The relation of the artist to the struggle of the people* (1972), (New York: Limelight Editions, 1991), p.7

25 Goodman, Paul. 'Art of the Theatre', p.vii

26 Pinter, Harold. *Landscape*, in *Plays: Three* (London: Faber and Faber, 1991), p.166

27 Ibid.

28 Since this chapter was written, Tim Crouch and Andy Smith have staged an infinitely more accomplished exploration of the same contradictory dynamic in their extraordinary play *what happens to the hope at the end of the evening*, in which 'Andy' addresses the audience directly, while his 'Friend', played by Crouch, remains always behind the fourth wall. See Tim Crouch & Andy Smith, *what happens to the hope at the end of the evening*, in Tim Crouch, *Adler & Gibb* (London: Oberon Books, 2014)

29 Barker, Simon. 'A Jarman Party', in *Punk's Dead* (Prague: Divus, 2011), n.p.

30 'Contemporary Living Rooms', Harley Gallery, Welbeck Estates, Nottinghamshire (28 May-24 July 2005)

31 Mitter, Shomit. *Systems of Rehearsal: Stanislavsky, Brecht, Grotowski and Brook* (London and New York: Routledge, 1992), p.78. These words are Grotowski's own.

32 Ibid., p.111

33 Ibid., p.125

34 Von Trier, Lars. *Antichrist* (Zentropa Entertainments, 2009)

35 Goode, Chris. 'All you get is sensory titillation', at *Thompson's Bank of Communicable Desire* (blog), posted 8 November 2007, http://beescope.blogspot.co.uk/2007/11/all-you-get-is-sensory-titillation.html [Accessed 2 April 2015]

36 Ridout, Nicholas. *Stage Fright, Animals, and Other Theatrical Problems* (Cambridge: Cambridge University Press, 2006), pp.97-98

37 Thanks, Ang.

38 Schmidt, Theron. *Some people will do anything to keep themselves from being moved* (Unpublished performance text, 2013)

39 A reference, of course, to Roald Dahl's *Charlie and the Chocolate Factory*

40 Sorkin, Aaron. *The West Wing,* episode 1.12, Warner Bros. Television, Original airdate: 12 January 2000 (See also: episode 4.03). In episode 1.12, the quotation is attributed to "a man"; the web suggests the man in question was either Harry S. Truman or Woody Allen.

41 Smith, Andy. 'Re: information sharing', private email to the Theatre141+ discussion group (18 January 2011)

42 Goodman, Paul. *Growing Up Absurd* (New York: Vintage, 1960), p.159-160

43 Ibid., pp160-168

44 Locke, John. 'Of Power', in *An Essay Concerning Human Understanding*, Book II, Chapter XXI (1689), available online at: https://ebooks.adelaide. edu.au/l/locke/john/l81u/complete.html [Accessed 2 April 2015]

45 Baudoin, Patricia & Heidi Gilpin. 'Proliferation and Perfect Disorder: William Forsythe and the Architecture of Disappearance' (2004), previously available online at: http://www.hawickert.de/ARTIC1.html [Accessed 2 July 2013; site apparently down 2 April 2015]

46 Ibid.

47 Adams, Douglas. *Life, the Universe and Everything* (1982), in *The Hitchhiker's Guide to the Galaxy: A Trilogy in Four Parts* (London: Pan, 1992), p.359

48 Stecyk III, C.R. 'Fear of Flying – Speed, A Strange and Tragic Magic' (1975), in *Dogtown – The Legend of the Z-Boys* (New York: Burning Flags Press, 2000), p.14

49 Berry, Bill, Peter Buck, Mike Mills & Michael Stipe (R.E.M.), 'Stand', from *Green* (Warner Bros. Records, 1989), track 4

50 Ahmed, Sara. *Queer Phenomenology: Orientations, Objects, Others* (Durham and London: Duke University Press, 2006), p.16

51 Brook, Peter. *The Empty Space*, p.119

52 Ibid., p.120

53 Ephron, Nora. 'What I Will Miss', in *I Remember Nothing and Other Reflections* (London: Doubleday, 2011), p.221. Thanks to Sam West for drawing attention to this passage in his wonderful speech at Pilot Theatre's Shift Happens conference (5 July 2012), transcript at: http://artsfunding. ning.com/profiles/blogs/speech-at-shift-happens-a-conference-organised-by-pilot-theatre [Accessed 2 April 2015]

54 Forsythe, William. *Improvisation Technologies: A Tool for the Analytical Dance Eye*, CD-ROM with booklet (Karlsruhe: ZKM Karlsruhe, 2003)

55 'Reorganizing: room orientation', in *Improvisation Technologies* booklet, p.62

56 Knight, Christopher. 'Labyrinth from the artist's mind' (*Los Angeles Times*, 13 February 2008), available online at: http://articles.latimes.com/2008/feb/13/entertainment/et-asher13 [Accessed 2 April 2015]

57 Merleau-Ponty, Maurice. *Phenomenology of Perception*, trans. Colin Smith (London and New York: Routledge, 1962), p.250

The naked and the nude

1 Whalen, Philip. 'The Slop Barrel: Slices of the Paideuma for All Sentient Beings', in *The Collected Poems of Philip Whalen*, ed. Michael Rothenberg (Connecticut: Wesleyan University Press, 2007), p.56

2 Bataille, Georges. *Eroticism.* (1957), trans. Mary Dalwood (London and New York: Marion Boyars, 2006), p.17 – though, wishing in this epigraph to depart slightly from Dalwood's version, I have quoted here the original French text: see: *L'Erotisme*. Paris: Les Éditions de Minuit, (1957)

3 Goode, Chris. 'O Vienna', in *Masthead*, 10, 2009, http://www.masthead.net.au/issue10/goode.html [Accessed 2 April 2015]

4 Burrows, Jonathan. *A Choreographer's Handbook* (London and New York: Routledge, 2010), p.195

5 Brook, *The Empty Space*, p.44

6 Burrows, p.184

7 Miller, Tim. *Body Blows: Six Performances* (Madison: University of Wisconsin Press, 2002), p.xxi

8 http://www.castingcallpro.com/uk/ [Accessed 2 April 2015]

9 A random sample accessed in April 2015 returned the following results: of 100 members (split evenly between men and women) whose profiles included an answer to the question 'Perform nude?', responses were: No: 32; Only professionally: 64; Yes: 4. In interpreting these statistics, however, it is important to note that transactions through Casting Call Pro relate to film and television work as well as theatre; screen nudity is an entirely different construction to nakedness on stage, and, as we learn to our continual horror from the dizzyingly exploitative callouts collated at Casting Call Woe (http://castingcallwoe.tumblr.com), the frequency with which young women actors in particular are required to shed their clothes for no pay in half-baked amateur film and video projects makes total sense of the need for 'only professional' self-protection.

10 Berger, John. 'Speech on Accepting the Booker Prize for Fiction' (1972), in *John Berger: Selected Essays*, ed. Geoff Dyer (London: Bloomsbury, 2001), p.254

11 Ibid.

12 Prynne, J.H. *They That Haue Powre To Hurt; A Specimen of a Commentary on Shake-speares Sonnets, 94* (Cambridge: privately printed, 2001), p.3

13 Clark, Kenneth. *The Nude: A Study of Ideal Art* (1956), (Harmondsworth: Penguin, 1960), p.1

14 Ibid.

15 Berger, John. *Ways of Seeing* (London and Harmondsworth: British Broadcasting Corporation and Penguin, 1972), p.54

16 Ibid.

17 Ibid., p.60

18 Wroe, Nicholas. 'Tate Britain: On the move', *Guardian* (3 May 2013), available online at: http://www.theguardian.com/artanddesign/2013/may/03/tate-britain-on-move-rehang [Accessed 2 April 2015]

19 This essay – first published in *The Drama Review*, 16 (1), 1972 – eventually became chapter one of: Kirby, Michael. *A Formalist Theatre*, (Philadelphia: University of Pennsylvania Press, 1987)

20 Kirby, Michael. 'The New Theatre' (1965), in *Happenings and Other Acts*, ed. Mariellen R. Sanford (London and New York: Routledge, 1995), pp.29-47

21 Kirby, 'The New Theatre', p.29

22 Ibid., p.30

23 Ibid., p.3.

24 Ibid., p.32

25 Kirby, *A Formalist Theatre*, p.3

26 Bresson, Robert. *Notes on the Cinematographer* (1975), trans. Jonathan Griffin, (Copenhagen, Green Integer Books, 1997), p.16. I am deeply indebted to Dennis Cooper, whose critical writing and eager conversation around Bresson has greatly influenced my own interest in and perspectives on the director.

27 Ibid., p.14

28 Ibid., p.19

29 Ibid., p.77

30 Ibid., p.64

31 Ibid., p.66

32 Ibid., p.97

33 No primary source for this quotation seems to be known, but it is widely attributed to Brecht, for example in: Geary, James. *Guide to the World's Great Aphorists* (New York: Bloomsbury, 2007), p.206

34 St John of the Cross. 'On A Dark Night', available online at: http://josvg.home.xs4all.nl/cits/lm/stjohn01.html [Accessed 2 April 2015]

35 Bresson, p.58

36 Ibid., p.85

37 Ricard, Rene. 'The Radiant Child'. *Artforum* (December 1981), available online at: https://artforum.com/inprintarchive/id=35643 [Accessed 2 April 2015]

38 'The Radiant Child'

39 Geldzahler, Henry. 'Introduction' to Keith Haring & Tseng Kwong Chi, *Art in Transit* (New York: Harmony Books, 1984), available online at http://www.haringkids.com/art/subway/geldzahler_print.html [Accessed 2 April 2015]

40 Schechner, Richard; Hoffman, Theodore; Chwat, Jacques; Tierney, Mary. 'An Interview with Grotowski' (1968), in *Re: Direction: A Theoretical and Practical Guide*, eds. Rebecca Schneider & Gabrielle Cody (London and New York: Routledge, 2002), p.237

41 ...Yeah, no, I'm not telling

42 Abrahami, Natalie. 'Sex on stage is best done through dance.', *Guardian* (4 February 2009, available online at: http://www.theguardian.com/stage/theatreblog/2009/feb/04/sex-stage-dance [Accessed 2 April 2015]

43 Arons, Rachel. '"Behind the Candelabra" and the Queerness of Liberace', *Los Angeles Review of Books* (27 May 2013), available online at: http://lareviewofbooks.org/essay/behind-the-candelabra-and-the-queerness-of-liberace [Accessed 2 April 2015]

44 Berger, John. *G.* (1972), (London: Bloomsbury, 1996), p.39

45 Berger, John & Silverblatt, Michael. 'Conversation 1, Episode 4', Lannan Foundation (2002), available online at: https://vimeo.com/10516169 [Accessed 2 April 2015]

46 Ibid.

47 Ibid.

48 Ibid.

49 Montaigne, Michel de. 'Of the custom of wearing clothes' 1572-74, in *The Complete Works*, trans. Donald M. Frame (New York: Alfred A. Knopf, 2003), p.202

50 Berger, John & Silverblatt, Michael. 'Conversation'

51 Stevens, Tassos. 'The experience of an event...', at *All Play* (blog), posted 29 December 2011, http://allplayall.blogspot.co.uk/2011/12/experience-of-event.html [Accessed 2 April 2015]

52 Akers, Matthew, and Jeff Dupree. *Marina Abramović: The Artist is Present*, HBO Documentary Films (2012)

53 e.g. Abramović uses the phrase in an interview included in *The Artist is Present*.

54 Sinclair, Iain. 'The Horse. The Man. The Talking Head (a note on Howard Hughes)', in *Suicide Bridge* (1979); *Lud Heat* and *Suicide Bridge* (London: Granta Books, 1998), p.231

55 Braco website [author not identified]. 'About the Gift', http://www.braco.net/about-the-gift [Accessed 2 April 2015]

56 'Braco – Gazing the 11/11/11 Oneness Portal', posted on YouTube (22 October 2011), https://www.youtube.com/watch?v=PqV0q_cHtRE [Accessed 2 April 2015]

57 Ibid.

58 Braco website. 'Ivica & Braco', http://www.braco.me/en/about/braco-ivica [Accessed 2 April 2015]

59 Benjamin, Walter. 'Little History of Photography' (1931), in *Selected Writings 1931-1934, vol. 2*, eds. Michael W. Jennings, Howard Eiland & Gary Smith (Cambridge, Mass.: Harvard University Press, 1999), p.518. I have slightly tweaked the translation.

60 Berger, John. 'Why Look at Animals?', in *Selected Essays* (1977), p.260

61 Ibid.

62 Tisdall, Caroline. *Joseph Beuys: Coyote* (1976), (London: Thames and Hudson, 2008), p.9

63 Berger, John. 'Why Look at Animals?', p.260

64 Ibid.

65 See: Blouin Artinfo website blog pages [author not identified]. 'Belgian Artist Jan Fabre is on the Lam After Cat Throwing Performance', posted 5 November 2012, http://blogs.artinfo.com/artintheair/2012/11/05/belgian-artist-jan-fabre-is-on-the-lam-after-cat-throwing-performance [Accessed 2 April 2015]

66 Agamben, Giorgio. *Homo Sacer: Sovereign Power and Bare Life* (Stanford, California: Stanford University Press, 1998)

67 Wittgenstein, Ludwig. *Philosophical Investigations*, trans. G.E.M Anscombe (Oxford: Basil Blackwell, 1958), p.223

68 Wittgenstein, Ludwig. *Tractatus Logico-Philosophicus*, 4.002, (London: Kegan Paul, 1922), p.39, available online at: http://www.gutenberg.org/files/5740/5740-pdf.pdf [Accessed 2 April 2015]

69 *Marina Abramović: The Artist is Present* [my transcription]

70 Carlson, Jen. 'Marina's Unexpected Nude Speaks Out', *Gothamist* (blog), posted 2 June 2010, http://gothamist.com/2010/06/02/marinas_streaker_speaks_out.php [Accessed 2 April 2015]

71 Ibid.

72 *Marina Abramović: The Artist is Present* [my transcription]

73 Abramović, Marina. Wounded Geode (Transitory objects for human use), Iron, amethyst geode (1994), 'Instruction for the public' documented at: http://www.few.vu.nl/~eliens/media/local/dossier/abramovic/text/backup/Interview_2_%20Marina%20Abramovic.txt [Accessed 2 April 2015]

74 Lodge, David. *Small World* (Harmondsworth: Penguin, 1985), pp.26-27

75 Stigh, Daniela & Jackson, Zoë. 'Marina Abramović: The Artist Speaks', at *Inside/Out: A MoMA/MoMa PS1* (blog), posted 3 June 2010, http://www.moma.org/explore/inside_out/2010/06/03/marina-abramovic-the-artist-speaks [Accessed 2 April 2015]

76 Bataille, *Eroticism*, p.12

77 Ibid., p.17

78 Ibid.

79 Ayers, Robert. '"The knife is real, the blood is real, and the emotions are real." – Robert Ayers in conversation with Marina Abramović', at *A Sky Filled With Shooting Stars* (personal website), posted 10 March 2010, http://www.askyfilledwithshootingstars.com/wordpress/?p=1197 [Accessed 2 April 2015]

80 Berger, John & Silverblatt, Michael. 'Conversation'

81 Bresson, p.64

82 [no named author] 'Eric Massa: Rahm Emanuel Is The "Son Of The Devil's Spawn," Lobbied Me In Shower', *The Huffington Post*, posted 8 May 2010, http://www.huffingtonpost.com/2010/03/08/eric-massa-rahm-emanuel-i_n_490058.html [Accessed 2 April 2015]

83 Interview with Bill T. Jones in Morgenroth, Joyce. *Speaking of Dance: Twelve Contemporary Choreographers on Their Craft* (New York and London: Routledge, 2004), p. 140

84 Kane, Sarah. *Cleansed* (London: Methuen, 1998) p.14

85 Ibid.

86 Goodman, Paul. 'Art of the Theatre', p.xi

87 Goodman, Paul. 'The Politics of Being Queer' (1969) in *Anarchism: A Documentary History of Libertarian Ideas, vol. 2: The Emergence of the New Anarchism (1939-1977)*, ed. Robert Graham (Montreal: Black Rose Books, 2009), p.490

88 Goodman, Paul. 'Wordsworth's Poems', in *The Paul Goodman Reader*, ed. Taylor Stoehr (Oakland, California: PM Press, 2011), p.245

89 Goodman, Paul. *Growing Up Absurd*, p.71

90 Goodman, Paul. *Five Years: Thoughts During a Useless Time.* (New York: Brussel & Brussel, 1966), p.91

91 Many of the works cited and examples of the tendencies discussed in these paragraphs can be found at: http://ryanmcginley.com

92 [no named author] 'Conversations on Art at the Whitney Museum of American Art with Larry Clark, Ryan McGinley, and Sylvia Wolf' (25 March 2003), Ryan McGinley's website: http://ryanmcginley.com/essays/larry-clark-2003 [Accessed 2 April 2015]

93 See: eds. Bonami, Francesco & Simons, Raf. *The Fourth Sex: Adolescent Extremes* (Milan: Charta, 2003)

94 Kupfer, David. 'Interview with Utah Phillips', *Southern Cross Review*, 29 (2003), http://www.southerncrossreview.org/29/utah.htm [Accessed 2 April 2015]

95 Anderson, Laurie. 'Say Hello', *United States* (performance, 1983), [my transcription from *United States Live*, Part 1, track 1, Warner Bros. Records, 1984], cf. text at Lyrics Wikia website: http://lyrics.wikia.com/Laurie_Anderson:Say_Hello [Accessed 2 April 2015]

Signal and noise

1 Sontag, Susan. 'Against interpretation' (1964), in *Against Interpretation and Other Essays* (Harmondsworth: Penguin, 2009), p.5

2 Creeley, Robert. 'In Conversation with Leonard Schwartz', transcribed by Angela Buck from the radio programme 'Cross-Cultural Poetics', KAOS 89.3fm (Olympia, Washington, 24 November 2003), in *Jacket* 25 (February 2004), http://jacketmagazine.com/25/creeley-iv.html [Accessed 2 April 2015]

3 Mancio, Marie-Anne. *An A-Z of The Ting: Theatre of Mistakes – M.*, eBook: Proboscis (2009), p.12, http://diffusion.org.uk/ebooks/ TheatreOfMistakes_M_us.pdf [Accessed 2 April 2015]

4 Allin, Michael. *Enter the Dragon* (Warner Bros. Television, 1973). The scene described can be viewed online at: https://www.youtube.com/ watch?v=LH1GFaw09hk [Accessed 2 April 2015]

5 *Surangama Sutra, vol. 2*. Buddhist Text Translation Society, trans. second edition (2002), p.61, available online at: http://online.sfsu.edu/rone/Buddhism/ Shurangama/ps.ss.02.v2.020526.screen.pdf [Accessed 2 April 2015]

6 Robinson, Ken. 'On Passion' (The School of Life: Sunday Sermons). Talk given at Conway Hall, London, 13 March 2011. My transcription from video documentation available at: https://vimeo.com/21195297 [Accessed 2 April 2015]

7 *Desert Island Discs.*, Julian Barnes interviewed by Sue Lawley [my transcription], BBC Radio 4. First broadcast 28 January 1996, available online at: http://www.bbc.co.uk/programmes/p0093nwl [Accessed 2 April 2015]

8 Sontag, p.10

9 Ibid.

10 [Interview montage: no single author named.] 'If that goes off again I'll kill you', in *The Guardian* (11 September 2008), available online at: http:// www.theguardian.com/stage/2008/sep/11/comedy [Accessed 2 April 2015]

11 Sontag, p.14

12 Ibid., p.8

13 Quoted in: Cloyd, Frederick. 'Kazuo Ohno: Great Butoh Expressionist Dancer Passes Away June 2010', at *Ai No Ko* (personal blog), posted 7 July 2010, available online at: http://tinyurl.com/ohno-garbage [Accessed 2 April 2015]

14 Prynne, J.H. 'L'Extase de M. Poher' (1971), in *Poems* (Newcastle upon Tyne: Bloodaxe Books, 1999), p.161-2

15 See: Porat, Marc. *The Information Economy: Definition and Measurement*, (Washington, D.C.: Office of Telecommunications, 1977)

16 U.S. Census Bureau. 'North American Industry Classification System: 1997 NAICS: Sector 51 – Information' (1997), available online at: https://www.census.gov/eos/www/naics/reference_files_tools/1997/sec51.htm [Accessed 2 April 2015]

17 Wittgenstein, Ludwig. *Zettel* (1967), eds. G.E.M. Anscombe & G.H. von Wright (Berkeley and Los Angeles, California: University of California Press, 2007), p.28(e)

18 Forrest-Thomson, Veronica. *Poetic Artifice: A Theory of Twentieth-century Poetry* (Manchester: Manchester University Press, 1978), p.x

19 Childs, Lucinda. 'Prematurely Air Conditioned Supermarket', from *Einstein on the Beach*. Music by Philip Glass, design and direction by Robert Wilson (1976), see: Holmberg, Arthur. *The Theatre of Robert Wilson* (Cambridge: Cambridge University Press, 1996), p.54.

20 Hurley, Kieran. *Beats* (London: Oberon Books, 2013), p.16

21 Ibid., p.13

22 Eno, Brian. *A Year With Swollen Appendices* (London: Faber and Faber, 1996), pp.194-95

23 Hall, John. *On Performance Writing: with pedagogical sketches: Essays on Performance Writing, Poetics and Poetry, vol. 1.* (Bristol: Shearsman Books, 2013), p.90.

24 Goulish, Matthew. *39 Microlectures in Proximity of Performance* (London and New York: Routledge, 2000), p.124

25 Eno, Brian & Schmidt, Peter. *Oblique Strategies* (19750, see: http://www.rtqe.net/ObliqueStrategies [Accessed 2 April 2015]

26 See the Discogs website entry for *Noisembryo* at: http://www.discogs.com/release/3071077 [Accessed 2 April 2015]

27 Hegarty, Paul. 'Noise as Weakness', paper given at Sonic Interventions (Amsterdam, March 2005), http://www.dotdotdotmusic.com/hegarty2.html [Accessed 2 April 2015]

28 Ibid.

29 Ibid.

30 [unnamed author] 'William Basinski, *The Disintegration Loops I-IV*', at the *Haunted Ink* website: http://www.hauntedink.com/25/basinski-disintegration.html [no date] [Accessed 2 April 2015]

31 Goode, Chris. *The Consolations*, unpublished performance script (1999). An audio recording of this sequence, which subsequently appeared on the CD 'Copy Of' by COAT [Chris Goode & Jeremy Hardingham] (S2N Recordings, privately pressed, 2000), can be listened to at: https://soundcloud.com/airtrance16/copy-of [Accessed 15 April 2015]

32 Sheppard, Robert. 'Bob Cobbing: Two Sequences', at *Pages* (personal blog), posted 23 March 2005, http://robertsheppard.blogspot.co.uk/2005/03/robert-sheppard-bob-cobbing-two.html [Accessed 2 April 2015]

33 Cheek, Cris. 'Domestic Ambient Noise/Moise', at the *Riding the Meridian* website (n.d.; 1999?), http://www.heelstone.com/meridian/cheek/damntheory.html [Accessed 2 April 2015]

34 Rebellato, Dan. 'Preface' to *Theatremorphosis* (Glasgow: Suspect Culture, 2009), p.5

35 Lucier, Alvin. *I Am Sitting In A Room* for voice on tape (1969), spoken text available online at: http://www.dramonline.org/albums/alvin-lucier-i-am-sitting-in-a-room/notes [Accessed 2 April 2015]

36 Web Dictionary of Cybernetics and Systems. 'Noise', http://pespmc1.vub.ac.be/asc/NOISE.html [Accessed 2 April 2015]

37 Still online at: http://www.institute-of-failure.com [Accessed 2 April 2015]

38 Burrows, Jonathan; Etchells, Tim; Heathfield, Adrian & McIntosh, Kate. 'The Imperfect Body' event, as part of *Parallel Voices* (London: Siobhan Davies Studios, 1 March 2007), footage online at: https://www.youtube.com/watch?v=c41jSv3gXH4 [Accessed 2 April 2015]

39 Ibid.

40 Ricard, Rene. 'The Radiant Child'. *Artforum* (December 1981), available online at: https://artforum.com/inprintarchive/id=35643 [Accessed 2 April 2015]

41 Lavender, Andy. *Hamlet in Pieces* (London: Nick Hern Books, 2001), p.193

42 Interview with Julian Maynard-Smith in: Kaye, Nick. *Art into Theatre: Performance Interviews and Documents* (Oxford and New York: Routledge, 1996), p.194

43 Mancio, p.12

44 Goat Island. *Schoolbook: Textbook of the 1996 Goat Island Summer School in Glasgow* (Glasgow: CCA / Goat Island, 1997), p.8

45 Ibid., p.9

46 Knowles, Alison. 'Proposition' (1962), in *The Fluxus Performance Workbook*, eds. Ken Friedman, Owen Smith & Lauren Sawchyn, eBook (Performance Research e-publications, 2002), p.69, available online at: http://www.deluxxe.com/beat/fluxusworkbook.pdf [Accessed 2 April 2015]

47 Basinski, Michael. 'UNREADADABABLELITY', in *Perforations*, 26, eds. Robert Cheatham & John Lowther (Atlanta, Georgia: Public Domain Inc.), [n.d.], online at: http://www.pd.org/topos/perforations/perf26/basinski.html [Accessed 2 April 2015]

48 Daniel, Drew. 'All sound is queer', in *The Wire*, 333 (November 2011), pp.42-47

49 Ibid., p.44

50 McLuhan, Marshall & Fiore, Quentin; co-ordinated by Jerome Agel. *The Medium is the Massage* (1967), (London: Penguin, 2008), p.48

51 Daniel, p.45

52 Scarry, Elaine. *The Body in Pain: The Making and Unmaking of the World* (New York and Oxford: Oxford University Press, 1985), p.4

53 Ibid.

54 *Bookworm* podcast: 'Dennis Cooper: *The Marbled Swarm*', interviewer Michael Silverblatt [my transcription], (Santa Monica, California: KCRW, release date 12 January 2012), available online at: http://www.kcrw.com/news-culture/shows/bookworm/dennis-cooper-the-marbled-swarm [Accessed 2 April 2015]

55 Basinksi, Michael. Untitled ['The Germ of Creativity'], in *AND*, 12, ed. Adrian Clarke (Sutton: Writers Forum, September 2004), pp.14-17

56 Cobbing, Bob & Upton, Lawrence, interview with Martin Spinelli [my transcription], *Radio Radio*, programme 16 (2004?), available online at: http://www.ubu.com/sound/radio_radio/cobbing_upton.html [Accessed 2 April 2015]

57 Ibid.

58 Burrows, Etchells et al. 'The Imperfect Body'

59 Kahn, Douglas. *Noise, Water, Meat: A History of Sound in the Arts.* (Cambridge, Massachusetts: MIT Press, 1999), p.22

60 Quoted in: Williams, Wendy R. 'Interview' with Robert Wilson and Katharina Otto-Bernstein, *New York Cool* website, interview (24 October 2006), available online at: http://www.newyorkcool.com/archives/2006/November/interview-robert-wilson.html [Accessed 2 April 2015]

61 Sutherland, Keston. 'Statement for "Revolution and/or Poetry"', *Poetry and/or Revolution Conference* (UC Santa Cruz & UC Davis & UC Berkeley, 3-5 October 2013), available online at: https://revolutionandorpoetry.wordpress.com/2013/10/15/keston-sutherlands-statement-for-revolution-andor-poetry [Accessed 2 April 2015]

62 Quoted in: Waters, John. 'Roommates', in *Role Models* (London: Beautiful Books, 2011), p.266

63 Ibid.

64 Barthes, Roland. 'Cy Twombly: Works on Paper', in *The Responsibility of Forms: Critical Essays on Music, Art and Representation*, trans. Richard Howard (1982), (Berkeley and Los Angeles: University of California Press, 1991), p.170

65 Pavis, Patrice. 'Preface' to *Theatre Noise: The Sound of Performance*, eds. Lynne Kendrick and David Roesner (Newcastle-upon-Tyne: Cambridge Scholars Publishing, 2011), p.x

66 Debord, Guy. *The Society of the Spectacle* (1967), trans. Donald Nicholson-Smith (New York: Zone Books, 1995), p.12

67 Ibid., p.20

68 Holloway, John. *Crack Capitalism* (New York: Pluto Press, 2010), p.9

69 Oppenheim, Dennis. 'Two Stage Transfer Drawing' (1971), see: http://www.dennis-oppenheim.com/early-work/153 [Accessed 2 April 2015]

70 Seeger, Pete. 'The Water is Wide', on *Sing-A-Long at the Sanders Theatre, 1980* [my transcription, Disc 2, track 8, Smithsonian / Folkways, 1992]

71 Ibid.

72 Ibid.

73 Bataille, *Eroticism*, p.19

The forest and the field

1 Shakespeare, William. *The Tempest* (1611), I.ii.429, ed. Frank Kermode (1954), (London and New York: Routledge, 1988)

2 Auden, W.H. 'Bucolics: II Woods', in *Collected Poems*, ed. Edward Mendelson (London: Faber and Faber, 1991), p.558

3 Shakespeare, William. *King Henry V* (1599), Prologue, pp.1-8, ed. J.H. Walter (1954), (London and New York: Routledge, 1990)

4 Prynne, J.H. 'English Poetry and Emphatical Language', *Proceedings of the British Academy*, 74 (1988), pp.135-69

5 *Henry V*, Prologue, pp.11-14

6 *The Tempest*, V.i.181-84

7 Ibid., III.ii.133

8 Ibid., II.i.139-152

9 Ibid., II.i.155-160

10 Ibid., IV.i.148-156

11 Turner, Victor. *From Ritual to Theatre: The Human Seriousness of Play* (New York: PAJ Publications, 1982), p.26

12 Crouch, Tim. *The Author* (London: Oberon Books, 2009), p.16

13 Ibid., p.27

14 Schechner, Richard. *Between Theater and Anthropology* (Philadelphia: University of Pennsylvania Press, 1985), p.113

15 Ibid.

16 Goodman, Paul. 'Art of the Theatre', in *Three Plays: The Young Disciple, Faustina, Jonah* (New York: Random House, 1965), p.xi

17 Wilson has been delivering this excellent aphorism, with occasional minute variations, for many years – as he is wont to do with his favourite apothegmata. My rendering of it here is lifted from notes made at a lecture given by Wilson at the Barbican Centre, London, some years ago; but it can be found almost identically at, for example: MacAdam, Barbara A. 'Wilson's World', at the Artnews.com website, posted 20 March 2012, http:// www.artnews.com/2012/03/20/wilsons-world [Accessed 2 April 2015]

18 Crouch, Tim, quoted in 'A Conversation about Dialogue (Symposium Voices)', in *Contemporary Theatre Review*, *vol. 21 issue 4*, ed. Stephen Bottoms (November 2011), pp.425-6

19 Ridley, Philip. 'The Passion of Darkly Noon' [screenplay], in *The American Dreams: Two Screenplays* (London: Methuen, 1997), p.102

20 The Wizard of Oz

21 B, Jazzie; Wheeler, Caron; Hooper, Nellee & Law, Simon (Soul II Soul). 'Back to Life (However Do You Want Me)', 7" single (Virgin Records, 1989)

22 Hammerstein II, Oscar. 'If I Loved You', from *Carousel* (1945), available online at: http://www.stlyrics.com/lyrics/carousel/ifilovedyou.htm [Accessed 2 April 2015]

23 Ibid.

24 Schechner, p.110

25 Shakespeare, William. *Hamlet* (1601), II.ii.590-601, ed. Harold Jenkins (1982), (London and New York: Routledge, 1989)

26 *Hamlet*, III.ii.260

27 Ibid., III.ii.227-28

28 Ibid., III.ii.229-30

29 Ibid., III.i.56

30 Simpson, O.J. & Fenjves, Pablo F. *If I Did It* (New York: HarperCollins, 2007), [subsequently withdrawn; accessed as a pdf via a file sharing site, November 2013]

31 *The Tempest*, V.i.262; 294-95

32 Ibid., III.ii.6

33 Ibid., V.i.268

34 Ibid., V.i.290

35 Crouch, Tim. 'Death of The Author: how did my play fare in LA?', in *The Guardian* (7 March 2011), available online at: http://www.theguardian.com/ stage/2011/mar/07/tim-crouch-the-author-la-tour [Accessed 2 April 2015]

36 *The Tempest*, Epilogue, 19-20

37 Sutherland, Keston. 'XL Prynne'. In *Complicities*, eds. Robin Purves & Sam Ladkin (Prague: Litteraria Pragensia, 2007), p.73

38 Goat Island. *Schoolbook: Textbook of the 1996 Goat Island Summer School in Glasgow* (Glasgow: CCA / Goat Island, 1997), p.10

39 *The Tempest*, III.ii.121

40 Schechner, Richard. 'Performance Studies: An Introduction – Liminal and Liminoid' [my transcription], posted on YouTube by Routledge Textbooks (17 December 2012), https://www.youtube.com/watch?v=dygFtTWyEGM [Accessed 2 April 2015]

41 Szakolczai, Arpad. *Reflexive Historical Sociology* (London and New York: Routledge, 2000), p.217

42 Ibid., p.214

43 Ibid., p.213

44 Shakespeare, William. *As You Like It* (1599), II.vii.140-41, ed. Juliet Dusinberre (London and New York: Routledge, 2006)

45 Shakespeare, William. *Twelfth Night: or, What You Will* (1601), III.i.24-25, eds. J.M. Lothian & T.W. Craik (1975), (London and New York: Routledge, 1988)

46 Ibid., II.iv.110-113

47 Ibid., IV.i.5-9

48 Joris, Pierre. 'The Millennium Will Be Nomadic Or It Will Not Be: Notes Towards A Nomadic Poetics [version 1.02b]', http://pierrejoris.com/nomad.html [n.d.; 1998?], [Accessed 2 April 2015]

49 Quoted in: De Mille, Agnes. *Martha: the Life and Times of Martha Graham* (New York: Random House, 1991), p.264

50 Joris, op. cit.

51 Critical Art Ensemble. *The Electronic Disturbance* (New York: Autonomedia, 1994), p.12

52 Ibid., p.25

53 Ibid.

54 See: *PORES*, issue 2 at http://www.pores.bbk.ac.uk/2/index.htm. Starting with issue 5 (the most recent to date), the designation "avant-gardist" appears to have been quietly dropped.

55 *PORES*, issue 2

56 http://www.pores.bbk.ac.uk/2/stefans.htm

57 Ibid.

58 Ibid.

59 Ibid.

60 Sekula, Allan. 'Artist's text. Waiting for Tear Gas (white globe to black)' (2000), at the *Tate* website: http://www.tate.org.uk/whats-on/tate-modern/display/alan-sekula/waiting-tear-gas [Accessed 2 April 2015]

61 Joris, op. cit.

62 Bergvall, Caroline. 'Via: 48 Dante Variations', in *Fig.* (Norfolk: Salt, 2005), p.67

63 Stevens, Wallace. 'Yellow Afternoon', in *Collected Poems* (1954), (London: intage, 1990), p.237

64 Mottram, Eric. 'Composition and Performance in the Work of Bob Cobbing: a conversation' (1977), (London: Writers Forum, 2000), [n.p.] p.8

65 Davis, Matt. Introductory text at the *Field* website, http://www.f-i-e-l-d. co.uk/FIELD.html [Accessed 2 April 2015]

66 *Field* website. 'Hastings Field', blog entry posted 24 October 2006, at http://www.f-i-e-l-d.co.uk/Hastings%20Field.html [Accessed 2 April 2015]

67 Ibid.

68 Berger, John. 'Field' (1971), in *John Berger: Selected Essays*, ed. Geoff Dyer (London: Bloomsbury, 2001), p.354

69 Ibid., p.355

70 *Field* website. 'Hastings Field'

71 Berger, 'Field', p.355

72 Ibid., p.356

73 Ibid.

74 Ibid.

75 Ibid.

76 Ibid., p.357

77 Ibid.

78 Ibid.

79 Goodman, 'Art of the Theatre', p.xii

80 Berger, 'Field', p.357

81 Ibid., p.355

82 Ibid.

83 Ibid., p.356

84 Friedman, Ken. 'Center Piece' [sometimes rendered as 'Centre Piece'], event score (2003), published, inter alia, in *12 Structures: Scores by Ken Friedman* (London: The Centre of Attention, 2004), p.14, [Accessed 2 April 2015]

85 *The Tempest*, II.i.139-141

86 Ibid., II.i.150-54

87 Bourriaud, Nicolas. 'Altermodern', in *Altermodern: Tate Triennial*, ed. Bourriaud (London: Tate Publishing, 2009), pp.11-12

88 Handke, Peter. *The Long Way Round.* (1981), trans. Ralph Manheim (London: Methuen, 1989), pp.88-89

89 Ibid., p.90

90 Ibid., p.91

91 Bataille, Georges. *Eroticism.* (1957), trans. Mary Dalwood (London and New York: Marion Boyars, 2006), p.19

92 Berger, 'Field', p.357

Coda: Changing the world

1 Kupfer, David. 'Interview with Utah Phillips', *Southern Cross Review,* 29 (2003), http://www.southerncrossreview.org/29/utah.htm [Accessed 2 April 2015]

2 Bennett, Alan; Cook, Peter; Miller, Jonathan & Moore, Dudley. 'The Aftermyth of War', in *The Complete Beyond the Fringe,* ed. Roger Wilmut (London: Methuen, 2003), p.71

3 Billington, Michael. 'My Name is Rachel Corrie', *Guardian* (14 April 2005), available online at: http://www.theguardian.com/stage/2005/apr/14/theatre.politicaltheatre [Accessed 2 April 2015]

4 Allen, Tim & Duncan, Andrew. 'Introduction' to *Don't Start Me Talking: Interviews with Contemporary Poets* (Norfolk: Salt, 2006), p.5

5 Goode, Chris, after Anton Chekhov. ....*SISTERS,* unpublished performance text (2008)

6 See: eds. DeSilvey, Caitlin; Naylor, Simon & Sackett, Colin. *Anticipatory history.* (Axminster: Uniformbooks, 2011), p.9

7 Ibid., inside front cover

8 Hopkins, Rob. *The Transition Handbook: From oil dependency to local resilience* (Vermont: Chelsea Green Publishing, 2008), p.15

9 Reynolds, Simon. *Rip It Up And Start Again: Post-punk 1978-84* (London: Faber and Faber, 2005), p.202

10 Holloway, *Crack Capitalism,* p.254

11 "Never doubt, she's said to have said, that a small group of thoughtful and committed citizens can change the world." Sorkin, Aaron. *The West Wing,* episode 4.15 (Warner Bros. Television, original airdate: 12 February 2003)

12 The source of this attribution is difficult to track: see: http://en.wikiquote.org/wiki/Margaret_Mead#Disputed [Accessed 2 April 2015]

Index

WWW.OBERONBOOKS.COM